I lived in Those Times:
Five Generations Of A Michigan Pioneer Family

JAMES FORD

Fortitude Publishing
Kalamazoo, Michigan

First Edition

Designed by Sean Hollins, Fortitude Graphics
www.Fortitudegdp.com

Includes biographical references and index.

ISBN 978-0-615-33110-2

1. Michigan-History 2. Pioneer 3.Biography-Memoirs 4. United States-History 5. Pioneers-Biography; Military-History 6. Civil War-History 7. World War I-History 8. World War II- History 9. Vietnam-History

Dedicated to:

My father.

Without his memoir, and
his love for his family, this
book would not have been written.

Contents

Do not forget the things your eyes have seen
or let them slip from your heart so long as you
live. Teach them, rather, to your children and
to your children's children.

Deuteronomy 4:9

Acknowledgements

I am indebted to many people who helped me with this book. For many years my brother, David, has been the guardian of family records and photographs, and the information that he accumulated made my research infinitely easier. My cousin, Edna, wrote the history of my great-great-grandparents' early years in Michigan, only a small portion of which is included here, and those stories will be a gift to future generations. My father transcribed the handwritten memoirs of my Great-Grandfather Henry, and my uncle, Bill Ford, transcribed the letters of my Grandfather Robert. Martha Jamieson encouraged me to include all five generations in a single book, when the scope of the project seemed to me to be unrealistically ambitious. Amy Arver typed my father's memoir, offered grammatical advice, and proof read an early draft. Sam Field also read an early, longer draft, and was candid enough to tell me which parts needed to be cut. My mother proof read the final draft, and provided various facts and dates known only to her. Cheryl Ririe-Kurz helped with proof reading. My law partner, Bill Murphy, tolerated the many hours I spent not practicing law. Sean and Sonya Hollins, of Fortitude Graphic Design & Printing, took a rough manuscript, and turned it into a real book. And, finally, my wife, Hattie, was ever supportive, as she has been for thirty-five years. I am grateful to them all.

James Ford
Kalamazoo, Michigan

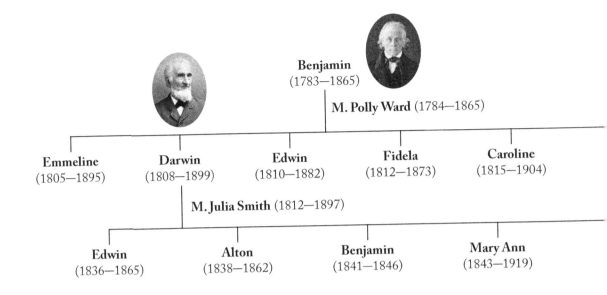

Benjamin
(1783—1865)

M. Polly Ward (1784—1865)

Emmeline
(1805—1895)

Darwin
(1808—1899)

Edwin
(1810—1882)

Fidela
(1812—1873)

Caroline
(1815—1904)

M. Julia Smith (1812—1897)

Edwin
(1836—1865)

Alton
(1838—1862)

Benjamin
(1841—1846)

Mary Ann
(1843—1919)

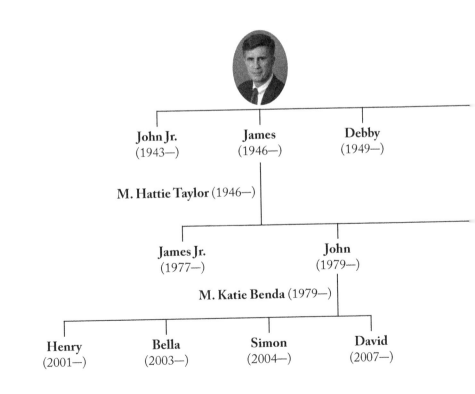

John Jr.
(1943—)

James
(1946—)

Debby
(1949—)

M. Hattie Taylor (1946—)

James Jr.
(1977—)

John
(1979—)

M. Katie Benda (1979—)

Henry
(2001—)

Bella
(2003—)

Simon
(2004—)

David
(2007—)

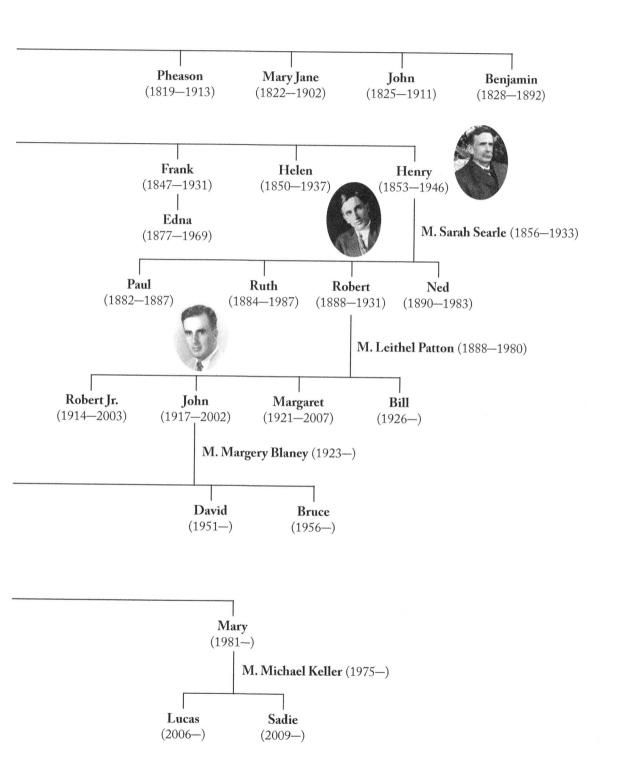

Pheason
(1819—1913)

Mary Jane
(1822—1902)

John
(1825—1911)

Benjamin
(1828—1892)

Frank
(1847—1931)

Helen
(1850—1937)

Henry
(1853—1946)

Edna
(1877—1969)

M. Sarah Searle (1856—1933)

Paul
(1882—1887)

Ruth
(1884—1987)

Robert
(1888—1931)

Ned
(1890—1983)

M. Leithel Patton (1888—1980)

Robert Jr.
(1914—2003)

John
(1917—2002)

Margaret
(1921—2007)

Bill
(1926—)

M. Margery Blaney (1923—)

David
(1951—)

Bruce
(1956—)

Mary
(1981—)

M. Michael Keller (1975—)

Lucas
(2006—)

Sadie
(2009—)

Prologue

I n West Texas the afternoon sun bakes the barren landscape during the summer months, and as the hot air rises it creates billowy cumulus clouds that soon turn into towering cumulonimbus. On many days these clouds reach thirty thousand feet or more. During the summer of 1969 I flew in this weather every day as I completed a year of pilot training at Webb Air Force Base in Big Spring, Texas. I was flying the T-38, the Air Force's advanced supersonic trainer which was also used by NASA astronauts for training, and later by the Air Force Thunderbirds flight demonstration team. At one time it held the world climb record, and it can roll two revolutions per second. Life can't get much better for a pilot than to spend a couple of hours in a T-38 on a summer afternoon. The flights were scheduled as aerobatic training flights, but for me they were play. I would pay big money for one more afternoon in a T-38.

The T-38 training areas at Webb were south of the field, and as I climbed out during a flight in late August I scanned the horizon for the area with the most clouds. After four months in the airplane I was confident in my ability to do loops and rolls and other aerobatics, so instead of practicing I spent much of my solo time chasing clouds. I loved to race through holes, climb up one side of a cloud, roll inverted as I came over the top, and then follow the contours as I came down the other side. No two clouds are ever alike so there are always plenty of nooks and crannies to explore, and the sense of speed is exhilarating. You can't see speed in a clear sky, but it is impressive to pass a cloud at five hundred knots.

On this day the greatest accumulation of clouds was one hundred miles to the southeast, so that's the area that I requested, and I spent the better part of an hour attacking one cloud after another. Then I rolled inverted and tilted my head back so I could look out the top of my canopy to see the ground below. Beneath me was the old abandoned runway at Goodfellow Field in San Angelo where my father had been stationed as an instructor pilot during World War II. As I looked down at the runway I thought of him spending many hours flying over this same countryside, and I imagined him doing many of the same maneuvers I was doing, albeit at a much slower speed, and at a much lower altitude. I was surprised to see that the runway still existed in 1969. It had been twenty-five years since my father flew there, and that seemed to be a very long time in my mind, longer than I had been alive. Twenty-five years is less impressive now, forty years later, but the nostalgia I feel is still as intense as I think of the adventures that we both experienced as young pilots during times of war.

Dad entered the Army Air Corps one step ahead of the draft in 1942, and I entered one step ahead of the draft in 1968. Flying airplanes sounded better to Dad than the trench warfare that he had read about from World War I, and it sounded better to me than slogging through the jungle in Vietnam. If I had to go to war, flying airplanes was the way to do it. Dad would never have joined the Air Corps if World War II had not occurred, but I might have joined even without Vietnam. I grew up listening to his stories of flying, and I was captivated at an early age. In the years right after the war I remember him wearing his leather flying jacket, and as I grew older the adventures he recounted seemed larger than life, so I always knew that if I got the chance I wanted to do what he had done. It is not uncommon for a son to emulate his father, but for me it was more than that. I had not only my father's example to guide me, but also the reputations of my grandfather and my great-grandfather.

When I was a boy Dad frequently reminded me that our ancestors never had money, but they did have intelligence and industry and character, and I understood that I had an obligation to maintain the family's good name. It gave me something to shoot for. But it wasn't until relatively late in life that I developed a desire to know who these ancestors really were. Old people are like that. The closer we come to our own mortality the more we begin to appreciate that we are just one link in a continuous chain. My interest peaked when Dad wrote his memoir. That inspired me to write my own memoir, and then to compile this history of five generations in a single source. I benefited from educated ancestors who left a record of their lives, and from the stories that my Great-Great-Grandfather Darwin told his granddaughter, Edna.

Darwin was born in 1808, and lived the last twenty-two years of his life with Edna on the family farm near Hillsdale, Michigan. The stories that Edna recorded, including homesteading in the wilderness, and the loss of two sons in the Civil War, convinced me that human nature has changed little in two hundred years. Technology has changed tremendously, but people remain the same. The fears and hopes and humor of my ancestors are not very different from my own. In part that may be because two hundred years is not so great a chasm as we may think. The same Edna who spent her first twenty-two years with Darwin spent the last twenty-three years of her life with me. She did not live with me, but we spent many holidays together, and I remember her well. Sharing this common companion with my great-great grandfather, born two hundred years ago, reminds me of how closely we are connected to those who came before.

The stories that follow are Edna's history of how the family farm was carved out of the forest, my Great-Grandfather Henry's memoir of life on the farm in the years before the Civil War, the letters of my Grandfather Robert, my father's memoir, and finally my own. They are stories of ordinary people who lived through some extraordinary times, including the opening of the wilderness, three wars, and the Great Depression. But mostly this is a history of what life was like in the nineteenth and twentieth centuries. People may not have changed, but our lives certainly have. Great-Great-Grandfather Darwin came to Michigan by oxcart; I flew supersonic jets. He was a farmer; I was a lawyer. He lived in a world lit only by fire; I wrote this on a computer. Which of us led the better life is not so obvious, but perhaps the stories recorded here can provide part of the answer.

Book One

Darwin Ford
1808-1899
By Edna Ford
1877-1969

For seventy-five years, from 1854 to 1929, all roads led to the farm that was the home of the Darwin Ford family and various relatives for all those years. The road to the farm began near Salem, Massachusetts where Martin Matthew Ford worked as an indentured servant in the 1680s. Several official documents from that era refer to him as a Frenchman, so it is likely that he was one of the many French Huguenots who immigrated to America in the late seventeenth century. Four generations later Benjamin Ford was born in 1783 in Middlefield, Massachusetts two months after his father, John Ford, a private during the Revolutionary War, was killed by a falling tree. John's wife, Jemima, was the stuff of which heroes are made. The authorities denied her permission to bury her husband until a debt had been paid, so she took things into her own hands, and after dark dug the grave and buried him herself. This was no easy task for any woman, especially in the winter, and for one expecting another child in two months. It must have been hard for her to manage for herself and five small children, the oldest only five.

In 1804 Benjamin married Polly Ward, and they soon became part of that great stream of pioneers moving west. Their first stop was in Cornwall, Vermont, where my Grandfather Darwin was born in 1808. Over the next twenty-five years Benjamin and

Polly moved numerous times throughout the Northeast, eventually settling in Medina, Ohio in 1833. They traveled to Ohio by boat from Buffalo, departing just a few steps ahead of the law. Benjamin owed four dollars for a plow, and knew that he was a wanted man, so when they got on the boat he went to the engine room, tilted back in his chair with a newspaper, and pretended to be a workman on break. The ploy was successful, as the sheriff came through the engine room, but passed him by.

In 1834 Grandfather Darwin married Julia Smith, my grandmother, and in 1836 Grandfather loaded his wife and baby, Edwin, and all their belongings onto an ox-drawn wagon and started for Michigan. When I was a little girl I loved to hear Grandmother tell stories of their early years in Michigan. One day she was picking berries in the woods when she gradually realized that there was someone on the other side of the berry bushes, and on investigation found a bear as busily engaged on his side of the thicket as she was on hers. Some time later she met two Indians while walking along a trail to what is now State Street in Hillsdale. They warily asked her where she was going, and she told them she was walking home. A short distance down the trail she stepped over a log, and discovered a bark full of honey. The Indians had found a bee tree, and were obviously concerned that she would harvest it before they could.

The Pottawattamie Indians in Hillsdale were friendly and well liked by the settlers, and were responsible for the survival of many of the earliest pioneers, but in 1840 federal troops were sent to remove the Indians to their new home in Iowa. It was a sad day for the Indians and the settlers when the Indians were assembled, with Chief Baw Beese in the lead, to start the journey west. One of the witnesses to this forced migration was my Aunt Caroline. Grandfather's parents, Benjamin and Polly, and his sister Caroline had followed Grandfather to Hillsdale in 1838. Caroline was the first school teacher in the county, and on the day the Indians left she let her students out of class so they could witness the sad event. She said it was a pitiful sight. The dejection of the Indians was great, but not a sound was heard. The women carried the papooses and the wigwam equipment, while the few ponies and horses were ridden by the men.

Grandfather and Grandmother did not remain in Hillsdale for long. Over the next eleven years Grandfather led them back and forth between Michigan and Indiana, never staying anywhere for more than a year or two. During these years Alton was born in 1838, and Mary Ann was born in 1843. A third son, Benjamin, was born in 1841, but died at the age of five. My father, Frank, was born in 1847. In 1849 the family was once again on the move, heading west with a team of oxen and a covered wagon, but near Michigan City, Indiana bad luck overtook them with the death of one of the oxen. Disheartened, they returned again to Hillsdale to settle close to Benjamin and Polly just a short distance from where the college now stands. Here their family was completed with the birth of a second daughter, Helen, in 1850, and a fifth son, Henry, in 1853.

By 1853 Grandfather and Grandmother had been married for nineteen years, and had moved a total of seventeen times. The eighteenth brought them to the end of the journey that had started so long ago in New England. In 1854 the family was once again loaded into the wagon, the oxen were hitched, and the seven mile trip to the farm began. It was slow progress over the roads and trails of that day, much of which led through woods. Avoiding stumps and fallen trees, plowing through sand, and rattling over corduroy stretches the family finally reached their new home. This was the end of the road, and here they lived out their lives and died. As a young girl in the 1880s I made many trips from the farm into Hillsdale, and my father would point out spots on the original trail that they had taken thirty years before. By that time a road had been constructed, but I could still see the outline of where the original trail had skirted a mud hole, and a stump field that marked the junction of the trail with the road.

The farm was one hundred and four acres of rolling terrain seven miles southeast of Hillsdale in a small community known as Jefferson Township. No timber had been cleared when the family moved in, other than a few trees that Grandfather and the two older boys used to build a temporary shelter. Through the years more and more land was cleared until only a few acres of woodland remained at the back. Wheat, oats, corn and hay were the main crops. They had cattle for milk, butter and meat, pigs for hams and sausage, and chickens for eggs and chicken pies. Horses did the work on the farm, and provided transportation. When they moved to the farm Edwin was only eighteen, and Alton sixteen, but they did a man's work in clearing the heavily wooded acres to make room for farm buildings, crops, and pasture land for the cattle. Grandfather often spoke of Edwin and Alton, the work they did, and the admiration and love he had for them.

There was always a garden to provide vegetables. An apple orchard was planted north of the house, and a few extra planted in the dooryard. Every fall bushels of Spies, Baldwins, and Greenings were carried into the cellar for winter use in pies, applesauce, and wonderful baked apples. In later years pears, peaches, and plums were planted, and there was usually a large strawberry bed. Raspberries and blackberries were plentiful in newly cleared spots and along fence rows, and the women spent hours picking, cleaning, and canning.

In summer the barn was filled with hay, and the granary bins with wheat and oats. In the early days corn was stored on the scaffolding in the big barn, but later a corncrib was built. As far back as I can remember the hens had a lean-to built on the back of the horse barn, but it must have been a very cold place, for we had very few eggs in winter. Later a real henhouse was built, and we were rewarded with many more eggs.

Times changed, and methods of work on the farm changed with them. In the beginning grain and hay were cut with a scythe and cradle. Later came the mowing machine and reaper. The reaper was a mowing machine with a large table bolted to it to catch the grain as it was cut, and four rakes in bright colors raked the oats and wheat to the ground. Men followed the reaper with hand-rakes to gather the grain into sheaves, which were tied with withes of grain. When the harvest was over the reaper was dismantled and stowed until next year.

In the early days grain was spread on the barn floor, and threshed by hand with a flail. A flail was a wooden bar called a swingle that was attached to a long wooden handle by a leather thong. The thresher grasped the handle with both hands, swung the swingle around his head, and brought it down onto the grain to separate the grain from the chaff. It always seemed strange to me that no one ever beat his brains out with it. It was a great day when grain could be threshed with a separator powered by a horse plodding around a central pivot for hours at a time. I could never understand why the horse didn't fall down from dizziness. After the horse thresher came one driven by a steam engine. Then came the tractor driven separator, and now the combine.

During the seventy five years that the family operated the farm they saw many changes. Ox teams gave way to horses, and then horses to tractors, trucks, and automobiles. After 1900 mail was delivered by rural free delivery to a mailbox beside the road. Prior to that mail was picked up at the post office in town. Eventually telephones provided social contact and daily weather reports until radios took over that function. Candles gave way to kerosene lamps, and these in turn to electric lights. Hand milking was replaced by milking machines run by gasoline powered generators. The stone churn and dash were discarded for wooden churns operated by a crank. In the 1890s farmers began putting up ice in the winter to store food in the summer, and the ice, in turn, was replaced by the electric refrigerator.

During the winter ashes from the heating stoves were stored in a large ash barrel in the yard. The barrel sat over a large iron kettle set in the ground. In the spring water was poured over the ashes, and before long water percolated through the ashes, and lye began dripping into the kettle. The lye was then added to a huge kettle of grease and fat that Grandmother had saved from the kitchen. When the lye dissolved all the grease the mixture was cooked over an open fire until it achieved just the right consistency. The final result was soap for dishwashing, floor scrubbing, and laundry. Killing hogs and cleaning up the greasy mess afterwards are not my most pleasant memories of life on the farm, though some of the hams and bacon and sausage would be very welcome now. Many present day products lack the flavor of homemade foods.

Days were long in summer, and short in winter, but no day ended without something being accomplished, and it is satisfying to know that we had a part, however small, in the development of the Midwest. When the family moved to the farm in 1854 they lived in a temporary shanty until a log home could be built, which didn't take long. The log house was a comfortable and beloved home. It had a large fireplace on the north wall, and a loft where the four boys slept. Grandfather and Grandmother and the two daughters slept downstairs. On the walls hung two pictures, one of Uncle Tom and Little Eva, and another of John P. Hale, the abolitionist senator from New Hampshire.

An earthen bank surrounded the house, and on this bank flourished cinnamon roses, snowdrops, and other shrubbery. Lilacs framed the front door, and a bed of purple iris was nearby. A pathway led from the house to a spring at the foot of the hill, and a number of the maples from the original timber were left to shade the dooryard. The family lived in the log home until 1868. By then the two oldest brothers, Edwin and Alton, had died in the Civil War.

Much of the farm's success was due to Edwin and Alton. Although they were both still teenagers when they moved there in 1854, they helped Grandfather clear almost one hundred acres of forest by the start of the Civil War. All those trees had to be removed, root, trunk, and branches, and disposed of by fire, by sale, or by use on the farm. Grandfather's ledger recorded six hundred cords of wood that were hauled to Hillsdale and sold. When the Civil War began both Grandfather and Great-Grandfather Benjamin were outspoken abolitionists who expressed their opinions freely. Feelings ran high, and there were some unpleasant confrontations. Grandfather's abolitionist spirit no doubt rubbed off on his children, with consequences that he could not have anticipated.

Alton was the first to enlist in September 1861. He left that same night for camp in Grand Rapids, and from there traveled to Mississippi where he participated in several battles near Shiloh. While in Mississippi he contracted typhoid fever, and was sent to Cincinnati. Grandfather got the message in Hillsdale, and left that night by train for Cincinnati. After a difficult journey they arrived home on May 18, 1862, and Alton was placed in Grandfather and Grandmother's bed in the southeast corner of the main floor. Four days later he died with the family gathered around him, and with Grandfather holding his hand.

In July 1862 Edwin, the oldest son, enlisted in the 18th Michigan Infantry. His regiment trained in Hillsdale at Camp Woodbury on State Street Road, and on September 24, 1862 they left Hillsdale to serve in Cincinnati and Nashville before eventually arriving in Decatur, Alabama in the summer of 1864. While in the army Edwin wrote several letters to his Aunt Caroline, talking of his loneliness and his hopes for the future.

Excerpts from a November 1863 letter to Caroline Ford (from Nashville)

Dear Aunt,

I received a letter from you some time since and have forgotten whether I have answered it or not – though I think that I have not as you are usually very prompt in answering my letters and I have got none from you in some time. There is nothing of much importance to write about. One day is just like another with us.

The weather is pleasant but rather cool. The regiment is in a good state of health as a general thing, and we are enjoying ourselves well – as well as soldiers can expect to. We have battalion drill in the afternoon and dress parade at night. We have got a new silver band which has been practicing about a week and is making splendid progress in learning to play. The other night it was up at the State House at the great congratulatory meeting held there the other night to rejoice over the glorious news from Pennsylvania (Gettysburg).

Several fine speeches were made by gentlemen from Ohio and Tennessee, the last of which was Andy Johnson. (Later to become President on the death of Abraham Lincoln) The speech of Governor Johnson did me more good than any other which I ever listened to in my life. He said that he was in favor of immediate emancipation and when the states were reorganized, of leaving out the disturbing element of slavery. Then we should have peace. What should be done with the negros was not clear to his mind now, but he believed that if we commenced on a true principle and followed it up all would come out right in the end. But I must

stop. I wrote to Aunt Mary a short time ago and must write to grandfather's folks too. My best wishes to all the friends. Answer soon.

Goodby,
Edwin

Excerpts from a July 1864 letter to Caroline Ford (from Nashville)

Dear Aunt,

I sit down to write you a few hasty lines. I have been writing letters nearly all day. It will soon be dark, but I will try & write something, although it doesn't amount to much. I wrote you last spring for which I never received an answer. I am sure that it never reached you. I have been having some photographs taken, & send back one in this letter. It is poor enough, but as good as I could get. The dark spots on the face were caused by perspiration, which it was of no use to wipe off. I am sorry that it happened, but it can't be helped now.

As Aunt Mary is not at home I will not send her one now, and will get one taken and send to her when she gets back. It is a good while since I received a letter from you or Aunt Mary either. A good many who were right anxious to correspond with me when I left Hillsdale seem to have forgotten that there is any such person in existence as my humble self.

We are having good times in the city, & probably will be here several months. There is no news to write from here that will be of interest that I know of. The prospects for the success of our cause & the complete overthrow of the rebellion is very bright now. The rebels have received heavier blows during the present month than before since the commencement of the war. I live in hopes that peace and prosperity will smile again on our torn & distraught country & that some of us at least may live to return to the homes we have left.

I wish that you will write to me, & write often as you can. I receive very few letters except what come from home. I suppose that Hillsdale will be so changed before we get back that it will seem almost like going into a new place. But I have written enough such as it is and will say good night.

> From your nephew,
> Edwin

In Alabama Edwin served as a scout, and on September 24, 1864 his detachment was sent to reinforce a garrison at Athens, Alabama. Two miles from their objective they were attacked by a much larger force under the command of General Forrest. After a five hour engagement, and with their supply of ammunition exhausted, the surviving members were taken prisoner, and were then sent to Cahawba Prison in Cahawba, Alabama where they remained for seven months until the end of the war. They were then released to return home.

For those left at home the war years seemed endless. The suspense and anxiety were tremendous as Grandfather and the two youngest boys were left at home to raise the crops and continue clearing the land. And as Frank grew older he, too, got the urge to enlist, although Grandfather and Grandmother both tried to dissuade him. Grandmother offered to make him a nice coat with brass buttons if he would give up the idea, and this served for a while, but the urge to enlist continued, and shortly after turning seventeen he enlisted on March 31, 1864. His training barracks were located in Hillsdale just behind where the Catholic Church now stands. While still in training he and some of his friends helped themselves to a neighbor's chicken. To conceal the deed they threw the feathers into the fireplace, whence they were whisked up the chimney and all over town, but no complaint was ever made.

After training Frank was sent to Virginia where he took part in the battles of Cold Harbor, North Ann River, and Petersburg. While serving sentry duty on the night of March 25, 1865 he challenged someone moving through the bushes, and gave away his position to the enemy. He and several others were taken prisoner, and were held for five days at Libby Prison in Richmond before being exchanged. He was soon discharged from the army, and returned home in late April. On his way through Hillsdale he stopped at the Post Office, and picked up a letter from Edwin saying that he would be home soon from Cahawba Prison. It was a time of relief and rejoicing! The long strain would soon be over.

The Union prisoners from Cahawba were repatriated on steamships up the Mississippi River from Vicksburg, and several ships had already departed before Edwin boarded the Sultana on the evening of April 24th. On the way north the Sultana docked in Memphis on the evening of April 26th. The prisoners were allowed to leave the ship while it loaded cargo, and Edwin was among those who took advantage of the opportunity. After several hours in Memphis he heard a whistle, and realized that he was about to miss the ship's departure, so he ran back to the river, barely getting on board before the gangplank was raised. Finally Edwin was on his way home after almost three years of war.

The next day Henry, then twelve, was walking home from visiting a friend when he was picked up by a neighbor coming from town. The neighbor told him that the Sultana had blown up on the Mississippi River, and that Edwin was reported to be among the dead. He was an excellent swimmer, but had been weakened by captivity, and was found clinging to a tree where the icy river had overflowed its banks. He was one of approximately sixteen hundred casualties in the worst maritime disaster in American history.

Three months after the loss of his oldest son Grandfather also lost his father and his mother. Benjamin died July 16, 1865 at his home in Hillsdale. His obituary noted his long history of opposing slavery, stating, "During the whole conflict his testimony against the mighty wrong has been as vehement as it has been incessant." Four sons and five daughters survived him, and for the first time in thirty-five years all of his children gathered in his home shortly before he died to accept his dying blessing. His wife, Polly, expressed relief that he was at rest, beyond the reach of every ill and suffering. As to the separation she said, "It can only be for a few days." It proved to be briefer than anyone anticipated, as she followed him in death eleven days later on July 27, 1865.

In 1860 a new home had been started on the farm just south of the old log house. The foundation was laid, and the frame was up, but with the three oldest boys off to war progress was slow. There it stood through summer heat and winter snows until some of the frame became warped from exposure to the elements, but finally it was completed in 1868. When my father, Frank, got married a new wing was added to the south for his family, with bedrooms and a separate kitchen and living area. It was in this house that I was born and grew up, and it was from this house that Grandfather and Grandmother were taken to their last resting place. It was here that Uncle John came to live out the last forty-six years of his life. It was here that Grandfather's sisters, Caroline, and Mary Mead, and his brother Benjamin would gather after they followed Grandfather to Hillsdale.

Life in the 1800's was difficult and precarious. Disease was an ever present threat. Grandfather and Grandmother lost a son, Benjamin, at age five in 1846, and lost Alton to typhoid at age twenty-three. Nor did the next generation avoid these sorrows. Father married in 1875, and had his first daughter, Edith, the following year. His older sister, Helen, was living in Kansas, but in December 1877 Helen brought her two small children back to the farm for a visit, and while she was there diphtheria ran through the family. Little was known about the disease in those days, and no precautions were taken to prevent it from spreading. The adults who contracted the disease survived, but four children died, including both of Helen's children, my sister Edith, and Mother's nephew. It was a horrible time. A few years later Henry suffered the same pain with the death of his five year old son from malaria.

Grandfather's sisters, Caroline and Mary Mead, followed him to Hillsdale, but always lived in town in separate homes connected by a raised walk. Being Fords, one could not expect them to live in the same house, and either one have any peace. After Henry got married he moved into a house across the street. When Grandfather visited Henry, and the time came for him to start for home, Grandfather would pick up his hat and remark, "I'll go across the street and stir up the animals."

Uncle John, Grandfather's younger brother, was born in 1825. He moved to Hillsdale with his parents, Benjamin and Polly, in 1845 and continued to live with them until their deaths in 1865. He then moved to the farm where he lived out the remaining forty-six years of his life. Uncle John never married, but on the farm he was one of the family, and earned his keep doing various chores. His main jobs were milking the cows and keeping a big pile of wood split for the kitchen stove. He was an avid reader and book collector, at one time accumulating three hundred volumes.

When we children were small Uncle John ordered magazines for us according to our ages. We have much to thank him for in the amount of reading material available. There was quantity aplenty, although the quality was questionable. Uncle John was a kind and considerate man, but not at all efficient. I can see him yet at family prayers holding onto the arms of his Boston rocker, swaying back and forth, sometimes pounding the arms of the chair as he prayed for "the President and all in authority." In the winter he sat in his rocker with his books and papers in the front corner of the living room by the big stove. From time to time he laid aside his reading, reached for the poker, and wrestled another big chunk of wood into the stove, puffing and blowing to beat all. Grandfather sat on the other side of the stove offering occasional sarcastic comments, few of which were helpful.

When spring came Uncle John's stoking job was over, but there was the garden to cultivate, potato bugs to pick, and cows to water. When the garden was up and flourishing Grandfather would take over, and Uncle John would be out. Then there were other jobs for him to do. One was digging, cleaning, and grating horseradish, which he did out of doors to prevent too much weeping. This job Grandfather did not offer to take over. In the 1880's he walked seven miles to Hillsdale three times a week to pick up mail and small purchases for the family and the neighbors. He continued this until the farmers hired a stage driver to deliver mail every day for the sum of two dollars a year from each farmer.

Uncle John was a favorite, not only of ours, but also of the other children in the neighborhood. After his death Aunt Mary Ann remembered the special bond he had with children:

Uncle John

Does he remember in the heavenly home
The pleasant Christmas days that used to be?
The pretty keepsakes and the many times
His little friends have sat upon his knee:

Does he remember in his gladness there
The happy voices of the children here?
Can he forget the touch of little hands
Or rosy faces that were once so dear?

And when he picks the golden violets
And lilies-of-the-valley fair to see,
Does he remember the for-get-me-nots
He used to gather in the grass for me?

Does he remember quiet walks alone,
The many paths, the clump of evergreens,
The two homes sheltered by the trees,
The smiling fields, and stretch of road between?

Oh, yes. I hope he still remembers all –
The shady run in summer where Johnny-Jump-Ups grow,
Pretty red robin swinging on the bough,
And four rosy faces, and voices soft and low.

Grandfather was driven by wanderlust all his life. There were always better things ahead. Grandmother had to be ready to pick up and move whenever Grandfather took a notion to look for greener pastures. There was a sterling quality about him, an uncompromising antagonism toward evil in any form, and a demand for honesty and uprightness of character, but my memories of him are not as pleasant as my memories of Grandmother. He was often harsh in his condemnation of wrongdoers, and difficult with his own family, and at times had lapses of memory which he tried to conceal. He once forgot the name of the Sexton of the Church during a business meeting, and attempted to cover up the failure by referring to him as Brother Bellringer.

Grandfather had an inventive genius, and was a self taught musician. He taught himself to play the flute and the fife, and late in life bought a violin that he also learned to play. He usually played only hymns. One exception was that he liked to play martial and patriotic music on the fife. With Grandfather on the fife, Henry on the snare drum, and Frank on the bass drum they furnished music for patriotic meetings during the Civil War up until the time Frank enlisted.

One of his inventions was a system of gears to make butter churn faster. It was a success in that respect, but it spoiled the butter. An invention that worked much better was a frame to hold one end of the crosscut saw so he could saw wood alone. The men who were hired to help thresh the grain were much interested in this contraption, and sawed a lot of wood trying it out. One winter he also built a simple toboggan for my brother and me. We took much pleasure sliding down the hill, through the gate, and part way across the field north of the barn. I don't know how it was made, but that did not matter to us as long as it whizzed down the hill with one of us on board.

Our greatest debt to Grandfather is his attitude toward education. For a man with very little schooling he had a deep interest in education, and he was a very proud man when he took one of his children to enter Hillsdale College. He also had a humble part in the building of the college. Before moving to the farm they lived within sight of the work that was going on to construct the college, and Grandfather used an ox team and wagon to haul stone and gravel for the foundations. One day Grandfather was loading his wagon when a passing neighbor called to him from the road, "Hey, Darwin, what are you doing over there in that hole?"

Immediately came back the reply, "Digging for gold." It was an apt response, for the construction of the college was a richer vein than was ever struck in any mine. In return for his contributions to the college Grandfather received two scholarships which have been used by many of his descendants to pay their three dollar matriculation fee. Three of his children, Edwin, Mary Ann, and Henry studied there.

Grandfather liked to read the newspapers and the church papers, and every evening there were family prayers before bedtime. After this Grandfather would say, "Julia, I wish you would bring me a few spoonfuls of bread and milk," and soon Grandmother would come in with a large bowl of bread and milk which all promptly disappeared. Grandmother accepted Grandfather's temperament, preferring to avoid a battle of words. She seldom reached the breaking point, but it did happen on rare occasion. One morning Grandfather had a ranting spell at the breakfast table, and Grandmother finally became fed up. She rose from her chair, held her coffee cup in a menacing position, and said, "Darwin, hold your tongue." He immediately subsided, and she sat back down to finish her coffee.

My memories of Grandmother are all pleasant. Frontier life was not easy for any woman: bearing children, keeping them clothed and fed, caring for them when they were ill, laying them away when death took them from her, and soothing her sorrow in labor and care for those who were spared. Three of Grandmother's children preceded her in death, Benjamin at age five, Alton at twenty-two, and Edwin at twenty-eight. When her children were young they would follow her as she worked in the garden, or picked berries in the fields, and she would sing to them and recite poems. But she never sang again after Edwin and Alton died.

God called Grandmother home on April 6, 1897. Grandfather followed two years later, and his last years were not easy. He missed Grandmother greatly. Only one letter from Grandfather Darwin still exists, written to Henry in the early 1880's.

It is very warm weather in southern Mich. The grass looks green, and the cherry tree's in full bloom. Apple bloom is a coming. On a fig tree the fruit appears before the leaves. They come late and Jesus says ye may know that summer is nigh. Franklin is marking out the corn ground. Plant some tomorrow. Sowed some cabbage seed today. Plenty of onions in the garden, or scallions as you are a mind to have it. The farmers all busy. It is agrowing time. Wish you were here to help us in harvest and have a good time. Since you have gone away there is no singing, no playing on the organ. John will sit in one corner and read to himself, and Mary Ann and your mother wash dishes and talk without any cessation like the ticks in the clock. Wheat will be two thirds of a crop. The price will be in proportion to the scarcity in the United States. If we should supply Europe with wheat would be worth ten or twelve shillings. It costs something to keep Europe in standing armeys. They must have bread, and so must we. Some farmers some ministers some tradesmen don't know the Earth is the Lord's and the fullness thereof and they dwell therein.

Book Two

Henry Ford
1853-1946

One hundred and fifty years before my father and mother moved from Hillsdale to the farm a cyclone of tremendous violence swept thru that part of the country laying low much of the primeval forest. Great trees, turned up by the roots, lay half decayed midst the second growth which had since sprung up. The township was thickly wooded with this new forest. The timber was young, tall, straight, and crowded: beech, maple, cherry, ash, walnut, butternut, elm, oak, and basswood. A wide spreading but shallow stream without banks ran throughout Father's one hundred acres from west to east, and on both sides grew the black ash timbers that furnished the rails for the new farm.

There was a sugar bush of one hundred trees or more, and one of the first awakening pleasures of spring came with the tapping of the trees. We first made a sharp undercut with an ax, and then drove in a spike made concave on the upper side to carry the sap into troughs of basswood. Against a fallen tree we built a fire, and swung a ten and a five pail kettle suspended by chains from a horizontal pole. Here through March and half of April we gathered the sap, carrying two pails at a time by a yoke comfortably fitting the neck and shoulders, and here we diligently boiled the sap all day until at night all of it was a thick syrup. This was taken to the house and reduced to maple sugar, and sometimes some of the neighbors were invited in to eat a dish.

This was one of the pleasures of farm life eagerly looked forward to. In the gathering of the sap there was rest and diversion. We would stop and peel up strips of basswood bark clear to the limbs thirty or forty feet above us, and by holding on to these, and backing up as far as we could, would give a run and jump, and swing through an arc of forty to fifty feet. Wild grapes were plentiful, and after a heavy frost walnuts and butter nuts covered the ground, and we often gathered ten or fifteen bushels. Edwin and Alton sold enough one winter to buy them each a calf. These nuts were often found in hollow trees or hollow logs where the squirrels had stored them for the winter supply. In the early days squirrels were so plentiful, gray, red, and black, that hunters would bring down two dozen or more in a two hour hunt. They were the pest of the pioneer farmer whose fields were surrounded by woods.

Deer, wolves, and wild cats were gone, but coon, fox, turkeys, geese, chucks, and pigeons were plentiful, too plentiful. I have seen Passenger Pigeons by the millions in a single flock fly over my head, beclouding the sun, and extending from horizon to horizon, and be several minutes passing over. Wild ducks were a common sight on our ponds. We thought nothing of it – and we owned no gun.

As late as the eighteen sixties I have seen turkeys, forty in a flock, come out of the woods into the corn fields in winter to eat the corn left in the standing shocks. One of my early recollections was seeing out of our north window two big wild toms, with long beards hanging down, come up thru our orchard from Uncle Asa's woods, whose objective was our log corn crib. This happened for several days in succession. The last visit they made, Edwin rushed out bareheaded, grabbed two sticks of stove wood, and fired straight at them, but missed. If he had only been an expert ball pitcher we might have had a turkey dinner.

I do not recall wild geese ever landing on our small ponds, but they would honk far above us in their "V" formation as they passed in a southeasterly direction in the fall, and northwesterly in the spring. In walking to town in the spring, just after the ice had gone out of Lake Baw Beese, one could see a thousand wild ducks with a sprinkling of wild geese and swans. It was not uncommon to see a Blue Heron slowly flapping its long awkward wings, and making some distant mud bank.

In those days, before so many anglers had depopulated our lakes, it was fun to fish, and we could be pretty sure to bring home a string of blue gills, bass, and perch. Spearing was then permitted, but this meant the wanton slaughter of two or three hundred fish in a single night. One June day Frank and I went to Lake Baw Beese and found an old scow that we had to bail constantly to keep above water. It was too dangerous for deep waters, yet we took chances and covered the lake in it, and found a school of blue gills, and took home a string of over eighty. Fish were thicker than game wardens in those days.

One day Father and I went fishing on a rather risky platform built over the swampy edge of Tamerack Lake. We threw out our hooks, and almost immediately Father hooked a large speckled bass, but just at the edge of the landing it wriggled off the hook. He was so excited he fell on his knees and plunged his arms their entire length into the water for that fish, which probably by that time was far enough away to be safe. It was a lake of not over twenty-five rods (one hundred thirty seven yards) across, a regular quagmire in the middle of Tamerack Swamp, a fearful black hole that made one fairly sit up in bed at night just to think of it, but it fairly swarmed with fish. How our footsteps quickened as we came nearer to the pond until we were on the dead run and arrived breathless to the water's edge. Could boyhood want or ask for anything better?

Our farm had many swales which were a blessing in disguise, for when cleared out and drained they became our best land around. The edges of these swales grew wild raspberries and blackberries. These water holes were a paradise for snakes – striped snakes, blue racers, black snakes, water snakes, and what will you. Mother was a bold attacker of these when going after berries. A racer six feet long had no terrors for her. I recall one Sunday afternoon when going to church with Father, Mother, Edwin, and Alton. Just before we reached the top of the hill two blue racers ran into a brush pile by the side of the road. The brush was set on fire, and the snakes killed as they ran out. In all our farm history of seventy-five years only one Massasauga rattler was ever found.

Father was born in Cornwall, Vermont in 1808, and his father, Benjamin, moved soon after to Union Hill, New York, where he built a farm, and ran a saw mill. The foundation of the saw mill can be seen there yet (1931), and the old farm is still standing, and in good repair. When Father was twenty-one the family sold out everything, and moved to Medina, Ohio where he and Mother were married in 1834. He was twenty-six, and she was twenty-two. When Mother was fifteen she bought a tea set which is in a perfect state of preservation to this day, all save the cream pitcher which Father kept on a girt in the stable with horse medicine until it was broken. Strange how little we prize some things. A bottle or an old teacup would have done as well.

I have visited Grandfather Benjamin's house in Medina. It is a very good looking frame house, and is still standing. Why he should leave it in 1838, and come to Hillsdale to buy a farm mostly marsh is not to be accounted for, except he possessed the Ford discontent and restless spirit of adventure. To be sure, my father, Darwin, and two other children had preceded him to Michigan, so that probably made the decision easier.

Brother Edwin was a child in arms in 1836 when Father moved from Medina to Michigan with ox team and wagon, and cow tied behind. Coming through the Maumee Swamp south of Toledo his wagon mired in the black muck. After some hours he got loose, and had proceeded two or three miles when he missed his pocket book. Mother suggested that he probably lost it back where he pried the wagon out of the mud, so he left mother and the baby with the oxen, and trudged back, and sure enough found it in plain sight. It contained three dollars, all the money that he had in the world.

That first winter they lived on a heavily timbered property in Adams, just east of Hillsdale. Beside a fallen log he rigged up a tent, and there lived, eating on basswood chips for plates. The cow was turned loose to browse in the woods while Father got out the timber for a log house. In a few days he notified what few neighbors he had that he was ready to raise his shanty. They came, and in a short time he was moved, and began keeping house in Michigan. As they sat one evening taking inventory of their possessions, and finding themselves reduced to a little flour and a piece of venison that one of the neighbors had sent, Father remarked, "Well, Julia, as long as we have a cow that gives milk for the baby we can make out someway." There was then a knock at the door, and a neighbor came with the bad news that he had fallen a tree that killed the cow. They were seemingly at the end of all things. I don't know what shift they made in this impossible state of affairs, but evidently Providence had a way out.

It was in this cabin that they heard wolves howl at night when they had only a blanket hung up in the opening for a door. During that first winter Mother was rocking the baby when a foot wrapped in a red rag suddenly appeared under the blanket in the doorway. At first she feared that Father had cut his foot, but when the blanket was pushed aside she saw Chief Baw Beese and several Indian braves from the local Pottawattamie tribe. They asked for food, so she gave them bread, and they went away without incident.

Father did not stay here long. He sold, and the next landing was a few miles north, near Homer Village, where Alton was born in 1838. But neither did he reign long there. Seized again by wanderlust, he left for Steuben County, Indiana where Benjamin was born in 1841. From there they moved to Rome, Michigan where Mary Ann was born in 1843. Sometime later they moved back to Indiana where Benjamin died in 1846, and where Frank was born in 1847. Two years later they moved to Hillsdale, a half mile east of the college on East Mechanic Street. But before leaving Indiana Father and Mother came out in a series of meetings conducted by Eld Staley, were baptized in Clear Lake, and joined a Free Will Baptist Church.

In 1849 Father loaded his family in a covered wagon, and with his brother Benjamin to drive the oxen, started on a long trip to seek their fortune in the far west. Poor Mother's heart longed to settle down and make a permanent home, especially during these years of bringing children into the world. For her it must have been a weary and hopeless life, and so needless, and so wandering and fruitless. What was this mania, this never wearied wanderlust that took possession of Father in those early years, and whence came of it? Was it the spirit of adventure ever seeking and never finding? Perhaps Abraham, who started out from home "not knowing whether he went", could explain. But that journey into the west was suddenly and perhaps providentially terminated before it had hardly begun, for somewhere between South Bend and Michigan City one of the oxen died. Becoming disheartened, they returned to Hillsdale where Helen was born in 1850, and I, the youngest, was born in 1853.

In the summer of 1853 the first laying of the cornerstone of the college occurred. Mother stood with me in her arms, looking over across the fields at the crowd assembled only half a mile away. I do not recall seeing the crowd, but have always claimed that I was an eye witness to the laying of both cornerstones in 1853 and 1875. Father, Mother, and I attended the last one. It was a great occasion. Professor Perrine facetiously remarked that he represented the tadpole period of Hillsdale College. Ex-President Fairchild, following, said, "If we came from the tadpole, and have advanced thus far intellectually, where in creation are we going to?" After the ceremony Mother spied Mrs. Emery, an old neighbor of hers, and wanted me to meet her. Mother said, "Mrs. Emery, this is my boy whom you used to see when he was a baby."

She looked me over from head to foot, and then remarked, "Well young feller, you've grown some since that mornin' I put the first shirt on ye." Embarrassed though I was, I bowed my belated thanks for that early service.

When Father moved to the farm in 1854 he was forty-six years old, Mother was forty-two, Edwin eighteen, Alton sixteen, Mary Ann eleven, Frank seven, Helen four, and I was one. We moved into a rude shanty, eighteen by twelve that Father and the two oldest boys had made ready to shelter the eight of us until a little later when we moved into a better built story and a half log home on the hill. For nine years thereafter the shanty was used as a cow stable and stood beside a log barn at the foot of the hill to the north. The barn consisted of a bay to the east, a horse stable on the west, a middle part used in the back to store grain, and the front for an entrance. It was here, during the last year of its existence that Father raved and shaved the shingles for the new house.

Many a skunk found his dwelling place under and around this barn, and met, also, the fate he deserved. The way old Jocko smelled gave evidence he tampered with the enemy. Old Jocko was a regular member of the family, a red, long, low bodied dog with short bandy legs. He was a bold chaser of thunder bolts, and became greatly excited in an electrical storm. He would plunge out of the door, and tear around the house and over the yard, howling as he went. Whether he ran against an obstruction or slipped or was struck by a thunderbolt in one of these escapades we could not tell, but he set up a terrible yelping, and one of the boys ran out and brought him in, and he went on three legs for a month or two, and never was quite himself after that. Poor chap, he was an unfortunate dog.

Having no corn crib, we hauled corn up to our two barn lofts by rope and pulley. One rainy day I lowered the basket to the floor, and put Jocko in, and hauled him up to the level of the loft, fastened the rope and mounted the ladder to swing the basket onto the platform, but the dog thought he could do it himself, and gave a jump. Alas, he only kicked the basket away from him, and came down twelve feet onto the bare floor, and broke his hip. He recovered after a long time, and could walk in a kind of sorry way, but he was practically done for. Thinking it best to miss some fireworks I never told how the broken hip happened. One morning in the winter of 1871 he followed me through the woods on my way to school, and that was his last journey. We never saw him more. This is a great deal to say about a dog, but he lived with us a number of years, and was death on skunks.

We children could not resist the temptation to play in the hay in the old log barn. This was taboo, especially on Sunday. There was to be no playing at anything on that sacred day, work or play. Father did not thrash the cider barrel for working on Sunday, but he would have prevented it if he could. One Sunday he spied us playing in the hay in the barn, and came running bareheaded and in his shirt sleeves. Frank and Helen escaped out the back window, and Frank was part way down the lane when Father appeared. Helen succeeded in getting out the window, and, lost in divine contemplation, was repeating some sacred texts of scripture as she walked along, apparently unconcerned. But I was cornered, for I was too small to climb out. I took a spanking, punishment for all three.

One Sunday morning while getting ready for church, Father was stropping his razor when Mary Ann, quite a Puritan herself, came bouncing into the house and said, "Father, Frank is singing something perfectly dreadful." The Sabbath desecrator was summoned to report in person without delay. "Franklin," Father said. Father always said Franklin when real business was at hand, and it was a kind of foreshadowing of doom. "Franklin, what have you been singing on this sacred day? Mary Ann says it's awful."

Frank stammered that it wasn't much of anything. "Come out with it, no denying it now," said Father.

"Oh it's just something I hear Bob Howell sing," replied the culprit.

"Well, sing it, I tell you," insisted the defender of the Holy Day.

"Why, I was just singing:

> *The Lord into his garden come,*
> *The calves stuck up their tails and run."*

Father, on hearing this parody of a good old church hymn, and struck with the incongruity of it, lost his dignity and shook with laughter. Father let him off with the promise never to sing it again. Frank, feeling that he had been let off easy, bounced out of doors, got down and rolled in the grass.

The log house at the top of the hill was surrounded by rose bushes, snow drops, and balsam, while two lilac bushes graced either side of the front door, and a row of sumacs surrounded the house about fifteen feet from the banking. Late every fall the outside of the house was chinked and plastered with mud-mortar to keep out the cold, but there was plenty of cold notwithstanding. There was a twelve by twenty-five lean to on the west side of the house that served as the kitchen. The living room was twenty by twenty-two, including the recess for the bed, which was curtained off.

The living room had a big fireplace in the north end that would take nice great big logs eighteen inches in diameter and three feet long. Father would walk them in on end. The hand irons were placed in front, and a fore stick laid on this, and wood piled in between. Often there would be two back logs, the smaller on top of the larger. When set ablaze the cheer it lent the room, with all the dancing shadows on the walls, made us laugh at winter winds and storms outside. The fireplace was the *piece de resistance*. It relieved the dullness and dreariness of many a day. But when the weather registered ten below we had to stand close to it, and turn around every minute or two like a pig roasting on a spit to keep from scorching on one side while we chilled on the other. This fireplace was the only heat we had, save that from the cook stove in the kitchen.

In the northwest corner was the door to the stairway, and in between that and the chimney was the wood closet. Helen and I had to see that it was well filled every

Saturday for the next day when no wood was to be brought in. This made us dread both days. Helen and I were not saints. Back of the living room were two recesses for beds, with a closet between them. This dark closet back of the living room was a place of horror. When we children were left alone for an evening, and in front of the fire when anyone would tell us ghost stories, Frank would say, "Henry, I dare you to go into that closet and shut the door."

Father and Mother slept in the east recess, and Mary Ann and Helen in the west. Edwin and Alton slept upstairs in the northeast part, in a little room they made by a simple board partition, and papered with the New York Ledger, and New York Tribune. Frank and I had our bed on the southeast side with the head next to the partition. The eves came down pretty close to our heads, with nothing but thin shaved oak shingles between us and the sky. How often we were lulled to sleep by the patter of the rain on the roof so near our heads.

> *"Oh the patter on the shingles has an echo in the heart,*
> *And a thousand dreamy fancies into busy being start."*

That chamber where we slept charms the memory to this day. Mother spun her rolls up there. From below we could hear her steady tread, back and forth, back and forth, to the hum of her spinning wheel, and the snarling of the spindle.

Suspended from the rafters along the west wall were bunches of smartweed, catnip, and ox balm, and peppermint Over in the corner was sure to be a cat or two with a litter of new kittens, and a bushel or two of corn piled around the chimney to dry for grinding. There were old chests full of interesting things, shelves for clothing, and there was the south window. How many days I've put my elbows on the sill and gazed out while the sun always shown in warm. Mother lost her shears one time, and went without them until one day I found them on that window sill.

Oh for a week back in this old house, to sleep there with that heavy red woolen blanket over us, and Mother to come up the last thing to tuck us in. I often got up when I heard Mother stirring the embers in the fireplace below, to keep her company in the kitchen, and to watch out of the west kitchen window, and wonder at the bright moon shining in. Mother told me about the man in the moon, and other things that aroused my childish imagination. She told me about a shining door in the west through which a beautiful boy went, and never came back. I suspect now she was thinking of her little Benjamin who left her when he was only five years old. Mother carried a burden of sorrow we children did not know about.

Mother had the poet's fancy, and as we walked together out in the fields she often quoted lines of poetry, half to herself and half to me, with a peculiar musical intonation and pathos. Her voice at these times had a great chorus for me. I adored Mother, and we were always chums. I was worried for fear I would lose her. One day out at the end of the lane I heard Alton and Edwin singing, "My Mother's Grave" set to a most doleful tune. I was seized with panic, and rushed down that lane losing my cap, which I never stopped to pick up, and plunged wildly into the house, and to my joy found Mother as usual at her work. Father, in his morning prayer, would speak of Jordan's swelling flood, and just across the "far banks of sweet deliverance." I would spring to my feet as soon as Father had taken us all to heaven, said "Amen," and going up to Mother would say, "Mother, let me see your teeth." When I saw they were all intact I was comforted to think she wouldn't have to cross Jordan right away.

Ah me. I am now old and gray, and Father and Mother and five of the family who knelt around that family altar night after night are now over in the Promise Land. Brother Frank has just arrived, and what a greeting and what a welcome he had from those kindred waiting at the gate. I imagine like Valiant-For-Truth (*a character in "Pilgrim's Progress"*), "all the trumpets sounded on the other side."

When in 1854 Father moved from Hillsdale to the farm, purchased for seven dollars an acre, it was reached by crossing over, or rather bumping over a quarter mile of corduroy road not yet dirt covered. A deep ditch lay on either side to drain the swamp through which it lay. Not a stick of timber had been cut, save what he cut for his first shanty just previous to moving in. As I try to throw myself into this situation I am deeply puzzled to know how a family of eight lived and got anything to eat before any timber was cut, or land cleared and a crop raised. They must have brought something from the farm they left, and Grandmother Polly may have seen that the family didn't starve. But under the best possible fortunes there must have been penury and hunger aplenty. Their pioneer start lacked a good many roses.

They began at once to clear the land, and get in a crop, a patch of potatoes, a small field of corn, and a garden, maybe for onions and turnips. Father must have been drawing cord wood almost at once to town. He has, to his record, about six hundred cords he cut and took to Hillsdale, and with the money could buy sugar and flour, shoes, and hardware. To get rid of the timber was a problem. One way was to draw together a great pile of logs, cover it with straw and dirt, and make a "coal pit." This would make charcoal that Father would sell to the blacksmiths. Another way was to make log heaps, and burn openly. Burning the log heaps and brush heaps after dark was a picnic. No Fourth of July fireworks could compare with it. The smell of the virgin soil, and the burning brush – who that has had his nostrils dilated by it can ever forget it?

A few neighbors preceded us. Old "Doc Latham" was one of those, with a home about two miles north of us, near the Lake Shore Railroad track. He was our pioneer doctor, and diligently dosed us with Golden Seal and quinine for "fever and ague," and there were plenty of those. The old doctor was an herb doctor, represented no school, never looked inside a medical school, and "knew more" than those who did. He needed no license. What good was a license in that mosquito infested country? He could be seen bending low in the fields and woods searching for herbs and roots with which he manufactured his own pills.

His old lame horse, which could be safely trusted to stand anywhere without tying, and when in motion had the speed of Aesop's tortoise, faithfully hauled his master's bulk, which was substantial, over the rough country roads. The doctor was a real character, so rotund he hadn't seen his own feet since middle age. I once saw him helpless astride a rail fence which he should never have attempted to climb. The balky leg just wouldn't go over until a good neighbor gave a friendly hoist. He was consequential to a degree, without the slightest inferiority complex. His vast self importance was matched by an unblushing pretentiousness as amusing as it was amazing. A neighbor once happened in just as the doctor's family was sitting down to supper at a table that had one of the table legs tied up with a splint. The doctor looked around over the table and inquired of his wife what she had done with all the silver spoons. A silver spoon was quite unknown in that primitive neighborhood. The doctor, like the rest, had a large family, a fantastic number as I recall, and got little from his practice. He owned little land, mostly marsh, and the rest hard scrabble, so it is doubtful if he could buy many silver spoons. Yet, he was a friendly man. The neighbors trusted him, and depended on him in accident or sickness, and he never failed to come day or night when called.

Father was fond of him, but could see through him, and they often bantered each other when they met. I witnessed a colloquy between them one day when the doctor was riding by, and stopped in front of the house. Father had just finished stacking flax in the front yard, and it did look neither like anything in heaven or on earth, except perhaps some pre-historic amphibian. The doctor spied it in the yard, and called out, "Darwin, what kind of critter you got there? Be sure to tie that up tonight so it won't sick the cows." Father retaliated by saying, "Doc, it looks like one of your patients who has just taken a dose of your handmade pills."

The doctor had come our way to let off some of his pent up enthusiasm. He had just returned from Illinois where he had been to look at some land for a future home. Father was a good natured listener to the doctor's grandiloquent bombast. The doctor sat bolt upright in his shaketty buckboard, and with grand flourishes of his arms, and waving his whip, described with eloquent voice the land he had located in the west. He "wouldn't trade it for all the land in Hillsdale County." Father had mounted a stump in the front yard the better to give absorbing attention, but pretended to be drawn irresistibly nearer. He got down from the stump and worked his way to the road. The doctor was still going strong and waxing more eloquent when Father suddenly grabbed a rail from the fence, and shoving it under the hind axle, gave a mighty hoist, and yelled, "Get up." The doctor was suddenly thrown off his balance, and came down out of the clouds minus his bilateral symmetry as well as his equanimity. I never saw the doctor peeved but this once. But when he moved away to Illinois everybody felt they had lost a faithful doctor and a genial friend and neighbor.

Steve Comstock, Dr. Latham's son-in-law, was hardly an admirer of the doctor's bombast, and after the doctor had written back from Illinois glowing over his newly acquired possessions, Steve facetiously remarked that the doctor had "acquired the whole south half of Chicago, and was about to close a contract for the north half." Steve was known for his dry wit, and he walked with his head down as if in meditation, perhaps thinking up a new joke.

In 1859 Mother's brother, Uncle Asa, and Aunt Betsy bought forty acres across the road from us. They gave Father a valuable horse for help in clearing the land, and Father, Edwin, and Alton were several months carrying out their part of the contract. They lived with us while putting up their log house. Later in 1863 they built the frame house now standing. They were good Episcopalians, and drove a yellow horse which they called "Rumphice and Milk" to town every Sunday morning. They diligently read their prayers night and morning. Uncle Asa loved books, was quiet and peace loving, but held his own opinions, and Aunt Betsy was the best of cooks. They were a great comfort to us, and he lent money to me several times to go to college. He was anxious that I finish my education, and they were scrupulously neat. Uncle Asa scrubbed his pigs with soap and water weekly, and one could eat off Aunt Betsy's back steps. And now they have lain in Oak Grove Cemetery for fifty years.

The first log school was built in 1849 about a mile north of the farm. It was built with whitewood logs eighteen to twenty inches in diameter, and was faced on the inside. It was a pretty good log schoolhouse, well built, and had four windows, two on the north, and two on the south. It had a single door facing east. A box stove occupied the center of the room, and desks ran the whole length on each side, with seats behind and low ones in front of these long desks. The teacher's desk stood at the west end. The building served for both school and church for fifteen years.

In the winter of 1867 a new stone school house was constructed across the road. In point of comfort the new building was no better than the log schoolhouse. The six windows were placed so near the ceiling that the sky was the only thing visible to the scholars. This made it a veritable prison. The noble thought on the part of the designers was to keep the children from having their minds disrupted from their books by any object outside. The seats were solid oak, narrow and flat, with the backs perpendicular so that we had about four inches of the seat to sit on, and our bones ached before the day was half spent. The whole thing was a torture chamber. Nothing worse could be devised, and proved the abysmal ignorance and stupidity of the building committee, whoever they were. I'm glad I don't remember. To be ignorant of a young child's simple needs and comfort through eight hours of study is a sin of the first magnitude. In those days the country schools were not graded. Each school taught what it pleased, and teachers were not required to attend any Normal (education) School, but could teach on a third grade certificate.

My own commitment to education occurred in 1867 as I sat listening to President Fairfield's baccalaureate sermon at the College, and I remember to this day an illustration he used to show the advantage an educated man had over an uneducated. The uneducated man was like one trying to lift a great rock by his hands. The educated man was like one who owned a crowbar, and pried over a fulcrum. I sat in the west gallery the Thursday following, and listened, and was thrilled over Henry Magee's graduation oration, as with a flourish of arms and the toss of his long brown hair he declared he had come to college without a dollar, had gone through, and was going out without a dollar. It sounded like "We brought nothing into this world, and it is certain we can carry nothing out." Anyway, sitting there, a lad of fourteen, I highly resolved to try without a dollar to obtain that coveted crowbar.

Our play at school in winter was skating, coasting, snow balling, fox and geese, and high sky. Indoors we played the needles eye, the miller and the mill, and Charlie is a nice young man. In the summer we swam in the beaver dam, and ate our noon lunch on top of Carustoch's Hill. What early scholar could forget it? From foot to summit grew great walnut, oak, and whitewood trees that the whirlwind missed. From the top of the hill the country could be seen for miles, including Baw Beese and its five lakes. This hill, with its towering trees, was a landmark seen from afar, and when the autumn poured her paint jobs out over the forests, this hill was a sight not easily matched for beauty. It was a spot that should have been preserved.

Religious activities were the heart of the community. The West Jefferson Free Will Baptist Church kept up an active existence for twenty years until it was absorbed by another church in 1876. The old log school was its cradle, for here all its public services were held, morning and evening preaching service, Sunday School Covenant meetings, and prayer meetings in the early days, until its services were transferred to the new school house. The date of its organization was about 1858, and Father and Mother were among its first members. In the late eighteen fifties there was a revival, at which time a number of the young people were baptized and joined the church. Among these were Alton and Mary Ann. In 1868 there was another revival, and among those who began Christian Life at that time were Helen and myself. There were seventeen in all, and we were baptized in Baw Beese Lake.

As candidates for baptism and church membership, we were examined by a number of ministers and deacons apparently wanting to make sure we had a genuine experience. In a semi-circle they confronted me, a boy of fourteen, for baptism and church membership. "My boy, are you fully conscious of these solemn vows you are about to make?"

"Yes," I answered.

"Do you realize you have been snatched as a brand from the burning?"

I didn't know exactly what that meant, but thought it must be all right, so I answered, "Yes."

"Do you know the exact moment and place when you experienced this sudden change, and the light shone in?"

"Well, no sir, but it was sometime during the meetings I felt a change."

"And so now are you sure you have yielded your will to the will of God?"

"Yes, sir, I am sure."

"But if it should be revealed to you that it was God's will that you were to die tonight, would you cheerfully say, 'Thy will be done'?"

And I suppose I said, "Yes," like any other youthful prevaricator who was almost scared to death.

But these old brethren were faithful souls. With growing fondness I think of them, these sponsors of religion in our pioneer community. They did have an affectionate solicitude for us who had just begun the Christian life. They diligently watched over us, and heartened and encouraged us. They were real people with warm hearts under all their rough exteriors. They were true soldiers of the cross in that they stood firm in the midst of ridicule and jest. They stood for the things of solid worth in the midst of much that was frivolous. They were the solid asset in that day. They were not always well balanced nor always consistent, but, all in all, they were the moral backbone of their times. They meant well, had warm hearts, stood for all that was best in their day, and long ago went up to Heaven in Elijah's chariot of fire. All honor to them, and their work will live and their influence go on.

Father Manning, as he was called, was for many years a missionary among the freedmen down "Caro way," and a man held in great affection by the colored people. Some years after Father Manning had left the mission I used to visit some of the colored churches he helped to organize. One morning in St. Louis I was eating breakfast with Deacon Brown when he reverently and solemnly said, "Brother Ford is setting where Brother Manning have set many times. You're setting in a big place, now let me tell you." And his wife added, "Indeed you is."

Father Manning was driven out by those who opposed Negro schools and "white nigger preachers." At Caro his school was burned. On one of his vacations in Hillsdale he held some revival meetings in our school house. It was the third of any consequence, judging by the results and the beginning of Christian life of those who became faithful and efficient in the church afterwards. Among them were Brother Frank and Aurilla Harris who later became his wife. They became an influential family in the community, and led their children who followed in their footsteps.

Two of the brethren who examined me for membership in 1868 were Father Baldwin and Father Hopkins. Those who never saw Father Baldwin have missed something unique. Nothing in the Heavens above or the earth beneath was ever just like him. To know him was to be reminded of the infinite variety of nature's product, and the amazing mixture of rare designs. His testimonies were quaint, but something to remember; his prayers were simple and seemed to indicate great intimacy with the Deity. When I was a lad I was present at a two-days' grove meeting, and heard him pray for rain. We were suffering from a drought, and he poured out his soul, and stormed the gates of Heaven, and said, "Lord, the creeks are dried up, the little colts and calves can't get any water, and even the squirrels and chipmunks can't get a drop to drink." The next day he was the preacher, and had his coat off and a smart shower came down, but he never halted. The harder it rained the harder he preached. He couldn't stop after praying for that rain; it wouldn't have looked respectful nor grateful.

In those days many ministers sat in the congregation while other ministers preached, and I had a Yankee, and possibly an irreverent, curiosity to watch the reaction of the sermon on the congregation. How plainly now I can see Father Hopkins, a little man with bushy white hair, straight back, and minus an inferiority complex, sitting upright on the front seat as if to give an air of respectability to the occasion, and resolved, live or die, he would keep awake. But, alas, half way through the service his head would suddenly drop, and as suddenly he would raise it as if giving full assent to what the minister was saying, and, repeating these motions several times, finally dropped off into continued and blissful slumber. The scriptures say, "He giveth His beloved sleep." During my ministry of forty-seven years I have had my full share of "beloveds" in my congregation, but their Sabbath siestas never irritated me, for it was visible proof I was doing some good when my sermons were soothing to peaceful slumber some over-tired "beloved."

For years Father led the congregational singing in our church, and his tunes were somewhat limited to such as Berlemny, St. Martius, Ortonville, Windom, Exhortation Communmeter, China, and a few others. As a boy I enjoyed Exhortation Communmeter. It had runs and broken time. The bass was quaint, and in places would hold its note while the air and time went galloping ahead. Then the air and alto would suddenly stop, and the bass would lumber on to catch up and push on ahead, and so on through the hymn. As he sang Father's chin whiskers would move up and down as if beating time.

One Sunday morning the choir was in the middle of an anthem, and going strong, when there was a sudden commotion in the pulpit, and looking up from our singing books we saw Eld Kearny had jumped from his chair, and was gazing straight up at the ceiling trying to locate a wasp that had lit on his bald head. The voices of the choir grew faint, and then ceased altogether, and with the anthem half finished, sat down in disgrace, scandalizing the service. But it was too much for humans whom God had made with a sense of the incongruous. Most everybody shook with suppressed laughter, but the deacons had a warning look that forbade no good.

Every Thursday there was an evening prayer and testimony meeting. It must seem strange that tired farmers, after a hard day's work, would walk a mile or more carrying their hymn books and bibles in their hands to hold a weekday prayer and testimony meeting. But these were well attended, for it was about all that was going on in the community. Brother Mullikin, always feeling a sense of the brevity of this mortal life, would rise and remind us that "a few more rising and setting suns would tell the story with him." Notwithstanding, he lived many many years to repeat this testimony until he reached the ripe age of ninety-four. Good old Sister Briggs would rise and "stand on Jordan's stormy banks" urging us to meet her in Caanan's fair and happy land. As she sat down, Father, who led the singing, would strike up:

> *"Amen, amen my soul replies,*
> *I'm bound to meet you in the skies."*

The faithful and tired old soul, after many trials and losses, finally did cross over, and her testimonies were heard no more.

Then it came Brother Vining's turn, but before rising to witness he would give a final squirt of tobacco juice under the old box stove, and follow it with a toss of his quid (*plug of chewing tobacco*), as if to dispose of all things earthy before taking his flight. Brother Vining had one eye hopelessly askew, so that while one was fastened upon us as if to search out our deadliest sins, the other automatically turned aloft, seemingly to discover the country "eye hath not seen."

The preachers, for the most part, came down from the college. Many were students, but much older than the students of the present day. Many a student preached his first sermon in our log school house. Some showed real preaching and sermonic ability, and afterwards rose to eminence. Others were not prophetic of future greatness. I recall one young man who thought he would do a real service to illuminate the minds of the untaught natives of the township by describing the mighty wonders of the Cosmos. In an eloquent and dramatic flight he declared that the "world was round as a horse's head."

Then there was one Collins, a "wonder" who betrayed no inferiority complex, and who could run off a perfect flood of words without saying anything. Well, he captured the whole community, Mother and brother Edwin excepted. It is no new observation that some people are too lazy to think, and some have nothing to think with. They are charmed by empty sound. But to do justice to the preachers and the preaching of that early day I must record that there were men of real character and ability who came down from the college to preach in our school house. Some were as ignorant as they were blessed, but they had "grace abounding."

I have a soft place, and an ever increasing affection for these dear old saints, and I mean no disrespect to them when I speak of their quaint ways. They have, one by one, finished their pilgrimage, and I trust found the country they started out for. The old school house where they worshiped was only an inn for these travelers on their way to Jerusalem. As I recall these primitive days, and these simple good folks, I am more and more seriously impressed that life with them was a great adventure, and a blessing to those of us who follow after. "Their works do follow them."

The people of a pioneer community could be depended upon for sociability. They were driven day and night with the work in clearing the land, yet found time to occasionally put on their Sunday best, and spend the afternoon taking tea with a group of neighbors in one of their houses. The women would take along their sewing or their knitting. The men, knowing less what to do with themselves, would sit uneasily in their starched clothes, and awkwardly pass the time feeling too proper, and glad when the time came to go home and get into their old clothes.

On one of these occasions taking place at "Uncle" Mike's, to which Father and Mother had been invited, I was entrusted to Mary Ann, who was fourteen going on twenty-five. She was duly instructed to keep watch and guard over me, and see that I did not leave the house. I felt desolate and forsaken, and watched for a chance to make a getaway, and go to the party. The chance came when Mary Ann went upstairs for a minute. I stepped slyly out, and was well on my way when from an upstairs window I was discovered, or rather my twinkling heels were. I saw her coming, and like the man chased by a bulldog prayed for "pep." I won out. In dirt and rags and out of breath I burst in upon the party to Mother's dismay, but "Aunt" Lida, the hostess, pled for me, and I was permitted to stay and play in the back yard, and eat at the second table. I always had a soft place in my heart for Aunt Lida after that.

The folks of that early day devised many ways to get together. There were logging bees, husking bees, apple peeling bees, quilting bees, wood bees, spelling school, singing school, concerts, sleigh riding, parties, skating parties, fishing parties, and corn roasts. When it came to getting enjoyment out of simple things the pioneer could not be outclassed. In the midst of penury and privation and entire want of luxuries, he satisfied and solaced himself with participation in these primitive social events and activities.

The minister's donation was the event of the year. Nothing could be substituted for this old fashioned festival. Many of the present generation never attended one, and thereby missed something to be regretted. Two or three Sundays preceding the event the names of the committee to put the thing over was read in church. When the parchment rattled as it was being unfolded, there was a flutter of excitement. Of course we knew every man and wife in the community were on that list. This was calculated to interest every family, and prevent any jealousy. A night or two previous to the donations every kitchen presented a busy scent, and from which sundry and savory smells issued. Cookies, fried cakes, baked beans, chickens, pies, minced, apple, and pumpkin pies, frosted cakes, etc., which foretold the grand feast about to be enjoyed. Children were too excited to sleep. There were hams taken out of the smoke house, vegetables and spare ribs all to go to make the minister's larder a joy unspeakable, and oats for the minister's horse. Chores were done early on the eventful night. A committee in the afternoon had put in tables and chairs, decorated the walls, prepared places for teams of horses out in the yard, and set everything in order.

The old folks came early to have a quiet visit and a cup of tea. Scarcely was it candle light before the first arrivals appeared, followed by an ever increasing stream. Teams filled the yard, cutters, bobs, sleigh bells, laughter, shouting, and tumult. The crowd, bundled in wraps and overcoats, came "stomping" in, big folks, little folks, middle sized folks, a merry rollicking crowd bent on a good time. They came lugging bundles, baskets, boxes, pails and receptacles of various sizes and shapes, containing all the good things country women knew how to cook. They were given into the hands of the committee in the kitchen who kept up a good natured bedlam of noise. There was the clatter of dishes, and a clatter of tongues, hurrying and scurrying here and there. High spirits reigned.

The young folks found a room where they could play their games, mostly the "needles eye." Tickets were sold for the first table, second table, third table, and there was enough for all, and abundance left over: pans of beans, countless fried cakes and biscuits, a chicken pie or two, and many frosted cakes. This is no exaggeration, for I attended a donation years ago when the pastor received two quarters of beef, five spare ribs, eighteen quarts of molasses, four chicken pies, and other leftovers to last the minister's family a long time. The good time everybody had was the talk for long afterwards. The good will donation is a joy of the past, and there is nothing left to take its place.

Our old community did not escape scandal. Strange as it may seem, while the neighbors loved to get together, and would give themselves unstintingly to each other in times of sickness and distress, nevertheless they did love to scrap and peddle gossip. Gossip had a ready market, and was strangely mixed with the social activities of these pioneers, who did their share of this deadly sinning. Once it resulted tragically, and forced a family of high standing, and one of the first families to settle in that community, to sell out at a sacrifice. Broken in spirit, they bid farewell to the associations of a lifetime, and departed after gossip sought to tear down the good name of a member of the family, causing immeasurable sorrow and anguish. Why did not someone in fiery and withering indignation stand up and protest this wrong? Well, I suppose there are saints in Heaven who were once not very saintly on earth. This case called for repentance and reparation, but it was never forthcoming.

One of the oft repeated phrases in my father's morning and evening prayers was, "Lord, break the tyrant's chains, and let the oppressed go free." He little realized what those prayers were going to cost him and the nation, for there were three sons kneeling at that altar who were going to answer those prayers some months later, two of them going to their graves as a sacrifice, and the other to fight hard battles, and pass through a southern prison. For many years the cherry stump stood, where one September day Alton stuck his corn knife into it, and said to Father and Edwin, "I'm done. I'm going to war." Father did not oppose, and the three of them came to the barn and harnessed the horses to the wagon, and took Alton to town. He enlisted in Co. G, 2nd Michigan Cavalry, Captain Fowler's Company, and was off to Grand Rapids to go into camp. An hour after he had enlisted he met Lon Mulliken on the streets of Hillsdale. Lon had a new harness on his shoulder which his father had just bought for him upon the promise he wouldn't go to war. Alton said, "Lon, I've enlisted, and I'm going tonight." Lon threw down the harness which his father picked up, and inquired where the place was to enlist, and both were off to Grand Rapids that night.

Before the regiment left for the South the boys had two days at home. I vividly recall that Sunday. While we were visiting, Father reached for the Bible, saying, "We may never be all together again, and I want to read and pray." Father read, "In my house are many mansions." It was a solemn moment, then we knelt and Father prayed. Just eight months later Lon wrote from Corinth, Mississippi that Alton was on his way to Cincinnati with typhoid fever. Father was in town when he got the news, went to Mitchell's bank and borrowed one hundred dollars, and ran his horses home in forty minutes. Mother got him ready, and he was off to Cincinnati that night.

As Father was climbing the hospital stairs in Cincinnati the nurse appeared above and said, "You are Alton Ford's father. He said you would come." Father talked with the doctor who said, "Alton is very sick with no chance for getting well, and he will want to die at home. Take him and go. He will probably live to reach there." Four men held his bed all the way to Toledo, and others stood ready to take their places. There was a long wait in Toledo for the Lake Shore train. En route to Hillsdale he came near going, but rallied. At Hillsdale Father found Shell Smith, who brought Alton home in his band wagon, and arrived Sunday morning. Fifty people came the Sunday he arrived. He lived five days, and died May 22, 1862. He was twenty-three years old, and his remains rest with those of his comrades in the soldiers circle at Oak Grove cemetery. I shall never forget those last moments when Father sat on the bed holding his hand and speaking words of encouragement as Alton entered the valley of the shadow.

Edwin enlisted in the fall of '62 in Co. D of the 18th Regiment of Michigan Volunteers. I recall the night he came home in his soldier's uniform. Mrs. Jones, a neighbor for whom Edwin had no great admiration, was at our house when he came. She rather flippantly referred to his outfit. Edwin shortly replied that, "George (her husband) has one just like it." She gave a whoop, and plunged out the back door and across the fields yelling as she went. The next morning she stood at her gate continuing the racket of the night before. The neighborhood impression was that she was glad to have George go, and her ado was all put on, but the neighbors may have been uncharitable.

For a short time the regiment was camped a mile east of town. Camp Woodbury was the name, and the day before the regiment was to leave the county was there. Long tables were spread, and a great feast was given. I remember getting lost and unable to find the folks. But Frank, who was put on the search, found me about two o'clock, and brought me a biscuit from one of the tables. Then he brought me to Aunt Cyphas' hangout, and she pitied me, and gave me a full meal from her basket.

The 18th broke camp the next morning to entrain for Dixie, and we all went up in the lumber wagon to bid Edwin and the boys good-bye. Frank and I left our folks, and went on foot up State Street past Dr. Talley's old place, and took our stand under a tree beside the road waiting for the soldiers. Soon, with flags flying and drums beating, and bayonets glistening in the morning sun the blue ranks of six soldiers abreast, keeping perfect step, came pouring over the hill opposite Grandfather's place. Fortunately we found Edwin on our side of the road, and the outside soldier of his rank. The thought of Edwin going away, the sound of the marshal music, and the sight of a thousand marching men thoroughly unnerved me, and broke me up, and I went along crying till we got to the station. Edwin on the train raised a window and talked with us as we stood clustered together on the platform until the train carrying one thousand soldiers pulled out of the depot. That was the last any of us saw Edwin.

I recall the winter day two years later when Father brought the work bench into the house, and was all day long making a box 30" x 36" out of rough unplaned basswood boards, which he planed down from 1" to 6/8". He hardly stopped to eat. It was a

Christmas box for Edwin who was stationed at Nashville, Tennessee. He did not ask for it, but we wanted to send it. Mother packed it full, and some of the neighbor women wanted to contribute. There were two stuffed baked chickens, sausage, ham, fried cakes, cookies, bread, biscuit, pork and beans, tea, coffee, sugar, butter and ginger bread made with sorghum molasses. A neighbor brought a glass can of preserves. Mother was fearful the glass might break, but the neighbor assured her that even if the contents did spill and run over everything, Edwin would still "get the good out of it." This salvaging of the jam failed to impress Mother, but out of courtesy the jam went in. There were other things put in that box, stockings, mittens, writing paper, buttons, thread, soap, and handkerchiefs. When the Christmas box arrived Edwin was on picket duty, and it was some hours before he was at liberty to look into that box. He had plenty of company for a while and as long as the contents of the box lasted.

Edwin was well posted on the war, and wrote long letters discussing its stages both in the eastern and western divisions. The long stay in Nashville was irksome to him, and he was anxious for real service, and the smell of gun powder at the front. He was to get his wish, for Hood came up from the southeast and invaded Nashville, and outside of the city there was a battle in which the 18th was engaged. In September 1864 he was taken prisoner after a battle near Athens, Alabama, and was imprisoned in the southern prison at Cahawba, Alabama. The conditions at Cahawba were grim, but not as grim as at other prisons, such as Andersonville. Their worst suffering was caused by periodic flooding. The prison was located on low ground along the Alabama River, and when the river overflowed its banks the prisoners had to retreat to the rafters until the flood waters subsided.

In January 1865 Edwin wrote to my sister, Mary Ann, trying to convince her that his life as a prisoner was tolerable:

Dear Sister,

As I have another opportunity of sending you a letter I will do so. I have nothing new to write. Everything goes on about the same from one day to another – about as it used to when I was with the regiment. I am well & I believe that the rest of my company who are here are the same. Amos Sawyer is back from the hospital all right. We are all doing well and in as good spirits as ever. I have plenty to eat, have an excellent appetite, and weigh more than I ever did at home. That don't look much like starving. It is four months to the day since we were captured. The time has passed very quickly to all of us. A little more than seven months and my time of service will close – not very long to wait.

It is no use to worry & be overanxious about those who are absent. I am all right and hope that Frank & all the rest of you are the same. Tell him for me that he must be a good boy & a good soldier as he resolved to in the beginning & not be discouraged. I suppose that you are in your new house. Don't think that I am suffering with the cold this winter for I am not – have plenty to wear and blankets enough, and pass the time just as comfortable as anyone can in a military prison.

I suppose that Father has his hands full this winter. Everything to do with no one to help him but Henry, but I will be at home next winter if nothing happens. Would like to hear from all the friends, but that is out of the question. Give them all my best wishes. Tell Washington Mann's wife that he is well and about as wild as ever. We are none of us very dispirited. In fact, have about as much spirit as ever. Are in no danger of dying of the blues. Can't write any more now. Why don't some of my numerous friends write to me now as they used to? Answer right away.

Yours,
Good by
Edwin

Edwin was in Cahawba prison for seven months until April 1865 when he was exchanged and put on a steamboat packed with 2100 other prisoners bound for the North. The steamer, the Sultana, was old and its boilers blew up, and the packet caught fire. Hundreds were thrown into the water by the explosion. Others jumped overboard, Edwin among them, and he and 1600 others found watery graves. There was little chance to survive, as the river at that time had overflowed its banks, and at this point was ten miles wide.

The soldiers, weak and emaciated from prison life were on their way home. A letter from Edwin, written at Vicksburg and sent overland informed us that he would be home three days after the arrival of his letter. The letter was read as we gathered before the old fireplace, and we were all in high glee. That very moment Edwin was a victim of the cold waters of the Mississippi. Next day Mr. Mullikin, coming from town, spoke of rumors that some kind of marine disaster had happened on the Mississippi, and that Andersonville and Cahawba prisoners were in it, but it was a floating rumor and nothing definite.

After Father and Mother had seen the Mullikins, and learned what they could, they started for town to find out what they could further. Joe Stevens, one of Hillsdale's boys, and one of those rescued, had just reached home. He told the sad news about Edwin; that he, Edwin, and Steven's brother-in-law roamed the burning ship together trying to devise some way of escape. All at once Edwin was missing. Stevens said that probably he had jumped overboard, as they all had to, for the boat was fast being consumed by the flames. The next day searching parties found Edwin lying at the foot of a sapling in three feet of water in the overflow where he had clung, probably until chilled and unconscious. He lies buried with hundreds of his comrades in the National Soldiers Cemetery at Memphis. Aunt Mary Mead, my son Rob, and I are the only relations to visit his resting place. The magnolia blossoms have floated down upon his grave for sixty-six years. I will not describe the days following in the old home. Uncle Elihu and Aunt Pheason and Uncle Ben hurried down after getting the news. I need not describe the meeting. Edwin had always been a favorite with Uncle Elihu.

Back in the winter of '61 and '62 Mother had promised Frank, then but fifteen years old, a double breasted frock coat with brass buttons, on condition he would give up all thought of going to war, for he was crazy to go, and talked and thought of little else. This staved the matter off for two years, but in 1864, just past seventeen, nothing could hold him longer, and March 3rd he enlisted in Colonel Richaby's company, and in May the company left Hillsdale for the front. A Baltimore and Ohio train bore him down past Harpers Ferry and Washington to join Grant's Eastern Division. Frank saw more real fighting than either of his brothers. He was in the battle of Cold Harbor and the battles before Petersburg on June 20, 1864, and witnessed the blowing up of the mine that destroyed the rebel fort.

On March 25, 1865 he was taken prisoner, but after six days in Libby Prison he was paroled, as Richmond was being evacuated, and General Lee's army was withdrawing from the city only to be captured a few days later near Appomattox by General Grant. Frank was fortunate to get only a taste of southern prison life. He arrived home on a thirty day furlough, and then had to report at Camp Chase at Columbus, Ohio to be paid off and discharged. When he came home on furlough he stopped at the post office and picked up a letter from Edwin that had been written at Vicksburg, Mississippi. Arriving home that evening he sat with us before the fireplace when the letter was read.

Coupled with these events occurred the great national tragedy: President Lincoln's assassination. We were at breakfast when Uncle Asa came in and stood for a moment, white and mute. His mouth worked, but he could not speak. Mother, alarmed, exclaimed, "Asa, what is it? What has happened?" And he replied, "Lincoln was assassinated last night. A man just brought the news." Father shoved back from the table, I can see him now, and got to his feet, and declared it wasn't so. In fifteen minutes with old Betsy hitched to the buckboard, he was speeding to Hillsdale. He found excited crowds on the streets, and the flags at half mast, for the nation's savior and chief lay cold in death in the nation's capital.

At the end of his furlough Frank went to Columbus in June to get his discharge, and on the day he was due home Father and Mother went into town to pick him up from the train station. Toward evening I was watching the road. As they drove in at the gate and up the hill only Father and Mother were visible. Heartsick, I said, "Didn't Frank come?" Just then he jumped out from behind. That was one happy day among all the sad and dreary ones that had preceded.

Events occurred thick and fast in July 1865. Grandfather and Grandmother died only ten days apart. Their nine children were present, meeting together for the first time in thirty-five years. All their children survived them. The next year, 1866, Uncle John came to make his home with us. He came with his books. He spurred us on to read, and go to college, and his personal influence had much to do with religion and education in our family.

During the war politics and policies were a disturbing and sometimes dangerous matter to discuss. Upon the streets of Hillsdale might be seen groups of men talking excitedly and sometimes angrily. Neighbors were at loggerheads and often became bitter enemies. The air was thick with imprecations. Such epithets as Copperhead, black abolitionist, sesest, nigger lover, nigger hater, traitor, Southern sympathizer, rebels at home, and enemies in the rear were bandied about and angrily flung at each other. There were frequent fist fights and knock downs. There was plenty of lying propaganda, accusations, vilification, mud slinging, etc. Blood was constantly at the boiling point. Primitive instinct showed up and had sway. People were bereft of their just and sober senses. Lifelong friendships were tragically broken. War rancor survived the civil conflict. Deep wounds were made that took years to heal. These were some of the serious results of war. Sherman was right in his definition of war (*war is hell*). He made it none too strong; that is what war is, and nothing else.

The Civil War made people of the North poor as well as it impoverished the South. Our community had been drained of seventy two strong young men. War took only the best. Women, mothers and sisters, and children had to work in the fields. Farming during the war was more or less slipshod. Taxes were heavy, and there was little to pay them with, so that the war left a run down state of affairs. In consequence, Frank, upon returning, faced a serious situation. Now that Edwin and Alton were gone he had to take upon his shoulders heavy burdens, sharing them with Father and Mother. I was but twelve, and in school. Frank was eighteen, and had little chance for schooling after his return. The farm required his time from there on, so that, except the fifteen months he was in the army, he spent seventy five years on the old homestead.

Everywhere can be seen the results of his labors. Everything speaks of him. He was called on to bear ever increasing burdens now that Father and Mother and Uncle John were wearing out, and fast ageing, and suffering failing strength. For years Mary Ann was an invalid, which greatly added to the already too heavy burdens of Frank and his wife. Their service of love and care extending over many years are beyond all estimate, but are all written in the book. The "Well done, good and faithful servant," can be said of them as to none of the rest of us, except of sister Mary who also with rare devotion gave her life unreservedly to the old home and the family.

Helen had married in '74, and was busy with a growing family in the west. And I, whose chance for education could never have been without the help of Frank and Mary and Father and Mother, had married in 1880, and was living away, so that the cares and burdens fell heavily upon those at the farm. Those who will occupy a front seat in the Heavenly Courts are not those who, fed by applause, live a somewhat public and spectacular life, but those who encouraged by no praise, and whose sacrifices are unknown, and have no personal ambitions, and who covet and want no praise, they are the ones who will someday be counted as most worthy.

Frank had not the privileges of the schools, but he possessed the sovereign grace of dependability and reliability, common sense and balanced judgment, and with it a sense of right as great or greater than any of his father's family. Mary, while a dreamer with a poet's mind and a restlessness for much that she longed to have, and longed to be, nevertheless in faithfulness to her own was never found wanting. Hers, too, was the full measure of devotion.

It will be conceded by all her children that Mother was the central joy. Without her the home would have been strangely empty and desolate. One incident alone, which may seem trifling and inconsequential to some, is sufficient to prove the beauty and holiness of her character. I once asked her what events in her life were the hardest to bear. She spoke diffidently of several, but one stands out in my memory, and one she told with a choking voice. It was to see her children suffer want, and go without some of the commonest and most necessary things that other children had. She did not mind, she said, going without things herself, but to see her children suffering and pinched by penury was hard to bear.

Mother did her best in those days of want. She worked away into the hours of the night, one and two o'clock to provide what would barely keep soul and body together. I never knew Mother to provide for herself what she could possibly do without. I remember, though sixty-five years have passed, a straw bonnet which she wore seven or eight years that she carefully kept in the upper bureau drawer. It had mortified her to wear it. She had skimped to save a penny here and a penny there until she had two dollars to buy another. But one day she put it into my hands for some need I had when in school, and thoughtless that I was I accepted it and Mother still wore the faded bonnet. Among the sins to confront me at the great Assizes, I hope the merciful judge will not bring forth that old bonnet of Mother's, and ask me, right before the assembled nations, if I recognize it.

In 1929 the old homestead passed out of the family possessions after being occupied by them for three quarters of a century, for the last occupant could no longer care for it on account of age and failing strength. Needless to say, parting with the old home brought poignant sorrow. The household goods were loaded, the empty rooms were swept for the last time, the keys were turned in the doors, and at the bottom of the hill the departing family turned and looked back upon smokeless chimneys and a home left to brooding silence. One can easily imagine the old farm, heart broken over being forsaken and left behind by those whom it had sheltered from infancy.

But let it be known and be assured that as long as one of its children remains, so long will it be enshrined in his affections no matter how long he may live or how far he may wander. For here Father and Mother came in their prime with us children. Here they cleared the land and cultivated the virgin fields, and wore a living from its responsive soil. Here they built the log home on the hill, and embroidered it with vines and flowers. And in that home, by candle light, Father read out of the family bible mornings and evenings, and knelt with his family to pray. And here with brave and cheerful hearts in the early days they faced toil, hardships, and penury. Here we children grew up in a home that sheltered us from storms. Here we waded in the brook, went to the woods and gathered cow slip in the meadows. Here under the trees we rested at noon time, and the big barn welcomed us on rainy days, and the hill afforded us a sliding place in winter.

From this home Edwin and Alton and Frank left for the war, and here Alton was brought back to die. To this home Frank returned from Libby Prison, and to this home Edwin was fondly returning when the cold waters of the Mississippi claimed him. Here Helen was married. Here Frank and Aurilla, his wife, began keeping house, and here their three children were born. Here during the dreadful winter of 1877 their little daughter Edith, and Helen's two children died of diphtheria. Here Uncle John came with his books to live and share our hearthstone for forty-five years, and to inspire us children with greater things. Here in Father's bedroom he slept his last sleep. Here Father and Mother, bent with age, and walking with faltering steps, laid down the burden, and moved into the Eternal Mansion. Here sister Mary wrote and toiled for the old folks until worn out in loving service, "fell in sleep." Here Frank and Aurilla for long and strenuous years assumed and took upon themselves unprecedented burdens, and with cheerful courage carried on until the infirmities of old age called a halt.

Such are the associations and memories of the old farm. How sacred that spot. How tenderly and reverently we recount the old days spent on that one hundred acres, section 18, Jefferson Township. It has been the brightest spot on earth to all of us.

> *"The heart has many passages*
> *Through which the feelings roam,*
> *But its middle aisle is sacred*
> *To the old old home."*

Epilogue
By James Ford

H enry, the youngest child, was born in 1853, and lived on the farm until entering Hillsdale College in 1870. His education was frequently interrupted when he taught school to help earn money for his college expenses, but he persisted and graduated in 1879. He was selected to give the commencement oration at his graduation ceremony, and in that speech displayed some of the intelligence, humor, and command of the English language that characterize his later writings, albeit without the gentle grace and doubt that would come with age:

The world's university cannot be found on any map. It has no particular latitude or longitude. It has no especial post-office address. But, like love, it is found in "The camp, the wood, the field and the grove." (The student) is day by day acquiring a knowledge never found between the covers of any book yet written, the knowledge of experience and observation. So the newly graduated is alone in the world with a diploma. That diploma is a good thing, but it only tells what has been done, and sometimes tells more than the whole truth about that. But admitting that it has been fairly earned, it is only a certificate, stating that the one whose name it bears is merely prepared for entrance into that greater, that higher school – the world.

The worthy man is, therefore, the self made man, and only as he is self-made has he honor. Honor is, therefore, the indirect result of genius- the genius for labor- an inheritance which nature would give to all the sons of men. But this genius for labor fails when it is spread over too much surface – when it attempts too many things. Concentration of effort in carrying out a single plan is the secret of great men's success. The grandest old hero that ever lived (St. Paul) had a motto – a good one for us all: "One thing I do, I press to the mark." As students, here or elsewhere, we shall succeed only as we bend our whole effort in one direction, having one mark and one goal; and the direction of our purpose here in school will determine the result of our lives in that greater, that higher school – the world.

After one more year of study he earned a divinity degree, and was ordained at Commencement in 1880. That same year he married a classmate, Sarah (Sadie) Searle. Sarah came to Hillsdale from her home in Kansas, and Henry was immediately smitten. When he decided to ask her to be his wife he did so by walking her through Oak Grove Cemetery, just north of the college. There at the family plot he proposed by asking, "How would you like to have your bones buried here?" No one knows how she responded to that romantic invitation, but she apparently liked the offer, for she did marry him, and her bones rest next to Henry's in Oak Grove today.

Sarah's wedding dress was made by her mother out of three cashmere scarves. No picture of her in the dress exists, but there is a newspaper article from the Topeka Daily Capital describing the Sept. 9, 1880 wedding:

"The bride wore a trained robe of white cashmere and white satin, a tulle veil which enveloped her completely, fastened with lilies of the valley and orange blossoms, and the groom was attired in conventional black."

Although we have no pictures of Sarah in the dress, we do know what it looked like, because it has survived until today, stored in an ordinary cardboard box. Stored, but not forgotten. From time to time the dress has been taken out, pressed, and worn by other brides, six by present count in addition to Sarah. They include my mother in 1942, an aunt, a cousin, my sister, and my wife, Hattie, at our wedding in 1975. Most recently it was worn by our daughter, Mary, in 2004. The dress is no longer white. It is now an attractive ivory, and with luck will someday be worn by other brides, even those with no desire to reside in Oak Grove Cemetery.

Following the marriage Henry started his ministry as pastor of the Free Baptist Church in New Lyme, Ohio, and it was there that his first two children were born, Paul in 1882, and Ruth in 1884. He then served as pastor in Lansing, Michigan for a few years until he was appointed State Agent for the Free Baptist Church Association of Michigan in 1887. While Henry looked for a permanent home in Hillsdale, Sarah took the children to visit her family in Kansas, and while there they suffered the same tragedy that Darwin and Julia had suffered forty-one years earlier, the loss of a five year old boy, when little Paul died of malaria. We don't know if that loss shook Henry's religious faith, but he certainly never gave any indication that it did.

After the death of Paul, Henry and Sarah had two more children, Robert (my grandfather) in 1888, and Franklin Edwin (Ned) in 1890. On Robert's twenty-eighth birthday Sarah reminded him of that cold February morning when he entered the world.

Dear Bob,

Twenty eight years ago in Topeka, Kansas there was no snow on the ground, and spring was coming, but that was a small matter beside the coming of "little Paul's brother." How welcome he was, and how we had hoped for a boy – not to take Paul's place, but to comfort us with a boy's life and ways, and we found Bob – just the very boy we wanted. Your father and I have been thinking about the February winds that blew in 1888, and what a little fellow you were to face the winds and storms of the world. Perhaps we have told you so often what each one of the family said about you that you know it by heart, but I go over it in my mind in the foolish way that mothers have. You may be sure that all the family, to the remotest twig, were glad you came. Bob, you have been a great comfort to us. Your father is going to write when he comes back from the Kentucky Association…..

It appears from his letters that Robert was somewhat less introspective than his father, more robust and adventurous by nature, and less subtle in his humor. Robert always regretted that his father was so often gone on church business during Robert's childhood, but there remained a special bond between this father and son that persisted through the separations and into adulthood when Robert became the absentee by moving to Texas. Each presumably may have admired the qualities in the other that he lacked himself. And Henry may have seen some of the same spirit in Robert that he had known in the two older brothers who had died so young so many years ago.

For the next twenty-five years Henry held various administrative positions in the Free Baptist Church, and was often away from home for long stretches while visiting churches throughout the Midwest. Then in 1911 he was instrumental in uniting the Free Baptists with the Northern Baptist Convention. Following that union he returned to pastoral work, first in Maine from 1912 to 1919, and then from 1919 to 1923 at the College Baptist Church in Hillsdale, thereby closing the ministerial circle that had started with his ordination there forty-three years earlier. There is no known reason for his resignation from the College Baptist Church, but it seems likely that he was too liberal in his thinking for that conservative congregation. Late in life he expressed admiration for some of the tenets of prayer in the Catholic Church, and at the same time expressed reservations about the virgin birth. He probably never expressed such reservations publicly, but he could not have concealed his gentle, humanistic view of the world that may have offended those seeking a simpler doctrine. And he was seventy years old, so it was time to retire.

For the remainder of his life he lived with his youngest son, Ned, on a farm in Brooklyn, Michigan, twenty miles east of Hillsdale. When the opportunity offered he would preach as a substitute pastor in local churches, and otherwise kept busy maintaining a garden, and helping with as much of the farm work as his health allowed. He was with Ned when Robert died in 1931, and when Sarah died in 1933. Shortly after her death he wrote of his regret at having spent so many years traveling for the church while his children were young:

> *"If I had my life to live over again I would not leave her twenty years, and go on the road, and leave her alone to bring up the children. She never complained, but I*

know now how hard it must have been to live that twenty years. It was too much to ask of her."

During his later years he spent time writing letters to children, relatives, and friends, discussing a wide range of topics, explaining his religious beliefs, and often reminiscing about the farm and the folks who lived there. The following are excerpts from those letters.

July 15, 1944
My Dear Linn (his brother Frank's son),

You had the good fortune to be born & raised in a religious environment & of religious forebears, and have appreciated & followed & are practicing & handing on down the faith & spirit of our culture. I have observed this in you with great satisfaction. This religious culture & testimony & treasure distinctly belongs to your two ancestral relatives, and you have a tremendous & eternal treasure. With all its primitive crudeness the bible is a wonderful book – doubtless the most beautiful ever written – made up of various manuscript writings of various religious authors – The Hebrew was a religious genius & specialist, and had the highest conception of God, and a spiritual study far beyond any other people. Much that was crude and primitive crept into their writings & their religious beliefs. I have been studying the bible for 70 years, and there is much that is puzzling – yet it is the best I know, and all we know of God and faith comes from that old book. I am interested to note that in reading the letters of St. Paul to the churches that you cannot understand & can't see much sense to. Well, you are not alone there. Paul's spiritual psychology is often baffling, but the churches he wrote to must have understood, because he was not used to speaking above the heads of his disciples. Paul was practical, but he sounded depths religiously & experimentally that we can't fathom. I think Paul was a wonder. The Christian

Church never gave birth to his equal – not even Augustine nor any of the great fathers of the early church compared with him.

Well, Linn, I'm down close to the finish. My work is done. How I wish it could have been done better. I conclude my work and look back with many serious regrets for failures and much that seems slipshod and ineffectual, and much that was foolish. I haven't practiced the life of prayer as much as I should. I have often been willful and had my own way. But my hope is in the infinite riches of God's grace.

Affectionately,
Uncle Henry

February 24, 19—
Dear Edna (Frank's daughter),

I am sending some more "Old Masters." But that old barn has many memories – we used to ride the horses to water and ride back & slide off just as they were shooting in at that stable door. The north window of the bay was up about 8 feet – the one Frank and Helen climbed out of & left me in the hands of the enemy. We had many a good time in that old bay. With these doors wide open Father shaved all the shingles for his new home in 1864. There was a pile of shavings outside. Well, that old barn makes me homesick for the old days & how well I can see the forms and faces that have since disappeared – 80 years ago. Helen and I gathered cow slips along the creek that overflowed – we had them for greens – bushels of them.

With love, Uncle Henry

March 29, 19—
Dear Linn & Clara,

Wish you or some of the relatives would buy back the old farm – would like to have it come back into the Ford family – so many fond recollections & a few not so fond. I'm hungry to go fishing & cast my hook into Baw Beese Lake once more just as Frank and I used to do. But there are not so many fish there as there once were, nor so many wild ducks & geese as I used to see when walking up the railroad. Mercy, how long has it been since I walked those ties – seventy years or more. Guess it was last summer Edna & I rode down the new highway between the lakes, and went to the farm & up to Warren's. The old neighborhood looks awful, the barns & houses wretched. Two years ago Jack and Willis McRitchie drove me down thru the old neighborhood, and I was so ashamed at the looks of things. All the way along I had to explain that our forebears kept things spick & span, and would turn over in their graves trying to go back to sleep after getting up and seeing decay everywhere. Well, the old folks are all gone.

Well, this isn't much of a letter, but come sometime and let us go fishing together. I believe there are a few more blue gills in Baw Beese Lake anxious to go into the frying pan. It is a good time for relations to keep in touch.

Love, Uncle Henry

February 21, 1945
Dear Linn & Clara,

My writing has become so impossible and bad for the eyes that it will be a kindness to make my letters short. Well, how do your children enjoy living on the same street? You must find it a great pleasure and comfort. You should pray to have that arrangement continue, to be near enough so you can drop in of an evening for a little visit. Why, it will make you young again, and you will renew *your youth. They will open the door and give you a cheery welcome, and that will be a life worth living. None of my children ever lived near enough so we could do that. But we did make journeys to see them, and how happy we were. Sarah was a blessed girl to travel with. It was such a pleasure to go with her into the dining car and have a breakfast. She only wanted a cup of weak coffee & buttered toast, but I wanted good coffee and some toast & Roquefort cheese. Then we would sit long and talk & look out of the window at the landscape as we rushed along. Oh what would I give for one such journey with Sarah now. It never can be until I journey by & by to go to see her. You and all the others will take all the comfort you can while you have each other & your children. You are happier than you know, and someday you will find yourself saying that.*

Love,
Uncle Henry

Henry journeyed to see Sarah on June 3, 1946 at the age of 93. In his last letter, written just a few weeks before his death, he mentioned his nearness to the crossing, and wondered if he would like the next world as well as he did this, and whether that world would like him.

Book Three

Robert Ford
1888-1931

obert was the second son of Henry and Sarah, born in Kansas on a blustery February day in 1888 just two months after the death of his older brother, Paul. Robert grew up in Hillsdale, across the street from his Great Aunt Caroline and Great Aunt Mary Mead, and graduated from Hillsdale College in 1911. During Robert's formative years Henry was often traveling on church business, leaving much of the child rearing to Sarah, a fact that was later regretted by both Robert and his father. While at Hillsdale College he was a successful athlete on the football and track teams, and liked to stand in all kinds of weather on the top of the bell tower that adorned Central Hall, apparently having inherited the spirit of adventure that motivated his grandparents and great-grandparents in earlier years.

In 1913 Robert married Leithel Patton, who had been a classmate at Hillsdale College. Before their marriage Robert taught for a year in Niles, Michigan, and then a year in Baton Rouge, Louisiana. After the marriage he spent two years as the high school principal in Napoleonville, Louisiana before returning to Michigan to be the superintendent of schools in Alpena. But he was never really satisfied with a profession in education, and in 1919 he moved to Wichita Falls, Texas to go into business with his father-in-law.

Robert and Leithel had four children, Robert Jr. (1914), John (1917), Margaret (1921), and William (1926). Robert's life was tragically cut short by diabetes and pneumonia in 1931 at the age of forty-three, but we do have some measure of the man from the letters that he wrote home to his parents every Sunday evening. Regrettably many of those letters have been lost, with the exception of one letter from Niles in 1912, a number of letters written from 1913 to 1915 while he lived in Louisiana, and another series written from 1920 to 1931 while he lived in Texas. The following are excerpts from those letters, along with a few that were written by his parents and his wife. The final series are the poignant letters and telegrams exchanged between Michigan and Texas at the time of his death.

The first letter was written by Henry to his son, Robert, in 1897 when Robert was nine. It was written from somewhere on the road while Henry was traveling on church business for the Free Will Baptist Church.

1897

My dear Rob,

I'm going to write you today. I've been thinking of you ever since you came to the depot with me. You are 9 years old. I remember when I was 9. It was 1862, the year Alton died. I rode up to Hillsdale in a lumber wagon with Frank who was 15 – we sat behind on a board, & Father drove. Mother sat with him, & Mary Ann & Helen on the middle seat & Edwin with us boys. We buried Alton, & the soldiers fired off 12 guns. We were all so sad that day.

You are 9 years old and now you must begin to be a man and think about what part of the work to take. You must think to help Mother, for I am gone and can't help her. You will have to take my place and think *what to do. She will have to depend on you. You are her man now. You have the making of a nice man if you want to be one, and I think you do. Now the way to be a man is*

To discipline everything that's mean and low
To be kind to Ned and Ruth and Mama & schoolmates
To be helpful. Try & help Mama
To be happy – Be just as happy as you can – Don't find fault or whine

If you do this, people will say, "Do you know Rob Ford, he's just a man, every inch of him."

Now I want you to remember another thing. We think of you and try to plan for you, and when we don't get you things it is because it isn't best for you to have them. Now we have a nice house, or will when it is all done, but we owe a lot of money on it which has got to be paid in June or the man can take it away from us. So we are saving our money to pay so we can keep our house. I want you to save all you can.

I'm lonesome away off here, but I can't come home now, but must work. I want you to go up to Harvey Reynolds & get his grapevines which he promised me & Mr. Ellis will set them out by the lattice. Don't forget. Perhaps Mama will write a note to send by you. I wish you could see these mountains.

Papa

Robert and Leithel were married for only seventeen years, and Leithel survived him by almost fifty years. I was thirty-four when she died, but one of my regrets is that I never talked to her in any detail about the grandfather I never knew. I do recall asking her once why she never remarried, and she responded, "I wouldn't take a million dollars for the husband I had, and wouldn't give you a dollar for another." I also recall her talking about his death. She said that the image she could not forget was how beautiful his hands looked as he lay in his casket. They were obviously devoted to each other, but I don't know why, and as I got involved in putting together this family history I wondered what it was about Robert that led Grandma to marry him. Perhaps some of the answer can be found in the only letter we have between them. He wrote it to her in the summer of 1912 while studying at the University of Michigan for his master's degree. A recent psychological study postulated that a woman chooses her husband at least in part by the way that he responds to children. The premise is that women can tell if a man truly enjoys children, and if he does this makes him a more attractive mate. The letter that Robert wrote in 1912 leaves little doubt that he loved children.

July 19, 1912 (Ann Arbor)
My dear "Little One,"

We are all frozen up here, the weather has taken a decided turn and everybody is shivering. Last night Bake took Russie and I down to supper, and he had little Francis there. We had a great feed, and afterwards Francis and I went to the moving picture show. He sat on my lap and we had a great time together. I imagined all the time that he was our boy, and I was as proud as could be. Won't I enjoy taking my boy to see things? We will be great old pals and we will be more intimate than father and me.

Bake told us that Della McIntosh's little boy had died of appendicitis. He was only two years old, and it seems pathetic to think of it. It makes me think that perhaps the ill fated hand may visit our home. But I hope nothing will befall us little girl.

You have been doing well little girl in regard to writing. I have been looking for a hello today, but none has come yet. I love you dear girl for yourself alone, and also for what you are going to mean to me next year and the years to come. You see how much your life is a part of mine? Sweetheart, I hold you close every day although you are miles away.

My love to you dear
Bob

Shortly before Robert and Leithel were married Robert's mother, Sarah, wrote to him, including some motherly advice.

> *1912?*
> *Dear Bob,*
>
> *Just a word to let you know. I wrote her (Leithel) today, and wanted to urge her to come down in vacation. We all want to see her. She is such a dear – I expect you don't deserve all the good things she does for you. No boy does deserve all the idealizing a girl does about him, but he begins to try to materialize that ideal, and he does quite a fair business at it by the time he's fifty if he works at it steadily.*
>
> *Daddy must not preach alone. Ned got a crick in his back yawning in church.*
>
> > *Love to you boy,*
> > *Mother*

The following are from letters that Robert wrote home to his parents every Sunday evening.

> *January 14, 1912 (Niles, Michigan)*
> *Dear Folks at Home,*
>
> *I was sorry to have waited so long before I wrote, but it seemed impossible. I am ashamed not to have done it before, but I am busier than a married man, and I don't know what I will do when I get married and have to watch the furnace, feed the chickens, build fires, chop wood, hold the baby, and a thousand other things all in half an hour.*
>
> *The school is going lovely, and I am not having a bit of trouble. I am reading David Copperfield, and it is great. The class is reading it for outside reading. We begin the Odyssey the latter part of this week, and I am in hopes they will enjoy it,*

but you can never tell what will appeal to them because their tastes are so varied. I am glad I read it in the original (Greek) because I think it will help me.

Love to you all, Bob

April 3, 1913 (Baton Rouge)
Dear Folks,

The weather is boiling here, and if it increases at this pace I will be parboiled by June. I am in my shirt sleeves and collar off, sweating to be the cars. School will be out here eight weeks from Wednesday, and those eight weeks will be hot and restless. I will leave here June 3 and get to Beeville June 4th at 5:40. Will marry at 7 a.m. and board train at 9:40 for Galveston, set sail Friday and get to N.Y. the following Thursday, and reach Pittsfield Saturday afternoon. That's doing the thing up in a hurry, but I can't waste any time down here in this hot climate when the cool breeze from the Maine woods calls us.

Leithel is writing regularly again, and is having good things to eat, and her people make her stay in bed a good share of the day. (she was recovering from goiter surgery) She says that she is gaining strength, and that she helped with the dishes one evening.

Ned is having his vacation, and I assume he is down with the farm folks helping them out in what he can. If I go to Michigan I will run down to see them.

With Love,
Bob

April 24, 1913 (Baton Rouge)
Dear Father,

This is your birthday, and no present so far, and as far as I can see there won't be any for some time, not until I arrive and then I will make up for lost time and past years. I don't know how the money is going to hold out, and until then I am going to be a little careful.

You are sixty years old today, and it only seems a little time ago when you were in your prime, and your hair had no grey hairs in it. You were young when we boys used to come to meet you as you came out from the depot, and use to walk down to the farm with us. Even mother went down to the farm with us. You are not so old yet, only it has been a good many years since I was a kid without responsibility and a "no care" attitude.

If you live as long as your father you have thirty two years yet for doing good, and there isn't any reason why you shouldn't live that long. By that time I will be almost as old as you are now, and I will have had a father longer than you did. I wish we might be closer together so we could really become acquainted and visit and make up for the time that I was interested in things of no account instead of spending more time with you. Perhaps you might have let some of the ministers go, and been a little more chummy with us boys, and given us good advice instead of finding it out through the vulgar talk of undesirable associates. It is a wonder we have escaped all the evil that is prevalent in the world, but we have, and there is no use to mention it now.

There are five more weeks of school, and then I am off, and will see you. I wish Ned could come for I was hoping that we could all be together once more as we were so many times in the old home. If I go to Ann Arbor Ned and I will room together, and have a chance to talk over old times, and perhaps by another summer we will be together.

> With Love,
> Bob

May 13, 1913 (Baton Rouge)
Dear Folks in Maine,

I was glad that something got you to write to me, if it were only the sad news of the death of Uncle John White. It is hard to think that death has begun on the second generation. Death has always seemed like the impossible until Uncle Will and Uncle John have gone in such a short time. The reality is gradually dawning on me, and it is not a pleasant mood to be in, because it means the severing of associations that are so essential to this life.

Three weeks from today school will be out, and I shall go immediately to Texas, and the wedding will be on the 10th of June. I can no more realize that I am going to see you people than I can of being married. By every conceivable method I am unable to pound into my head that I will be a married man in a month from now. Of course I know definitely that I am going to Beeville to see the girl, but my brain hasn't told me that I am going to take her away with me. We have waited long

enough so it ought to have soaked in that the inevitable year has arrived, and that life has just begun for us.

> With love,
> Bob

September 27, 1913 (Napoleonville, La.)
Dear Folks at home,

One week of school is over, and it has gone pretty well. Everybody knows me and speaks, although I have not met them. The town of Napoleonville has a population of about fifteen hundred counting the Negroes. The walks are of boards (Cypress) and the town is scattered all over. Some of the buildings are modern, and some are simply shacks. If it wasn't for the business ability of the few I don't know what the South would do.

No furniture in sight yet, but we have a house, and the man has put in electric lights and a bathroom. We have to pay $13.50. He wanted twelve without the improvements, and I knew it was worth a dollar and a half more for the lights and substitution of the backyard and washtub. We have bought a wood stove for $11. Leithel wanted gasoline, but I thought it wouldn't be warm enough for winter.

They drink rain water here, and usually have covered galvanized tanks which hold two or three thousand gallons. We shall boil our water or get a filter.

The mosquitoes are thick here, and Leithel fights herself tired every day, and I wrap my legs if I care to get any comfort reading the paper. Their days will soon be over, but they can make life mean while they exist.

With love,
Bob

October 1913 (Napoleonville)

Dear Folks at home,

This morning we didn't get up until eight, long after the bread and milk men had been here. I did the chores, and then shaved and went after the mail. Before I went I got ready for church. I came back, and we had liver and shredded wheat, and bananas and coffee. I read to Leithel while she did the dishes, and then eleven o'clock came and she wasn't ready for church, and so I went on, and when I left she had a few tears, and said she would tell me why when I returned. I found no church, as it was rainy. Of course when I returned she told me I was like all men – dress for church early in the morning, and then expect their wives to have all the work done, and be ready on time for church. I can see that I am like all married men, and especially like Daddy. A good many times I have waited on myself, and Leithel has asked me if the meat is good, and I say "Of course."

With love,
Bob

December 7, 1913

Dear Folks in Maine,

This is Monday, and no school, for it is one of the many Catholic holidays – Immaculate Conception. Yesterday before we were up there was a pounding at the front door, and I got up and put on my bathrobe, and found a man with grapefruit – 3 for ten cents. I bought six and have ordered a dozen more. This morning a load of wood came before we got up and I had to dress to give him a check. He couldn't talk English and my insufficient French didn't go very far, so I called to my neighbor who helped me out. I am getting so I can understand the French, but I can't speak it.

With love,
Bob

February 22, 1914 (Napoleonville)
Dear Folks at Home,

Yesterday I put a cord and a half of wood in my woodshed, and the first of the week another cord, so I have two and a half cords to run us. Ever since I have been here I have felt that our wood has gone faster than it should, so last night I bought a padlock, and hope to be able to use all the wood without the help of the Negro brethren.

Last Sunday we had just returned from church and were reading when lawyer Guion came up with his automobile and took us for a drive to Donaldsonville. We saw old antebellum colonial mansions with the tall large columns in front, and a front yard with five or six acres filled with live oaks from which hung Spanish moss. The people who lived in these houses would give house parties for weeks at a time, and when the cane was cut and ground the old planter would load his family together with his slaves onto a steamboat and go to New Orleans and spend thousands of dollars and perhaps gamble his plantation in a single night.

With love,
Bob

February 22, 1914
Dear Folks in Maine,

Yesterday we were invited out to a Mrs. Lanier's about two miles from town, and whose mother is a hard shell Baptist. She came from Virginia just after the Civil War as she met Mr. Monon while he was a soldier there. The old lady related to us incidents of the war, and especially of one skirmish which happened about her house. They had to go down in the cellar, and they could hear the bullets and cannon balls crash through above them.

After dinner we walked down past "Madewood," the name of a famous plantation and it consists of an old colonial style architecture, galleries running around the entire house both upstairs and downstairs. The house contains thirty rooms, and each room as large as an ordinary house. Back of this mansion were thirty Negro huts where the slaves lived. Some of the old slaves are still alive, and when a white person passes them they will tip their hats. Those kind of Negroes are quite desirable as they are honest and polite. The coming generations of Negroes are very insulting, and they are the ones that cause the mischief.

With love,
Bob

November 15, 1914 (Napoleonville)
Dear Folks in Maine,

You probably have the telegram by this time telling you of your new position, that of grandparents. When the doctor came he helped Leithel with her labors, and progress seemed to be made up to four o'clock this morning and then stopped. From four to eight we worked with no results and Leithel's strength was going rapidly. I was getting nervous and I saw that the doctor was, and I imagined things were in critical shape. The doctor proposed putting one blade of forceps under the baby, but the thing was too painful for Leithel to stand, so I went for another doctor to administer chloroform, and the tears trickled down my cheeks. I found the doctor was away on a baby case, and so came back home and by that time the doctor had made headway with Leithel's help, and in fifteen minutes we heard the baby crying and we were elated. The baby was a boy and you may know how my heart leaped up when the discovery was made.

With love,
Bob

November 20, 1914 (Napoleonville)

Dear Folks,

He is getting so he looks quite bleached and human. A number of people have said he looks like me. You see he can't look like much. The doctor came out with a card to make out to send to the state, and Leithel said his name was Robert Darwin Ford Jr. This happened while I was at school, so the baby is named after his two great grandfathers and his father.

Leithel is chipper and looks pretty well. Her eyes are sunken in a little, which formerly were quite protruded after the baby came. It was an awful strain. A boy would never speak cross to his mother or be insolent or forget himself if he knew what his mother endured at his birth. He never will know until he has had the experience.

Monday morning when I went to school the kids looked silly. The boys and teachers congratulated me, but the girls were terribly embarrassed and wore silly smiles.

I came home tonight and found that a cow had eaten 25 heads of lettuce and all my radishes and onion tops. I felt like cornering that cow and milking her.

Bob Jr. helps a little with the chores, that is he helps with the milking and spreads the manure.

With love,

Bob

January 3, 1915 (Houston)
Dear Folks,

I guess we should have stayed home instead of coming to Texas for Christmas. Ever since we started we have had trouble with trains and connections.

Since I wrote last I have done something that I never did before, and I have thought about it since a great deal, and I have come to the conclusion that I ought to make the confession, although it makes me blush even as I think of it. I realize that you have tried to bring me up correctly in habits and that heretofore I have done nothing to cause shame to either you or myself. You have waited with anxiety so long that I will put down in my own handwriting the one thing that I have never been guilty of and of which no one has ever accused me of and that is I took my mother-in- law to a concert.

I am getting a little excited over irrigation land and raising alfalfa and hogs. I am calculating that four more years in the teaching business will wind me up and that I will be in something I can work with all my soul and not feel that I am in

the wrong fellow's job. I want something I can work at the year round. All this is a daydream and will probably not materialize, but there is fun planning.

Love to you,
Bob

March 15, 1915 (Napoleonville)
Dear folks at home,

Leithel has gone out in the rain for a little fresh air, and the boy and I are here alone. He is yelling like a painter, and I am attempting to write to you. He gets cuter every day, and does a thousand and one things that make us smile and adore. He is perfect in our eyes.

There is a good deal of pneumonia and diphtheria around the community, and a good many people have died this winter. The sickness is playing havoc with our school. Half the regular enrollment is present.

Last Friday was my birthday, and for breakfast Leithel put a necktie under my plate, and for dinner two pairs of silk socks at 15 cents a pair, and for supper a handkerchief in the center of an angel's food. Leithel dressed in her best pink dress and sat across from me, and I tell you she looked like a lady from 5th Ave. She made me feel that day was something extraordinary. Well, we are happy, and that's what counts most in life.

With love,
Bob

At the end of the 1915 school year Robert accepted a job as superintendant of schools in Alpena Michigan, where a second son, John, was born in 1917. But he remained dissatisfied with the teaching profession, and in 1919 he moved to Wichita Falls, Texas to go into the furniture business with his father-in-law.

August 8, 1920 (Wichita Falls)
Dear Folks,

It has been a week since I received that can of ham. That tasted like we used to get on the farm. It hit the right spot, and I ate it all myself. It is hard to think of anything good to eat when I go to a restaurant, and the prices are out of reason. I manage to get along on $1.10 to $1.25 a day. Board used to be $2.50 a week.

Father must be used to making over houses, and especially when he goes to see his sons. I was mighty glad to get his help. Tell me how Ned's (his younger brother) house is going to look. Hope his crops look good, and will be a good year for him. Nobody knows whether he has 10 cents or $500 in the bank.

I am glad the boys like you, and that you like them. I thought you would when you knew them. Leithel has made you a long visit and now you must make plans for Texas next year.

Love,
Bob

The following letter was written after discovering that Leithel was pregnant with their third child, and she was not happy about it.

January 10, 1921 (Wichita Falls)
Dear Folks,

You had a first class letter written to you a few days after Christmas, but Leithel decided to write (on the back side) of it, and she wrote such a mean one I wouldn't send it. I don't know as the present one is improved, but you know Leithel and understand her sputter. She is putting all the blame on me, and has been a bear

to live with since she found out the news. Of course I don't know as I can blame
her, for the boys were at the stage when she was getting some comfort out of them,
and now to think of being tied down with diapers and vomit and all else that goes
with a baby. Even I will hate to think of doing night duty again.

I told Leithel that my large part in the transaction was for her. That she would
thank me to her dying days when she was presented with a blue eyed, golden
haired girl. She immediately said, "Twin boys." When this is over she threatens to
have a partition built through the center of the bed with barbwire on top.

We have worked out our financial statement, and find we have lost between
four and five thousand dollars. No use to waste time thinking about it. We are
planning on a bigger year than ever.

Love,
Bob

January 9, 1922 (Wichita Falls)
Dear Folks,

I asked the real estate man what my house was worth, and he said about
$5260.00, but that he didn't have any calls for that price. There seems to be very
little money in circulation, a good many not having, and those that do are holding
on to it. In six months from now I imagine that the property would be worth a
great deal more money, but a person could have starved to death between then
and now.

Love,
Bob

July 5, 1922
Dear Folks,

The revival starts up again Sunday. It doesn't seem that much judgment has been shown. Winter is the best time. They are very evangelistic down here, and when they can't think of anything else to do they put on a revival.

A week ago Sunday a boy four years old was staying with his father who was drilling a well (oil), the mother was in the hospital and the father was taking care of the boy. He had just raised a tool out of the 180 foot well when the boy ran across the 12 inch opening and fell in feet first and his hands upraised and gave a cry as he went in. The father could hear the boy crying daddy from the bottom, but he couldn't get the directions that the father gave. They threw a spot light down on him and let down a rope, but he was so hysterical he didn't know enough to grab hold, and there is a question whether he could have held on all the distance. Thousands of people went to the scene to give aid and suggestions. The salt water was running in all the time. The boy fell in about six o'clock in the evening, and they heard him calling daddy up to about ten o'clock, and then all was still, and they knew the water had covered him. Two hours later they pulled him up with grab hooks badly mutilated. The father is half crazy, and still calls to the boy. This is the worst tragedy that has occurred around here. The father will always hear the boy's voice as long as he lives.

We are feeding Jack two quarts of milk, or as near that as we can force down him. He is getting taller, but not gaining anything in weight. We are in hopes that milk will make him improve. His tonsils may have to come out if he doesn't do better. In order for him to eat we have to treat him like a baby, and feed him. He is not like his father on the question of eating.

Love, Bob

December 20, 1922
Dear Folks,

Today I bought "An American Boy", a paper published in Detroit and devoted to boys' interest. I took it when a boy, and I believe I had one of the first copies printed. I thought perhaps Bob would like it for Christmas. While Leithel was doing the dishes I read to the boys a story about tiger hunting in India, and when I was through they were so scared they couldn't go to bed. I offered Bob a nickel to go out and shut the chicken coop door, but he said he didn't need any money.

Love,
Bob

July 2, 1927
Dear Folks,

It was thoughtful of Mrs. Rumels to invite you to dinner. The last time we saw her was when she was with her mother. We were on our way to Sebagus Lake. That was a wonderful drive, and Leithel and I often talk of driving through Maine and up to Nova Scotia. We plan lots of trips, and when the family all arrives and is somewhat grown we may be able to realize some of our dreams.

A man who lives two doors down from us is a carpenter, and he owes us $15.00, and so I am going to have him help on the 4th to put up the framework of the back bedroom. That is the only way we will get our money.

Two weeks ago tonight I went home and milked about nine thirty, and then went over all the chickens and picked out three that were not laying, and put them in the feed box, and decided to clean them in the morning. About twelve o'clock a woman next door was screaming her head off, and I rushed out the front door in my night shirt, and she said my garage was on fire, and I rushed to the back and found it was the chicken house, and was practically destroyed by the time five fire trucks arrived. The only good thing saved was the lumber under the floor that I can use on the addition of the house. The three chickens and one other were all that was saved.

Love,
Bob

In 1928 Robert was diagnosed with diabetes. That summer he and Leithel took classes at the University of Colorado in the hope that they could find teaching jobs.

June 18, 1928 (Boulder)
Dear Folks,

You probably saw by the envelop that we were here at Boulder, Colo. A month ago I had come to a point where I got a little worried over myself so I took a specimen of my urine to Dr. Hargraves. He called me up and told me they had found sugar. What gave me warning was that I had lost 22 pounds, and was urinating too much. I had practically remedied the latter disturbance, but couldn't keep my weight. The Dr. had me come to the hospital and put me in bed Monday morning (3 weeks ago) and put me on a diet and weighed the urine and weighed the food to see my sugar tolerance. At the end of two days he still found sugar and the blood showed 265 sugar when it should be 135. He found it necessary to use insulin and that cleared up the sugar in the urine and the blood sugar has been reduced to 235. I am to have another test made soon. I was in the hospital from Monday A.M. to Friday A.M. and lost six pounds more. I have gained back 4 or 5 pounds and expect to gain more in this climate. The food has to be weighed and given to me in the right proportion as to carbohydrates, protein and fats, and so much insulin taken three times a day before each to take the place of the work of the pancreas.

I told the Dr. that he didn't know the Fords, and that I would fool him. I expect to get away from the insulin and be a normal man in 5 or 6 months. I believe at my age and by following the Dr.'s instructions I can come back. I have no sugar and practically no starch foods and drink my coffee and tea plain.

Leithel and I talked it over and decided that while I was getting well that we would come up here and go to school and probably get back into school work. She is taking work too, and Margaret and Jack are going to school that is conducted by the university. We brought them because we thought the climate would do them good. Mr. and Mrs. Patton are taking care of Bob and Bud. It was pretty hard to leave them. We rented out the house furnished, and sold the cow, and gave the 12 chickens we had left to the Pattons.

We will be here for at least five weeks, and probably ten for there are two terms. I hope to have a good position by fall. The teaching work seemed to offer the shorter hours, and so with everything considered we came up here. We are looking forward to a pleasant summer, and I feel like a new man to be away from Freers (the furniture store). I wasted six years there.

Too bad about Ned's calf. Hope his crops are coming fine. Tell him to go easy with the sugar.

Love,
Bob

June 28, 1928 (Boulder)
Dear Folks,

We hear from Wichita Falls every few days, and the baby seems to be happy although he doesn't like to go over to the old house. He feels and gets queer and hangs onto his grandmother and feels better when they leave. We notice all the two year old boys along the street, but they don't look like our boy.

Don't worry about me, for I am not worrying. I think I am better. As soon as I get the blood sugar test I will know better what to do, and will also know how I have progressed. I shall come back all right and show the doctors they don't know Ford stock. I appreciate all you say and offer. I may have to call on you in the next year or two if I don't get work, but I have only one purpose in mind, and that is to get well.

Love,
Bob

July 7, 1928 (Boulder)
Dear Folks,

I imagine the crops in Michigan are about as they are here. The corn is about knee high, and the peas are coming on. The hay is in, but the wheat hasn't turned golden yet. This hot sun should ripen the wheat.

I am enclosing an encouraging letter from Dr. Hall that I thought perhaps you would like to see. I still don't believe the insulin but I am obeying orders. I am in hopes in another month that I can forget the insulin and then gradually get back on a more regular diet. I am still hoping the doctors are wrong. There is something about a father that he wants to take all the bad luck that falls on a son or daughter – but it has to fall where it does, and I guess it is right.

Last Sunday we drove out by these palisades and roasted a round steak on a hot rock and afterwards while Leithel slept Margaret, Jack and I climbed the mountain. Margaret and Jack are like mountain goats, and don't know what danger is. Last Saturday we wound around one of the highest peaks here, and looked out across the circle and it was a wonderful sight.

With Love,
Bob

August 8, 1928 (Boulder)
Dear Folks,

In my last letter I told you I would tell what Dr. Kemper said at my last interview. Last Saturday we got up at 5:30 and got off at 7:15 for Denver, and at exactly 8:30 I was weighed and measured and put to bed and told not to move, not even my hands and feet. At 9:30 the doctor took a blood test, a urine test, and made me drink a glass of glucose (sugar syrup) and at 10:15 he took another blood test, and at 12:30 another blood test and urine test. At 1:15 he was through with the findings and told me I didn't have diabetes, and never had had it. You can imagine I felt like I had been freed from the electric chair. He told me to eat like I always had, and so we went to Leithel's cousin and I ate potatoes and bread and a piece of cake. The first I had in three months. The doctor said that the doctor in Wichita Falls had made a mistake in the diagnosis.

We have put away the scales and the hypodermic needles. And we are eating and thinking. When I received the report I felt like sending you a telegram. I go back *to him for one more test. I am testing my urine every day and it is showing clear. Jack thinks I can eat a banana and a hamburger.*

The Pattons and the boys (Bob and Bill) left Wichita Falls today, and should be here tomorrow and we will be glad to see them.

Love,

Bob

After completing their courses in Boulder the family drove to Michigan to visit the Ford relatives, and then returned to Texas to seek teaching jobs. The search was fruitless, and Robert returned to selling on commission in a depressed economy, although Leithel was hired to work in the library of the local junior high school, which gave them some help. The following is a letter that Leithel wrote to Henry and Sarah in the fall of 1928 describing their financial struggles.

Fall 1928 (Wichita Falls)

Dear Folks,

There have been several weeks where Bob hasn't made a dollar. I thought this fall that he should try to find something else to do, but I'm not so sure. Conditions here are bad. He has found nothing. He better be working at that than to be doing nothing. He tried for a year to get teaching work elsewhere, but had no encouragement anywhere. Please don't think I'm holding him here. When there are 50 applicants praising last year's record, a man who hasn't taught a day for ten years is at a handicap, especially where he is not known.

I want Bob to use some of your money for a suit. His summer suit will soon be too tight. His last years and year before that suit (same one) is frayed. He must be presentable both for his self respect and for his impression on the public. If we can hold on through the winter I think he will begin in the spring to reap his reward from his summer's work.

For a year and a half we have not been able to meet expenses. Taxes and insurance and all sorts of things are in arrears. I really don't dare think. We would have lost our home if anyone else held the papers. We have two and three year old dental and doctor bills. I'm only telling a few interesting items to let you see why I hadn't urged you to come. When you are living in an avalanche you don't want to invite anyone for pleasure for the avalanche might be too exciting. If you know me and how I feel for you, you will not be questioning my hospitality and love in urging you to share the avalanche. Again I want you to know you were never more welcome than now. We have so far eaten, and I'm not miserably despondent. Somehow ultimately I'm expecting real improved conditions in our business of living. This week I have engaged Terry for the laundry. I couldn't sleep for fatigue, and I was frightened into the extravagance.

I think I still feel that the Lord is on our side and things will have to be better. I know my feeling so is a saving grace for Bob. He is also trying to sell radios for the same service. He sent one out on trial the other day.

I'm so sorry farm times have been so bad. Both cotton and wheat were failures here. Wheat was fine in the Panhandle, but a failure here. Drought ruined both crops. That doesn't help business. Lavern's husband finished the Wichita business, and was let out with two and a half months pay. He has combed the town and found nothing. He is frantic.

The children are not taking music, though I'm keeping them practicing an hour a day, and helping them some. Love to you, and a welcome always.

Love,
From Leithel

In January 1929 Robert was hired as the principal of a small school outside of Wichita Falls. It paid little, but got him started back in the profession he had abandoned ten years earlier.

May 3, 1929
Dear Folks,

I guess I haven't written to you since Leithel wrote to you that I was applying for the Hillsdale job. I really didn't expect to land it, although I thought it would be a good beginning to get back into the work. I am not disappointed nor down hearted. I guess I am getting toughened to adversity. We still have three meals a day.

I have had quite a good deal of mental satisfaction in my work. There hasn't been much pay, but I am convinced I could do good work and would be enthusiastic about the profession. I had most of my experience in Michigan and I am 1500 miles away, and have been away nine years. However they know about my work. I am in Texas, and they don't know about the kind of work I can do. Whichever way I look I have obstacles to overcome.

This summer I am working for the Noble-Little Hardware Co. That is I'm selling their General Electric Refrigerator. I begin work at 9 and am through about 4:30. I am out in the open all the time, and hours are short. I am in hopes I will not starve to death.

I went to Dallas and Ft. Worth two weeks ago last Saturday, and interviewed the Supt. again. There may be something by the middle of July. I got up at 5 o'clock, milked the cow and was off at 5:30 and reached Dallas at ten o'clock – a distance of 150 miles. I saw my man in Dallas and then back to Ft. Worth, and 3 hrs.

interviewed with a man, and left 4 o'clock and reached home at 7 and milked my cow before dark. I covered 300 miles and had six hours of interviews.

Love,
Bob

Winter 1930
Dear Folks,

It is depressing to go down town, for all one hears is depressing stories. Stores are closing their doors and others are hanging on by a thread. Of course this had to come, and if we can live over this we will be all right.

Ruth and John are getting along some way and he should be thankful for any kind of job. Those receiving a small salary think they are unfortunate, but those without work know the real situation.

Love,
Bob

March 2, 1930
Dear Folks,

I found a man with a white horse who said he could plow my garden. He arrived at one o'clock and started in with a rusty plow and boards for handles that were wired on. For lines he had a rope, but that wasn't long enough so he tied on a ribbon and when he found that wasn't long enough he used another piece of wire. He used more wire to attach the single tree to the plow. When he was all hitched ready to go he remembered that the man from whom he bought the horse said she wouldn't plow. He started up and the first thing that happened the single tree

came off and then the lines broke. The man never got out of patience and took lots
of time to repair his junk. It took the horse longer to turn around than to go the
length of the furrow. It took him just 2 ½ hrs. to plow the garden. The garden
measures 50' x 75' with a chicken coop in the corner. In the garden part his horse
couldn't pull the plow through the Bermuda grass so I did using a garden fork and
rake. When he was through I asked him what he paid for his horse and he said
$6.00. That perhaps gives you an idea of the rig. You put a white tramp behind a
$6.00 horse and you haven't much.

Yes I had a birthday and I don't appreciate their coming around. I suppose it is
human nature to always want to be young. Your dollar is still in my vest pocket
and I believe I am going to buy a necktie. Mrs. Terry bought me a shirt and
Leithel and the children put a new crank in the Victoria and so we have music
once more.

Love,
Bob

March 1930 (from Leithel)
Dears,

The cow does so well that Mrs. Couch is teaching the two, Margaret and Jack,
music lessons. Jack is learning the shepherd boy. He got into a little scrape at school
yesterday over some notes. He was a subdued shamed little boy. I was glad it came
to a head for the teacher said she felt it was a bad influence of a fat boy we have
been disapproving of. I think it's been a lesson to Jack.

Bob's refrigerator business is looking up. We would be glad for a chance to square
up with society.

Love,
Leithel

May 1930 (from Leithel)

Dears,

Bob looks well. I believe things are on the mend for us. If his salary had been even the minimum we might hope to pay back taxes. I hope they will consider him off the substitute list before the year is up. I think he was afraid not to put Bob on, and is a big enough man to do it graciously and is putting the screws on. It's saving Bob's nerve when busy, and he is enjoying the work and if we don't let ourselves be frozen out the salary will have to come. No married women are given school contracts here so I will not know until school opens if I am to teach. Mr. Glass wants me, and I shouldn't be surprised if I shall, if we are here.

The children were never so much pleasure and we are happy, but we haven't the income to meet old obligations, and that's a worry. I am thankful to have food and clothes and shelter, but I do wish I could have someone to keep my house clean. Sometimes I get so tired, it worries me, but I'm feeling better than a few weeks ago.

Jack looks well for him, but I hear him coughing. He has been working on his pigeon pen. He is a character. I think you would enjoy them all. They talk much of you.

My Bobs are due home from church. I must do some ironing. I'm sure enough a heathen since I'm a working woman.

Love from Leithel

May 25, 1930 (from Robert)
Dear Folks,

School is over and the entire family is relieved. Leithel's nerves were getting on edge and I hope she can rest and relieve the high tension. Buddy is glad to have a mother again. Bob can read all he wants to and Margaret can cut out and play with a thousand dolls, and Jack can keep everybody stirred up. I wish Bob was up there so he could work on Ned's farm. It would do him good. There are so many boys here desiring work and so few jobs for them. The unemployment among the men is still great. Lavern's husband, who has been practically idle since Sept. 1st, goes to work in the morning. The men who left the farms to work for high wages in the city must return to the farm in order to relieve the present condition.

It is some job to raise a family of kids. When one gets them to majority one must feel he has accomplished something. Bob finishes high school next year and Jack comes over to the school where Leithel is and Margaret enters the 4th grade.

Love,
Bob

June 5, 1930
Dear Folks,

Seventeen years ago I arrived in Beeville and we were married the same day. I left Baton Rouge at 1:30 A.M. on Wednesday over the Frisco to Houston and the wheels of the train were in a foot of water practically all the way. It was the first train through in weeks. I arrived in Houston in the late afternoon and bought a clear cooler and some white roses for the bride. After riding all night on slow train to Beeville I jumped off the train at 6 o'clock and Leithel was there to meet me, but I hardly knew her, for the goiter had changed her appearance. She only weighed 80 lbs. and her eyes were bulgy. I didn't have enough sense to hire a taxi, but we walked up to the house, about 6 blocks. Mr. Patton was just building the kitchen fire, and the rest of the family wasn't up. We packed our belongings that day and while working my shirt tail came out, and I kept on and Leithel was so embarrassed and so modest she didn't dare tell me. The neighbors kept coming in and that made the situation worse. We were to have a big fat hen for our wedding dinner, but she ran under the house, and so I had to run down my meal.

The next morning I had to wrestle my father-in-law, and we rolled down the 12 ft. embankment and I landed on top, and he lost his new pencil and glasses which he never found. He had tried to hold me so the girls could pour rice down my back. The train waited while the performance went on and all the passengers got off and became sympathetic spectators.

I recall the letter, Father, that you sent to me after I had visited Topeka, and in it you had recounted some of your experiences when you landed there. I don't believe you had to trounce your father-in-law before the train left.

We are getting along pretty well. Your letter came today, and you seem to be worrying more than we are. I am selling some refrigerators – enough to pay the grocery bill and pay a few debts. When we get in a jam and can't wiggle we will let you know. Don't spend any time worrying about us.

If we had had the money we would have bought a new Packard automobile – come to the Hillsdale celebration and given a million to the college – bought great grandfather's place and put up a mansion and made an artificial lake in the ravine in back of his place etc. We may do it yet.

> With love,
> Bob

July 10, 1930
Dear Folks,

Mother's note and father's two letters with a check all have come since I have sent you a scratch. When a man is a bachelor or is a widower with four children he should be excused for most anything he does or doesn't do. Leithel went to Denton (to take a college course) six weeks ago, and four weeks ago we all went down there and surprised her. We arrived about seven, and found Leithel had gone to Dallas with Harriet Bishoff and her family. When we didn't find her Jack wanted to know who the joke was on.

I told Leithel while she was home that I was quite sure that I would get married the second time. I shall be relieved when she returns and plans the meals. I hate to come home and have to cook the meals. Other men have lived through it and I guess we will. Leithel took your check and it will pay her room rent for the balance of the time. It came in handy right now. We will get out of the woods sometime. The refrigerator business is going better naturally. The terribly hot weather is making people buy.

Jack has 6 duck eggs under his banty.

Love,
Bob

August 1930
Dear Folks,

I am purposely writing this letter at this time so that it will reach you by Monday, your golden wedding anniversary. We wish we were living near so we could help you celebrate. We wish we could make it a big event and invite the friends in and really make you feel you had accomplished something. I hope someone will remember it and do justice to the occasion. We would like to drop in and bring a large broiled steak and plank down $5000 in gold. If my dreams had come true that would have happened.

My getting in the schools here is a dream, and may never come true. I shall know in the next few days.

Love,
Bob

August 1930 (from Leithel)
Dear Father and Mother,

Fifty years, what a stretch of years. Can Bob and I live peacefully or peaceably under the same roof 33 more years. One would either love or hate pretty intensively by that time. I should think I can't think of one of you without the other and I guess you can't either.

I'm going to let Bob see what he can do about sending you a present. When the money isn't adequate I don't spend a dime. I haven't remembered my cousins' boy's graduation or K. Suhr's wedding. That hurts me. I have deposited my checks to Bob's account and then I write checks for groceries.

Love and memories of hundreds of happy hours you have given is all we treasure and remember especially now. We give our gratitude and thanks. We should all be doing for you to make your day comfortable and easy and here we are still being helped by you. How I wish it were the other way around. You might not be any happier, but I know who would be.

Love from Leithel

December 1930

Dear Folks,

Well, we are moving along slowly. We are gradually paying up a few of our debts. There is some talk of doing away with the junior college, and if that is the case it will make a problem for us, because Bob graduates in May. It is a question if the bond issue would carry under the financial conditions.

Jack has 15 pigeons that he realized through the trading of four ducks. He is quite confident that he has the big end of the trading. The ducks kept the neighbors awake at night and ate more feed than the chickens, so perhaps the trade is agreeable. We are wondering what the next pet will be.

The times are so tight that I haven't been able to sell any refrigerators. I have expected to sell a few for X-mas presents, but I may not. It may be next spring will be as soon as the housewife gets in the right frame of mind.

I am having some trouble with the Supt. over the amount of my salary. I will tell you more about it later. The Suhr's sent me a blue serge suit of Uncle Otto's and for $13.00 I had it made over and it gives me a Sunday suit. This is the first since 1915. I mean the first dress suit.

With our good looking capons we lock our chicken house. We never lock our own house, but we do the chicken house. Nobody would be interested in old clothes, furniture, or books, but would take a good looking chicken.

Love,

Bob

March 26, 1931

Dear Folks,

I realize that you watch every mail for a letter. I suppose that since I find it hard to find time for a full letter, that I might send you just a card. Every afternoon after school I sell refrigerators and in the evening I study. You see where my time goes. Perhaps you can make excuses for me.

My birthday came a month ago today, and I received your dollar mother and yours, father, sent from Toledo. It came in handy. I only wish it were possible to send you a check in every letter. My 43rd year went off peaceably as it could with a household of kids. It seems as if I were plugging along with not much in the future. Perhaps another year will show some sunshine. So many people are out of work, and so many stores going under, one feels a little satisfied with any kind of job.

If we had remained in the furniture business we would have been finished by now. Even those who have been in business for 20 or 25 years. If these conditions continue for another six months there will be few business houses left. People can live on reduced salaries, but they can't pay indebtedness that was made on the basis of old salaries. It may mean we will have to take a new start.

We went to hear a quartet the other night. Dr. Selectman represented the Protestants. Mr. O'Brien the Catholics, a Jewish Rabbi from Ft. Worth, and Clarence Darrow the agnostics. They were allowed thirty minutes apiece to represent his side. Darrow took the hide off from Selectman. The Jew presented his side in the most logical order.

Love,

Bob

April 9, 1931 (Last Letter)
Dear Mother,

If our house doesn't burn up tonight your birthday letter will arrive on time. Your seventy-five years must seem imaginary, for they go so quickly, but when you look about you and see the grandchildren, almost a dozen of them, you can appreciate the times.

There are six weeks of school, and then for a few months vacation. We are out on the 22ⁿᵈ of May and school starts Sept. 14ᵗʰ. I am in hopes that the refrigerator business will pick up. There are so few people who have money to buy additional furnishings. If there were money I think Leithel would like to come to Ann Arbor, but we may have to let her go to Denton. Perhaps another year will let us see the light. If we had been on a regular salary our debts would have been paid up.

Glad you are stronger, and hope to see you next fall.

Love,
Bob

Ten days later the "ill fated hand" that Robert feared in his first letter back in 1912 did come to visit their home. On the evening of April 19, 1931 he got chilled while milking the cow in a cold rain. Weakened by diabetes, he developed pneumonia and died five days later on his father's birthday, April 24ᵗʰ. It was a wound that never healed for Leithel or the children. We see in his letters a man who saw himself as an economic failure, but he was clearly much more than that. No failure is loved as Robert was loved by his parents, his wife, his children, and his students. One of the first clear memories of my childhood is April 24, 1951 as my father watched the clock approach 9:15 P.M. and the twentieth anniversary, to the minute, of his father's death. It was only then that I began to realize the depth of his love for his father, and the extent of his loss. Many years later, as my father lay on his own deathbed, I told him that no son ever had a better father. His simple reply was, "Except me."

The following telegrams and letters were exchanged between the family in Texas, and Robert's parents in Michigan after Robert became ill.

WESTERN UNION TELEGRAM
Wichita Falls, Texas
April 21, 1931

To: Rev. H.M. Ford
Diabetes controlled and condition better. Has good chance of having beat case.

J.A. Patton (Robert's father-in-law)

WESTERN UNION TELEGRAM
Wichita Falls, Texas
April 22, 1931

To: Rev. H.M. Ford
Bob had a restless night. Both lungs involved in consumption.

J.A. Patton

WESTERN UNION TELEGRAM
Wichita Falls, Texas
April 23, 1931

To: Rev. H.M. Ford
Bob improved through the night. Not so well now.

J.A. Patton

WESTERN UNION TELEGRAM

Wichita Falls, Texas

To: Rev. H.M. Ford

April 25, 1931

Bob died today nine fifteen P.M. This will be our home. Am planning service here Sunday afternoon three o'clock at church. Burial beautiful cemetery. A host of friends stood by consistently. Letter follows. I realize journey is too great.

Love

Leithel

(The date shows April 25. Robert died April 24, but the telegraph office probably sent it the next morning on Saturday, April 25th)

The following letter is from Henry.

1931

April 26

Norvell, Michigan

Dear Ones in Texas:

This is Sunday morning–the sun is breaking through gloomy clouds that have been over us for days–such a quiet friendly sun. But the glory of living and the glory of life have departed. Life can't be the same from now on. In our unspeakable sorrow we are thinking of you and the children and your father and mother. We can see you out on Avenue F in the lovely house beginning to prepare for the sad things of the day. If only we could be with you. We know your friends and the church will do all possible–you are having callers and they are giving consolation and saying loving things about Bob. I can't think of a world with Bob not in it. How peacefully his sick and tired body will sleep across on the hill yonder so free of pain-and his spirit so much awake in the Blessed Country. It will be all new to him and doubtless strange but he will be at peace and he will wait 'til you and the children come. It will not be long before Mother and I will be at peace with him.

Sunday night
April 26

This eventful day, one always to be sadly and sweetly remembered, is now past. Did you think there was a moment from daylight to the hour-8 P.M. that we have not been with you-with my mind's eye I have seen you in the little house trying to eat breakfast. Seeing people coming in. Seeing you making preparations for the funeral in the afternoon. Seeing you at 12 and 1 and 2 getting dressed and the children ready. Seeing the good women and their help-at 2:30 seeing people beginning to gather at the church-seeing the innumerable cars parked around the church in front of the Junior College. Seeing you come down the aisle with your children and Father and Mother-seeing the great congregation-the casket and banks of flowers-hearing the service and all so appreciative of Bob-seeing and hearing the choir sing, and maybe some broke down and couldn't sing-Bob was loved and the whole service told you Bob was appreciated and had won the hearts of a great multitude-soon the procession down the street and on to the cemetery. Bob sometimes felt he was not a success-what is success? That he won so many hearts and so many loved him and his teaching influence from this time would speak of success beyond all estimates.

This morning was stormy - but about 9:15 a.m. Mrs. Van Wormer drove into the yard. More were coming but too stormy. Edna sat with us and told what she had done at Hillsdale. We wired her your last message and she phoned the pastor of College Church and without a doubt, he announced it in church. She at once prepared for us items for the Daily-so people all over the city would know about Bob in the morning. By tomorrow I will begin to get letters from Hillsdale and you too will receive the same that a number had phoned expressing sorrow. I sent the message to Ruth, Aunt Helen, Vernon Main, Aunt Belle, Aunt Kit. In fact, I have been writing and sending out letters since Monday night, April 20. Well we had dinner at one and 2:30 we settled down in the parlor. I read PS. 90-1 Cor. 15, 2 Cor. 5" 1-8. I Thes. 4: 13, 14. Mrs. VanWormer made a prayer. A very tender and touching one and then Edna played softly our family hymn, "The Beautiful Land," prefaced by remarks to the effect that for 30 years this had been our family hymn and that the last time Bob was with us we had gathered in that same room and sang it- and it was the last time it had been sung. None of us could sing, but Edna played it fine and we could hear Bob's voice singing and we all broke down. We wanted to have this service at the same time as yours, but a storm was brewing and Edna wanted to start home soon.

To have riches and die without friends is not success but the sorriest kind of failure. I wish Bob could know how much he was thought of. Why can't we let people know while they are living how much we appreciate them? Our tongues are tied until our friends die and then our tongues are loosened. Well, we thought of you and saw you this day and our eyes have continually streamed and several times a day we break down.

We hope as soon as you find time and would tell us all about Bob from the time he was taken sick to the time of burial. We particularly want to know:

1.   To what hospital was he taken?
2.   Did he have any lucid moments?
3.   What did he do on Saturday 1st and 2nd. Did he go to church and sing or was he feeling too sick?

4.   *Did he realize any time his situation?*

5.   *When was he last conscious?*

6.   *Did he seem to suffer much consciously?*

7.   *What was the music at the funeral and who sang?*

Any little thing you may say will be of interest – anything.

Soon we must talk over your plans for the future. Tomorrow your father will get an airmail letter, containing a message and a check. I am going to send you yours and Bob's note to me and I will cancel and call it paid. It was given some years ago and a small amount was paid and now we will call it all paid.

Let me tell you what we did today: I feel we ought to go – I keep saying we want to go and feel as you do, but the money we would only give to the R. R. This will benefit you more.

                                        With great affection,

Monday morning.

How hard this morning will be for you and the children. It is hard for us. I got down to the piano and tried to sing Bob's "Mavourneen." I heard his voice in the last high note. We have several pictures of him on the piano. How strange, how strange and incomprehensible to realize he is away.

But we must think of present duties. I am wondering how much the insurance was drawn upon and how much of it lasted. I know at one time he had $10,000 on his life. But when he was sick and went to Colorado I think I remember he said he drew on it. I don't know how much and I imagine he could not keep much of the payments going. How I wish I had offered to do it.

But then there is so little money for any of us to use and Ruth has had so much sickness we had to help her a bit – only a bit, for I had only a bit – but I could have squeezed out a little more. I should have done it. Oh you have been brave and all was done for Bob that love and strength could do. If he only knew how much.

The following letter was written by Leithel to Henry and Sarah.

1931
April 27
Wichita Falls, Texas.

Dear All:

The heartbreaking inconceivable thing has happened. Bob had been feeling badly for a week tho' he taught all week and sang Sunday morning. At five o'clock we called on our janitor whose son had been killed Saturday night. He came home and went to bed with a chill. I doctored him thru' a restless night for a sore throat. In the morning he complained of a gas pain. I asked him where. He put his hand across his back and I feared all that came to pass. The doctor came out and asked about his diabetes. He said if he is sugar free he has a chance. If he isn't, he has but one chance in a million. In a little while he came back with the statement that the urine was full of sugar. He called the ambulance and we went to the hospital. He didn't expect him to last the night. He failed until Tuesday afternoon when they said he was dying. Late afternoon he rallied. I thought it was the end, but they gave him oxygen and he had a good night and was bright Wednesday morning. About noon he began to fail. We kept oxygen for him until the end. It gave him more ease and kept him from having such a hard death. He took nourishment fine until Friday noon. No sugar showed in the last two days. It was just wonderful to see his patience and courtesy thru' it all. The doctors were ineffably tender. Dr. Commack stayed day and night. We kept two nurses the last two days. They all loved him. He and I never talked. He was too sick and I feared to say anything to lessen his fight resistance. He said he didn't want me to lend any money to Papa. I was glad. It may help me to refuse some day. He said once, "It is such a little while since our wedding day" and again, "We must fight this thing out together". He joked with the Negro porter Tuesday morning. He said, "I'm still here. If I weren't, you wouldn't be either," and laughed. Thursday and Friday morning his mind wandered. He was teaching school, helping boys with their oration, and once he said, "It is only a little way to the cemetery." The lobby of the hospital was full of people all the time. They said they had never seen anything to compare in this hospital. Flowers were sent in abundance.

His death was a sleeping away peacefully. Jack was just heart broken. The children have been fine. Bill doesn't comprehend. Sunday morning he lay and threw kisses to his Daddy in heaven. When we left the cemetery Jack said he wished he could be with Daddy too. They are trying so hard to be good to me.

Flowers were sent in abundance. I counted cards-there were 75 gifts-40 gifts of flowers I believe. I got lavender sweet peas, pink snap dragons and orange pink roses. Your beautiful spray and mine were on the gray cypress casket. The lavender and pink were beautiful. I had them use the beautiful blue serge suit Aunt Kit had sent him. There was majesty in his countenance. He was beautiful to me. We had him in state at the undertaking parlor and I didn't have the casket open at the church knowing so well how he felt. The friends who cared most went to see him.

Dr. Painers gave the opening prayer. The new minister spoke a few words of tribute and Dr. McKinney of the First Methodist Church gave the scripture reading you sent. Mr. Henry gave a most touching and feeling of appreciation.

Harriet Bradley sang beautifully. The Scottish Rite Choir of which Bob was a member sang Come Ye Disconsolate, Lead Kindly Light, and at the close, It Is

Well With My Soul. Wm. Young sang I Am A Pilgrim, I Am A Stranger. The service was the most beautiful I ever attended. The choir was exquisite. It was a fitting setting for Bob. There were about a thousand people present. For a poor unpretentious man, it was a triumph. The sun shone as we buried him on the side of a hill at Riverside Cemetery near some cedar trees. At the grave, Mr. Henry spoke of him as of great nobility, courtesy, and courage. If there can be healing at such a time, God made it all a beautiful occasion and one of dignity and majesty.

There were about a thousand people at the church. The most beautiful things were said of him. His life counted much for Wichita Falls. The students wept. They said they had never known such a teacher. They said he understood them and taught them how to live. I wish I could talk to you. There is so much I should like to tell. The hundred dollars you sent, I do not have to have. I'm not sure what the exact amount of the insurance will be and do not know what to do about the house. I'll have 150 salary (per month) next year and perhaps 175. If I keep well we will keep going. I don't know yet what my doctor's bills will be but I suppose it will be big. I have no idea. You ask me any questions you want and I'll tell you more when I write and know about business here.

I don't know how you could come and I've suffered greatly on your account as mine. I know how dearly you loved Bob. I never left the hospital after Tuesday. They were so good to both of us. I can't tell you how puzzled and paralyzed I felt. I went back to school this morning. It seemed best. I must be busy. I just can't feel that it is forever and I don't dare give way with four children.

There is so much I should like to remember to tell. We never were quite so near as these last three years. Our earlier fright made us both so fearful of this day that we prized each other even more.

I must go to bed for there is much work on the morrow. Love and blessing on your sore hearts.

I'm wondering if I can't reimburse you for the thousand dollars we owed you. It has distressed us both. The insurance had lapsed. Some had been reinstated and I'll know later. Don't hesitate to ask me anything.

I would keep the check if it comforted you to have shared in relieving his wretchedness but not just now because I have to have it for bills. Let me know how it is. You may need it just now worse for other things and I want you to be frank. I'm glad and happy to spend my all for dear Bob and gave so gladly and freely and gave every aid the doctors could devise. They were ever faithful. He was sugar free the last two days.

I'm glad that Bob was my love all these years, that you belong to me and that there are four fine children who bear his name and likeness of their wonderful Father. Bob Jr. said of all the men he knew, his Father was the finest gentleman. So we all feel.

Yours,
Leithel

The following letter was written by Leithel to Henry and Sarah following the funeral.

1931

Sunday, May 3

Dear, dear Ones and All:

Your letters have been balm to my heart. Your loss approximates mine. The children are finding their way about. People tell me how fortunate I am in many ways (and it is so), but no one here feels the heart hungers. No one knows how utterly I loved him, how all sufficient we were to each other. I feel as if the better part of me, the joy and song of life were in the grave with Bob. People call me brave, but I'm panicky in my soul - not with fear of the problems to face but with the horror of a great loneliness that can't be filled. I am thankful for the beautiful memories, for the four dear children so like him and the host of friendly, kindly townspeople. Someone said it was the largest funeral of a private citizen ever held in Wichita Falls.

Last Friday night Mr. Downing died. He held the note on this house. There will be nearly $4,000 due on it, back taxes and all. Many advise me to let them have it. They tell me I could buy better for much less. I'm so uncertain. They may not want it back and can I let it go. The location is perfect. It needs new paint, roof, and so on. I thought they might be glad to settle for less. I don't know how much insurance I will have - I hope they will not fight some reinstatements on the diabetic principle. The undertaker's bill will be $325. I don't know the doctors. We have a $200 dental bill...and so on. I'll know more soon. We had borrowed a good deal on our insurance. I wish now we had turned the house back a couple of years ago when they would have accepted it - and yet, can I leave it? Do you see the way clear? It might be best for me to rent. Of course, I have a place here for the future. But might I hope to move later where the children's education would come easier.

My job will pay $150 next year. I'm insisting on a H.S. position. The new supt. and Mr. Glass (my fine principal) called here last night. I know that Mr. Tilches will be my friend, but I have to wait another year to get a senior high position, but I'm sure I'll be taken care of. Now I'm thinking of attending Ann Arbor this summer or possibly U. of Chicago though I think A.A. Bob Jr. hopes he has work with the Dixie Tire Co. and feel that if I'm to gain ground in the schools that I best get a masters. It's getting to be almost a requirement. It will pay me back. I thought I might in time get a position in Southern Michigan and find the advanced education of the children easier. All my plans will shape up when I find out about the insurance, house, and so on.

Mr. Glass took the picture of the grave. Just at the right are three pretty cedar trees. The hillside is covered with wild flowers. I wonder if I should have taken him north. All depends on where we remain. He always said not to.

Did you notice the inside of the Wichitan...the tribute of pupils? The children are dear. Bob Jr. is just trying to take his place. He is blessed. Jack is most like Bob in disposition. Margaret often says, "Do you want me to do anything, Mother?" Bill stayed at church this morning and tried to be good.

There are many things to decide and I'm not sure of my wisdom. Is the keeping of the cow and chickens so valuable for the boys' income as to justify the added work? We are fixed for them here. We wouldn't be most places.

I'm saving flower cards, telegrams and letters that I will send you to look over one of these days. I deposited your hundred dollars. Do not send more. I hope I can hand it back to you. I haven't written to Ruth. I'll try to send a card. From school out until bedtime people call until it's a case of a woman killed with kindness. My heart is with you. How dearly a love you are. We had dinner at Mothers.

Yours,
Leithel

The following letter was from Leithel's father to Henry and Sarah.

May 9, 1931
Wichita Falls, Texas

Dear Brother and Sister Ford;

Just received your letter of the 4th this morning, and so glad to hear from you. I know how heart-broken you both are over Bob's death. It just seemed too bad that he had to be taken in the prime of life. Everything was done for him, that could possibly be done. I never saw doctors work harder over anyone than they did over Bob. One of the doctors stayed 3 nights in succession and he never left the building, and then he was in every few minutes to look after him. Doctor Hargrave said from the very start that Bob was a very sick man and he did not think that he would pull thru. He told Leithel he wanted to be honest with her and on account of his diabetic trouble, his resistance was very low and that they rarely ever got well where they had pneumonia with it. They used 7 tanks of oxygen on him and kept him alive the last 36 to 48 hours, I am satisfied, with the use of it.

The church people were wonderful to them during Bob's sickness. They furnished a special nurse at night for him. There was a crowd of them all day and until they closed the hospital at night. They carried chicken, roast beef, pies, cakes, etc., enough to feed a bunch of harvest hands. The school faculty was also very fine and did everything to help in every way.

I knew Bob and Leithel were well liked but had no idea they had so many friends until he was stricken. The hospital said they never had a case like it, and one of the doctors asked what kind of people these Cameliters were and said he belonged to the Baptist Church but that they never had anything like that in their church; and if they would let him belong he wanted to be one of them. It made me feel proud to think that he was my son-in-law.

Leithel has quite a problem on her hands but I think she will be able to manage it alright if she keeps her health. Think she will get some $8500 insurance all told. I want her to let her place go back as they owe around $4000 on it and the house is where it is going to need a lot of repairs in the next year or two, and it is a cheap built house to begin with. Property has declined so much and one can buy a place very cheap now. Think with $2000 to $2500 she could buy a much better house than she has, and in the same neighborhood.

Leithel expects to keep the children all together and we will help her all we can while we live. Mrs. Patton has been staying with her at nights a good share of the time and seems she wants her in preference to anyone else.

I did not intend for you to send a check for these telegrams, as I expected to pay for them myself. I was only too glad to keep you posted and you can rest assured that everything possible was done for Bob, and we feel very badly over him being taken from us. The church will miss him as he was a fine choir leader and was a deacon in the church.

Hope this finds you folks well. Mrs. Patton joins me in extending to you our sincere sympathy and best wishes. I remain

> Yours sincerely
> J.A. Patton

P.S. Leithel has born up remarkably. Bob and Jack will be lots of help to her. Jack is going to be the business one of the family and is a real trader and schemer and everyone is his friend. He is shrewd and likes animals, has his own pigeons and built them a house and screened in and sold $1.50 worth of squabs last evening.

This letter was from Leithel to Henry and Sarah.

1931

May 12

Wichita Falls, Texas

Dears in Michigan:

It looks now as if I would have my insurance. I'm still uncertain about keeping the house. One day I think so, and again I question. I'm planning definitely on going to school in Ann Arbor and getting a Masters degree. It is necessary to teach in senior high school now. I don't know whether there would be a chance to locate in Southern Michigan or not but I should like to be there. I wonder, if not now, if in a year or two. There might be a chance to be in Hillsdale H.S. or College. It would mean so much to live in a college town as the children grew up. I thought I would attempt to find out the situation. Leastwise I think my three and a half months wouldn't cost me more that way than here. I will have to be doing work on a Masters to get into senior high. They have offered $150 per month here. I'm asking for Bob's job. I don't know how it will turn out. It would be worth more and increasingly so. Then being connected with the senior high school should make it easier to later connect in Michigan if I feel I want to. I should like to be near Amy (a close friend).

Tell Ned his dear letter came and I appreciated it. I would like to have papers drawn up making him and Amy joint guardians of the children if anything happened to me, if he would accept the responsibility. Please keep this as a temporary record of my wishes. I shall leave whatever money I do not use for the house with the insurance company on interest. If the house price is not cut so I can hold it, I may not try to buy, just store my furniture for the summer. Papa would keep my chickens. We had planned to sell the cow and buy a younger one so the cow doesn't worry me. The church paid $50 for the night nurse.

The doctor charged $202.24, the undertaker $334 which included the lot with room for four.

I'm wondering if I shall wish I had taken him to Michigan. As time goes on it seems that it might be easier to live without him there than here. A summer there will help me to know my mind. I could have him moved.

I saw a beautifully furnished house here-new-6 rooms, garage, three doors from my school for the price mine is. There is no comparison. And that is furnished completely. It makes me wonder if I ought to rent a year until I know my mind. We are sentimental about our house, but I wonder if I would adapt myself better in new surroundings. Well, you see do you not, how I mill around in my mind. People come to the house to see us and I can hardly get my work done. It's hard to squeeze in so many letters. I've written a hundred thank-you letters.

I wonder if I went to Ann Arbor, if we could leave a visitor or two at Ned's part of the time.

Your letters have been so faithful. I know how it saddens you. It seems to me it grows no easier. I don't see how it can be. He was the most alive person I knew. If it weren't for the children, I don't see how I could live at all. I feel weak and gone. I'm glad I have to keep so busy.

I love you all. I'll keep you informed. We have one more week of school. I hope I can leave a week later.
This is all for now. I've paid doctor and undertaker and owe $100 dentist bill.

Bob's last year has been a happy one for all. I'm saving a box of letters, cards and so on, for you. Such letters of appreciation! We may all well be proud of him.

Yours,
Leithel

1931

May

Wichita Falls, Texas

Dears:

Yesterday was baccalaureate at the auditorium so I saved your letter until next Sunday. I am going to ask Harriet Bradley to sing "There Is A Land Mine Eyes Hath Seen".

School closes this week and it is a very busy time.

The sickening reality of my loss has just been terrible this week. I can hardly stand it. I still plan to come. I'll write again very soon.

Dear Father, you are so dear to try to write me daily. Oh, Bob was so precious to me and I can't tell you how bereft I feel. We keep beautiful flowers on his grave.

Love from,

Leithel

1931

June

Wichita Falls, Texas

Dears:

School is out. The Downings will accept $1000 less on the place, so I have agreed to take it. I figure that I can hope to get $3000 out of it. It will cost me about $3000 after I roof it and that may paint it too. I hope to get away at least in a week *but can't tell. I'm trying to rent the place and it's a problem to finish up things. I haven't set a date for leaving. I thought I would go by way of Aunt Helen's and Ruth's. I shall have to write today asking if it would be convenient.*

I have six refrigerators to sell. Bob had taken them in on the electric one. There is so much to do – so many calls at door and telephone. I can hardly get anything accomplished.

I do love you and hope to see you soon.

In haste,
Leithel

Book Four

John Ford
1917-2002

Foreword

I remember my dad sitting at the table each Sunday afternoon writing letters to his parents, and, fortunately, his parents kept most of them. I remember Dad vividly, but I knew him as a child knows his father, not as an adult knows his father. His letters let me come closer to knowing him as I might have if he had lived.

As my days now dwindle down to a precious few I find myself wondering about the descendants who will follow me through life. Where will they live, what will they do, whom will they marry, what successes and disappointments will they experience? My ancestors must have wondered the same thing at this stage in their lives, and I wish I knew more about them. I wish they had written their own memoirs telling of their experiences, and their joys and disappointments. There are so many questions I could have asked that went unanswered because, like most of us, I was too interested in my own life to even consider the interesting stories those old people could have told. My parents and grandparents were not people of wealth, but they were people of character, high moral values, and intelligence. I have always felt fortunate to have been born into this family and I have always been proud of them.

My intent, when I started this project, was to make myself real to the descendants who will never know me, but now I suspect I really wrote it for myself, to re-live those wonderful days in my memory. At my age memories are like a cozy fireplace that warms me as my mind lets me return to all those happy, interesting years.

I have three passions that will be evident in this memoir: first and most important is my love for my family, then my love for music, and finally, an appreciation for humor. For me, life without any one of these three would make for a very gray life indeed. Luckily, my life has been enriched with them all.

My Early Years
Texas
Through 1931

___

Dad was particularly well suited to be a school administrator. He had the respect of his teachers and students and had a ready and wonderful sense of humor. But he thought the teaching profession received little respect, so he welcomed the opportunity when his father-in-law suggested that they open a furniture store together in Wichita Falls, Texas. It meant a long move across the country from Alpena, Michigan where he was the superintendent of schools, and where I was born during a blizzard on New Years Eve in 1917.

Dad left Alpena at the end of the 1918-1919 school year, taking the train to Texas, leaving Mother to finish packing, close the house, and follow him there with my older brother Bob and me. Recently I went back to Alpena, stopped at the railroad station, and tried to imagine Mother with two little boys boarding the train for that long trip to Texas. It must have been an exhausting ordeal.

Wichita Falls is just south of the Oklahoma border at the base of the Texas Panhandle. It was one of the boom towns built around large oil deposits that were discovered there between 1900 and 1930. It experienced explosive growth, with lots of money being made by the lucky, and lost by the unlucky. Texas is a big state, but most of it west of Dallas is typical West Texas, with rolling landscapes, mesquite trees, cactus, scrub brush, and a few cotton wood trees along the infrequent streams. There was no grazing land worthy of the name in that part of Texas, but the rangy long horn cattle were plentiful, and thrived on what little there was.

Wichita Falls is in northern Texas, but all of Texas experiences hot weather during the summer, and summer can extend from late February until Christmas. We had some cold days, but I remember warm days in late February when we teased to go barefoot. From May through October we enjoyed real summer with high temperatures, hot winds, and occasional dust storms. As a kid I don't remember ever thinking about the heat. We just accepted the days as they came, and found ways to enjoy them. The adults, however, did suffer from the weather, and Dad occasionally got so hot in the night that he filled the bathtub with cool water, and soaked the heat away. No one had air conditioning, so open windows and fans were the only way to get relief. Churches had small cardboard fans in each pew so people could fan themselves during the service.

Because Wichita Falls was a boom town, homes were built as quickly and cheaply as possible to accommodate the rapid growth. Houses were built on cedar posts three feet above ground level, and only the most expensive homes had plastered walls. Inside walls were simply boards nailed horizontally on the wall studs. Outside walls were made of lap siding with no insulation of any kind. In order to make wallpaper adhere to the inside walls, cheese cloth was tacked to the walls from ceiling to floor, and when the wind blew we could watch the wall paper moving with the wind. We once took all the old paper off to re-paper, and could see daylight coming through the wallboards.

During the winter we sometimes would get a "norther" with snow and freezing temperatures. This caused the milk to freeze in the glass milk bottles delivered by the milkman in the early morning hours. Then the milk would expand, pushing the cream at the top of the bottle upwards for several inches. We eagerly watched for that as Mother would give us the frozen cream mixed with sugar. Houses were heated with small natural gas space heaters, as natural gas was inexpensive in oil country. On some cold winter days we spent most of our time around a small space heater while the wind howled outside, and blew through the drafty walls.

The Red River flows just north of Wichita Falls, and is named for its red color which comes from the soil. The land is mostly clay, and becomes very sticky when wet.

In the 1920s most roads were not paved, and when it rained the clay became so slippery that if a car stopped on a crowned road it would start slipping sideways, and wouldn't stop until it was in the ditch. Drivers had to keep going until they found a driveway or stretch of road that wasn't sloped. Once in the ditch the only way out was to ask the nearest farmer to hitch up his team of mules or horses to pull you out.

When we walked in the wet clay we could accumulate as much as an inch of clay on the bottom of our shoes, so we always kept an old table knife at the back door to scrape the clay off our shoes before entering the house. We didn't have rain often in that arid country, but when it did rain it often came in cloud bursts. Then the Red River would overflow its banks, and flood the lower areas of town.

During the hot dry season great walls of red dust periodically rolled in from the western horizon, reaching well above ten thousand feet. No matter how hot it might be, when we saw those dust clouds coming we closed all the doors and windows, but when the storm hit the dust got in anyway, and covered everything with a thick layer of fine red soil. In the morning after a dust storm I would find my white profile on the sheet, and the rest of the sheet red with dust. The last time I experienced this was during World War II when I was sent to Enid, Oklahoma for basic flight training. On our first night there a dust storm hit, and the next morning the sheets were red with dust everywhere except where our bodies had lain.

Wichita Falls was the town where my Dad opened a furniture store with my Grandfather Patton in 1919. At first the business did well. The future looked bright, but a severe recession occurred in 1921, and when loan payments could not be met the banks foreclosed. Their furniture store was a victim of the recession, so my dad and my grandfather had to look elsewhere for a living. Dad was hired by the Freer Furniture Company on the southwest corner of Indiana Avenue and Tenth Street. The building still stands today, but the Freer Furniture Company is long gone.

My brother Bob was four and I was one when Mother brought us to Wichita Falls from Alpena. Our home was located at 2148 Avenue F on the south edge of town. There was virtually nothing south of us. The streets were still unpaved, and a couple of blocks south were open fields where only an occasional small house might be seen among the mesquite and cactus. The residential areas of Wichita Falls now extend for miles south of where we lived, but in 1919 it was all wild and open country. Since we lived on the frontier, Bob and I liked to go hunting for rabbits and birds which were plentiful. My mother, who could easily see us as we embarked on our exciting hunting forays, gave us two table knives as weapons. Off we went with high hopes, but of course little luck.

My earliest memory is sitting in a high chair when we had a dinner guest, and asking for "lulu" and "doggin." My parents explained to our guest that I was asking for sugar and milk. I remember using those words, and "lulu" still seems kind of right for sugar.

I may be one of the few adults who remembers being toilet trained, and for good reason. To make it easier for me my mother kept a little metal potty under the kitchen stove. Kitchen stoves in those days didn't rest on the floor, but stood on four legs, leaving an open space of about thirty inches between the bottom of the stove and the floor. One day Mother was scrubbing the kitchen floor, and set the potty on top of the oven, in which she had something baking. When she finished scrubbing the floor she took the potty from the top of the oven and put it back under the stove. Shortly thereafter I backed up and dropped my full weight on it. I can still remember shrieking and being unable to stand up fast enough. That incident is burned in my memory, as well as elsewhere. I suppose the experience set my toilet training back at least a month or two.

When I was three years old I liked to play with matches. We had gas kitchen stoves and space heaters that were lit with matches, so there were always matches in the kitchen. They were not the safety matches one sees now, which must be struck on the side of the matchbox. Kitchen matches could be struck against any surface that provided a little friction. I knew I shouldn't play with matches, but one warm summer day I sneaked out of the house, squatted down at the edge of an empty lot, and struck a match. I didn't mean to set the grassy lot on fire, but I did. After some frantic attempts to stomp the fire out, I realized it had gotten beyond me and I was in serious trouble. I high tailed it past our two neighbors, into our house, and into my bed. Mother didn't observe this, but she soon heard the fire engine and realized the field was on fire. Wanting to make sure I was safe, she came looking for me and found me in bed in the middle of the afternoon. I never wanted to take a nap, but there I was, in bed and awake. It didn't take Sherlock Holmes to make the connection between the fire, my history of playing with matches, and my being in bed at that time of the day. Many years have passed since that fire, and maybe my memory fails me, but I don't recall ever playing with matches again.

Rearing children is a trip full of love, laughs, worry, fatigue, and exasperation. As a young boy I'm sure I caused my parents all of those emotions. In 1921 my sister Margaret was born. She and I played together and had the usual disagreements between siblings. One morning while playing in the front yard we had an argument, and Margaret ran around the house to the back yard. I picked up a small stone and threw it over the corner of the house, thinking, "I wish it would hit her," but knowing there was no chance it would. Suddenly I heard her yell, and knew the gods had answered my prayer. Margaret ran in the back door and told Mother that I had hit her with a rock. When Mother questioned me, I put on my most innocent look and said, "I just threw a pebble over the house, I couldn't even see her." This was the absolute truth, though I didn't mention my secret wish. It just didn't seem important at the time. Fortunately for me, Mother bought that explanation, but she admonished me to be more careful when I threw things in the future. I agreed with her that this would be a good idea...in the future.

One hot summer day when I was three Mother gave Bob and me a bath and dressed us in freshly washed and ironed white outfits. She then asked Bob to walk a half block to the grocery store, and to take me with him. When we got to the street it was in the process of being coated with hot tar. Nobody had said anything about hot tar, so we marched right across the street, got what we were sent for, and returned by the same route. By the time we got back tar covered us, our shoes, and our suits. My poor mother must have felt like crying. Instead, she got a laundry tub and some gasoline, stripped us, scrubbed the tar off, and then tried to clean our clothing. Mother must have had many moments of despair, and I'm sure this was one of them.

When I was four I was visiting my Grandma Patton. I walked half a block from Grandma's house to the corner of Eighth Street and Broad, where I met another little boy about my age. We stood on the corner watching the cars go by, and then decided to start throwing rocks at the cars. Our aim was terrible and we didn't have enough strength to hit the cars, but suddenly my distance improved, my aim was right on target, and I put a rock through the windshield of a passing car. Actually it was more than just a passing car. It belonged to an off duty police officer who was riding with his little girl. Once again finding myself in an activity that was way over my head, I took off running back up the hill to my grandma's house.

I don't know where the other little boy went. It was every man for himself. I ran into Grandma's house, through the house to a back room, and hid behind an icebox. Actually, I was so scared that I think I could have squeezed behind just about anything. The driver, of course, saw where I ran and followed me to Grandma's house. He explained to her what had happened and then he and my grandmother came through the house with Grandma calling, "Jack...Jack...Jack." But Jack wasn't answering. I'm surprised that they couldn't hear my heart beating. I was terrified and wouldn't answer. Grandma paid him five dollars for a new windshield, and then came calling to me that he had gone.

When I came out my grandmother earned my undying love. She realized how terrified I was and took me into the front room, sat down in a big rocker, took me on her lap, and comforted me. I'll never forget her love and her kindness. She of course made me see the danger in what I had done. The little girl was sitting on her father's lap in the front seat and could have been badly injured or killed. Windshields in those days were not made of safety glass, so if a windshield shattered the results could be tragic. Of course we weren't trying to break windshields. We were just trying to hit the cars, never thinking of the damage we might inflict. I've remembered Grandma's kindness through all these years, and love her for it.

At age three I set fires. At four I threw stones. At five I talked my way into trouble. I was at the dinner table one evening when I had a difference of opinion with my mother. I don't know now what it was, but I responded, "Well, you're a damn fool." I didn't understand the seriousness of my remark, but I began to realize that something wasn't going quite right when I saw the look on my dad's face as he stood up and began to take off his belt. My remark must have been especially shocking to my parents, because I never heard profanity or discourtesy spoken in our home. I wasn't the smartest kid in the world, but I was quick enough to see that things were getting badly out of hand in a hurry, and I needed to correct a potentially fatal mistake. Not wanting to lose too much face I thought I softened my remark considerably when I said, "Well, maybe you're not a damn fool, but you're a darn fool." That retreat didn't slow things down a bit. The last thing I remember is being rocketed out of my chair by one arm and hustled from the kitchen through the door to the dining room, which at that time of the evening was pitch black. I have no memory of anything that happened after going through that door. My dad wasn't cruel or abusive. He had a wonderful sense of humor and he loved us. But after going through that door everything is a blank.

My childhood days in Texas were carefree times. Except for the constraints that all kids have from good parents, every day was play time. My older brother, Bob, was imaginative and creative, and always had some project going. In the early 1920s he made crystal set radios in which a small wire touched the crystal. He could get different stations by moving the wire to a different position on the crystal, and I remember him putting an aerial on the roof of our house to get better radio reception. He also had a real interest in airplanes. He made an airplane, using two by fours for the fuselage and a one by six piece of lumber for the wings and tail. Then he suspended it from a tree with ropes so we could sit on it and swing back and forth as we dreamed of flying through the sky. With a little imagination, of which we had plenty, we could be shooting down German pilots in World War I.

Bob carved little propellers out of wood and drilled a hole in the hub through which he put a small round stick about six to eight inches long. When the stick was spun the propeller would rise off the stick and fly through the air, a forerunner of the helicopter. He also made a tractor from an empty thread spool, a matchstick, button, small piece of soap, and a rubber band. They were cheap, worked great, and were lots of fun. He showed me how to cover a comb with tissue paper, and then hum through it to play a tune, a homemade kazoo. He was strong on model airplanes that he could power with rubber bands and actually fly. We also dug caves in our backyard by digging a hole and covering it with boards and dirt while leaving a small tunnel for the entrance.

Bob was an interesting older brother, but he wasn't perfect. One day he caught a fly, and told me he would give me a penny if I ate it. I was only four years old, but I knew the value of money, and I didn't have a penny. So I ate the fly, and to this day I can recall the awful taste. He never gave me the penny either. He probably didn't have a penny. Through the years I often reminded Bob of his failure to pay that debt. Finally after nearly seventy years Bob pulled a penny out of his pocket, gave it to me, and said, "Here's your penny. Now stop hounding me."

Not long after the fly incident I was walking down a dirt road with Bob, and as we walked along he said, "Close your eyes and open your mouth and I'll give you something good." After eating the fly, and knowing he didn't have anything good, you'd think I wouldn't fall for that line, but at four years of age most of us are pretty naive (dumb) and trusting. So I closed my eyes and opened my mouth, and was rewarded with a dried "horse apple" stuffed into my mouth. As I reflect on those two incidents, I have come to two conclusions:

1.   *It could have been worse...it could have been a fresh horse apple, and*
2.   *The horse apple didn't taste nearly as bad as the fly.*

Bob had ambitions and goals, while I was content to drift along with the breeze. He became an Eagle Scout and literally dragged me into the Boy Scout program, which I enjoyed, and he led and pushed me to the level of Star Scout. I think I might have become an Eagle Scout if Bob hadn't started college, but when I lost my motivator my forward progress stopped. We moved to Hillsdale, Michigan in 1931, and they didn't have the same vibrant scouting program in Hillsdale that we had in Wichita Falls, so my interest waned.

Summers were carefree times. We went barefoot, swam, played games, made rubber guns and sling shots, dug caves, and did whatever came to mind. We certainly weren't entertained with TV, electronic games or adult planned activities. We had empty lot ball games and I suspect we had more fun than the organized Little League organizations kids have now. One summer Bob and his friends put on a carnival and charged a nickel to see it. One kid dressed up as "The Wild Man of Borneo" by staining his face and arms with the oil of pecans. I wonder how he ever got that stain off. He was dressed in something that resembled an animal skin, made animal like noises and hopped around.

Another summer attraction was the ice wagon that came past our house every other day. It was a covered wagon pulled by two mules. Hardly anyone had an electric refrigerator in the 1920s, so people kept their food cold with ice. Each customer had a card to put in the window to tell the iceman how much ice the customer wanted. It was a square card with four sides. On each side was a number showing the amount of ice needed: 25, 50, 75, or 100 pounds. The iceman wore a heavy leather cape that covered his back. He would grab the block of ice with his ice tongs, swing the block of ice over his shoulder, and walk to the rear of the house to deliver the ice to the icebox in the kitchen. The iceman had to chip one hundred pound blocks of ice into twenty-five or fifty pound blocks, so there were always chips of ice for the kids, and these were a real treat on a hot Texas summer day. While the iceman was delivering ice to a house the kids would scramble into the back of the ice wagon to get a chip to suck on. The mules knew the route as well as the iceman, so they really didn't need a driver, but we heard that sometimes the iceman would let a boy drive his mules. We even heard he got paid fifty cents a day, but it was too much to hope for. I never knew anyone who got that job, but the rumor persisted.

We had a cow that gave more milk than we could use, so we bottled the extra milk and sold it to neighbors and friends. But the cow would go dry when she was pregnant with a calf, so during those dry times we bought milk from the milk man who delivered milk early in the morning. His wagon was much smaller than the ice wagon, and was pulled by a single horse. The milkman never had to drive the horse. He would fill two wire carriers with milk bottles and then deliver them on foot from house to house down the street. The horse would pull the wagon down the street by itself, and stop at the place where the milkman needed to refill his carriers. The horse had been on the route so long that he knew the milk route as well as the milkman.

My early childhood days in Texas were happy and carefree, but when I reached school age I suddenly found my freedom seriously restricted, and it came as a shock. On my first day of school Mother had Bob take me to school with him. He was three or four grades ahead of me and attended the same school. The school was the Alamo Elementary School, and it was about a mile from our house. It was, of course, named after the Texas shrine that is revered by all Texans, and the facade was the same as the original, with a bell shape over the center entrance.

I followed Bob into the school where all the kids were waiting for school to start. Then the principal, Mr. Parks, came into the hall from his office, stood up on a chair, and led us in the Texas "national anthem," "The Eyes of Texas Are Upon You," before sending us to our rooms. The tune is the same as that of "I've Been Working on the Railroad," with the following lyrics:

> *"The eyes of Texas are upon you,*
> *All the livelong day.*
> *The eyes of Texas are upon you,*
> *You cannot get away.*
> *Do not think you can escape them,*
> *From night 'til early in the morn.*
> *The eyes of Texas are upon you,*
> *'Til Gabriel blows his horn!"*

This happened every morning. I don't remember ever singing "The Star Spangled Banner," but we sang "The Eyes of Texas" every single morning.

When Mr. Parks sent us to our rooms that first morning kids scattered in all directions, Bob included, and I found myself alone with no idea where to go. I was five years old, feeling lost and abandoned, and had no clue what I was supposed to do. I finally sat down on the steps across the hall from the principal's office and began to cry. Soon a teacher asked me what was wrong, and when I told her I didn't know where to go she took me down to the end of the hall where Mrs. Davis taught first grade. Mrs. Davis was a kind lady and I liked her, so she was not responsible for what happened next. In the middle of the morning that first day of first grade I discovered something I hadn't anticipated: recess! Recognizing opportunity when I saw it, and already realizing that school was going to seriously infringe upon the free life I had known up to that time, I decided to blow the joint. So I left the other kids playing games in the school yard, and headed back home to the life I liked.

I found my way home by myself, and when I arrived I discovered my mother had gone grocery shopping. We had a servant house attached to the garage behind our house, where a black couple lived in exchange for house and yard work. The woman was there when I arrived, and welcomed me with the statement that my mother wasn't going to let me stay home. I had been dressed in my school clothes that morning, and was in the process of shedding those uncomfortable clothes in exchange for my coveralls when my mother returned. She asked me why I was home, and I told her I didn't want to go to school anymore. I had seen that school was going to seriously interfere with my freedom, and I didn't want any further truck with that organization. Mother straightened out my faulty thinking on the spot, got me redressed, and escorted me back to Mrs. Davis' room where she spent the rest of the morning observing. From that day until my last day in high school I never skipped school again. Either my mother was a convincing enforcer, or I was an easy pushover. Considering my disillusionment with public education, it is ironic that I spent thirty years as a high school principal, and three years as a pilot instructor in the Army Air Corps during WWII. The gods have a sense of humor.

In first grade I noticed that for some mysterious reason girls were different from boys. I was particularly taken with a little red haired girl who sat half way back from the front in the third row from the windows. I can't remember what she looked like, or her name, but I took every opportunity to walk past her desk . . . slowly . . . to go to the pencil sharpener and the waste basket.

Most schools have a bully, and the bully at the Alamo school was a couple of years ahead of me. When I was in the third grade I went into the boy's bathroom one day thinking how I'd like to punch that bully right in the nose. There was a wooden divider on the right side that we had to walk around, and as I came around the end of that wall I imagined the bully coming the other way. Like Walter Mitty I swung my fist as hard as I could right where I thought his nose would be if he were really there. As unbelievable as it seems, the bully WAS coming around the wall at the exact moment I threw my punch, and I nailed him dead center right in the nose. He staggered back and I nearly collapsed as I wondered how long it would take him to kill me and how much it would hurt, but he let me go without taking revenge. He either thought this little kid had a punch like Jack Dempsey, or else he bought my terrified apology that it was an accident, which I guess it really was as I would never have done that on purpose.

My homeroom teacher at the Alamo School was a dour unsmiling teacher named Miss Dickenson. She taught us all subjects except art and music. The art teacher was Miss Scott, who made a perfect mate for Miss Dickenson. They both had me believing they hated the world. Miss Dickenson didn't have much empathy for a student like me who enjoyed laughs, jokes, and a good time. I'm sure I must have been a trial to her, and I can imagine she was convinced that Jack Ford would come to no good. One day our class was having music, and we were in our seats with our music books open. I was seated on the front row (smart teacher) and the music teacher was standing nearly in front of me telling us something about that day's music lesson while I chewed a small piece of paper with no thought of making it into a spitball or of doing anything with it. It was a spitball all right, but I had no ulterior motive as I idly put it on my open music book. After leaving it there for a little while I casually flipped it by holding my finger against my thumb and then snapping my finger forward. This propelled the spitball, about the size of a BB, towards the front of the room. I watched in growing horror as the spitball, seemingly in slow motion, headed straight for the teacher, and then right into her open mouth. She dropped her book, gagged, and finally spit it out.

She knew where it came from, as she had probably tracked it from my book to her mouth. Even if she didn't, my horror stricken face was a dead giveaway. And if she didn't notice my face she probably felt it was a safe bet that I must have had something to do with it. She grabbed me by the arm and marched me down the hall to Miss Dickenson's room. I can imagine Miss Dickenson licking her lips as she heard the evidence, because she took me by the other arm and marched me back down the hall again to the bookstore across the hall from the music room. The bookstore brought fear to the hearts of kids who had misbehaved at The Alamo School, because it had more than just one connotation. It was used to store schoolbooks, but it was also where the school paddle was kept.

I'm ashamed to admit that I had visited the bookstore a number of times, and not to get books. The bookstore and I were on something like a first name basis. I wasn't escorted there frequently, but I was no stranger to it either. I honestly can't remember any of the previous charges that were leveled against me, but I had always escaped with a warning, probation as it were, so I had a rather ho-hum attitude as we once again made one of those nuisance trips to our friendly bookstore. It was a minor inconvenience to me, and I knew the script: look contrite and listen to their scolding and warnings. But on this occasion the court had apparently had enough. The warning was not forthcoming.

The first words out of Miss Dickenson's mouth were, "Bend over and grab your ankles." As I bent over to grab my ankles I still hoped for a reprieve from the governor, but it was not to be. Miss Dickenson vented some of her pent up frustration with a swat that made me reach for the ceiling. She invited me to bend over twice more, and gave me two more swats that straightened me up the same way the first one had. In my defense I have to repeat that it was an unintentional occurrence (although a beautiful shot), but my past was catching up with me. It was God's way of averaging things out. As I think about it, I may have come out a little ahead of the game. It was my only physical punishment during my school years, and the bookstore and I had no further contact with one another. My parents never heard a word about this incident, as I knew I would find no sympathy at home, and I didn't need more trouble.

Two blocks west of Alamo School was a small neighborhood grocery store run by a couple who owned a pet crow. In 1928 I was walking to school with friends on one of our rare snowy days when I saw this crow perched on an electric line. He was a tempting target for a snowball and I threw one at him, but missed. I threw several more but missed each time as he scolded me. When I turned my back to rejoin my friends I felt something strike my head, and turned to find the crow diving at me. After that the crow knew he had me spooked, and he attacked me every day when I went to or from school. He made my life so miserable I began to go to school by a different route.

I attended Alamo School every year except one. That year my parents rented out our house in town while we rented a place in the country so my dad would have more room for our cow and some chickens. Mother always said Dad would have made a good gentleman farmer, as he enjoyed being in the country and working with his hands. Our country house was a modest little house, but it was in good repair and we were happy there.

While we lived there Bob and I attended the Fanin School, usually walking there and back each day as there were no school buses. This house didn't have the conveniences we had in town. We got water from a nearby irrigation ditch, and electricity from a Delco unit in a shed in the back yard. The Delco unit was a gasoline powered generator. Our Delco was a temperamental gadget, and we could never be sure it would cooperate. The water from the irrigation ditch was not fit to drink, so we had to buy bottled water for cooking and drinking. We used the ditch water for taking baths. There was a screen to filter the water, but more than once I found small minnows sharing my bath with me. Our stove was a kerosene stove, which seemed adequate to cook on. These inconveniences must have been difficult for my mother, but we kids went our happy carefree way with hardly a twitch. We roamed the fields, hunted meadow larks, swam in the irrigation ditch, and thought life was grand.

A nearby family named Fore had a son named Burton who was about the same age as Bob. The Fore family planted a field of sorghum, and we enjoyed cutting a stalk of sorghum and sucking the sweetness from it. The Fores also had horses and quite a few of the famed Texas longhorn cattle. When we went over to their house we all had our own horse, and we'd go riding together. We lived in Texas, home of the cowboys, where everyone wore a six shooter and a ten gallon hat, and rode the range. Actually we were no nearer to being cowboys than kids in any other part of the country.

Burton Fore was just three years older than I, but he was an experienced tobacco chewer who talked me into trying a chaw. He said he liked it, and assured me I would too, but it took only a second or two for me to discover that this was a man's game. It burned my mouth and tasted awful. I tried water and then milk, but nothing put out the fire, and I suffered until time helped me recover.

When we lived in the country my mother was pregnant with my brother Bill, and Grandfather Henry and Grandmother Sarah came down from Michigan to Texas to be with us. I remember the day, March 9, 1926. I was playing in our front yard with some toy cars when Dad came down the road, sailed into our driveway across the grass to the front porch, jumped out of his car, cleared the porch railing in one jump, and yelled, "It's a boy." Dad had enthusiasm and a zest for life that showed in everything he did. He enjoyed his children and was amused by us. He was fun and exciting to be around. When he came home at the end of the day Bob and I would sit, one on each foot, and he would walk around giving us a ride. He would get down on all fours so Bill could struggle up on his back for a horse back ride. Dad died when Bill was just five years old. I once asked Bill if he remembered Dad, and he said, "I just remember somebody." That almost breaks my heart, because Dad would have so enjoyed Bill. It is a tragedy for a little boy not to know his father, especially that father. A boy needs a dad, and Bill really never had one. They both missed so much. We all did.

When Bill was four months Bob and I were outside playing when we found a dead snake. Bob suggested we sneak the snake in and put it in the baby's bed. We managed to get the snake in without being observed, and coiled the snake in the crib in a life-like position. We then went outside and watched through the window, knowing they would soon be bringing the baby back to his crib. Dad carried Bill into the room, and we watched with big grins as Dad saw the snake, jumped back, and left the room. A moment later he returned with a long two by four and began hitting the snake. He soon discovered it was a dead snake, and it was no trouble for him to figure out how that snake must have gotten there. Dad made it clear it wasn't nearly as funny as it seemed to us, but knowing him as I do, I'm sure he had to be amused.

Life was often more interesting than I really wanted. During one recess at the Fanin School I saw a group of boys at the back of the school watching a fight. I came up to the crowd as an interested spectator, and saw one boy sitting on top of another boy while he punched him in the face. My sympathy is usually with the underdog, and this outraged my sense of fair play. I wasn't outraged enough to get involved, but I had to express my sentiments, so I said to a boy standing next to me that if the boy on top hurt the other boy I was going to beat him up. I was just saying what I would like to do, as there sure wasn't any question that the boy on top was hurting the boy on the bottom. I didn't expect my confidant to tell the whole world what I had said, but he could see that the present fight was about over and here was a chance to watch another one. I froze as I heard him tell the winner that I said I was going to beat him up. The winner was flushed with victory, and ready for all comers.

I wasn't the fighting type. I try to avoid pain, and fighting usually causes pain. I think it hurts me more than anybody in the world to get hit in the nose, and here was a guy who obviously could fight, because he just won the first one. I didn't want to change places with the kid on the bottom, but I expected to as the winner slowly got to his feet and sized me up. He had his reputation to consider, so he started in on me, and there was nothing for me to do but fight back, which I did out of sheer desperation. I recall a soldier during World War II who said he wouldn't fight. The army's response was, "Okay, but we're going to take you to where the fighting is, and let you use your own judgment." Like that soldier I suddenly found myself where the fighting was. I must have gotten lucky, because all of a sudden the other boy broke and ran away. I had whipped him! I was a hero. I had an instant reputation in this school. Walk softly around me and be careful what you say.

As he turned the corner of the building I hollered after him, "Yeah, you big sissy, you big coward." This pushed some button on that kid, because he turned without missing a step and came back at me, and the fight began again, only this time with new vigor. I quickly realized he was a boy with a new purpose, so I started running in the opposite direction as he yelled, "Yeah you big sissy, you big coward." That sounded familiar, but I wasn't at all offended as I turned the corner and headed for the front of the school where kids were lining up on the sidewalk to go back to their rooms after recess. "Words can never hurt me," but that kid was murder the second time around.

As I got in line on the sidewalk I found a pretty little girl named Elizabeth Moore standing in front of me. The fight that I had both won and lost was forgotten, and since fighting held no future for me I thought I might try my hand at romance. I leaned over and kissed Elizabeth on the cheek, whereupon she called out in a loud voice, "Teacher, make Jack Ford stop kissing me." If people just wouldn't talk so much. Elizabeth's older sister told Bob that Elizabeth liked me, which just shows that girls start playing hard to get at an early age.

As I reflect on some of my misadventures, setting the field on fire, throwing rocks at cars, telling my mother that she was a damn fool, believing that Bob would give me something good to eat if I opened my mouth and shut my eyes, quitting school during the first recess in the first grade, and both winning and losing the fight behind Fanin school I am reminded of something I read in Alamo Elementary School. I sensed immediately that whoever wrote it had me in mind. It said, "Experience is a dear school, but fools learn by no other." Through the years that saying has flashed through my mind many times.

We lived in the country for a year, and then moved back into town to our home on Avenue F. That house seemed spacious when I was a boy, but when I go back to see it now it really is quite modest. The front yard that seemed large enough in those days now looks minute. In the late 1920s Dad added what I thought was a large room on the back of our house, but I now see that it is in no way a large room. Before Dad added that room Bob and I had double deck bunks in the kitchen, and I can remember waking up to see my dad cooking breakfast for us, usually Cream of Wheat or Ralstons. If he emptied the cereal box he would throw it at us in fun. He was always in good humor, joking and playing. Dad enjoyed us and enjoyed life.

When I grew older I tried various business activities to earn spending money. Knowing I liked pets, my Grandpa Patton gave me some Bantam chickens. They were no trouble, as we had chickens anyway, and a few Bantam hens and a rooster were no more work. After I had the Bantams for a while my grandfather brought six duck eggs to me, and suggested I put them under one of my Bantam hens. A hen won't naturally sit on eggs that aren't hers, but if you put a hen on eggs and put her in a confined nest where she can't get off, in two or three days she thinks they are hers and she will stay with them. The little hen I put on those duck eggs spread herself out as wide as she could to cover all the eggs. Four of the eggs hatched, three ducks and a drake. She did a motherly job of raising those ducklings and they waddled and quacked after her as she led them around the chicken yard. They grew into adults and took to the only water available, the tub of water my dad had for the cow. One night Dad came in from milking our cow and told me he was sorry, but I was going to have to do something about the ducks, because they were fouling the cow's tub, and the cow wouldn't drink from it.

Johnny Proctor had a large flock of pigeons in a pen in his back yard, and when I told him I had to do something with my ducks he offered to trade some of his pigeons for my ducks. I got ten or twelve of his pigeons for my four ducks, and built a pen on the back of our garage in the chicken yard. It was five feet by eight feet and about five feet high, with chicken wire over the top. I had a small protected area against the garage as shelter from the weather, with some nests and a place for them to roost. I fed them chicken feed, and they soon became quite tame. I kept them in this pen for about six months until they accepted the pen as home. I heard that I could put fence wiring on top of the cage that was large enough for other pigeons to drop through to be with my pigeons, but too small for them to fly back out. I had seen other pigeons perched on top of my pen, so I got some fence wire, and sure enough it worked like a charm.

I then began to let my pigeons out in pairs. I knew which pigeons had become pairs, and I picked out the two tamest pigeons and set them free. That evening I found them back in the pen. I began to let others out, and soon took the top wire off the pen so they could come and go as they wished. Little by little other pigeons joined them until I had about fifty pigeons. I nailed boxes to the garage as nests and I soon had young pigeons, called squabs, which became my main source of income. I cleaned and dressed them and sold them to neighbors and friends for twenty-five cents apiece. Four of them meant a dollar, and a dollar went a long way during the depression.

After my father died in April, 1931 I realized Mother's Day was approaching, and I knew this might be a hard time for her, so I sold some squabs to earn money to buy something for her. I was aware that Dad would have done something for her on that day, and he wouldn't be there to do so this year. I had a dollar and a half, and I went to the five and ten cent store and bought a grocery bag full of small items. I can't remember everything I bought, but I do remember buying a barber comb and hair cutting scissors, because our folks always cut our hair. I should have bought a new set of clippers, because the old set was missing some of its teeth, and every pass with those clippers pulled our hair. I realize now that one nice present would have been better than many small ones, but I know Mother appreciated the effort. It was the thought that counted. After Dad died we moved to Michigan, and the pigeons, being free, probably left for better fare.

I enjoyed animals, and was forever bringing home stray pets. I barely remember the first dog we had, but I do know he was sent to dog heaven for killing chickens. The first dog I remember well was a little part collie puppy that Grandpa Patton gave us. He was a cute little fellow and we named him Sport. We had him for many years until he started to become aggressive. Some boys used to come by the house and throw rocks at him as he lay on the porch, and he nipped a couple of them. Unknown to me my parents asked Grandpa Patton to shoot Sport because they felt they couldn't keep a dog that was aggressive towards people. My folks had me visit Grandma and Grandpa on the weekend when the deed was to be done. Grandfather knew how much I loved Sport, but for some reason he told me he had shot Sport, even describing in detail how he had put some meat down for him, and how Sport looked at him as he pulled the trigger. It wasn't necessary to tell me that, and I don't know why he did. At any rate, I forgave him and remembered how good he was to me.

It didn't take long to replace Sport. A neighbor two doors down from us, Mr. Cavanaugh, had a purebred Fox Terrier with a litter of pups, and he gave one to us when the puppies were about six weeks old. We named the puppy Duke. Actually, Bob named all of our pets, and I agreed with anything he suggested. Fox Terriers make wonderful pets for children, and Duke was no exception. He was a bright peppy little dog, and he was a great companion to us for years. I never knew what happened to Duke, but recently Bob told me Duke was shot for killing chickens. I wonder who did the honors that time.

My next dog, Queenie, came to my grandfather's house as a stray. She was a terribly frightened and shy little dog, and it took us a long time to gain her confidence. The first night we had her we let her out before we went to bed, and I wasn't sure we would ever get her back in the house. Mother suggested we get some bread soaked in bacon fat, and that coaxed her back inside. Queenie was a popular girl in the neighborhood, and we always had at least one litter of pups every year. It was my job to give the pups away. After Dad died we left for Michigan in June 1931 so Mother could get a masters degree in library science from the University of Michigan. We expected to be gone for the summer, so we found a couple to take care of Queenie until we returned. It was the same couple who had the pet crow that tried to ambush me every day on my way to school. As it turned out, we didn't return, so the couple simply kept her. Two years later we returned to Texas for a visit, and while driving down their street I saw Queenie trotting towards their store. When I gave the whistle I always used she stopped and her ears went up, but when I called her my voice had changed. She didn't recognize me, and continued on towards the store. That was the last time I saw that little dog that meant so much to me.

One summer afternoon I found myself visiting with our neighbor, Mr. Cavenaugh. Mr. Cavenaugh was sitting in a chair shaded by large ivy leaves, with a B.B. gun in his lap. He was always friendly, and he asked if I would like to shoot it. I eagerly accepted, but before he let me shoot it he pointed out a particularly large leaf that he cherished, as he said it gave him shade when the sun was a certain spot every afternoon. He told me I could aim at any other leaf, but to be sure not to hit that leaf. I took careful aim at another leaf and pulled the trigger. The B.B. went through the heart of that cherished leaf, and I couldn't have hit it more dead center if it had been laser guided. Poor Mr. Cavenaugh couldn't believe it, and for that matter, neither could I. I told him I hadn't aimed at that leaf, and he didn't scold too long, considering it was his favorite, but I didn't get any more practice with his B.B. gun.

As we get older our short term memory seems to fail us. Recent names are difficult for me to recall now, although I can clearly remember the names of classmates from elementary school: Frank Rusk, W.D. Tollet, Mary Jo Ellis (a little blond girl who made my heart beat faster), Elizabeth Perkins (a little brunette girl who made my heart beat faster), Ina Jo Ogle (maybe they all made my heart beat faster), Pete Nix, J.B. Garret, Jack Hill, Robert King, J.E. Duncan, and C.C. Jones. My grandparents' address was 1310 8th Street and their phone number was 6689. Our phone number was 8486. All this stays with me, but I wonder what happened yesterday.

C.C. Jones was called Sissy Jones. If you said C.C. fast enough it sounded like sissy, and the fact of the matter was that C.C. wasn't very masculine, and he walked on his toes in little mincing steps. During recess at the Alamo School we often played a game called work-up. It was a softball game where there were no sides. We played as individuals. A player started in the outfield, and worked his way up to being the batter as those before him flied or grounded out during their turn at bat. If the batter got a hit, and could run to first base before being thrown out, he returned to the batter's position to bat again. One day C.C. was in the field and I hit a fly ball straight towards him. Everyone could see it would be an easy out. But when C.C. saw the ball coming his way he put his hands over his head and started running away from where he thought the ball was going to land...and in those little toe dancing steps of his. As luck would have it he ran exactly the wrong way, and the ball hit him dead center on the head. Since he cost everyone else a chance to move up, they normally would have berated him, but it was so funny to see C.C. dance away with his hands over his head, and then get hit dead center, that they all felt it was worth the sacrifice.

Kids can be unkind because they don't empathize. I wish we had been kinder to C.C. back in the early 1920s. He was a nice boy and a good student, and he deserved better treatment from us. In the fifth and sixth grades my best friend was a boy named Thomas Caldwell. We all called him Fats for obvious reasons. I never thought of his feelings and he never seemed to mind, although if he had we probably wouldn't have realized it.

We also gave no thought to the names we gave things. We all had slingshots made from the fork of a branch, some heavy rubber bands from an old inner tube, and the tongue of a shoe. We called them nigger shooters. That name had absolutely no significance to me in reference to colored people. As far as we were concerned it was simply what we called a slingshot. Even the black kids I knew called them that. I don't think any of us thought of that term as anything but the name of a slingshot. It sounds terrible now, but there was no intent to demean colored people.

In 1928, at the beginning of the Great Depression, Dad lost his job at the furniture store. At the same time he discovered, at the age of forty, that he had diabetes. Until about 1922 diabetes was a fatal disease that could be controlled only by reducing food intake to a starvation level. Diabetics would starve to death over a short period of time if they observed their diet, or die over a painfully longer time if they did not. So the public concept of diabetes was much more frightening then than it is today. By 1928 insulin was available to control diabetes, but for my parents to face both the loss of their family income and diabetes must have been a stunning blow.

Today we have government safety nets such as Social Security or Food Stamps for people in trouble, but in those days when the head of the household lost his job there was simply no money coming in . . . none! My parents had four children, the youngest only two years old, and the oldest thirteen, and I can imagine how desperate they must have felt. My mother told me years later that when she discovered that my dad had diabetes she prayed for three years to prepare herself to take care of our family. Dad died three years later.

Both of my parents graduated from college, and my dad had a master's degree from the University of Michigan. Both had experience in public education, so it was logical that they would look to return to that profession. They borrowed money from my Patton grandparents, bought a used 1922 Dodge four door touring sedan, left my brothers, Bob and Bill, with my grandparents, packed Margaret and me in the back seat, and drove to the University of Colorado where they took classes to prepare themselves to return to teaching. It must have been awfully hard for my parents to leave Bob and especially Bill, who was such a little fellow. Thirty one years later my wife and I took our three oldest children on a trip to California, and left the two youngest with my mother and my sister, Margaret, as we knew they were too young to enjoy such a long hard trip. I remember how hard it was for me to leave those two little fellows. It was especially hard to leave the youngest, Bruce, because he was only three years old, and didn't understand that we weren't leaving him for good. Bruce was a daddy's boy, and as we drove away I could hear him calling to me, "Daddy, don't leave me. Daddy, don't leave me." I stopped the car and thought, "I can't leave that little boy," but Marge reminded me that he was too young to enjoy the trip, and if we took him we wouldn't enjoy it either. It took me some time to recover from the awful feeling his little cry had given me. My parents must have had similar feelings in 1928.

Most roads are now hard surfaced, but in 1928 that was not the case. Many of the roads in Texas were clay. Naturally we had rain the first day. When clay gets wet it becomes greasy, and on that first day our car slid off the road and into the ditch. We finally got out of the ditch when a farmer with a team of horses pulled us out. We spent the first night in Amarillo, Texas, a distance of no more than three hundred miles. That doesn't seem far for an all day trip, but cars did not travel very fast in those days, and the accident in the ditch slowed us down. The second day we reached Raton Pass between New Mexico and Colorado after dark, this time slowed down by a leak in our oil pan that had to be repaired. We drove over that pass at night, with primitive roads and dim headlights, finally reaching Walsenburg, Colorado around midnight. My folks expected to make the trip in two days, but we arrived in Boulder on the third day, and moved into a little cabin on the corner of Arapahoe and Seventeenth Streets. It was a beautiful place with pine trees, a mountain stream that ran past our cabins, blue skies, and majestic mountains just to the west of us. I loved my summer there, and fell in love with the Rocky Mountains. Boulder High School now sits on the property where our cabin was located.

My parents enrolled Margaret and me in some classes to keep us busy. I took a shop class, and made a hobbyhorse for Bill. The horse was made from a broomstick with a horse's head painted with a bridle and mane and eyes. We took our classes in the morning, and then came home for lunch and an afternoon of play. I thought it was a wonderful summer, certainly the most memorable of my childhood, and I wondered how heaven could be more beautiful than Boulder, Colorado. I'm sure my folks had plenty of worry on their minds, but Margaret and I had a carefree vacation.

On the weekends we often took a blanket or two, a bottle of water, a picnic basket, and some round steak, and drove up into the mountains. We made a small fire to cook the steak on a flat rock my folks found, and then after lunch Margaret and I explored nearby areas while our parents studied. I enjoyed the beautiful scenery and thought it must be the most beautiful place in the world, in sharp contrast to the flat arid landscape of West Texas. I cherish those memories and I still love those mountains.

The summer we spent in Boulder in 1928 has so many poignant memories for me that in 1988 my wife and Margaret and I flew to Wichita Falls, rented a car, and took that same trip via the same route that my folks had taken sixty years earlier. Most of the route is now super highway, but we could still see sections of the old highway down below us, both in Texas and in Colorado. The trip that took my parents three days we could have completed in one, but we elected to stop at Colorado Springs, and went on to Boulder the next morning.

On the fourth of July we took a day trip from Boulder to Rocky Mountain National Park. Long before we arrived we could see snow-covered peaks, and when we reached the mountains we got out of the car and had a snowball fight. On the fourth of July! It was hard to imagine for two kids from Texas. We were in Colorado for six weeks that summer, and took several drives to see interesting parts of the state. One memory that stays with me is the fragrant smell of the pine needles in the mountains. I still enjoy that fragrance when we return to Colorado these many years later.

We drove to Denver a couple of times that summer so Dad could have his blood sugar checked. In those days there was no way for an individual to check his own blood sugar. Diabetics had to go to a doctor's office to have a blood sample taken, which was then sent to a laboratory to be analyzed. I found I had diabetes in my early sixties, but I can check my own blood sugar as frequently as I wish. The trips to Denver were fun for Margaret and me. We started for Denver by driving several miles east on Arapahoe until we came to the end of the road, and then turned right. At this corner my dad would stop to buy a package of Black Jack chewing gum. It didn't take much to give us a treat in those days. We would eat lunch in some little restaurant, and then visit the Denver Natural Museum of History to see the stuffed animals in natural settings.

I particularly remember the sea lions. In recent years I have returned to that museum, and many of the same displays are still there.

Towards the end of that summer my grandparents brought Bob and Bill from Wichita Falls to Boulder to visit us. For several days we showed them around Boulder and through some of the scenic areas. After my grandparents returned to Wichita Falls my parents packed up the old Dodge, and we returned to Texas via Kansas, Nebraska, and Michigan. Along the way we stopped at Salina, Kansas to visit my Grandfather Henry's sister, Helen, and her daughter, Mary. Many years earlier Helen had lost her first two children to diphtheria while visiting the family farm in 1877. They made us sandwiches before we left, and when I looked in my sandwich I could see they had sliced a green bell pepper to look like a shamrock. I thought that was a neat idea. When we drove into Lincoln, Nebraska we crossed a bridge during a heavy rain, and in the middle of the bridge the car slid sideways and then turned end for end. We fortunately kept moving down the middle of the road rather than sliding into the side of the bridge, and luckily there were no cars coming the other way.

We were on our way to Omaha, Nebraska where my dad's sister, Ruth, and her husband lived with their four daughters and one son. Dad stopped the car around the corner from their house, and told me to knock on the back door. When Aunt Ruth answered I pretended to be a homeless child, and asked if she could give me something to eat. I don't remember ever having seen her before, but when she saw me she gave me a hug, and said, "I'd know those black eyes anywhere."

Their children were near our own ages, and we got along with them famously. Their son Robert was named after my dad. He was just a year younger than I, and in a short time we were rolling around on the floor in a friendly wrestling match as our parents watched and laughed. There were nine children altogether, so things were interesting. In the evening we played hide and seek and other games that always seemed more fun at night. One evening we were running around the yard, and I knew there was a chicken wire fence somewhere in that dark yard, but I wasn't sure just where. I picked up a hoe that was leaning against the house, and held it in front of me, so I wouldn't run into the fence. It was a good idea, but the technique needed some refinement. I held the hoe with the handle pointed away from me, and when I finally came to the fence the end of the handle slipped nicely through the chicken wire, and I hit the fence full speed. I wasn't hurt, so I picked myself up and took off again, but this time without the hoe.

From Omaha we drove to Michigan to visit the Ford family farm seven miles southeast of Hillsdale. I visited the old home several times at the end of World War II, and walked through it trying to imagine the people who had lived there. Some I knew, but most I had only read about or heard about. Edna gave us all a wonderful gift when she wrote her history of the Ford family. She had knowledge no one else had of the relatives who lived there during the 1800s. She wrote about a window pane in the pantry of the old home which had an imperfection in it that looked like a little hatchet. She wrote that the "small fry" were fascinated by the pane, and that they all loved to stand and look at that imperfection. When I heard that the old home was going to be demolished I went to it one day, removed the pane, and had it framed with Edna's quotation. My son David now has it.

While we were in Hillsdale that summer Dad learned that the Jackson Public Schools were looking for a new superintendent. He went for an interview, but was told that he had been out of public education too long to be considered for that position. That was a disappointment to my parents, as they would have liked to have had my dad employed back in a profession in which he was experienced and qualified, and back in Michigan where his family lived.

On the way back to Texas we stopped to visit friends who gave us a bushel of pears. The Dodge was loaded inside and out with luggage, and the only place for the pears was on the floor of the back seat with the kids. Riding all day in the car with nothing to do, we nibbled on pears until I got so sick of pears I couldn't stand even the smell of them. It was thirty-five years later, when we had an orchard of peaches, plums, and pears, before I could eat a pear, and then only occasionally.

On the trip home we found ourselves once again driving in the rain on those ever present greasy clay roads. Bob and Margaret and I were in the back seat with the pears while Mom held Bill in the front seat. She suddenly realized Bill was turning blue, and was unable to wake him. They realized then that Bill, lying in Mother's lap, had been breathing carbon monoxide that hadn't reached those of us higher in the car. Dad couldn't stop the car immediately because the slippery roads would cause us to slide into the ditch. So my parents rolled down the car windows, and held Bill up to the fresh air until they came to a place where they dared to stop. He soon began to recover and opened his eyes, but if Mother had not noticed his color he could have died. For that matter, we could all have been overcome.

At the end of the trip we drove all night to get to Wichita Falls, because my folks only had one nickel left after filling the car with gas. We didn't have any supper that night, because Mother explained to us that we had only one nickel, and Dad needed a cup of coffee to keep him awake. We understood the situation and accepted it. The other kids had pears, but just looking at them ruined my appetite.

Early in the evening we were driving on a road that ran parallel to a railroad track. At one point the road made an "S" turn that took us across the railroad track, and then ran parallel to it on the other side. Automobile headlights in those days were very dim compared to today's lights, so visibility was not very good. Instead of crossing the track and proceeding down the other side of the railroad track, Dad turned too soon, and we found ourselves bumping along down the railroad track itself. Cars were so high off the ground back then that we didn't get hung up on the tracks. I remember Dad jumping out of the car and looking up and down the track to make sure no train was coming, getting back in the car, and then jumping out again to take another look, as he could see lights coming towards us. He finally realized the lights were from cars coming down that road next to the tracks. He got back in the car, and we bumped our way back to the crossing and were again on our way, on the road this time.

The next morning we were just coming into the outskirts of Wichita Falls when the car in front of us slowed down to make a left turn. When Dad tried to stop he discovered that we had lost our brakes. He couldn't stop and he couldn't pass in the left lane because the car in front had already started across that lane. There was nothing to do but to turn with the other car. There were two telephone poles on the left side of the road, and Dad had just enough room to squeeze in between them. The other driver locked his brakes as we sailed past him heading back to the road, and Dad called out, "No brakes!"

When we returned home from Colorado Dad set out to find a job. It wasn't easy, because jobs were nearly non-existent in the early years of the depression. Mother wrote a letter to Grandfather and Grandmother Ford in which she said, "There have been several weeks when Bob hasn't made a dollar." Those were really desperate times for my parents, and they weren't alone. All over the country families were facing a similar crisis. For a short time Dad worked for Grandpa Patton who had a mattress factory. I'm sure that job was a way for my grandparents to help us after Dad had gone looking for work for weeks, only to come back empty. He finally got a job with Noble Little Hardware selling General Electric refrigerators on a commission basis. He took iceboxes on trade-in, and sold them from our house. I remember seeing several iceboxes in our backyard, and people coming to buy them.

In January of 1929 Dad was hired as principal of a small school system outside of Wichita Falls. That fall he moved to a larger system as principal, but still outside of the Wichita Falls school system. Then in 1930 he was hired to teach English in the local high school close to our house. We could look out of our front window and see the high school just two blocks away. Dad was happy to get into the Wichita Falls school system, and hoped to move into administration. Mother was also hired to work as an assistant librarian in Zundelowitz Junior High School. Zundelowitz was about four blocks from our house, and it was the junior high school I attended after leaving Alamo Elementary School.

In Zundelowitz I met a math teacher whose memory I cherish. She was Margaret Vance. I came to love her and looked forward to my arithmetic class each day. I can't remember what she did, or how she may have done it, but she did something that captured my interest and made math my favorite subject. She made math easy, understandable and fun. I had another teacher in high school very much like Margaret Vance. Virginia Grommen taught American History, and she made history fun for me. Most of my other teachers have faded in my memory, but those two stand out. A third favorite was my own mother, who was my teacher for English Literature during my senior year in high school. She was an outstanding teacher who was loved and respected and admired by her students over a period of three decades. Many of her students returned to thank her for the wonderful preparation she gave them for college, and for the values and personal standards she tried to instill in them. Most boys don't readily take to poetry, but I learned the beauty of poetry and learned to love and enjoy it from her teaching.

Near the end of our time in Colorado Dad's doctor told him, "You don't have diabetes, and you never did have it." Thrilled with the good news, he wrote to his parents, "I feel like I have a new lease on life." He had all the classic signs of diabetes, excessive thirst, frequent urination, and unexplained weight loss. He did have diabetes, and it became obvious to all of us three years later. One wants to believe good news, and when Dad was told he was not diabetic a heavy burden was taken from his shoulders. When he was originally tested for diabetes another man was tested the same day. Dad was told he had diabetes, and the other man was told he did not. At the end of the summer in 1928 my folks learned the other man had died. They hoped that perhaps the laboratory tests for my dad and the other man had been mixed, and that the other man had diabetes and my dad did not. When the doctor in Denver told Dad he did not have diabetes it all seemed to fit together. It turned out to be wishful thinking.

Three years later, on Saturday and Sunday, April 18 and 19, Bob and I attended a Boy Scout camp at Diversion Dam, a few miles from Wichita Falls. My folks had a big Sunday dinner at my grandparent's house with rich foods and desserts. Since he believed he did not have diabetes, Dad ate with relish. That evening he went out to milk our cow in a cold drizzle and got thoroughly chilled. Then he came in and took a hot bath before going to bed. I remember the next morning, April 20, 1931, seeing Dad sitting on the edge of his bed with his arm bent up behind his back showing my mother where he had a severe pain under his shoulder blade. He was going to try to go out and milk the cow, but Mother convinced him to lie down, and called a neighbor boy to do the milking. Mother's nursing training made her fearful of pneumonia, although she didn't share that worry with us.

I rode our old bike to school, and during the morning realized Mother hadn't come to the library. At noon I rode home to see how Dad was, and when I got there found the house empty. Mr. Cavenaugh came over to tell me that Dad had been taken to the hospital in an ambulance, and Mother had ridden in the ambulance with him. I returned to school for the afternoon, but my mind was not on my schoolwork. My Aunt Lavern took Margaret and Bill to her house, and we learned from her that Dad and Mother were at Walker-Hargreaves Hospital. Our 1928 Ford Model A was still at home, so Bob and I drove to the hospital. Mother did not tell us that the doctor verified Dad had pneumonia, and added, "If he shows sugar, he doesn't have a chance in a million." Of course his blood did show sugar, and they started him on insulin to bring the sugar down. In the days before penicillin pneumonia was a deadly disease, and even more fatal for diabetics. Our next door neighbor had died of pneumonia, and a little twelve year old boy across the street from us died from it, all while we lived there. My folks were well aware of the near finality of pneumonia, and Dad once told my mother, "If I get pneumonia, I'll just cash in my chips."

Late on Tuesday he began to drift in and out of a coma, but Wednesday evening he became quite lucid and recognized a friend who came to see him. Mother told us, "Maybe you'll have a daddy after all." But he lapsed into a coma again on Thursday and continued failing until he died at 9:15 Friday evening, April 24, 1931, his father's birthday. My Ford grandparents, Henry and Sarah, particularly loved and enjoyed my dad, and his death was a terrible blow to them. Happening on Henry's birthday was especially sad.

Bob and I went to the hospital every day, but on Friday Mother felt it better that I not go. Grandmother Patton was with me in the family bedroom Dad had built, and I now realize that everyone knew Dad was going to die that night. The phone rang about 9:15 and Grandma answered it, hung up, and came over to the bed where I was sitting. She sat down and put her arms around me and told me that Dad had just died. Grandma gave me the only comfort anyone could have given me. She was there and she held me. It was a terrible time for me, and it floods back over me as I write this. I remember Grandmother's love and her tenderness and kindness that night. There was no wind that evening, but as we sat on the bed in the dark a window across the room from us rattled for just a moment, for no apparent reason, and that was the only window that rattled. Grandma, a good Irish girl with a little Irish superstition, considered that a signal from Dad. Could it have been? There is a little Irish in me, too.

Grandma stayed at our house until a few days after the funeral and slept with Mother Friday night. Mother awakened the next morning, saw my grandmother's gray head, and for a moment thought it was Dad, and that it had all been a terrible dream. Saturday morning, as arrangements were being made for the funeral, I said I didn't think I could bear going to the funeral. Grandma understood that I dreaded the pain and the ordeal. She put her arms around me and told me it would be the last thing I could ever do for my dad. Grandma was a wonderful help and support to me and to Mother in those hours. I suppose we were all trying to deal with our own loss and pain, and were not much help to each other. Mother asked me if there were someone I would like to invite over that Saturday. I asked for a friend of mine named Billy Neel, a boy who had lost his parents and was living with an aunt and uncle. I guess I felt he would understand my loss.

It was sixty six years ago that Dad died, but I clearly remember those days and the devastating loss I felt. He was buried on Sunday, April 26th. It was a beautiful sunny day with blue skies and mild temperatures, and the rest of the family sat at the grave site during the service while Bill, who was five, played on a nearby hill. Exactly fifty years later I stood at the same site on Sunday, April 26, 1981, and buried my mother on a beautiful sunny day with blue skies and mild temperatures.

Dad's parents were unable to come to his funeral. They were elderly, and there was no commercial air travel in 1931. It would have been a three day train trip, and in those depression years money was scarce. I can only imagine their anguish. If there would be anything worse than losing a loved parent or spouse, it must be losing a child. And they had lost two, Paul, a little four-year old boy, and now my dad. His parents and his brother Ned and his family held their own service in Uncle Ned's home to coincide with the church service being held in Texas. Uncle Ned told me that it was a cloudy day in Michigan that April 26th, but the sun shone through for a moment and lit squarely on a picture of Dad on their piano. It was the only time that day that the sun broke through the clouds.

Mother took us to the funeral home to see Dad for the last time, as he had often said he didn't want an open casket at the funeral. I remember the gray casket and Dad, who looked so natural, as if he should open his eyes and speak to us, with his nearly white hair and a blue serge suit. He looked beautiful to me. Mother bent over and kissed him on his forehead. I was behind her and I too leaned over and kissed him goodbye. Dad was only forty-three when he died. At thirteen I didn't realize how young he was until I reached that age, and then, shockingly, when my own children reached that age. I remember when our son Jim told me that he was exactly as old, to the day, as my dad had been when he died.

A tremendous crowd filled Highland Heights Christian Church, and many stood outside in testimony to the high regard in which my parents were held in that community. Dad was well known in business circles, and in public education, and for his music. He had a beautiful well-trained voice, and sang both professionally and for community service. He was admired and respected for his gentleness, his grace, his humor, and his music. Fifty-seven years after Dad died Margaret and Marge and I attended Sunday morning service at Highland Heights Christian Church where Dad had directed the choir and sung so many solos. The minister introduced us and told of our background. After the service two ladies came up to us and said they had just recently been speaking of Mr. Ford and remembering his beautiful voice.

I clearly remember the slow ride behind the hearse to the cemetery as we drove up Monroe Street and Ninth Street. I saw people going their happy way, people laughing and talking, and thought, "They don't realize the light has gone out of our world." Cars pulled over to the curb as we passed by, and I was grateful for their doing so.

It was a sad time as we stood around Mother when the casket was partially lowered to ground level. I was glad they didn't lower it fully into the ground while we were there. I don't remember anyone going home with us after the funeral, but I'm sure my grandparents and Aunt Lavern and Uncle Waldon must have done so. I do remember how empty the house seemed without Dad being there, and knowing I would never again see him. Sunday evening I went to the evening church service, sat where I had sat that afternoon, and thought of Dad.

There have been many times through the years when I've wished Dad could be here so I could share things with him. He would have been interested and pleased with my study of voice, my musical accomplishments, and my scholarship at the Conservatory of Music in Chicago. He would have enjoyed my flying experiences during World War II, the three grandsons who were military pilots, the grandson who was an FBI Agent, and the granddaughter who is musically gifted. He would have certainly been interested that I followed in his footsteps as a high school principal. He loved to build, and would have been fascinated with the building of our home on Lake Michigan. He would have especially loved his grandchildren and their mother. I know he would have thought that my wife, Marge, was something pretty special. I wish our children could have known his zest for life, his enthusiasm, his sense of humor, his amused smile, his ready laugh, and his dancing dark eyes. My mother made a concerted effort to keep his memory alive for us through the years, and for me, at least, she was most successful.

I write this in 1998. It is one of those years when the days of the week fall on the same calendar date as in 1931. Yesterday was Friday, April 24, and Dad's death was on my mind all day as I relived the days leading up to his death and the days that followed. It has been sixty-seven years since I lost my dad, and the ache is still there.

Hillsdale
1931 - 1942
High School. . .College. . .Teaching

School let out in late May, and Mother was the lone parent of four children. The youngest was five years old, the eldest sixteen and just graduated from high school. Mother had been working as an assistant librarian at Zundelowitz Junior High School for two years, a job that paid little, certainly not enough to support a family of five. I can only imagine how overwhelmed and alone she must have felt. The whole world was in the throes of the Great Depression. She had no savings, a job that could not support her family, a nearly nonexistent job market, and a seemingly hopeless future. Dad left a ten thousand-dollar insurance policy that gave her some help, but it was not enough to rear and educate four children.

Mother didn't collapse and give up as some did, and I constantly admire her courage and strength of character. I wish I had been more sensitive and helpful to her, but at age thirteen we are too involved with our own interests and problems and sense of loss to fully recognize the needs of others. I just assumed our day to day life would continue to go along as it always had. We were not an affluent family, but I never worried about family income or paying bills. I had a place to sleep, enough food to eat, and clothes to wear. In the lives of most kids what else is there? Many years later I read one of Mother's letters from those difficult days in which she wrote, "I think I can keep all the children." I had never realized there was even a possibility that she might have to send some of us to live with friends or relatives. Her letters show the depth of Mother's grief and loneliness and worry.

Mother often said that her kids were her salvation during those days. Her family kept her thoughts occupied, and lessened the time she had to dwell on her loss. She intended to stay home for a few days after the funeral to sort out her situation and to grieve, but her principal said, "Mrs. Ford, I think you should come to school tomorrow." He knew that several days alone would be terrible for her, and that it would be best if she didn't have time to agonize. Mother later said that it was the best advice he could have given her, and she was always grateful to him for it. I remember Mother saying to me that the hardest part of being alone was not having anyone to discuss her problems with, or to help make difficult decisions.

Mother hoped she would be given Dad's teaching position at the high school, but in those days of intense competition for jobs she needed a master's degree to have a chance. School let out in late May, and a week later we packed our 1928 Ford Tudor and set out for Michigan so Mother could enroll at the University of Michigan. Bob and Bill stayed at Uncle Ned's farm near Hillsdale, while Margaret and Mother and I stayed with friends in Dearborn. It was a small apartment, but they generously invited Mother and Margaret and me to stay with them, and Mother enrolled us in summer school classes in Ann Arbor to keep us occupied while she was in school. Each morning we got up, made our beds, and took the forty five minute drive to Ann Arbor in an old Ford Coupe that had only one seat. In addition, what looked like a trunk lid opened into a small two passenger seat called a rumble seat, and that's where Margaret and I rode. It was outside and had no protection from the wind or cold or rain. The wind blew through our hair, and we thought it was a great treat. Margaret and I loved it. That summer I took Algebra, Latin, and a shop class. My favorite was the shop class, a love that eventually turned into my hobby of making furniture.

Mother came to Michigan that summer fully intending to return to Wichita Falls, but on a trip to Hillsdale she met the superintendent of schools, Percy Holiday, who had been a college classmate of my parents. When he learned of Dad's death he offered Mother a job teaching English and managing the library at Hillsdale High School. She accepted, as it paid a much better salary than she would get at Zundelowitz Junior High School in Wichita Falls. Plus, she had never liked living in Texas with the hot summers and barren landscape. So for the second time that year our lives took a dramatic turn.

Mother faced many problems. The most pressing was finding a place for us to live in Hillsdale. There wasn't time to return to Wichita Falls to collect our belongings, so she arranged to have that done for us. She also had to prepare for her teaching assignment while finishing her work at the University of Michigan. It must have been overwhelming.

Grandpa Patton took over the job of getting our things in Texas boxed up and sent north. Mother found a two story house at 72 W. Bacon Street in Hillsdale to rent for fifteen dollars a month. I was there when the Red Ball moving van arrived. It was a large house with three bedrooms, and a full basement with a coal furnace and hot water tank that burned wood or coal. When we wanted hot water we had to go down to the basement to build a fire. We didn't have the luxury of hot water twenty-four hours a day. We had to be careful, because if the fire got too hot the hot water would turn to steam. If that happened the hot water pipes could burst, or it could back up into the cold water pipes and break the toilet. We tried to be careful, but sometimes we would hear the pipes begin to rattle, and had to rush to open a faucet to release the steam.

The coal furnace had to be fed manually. Someone had to go down to the basement and shovel coal into the furnace and shake the ashes out at the bottom. The ashes periodically had to be carried out and disposed of. We burned soft coal which is much dirtier than hard coal, but it was also cheaper, so that was what most people burned. Soft coal gave off black smoke, but no one spoke of air pollution in those days. Cost was the most important consideration. So much soft coal was burned that snow never stayed white for long. Soot from the coal smoke would dirty the snow as well as any clothes that were hung out to dry. I had never heard of a clothes dryer.

Salaries in 1931 were a fraction of what they are today. Anyone making two hundred dollars a month was considered well off. Mother earned fourteen hundred dollars a year, and was paid only during the months that school was in session. Her salary was reduced the next year to twelve hundred dollars because of the country's economy.

While salaries were low, prices were also low. Mother could buy enough groceries to feed our family of five for five dollars a week. This came to one dollar per person per week. Mother paid seven dollars a ton for soft coal, six cents a quart for milk, and six cents for a loaf of bread. I remember seeing ads in the paper showing a new Ford or Chevrolet for six hundred and ninety five dollars.

People found ways to economize and do things for themselves. The year we left Texas it cost twenty five cents to have a three piece suit cleaned and pressed. As inexpensive as that seems now, most people did their own dry cleaning with Naphtha and something called Reneusit. We cleaned all our woolen clothes and then hung them out to dry, but we never really got rid of the odor. We always smelled of Naphtha, but so did most of the other kids. Most people who lived during those years have thought, "If only we had those prices with today's salaries."

I don't remember missing my friends or our house in Wichita Falls. Everything was new and we were busy adjusting to our new surroundings, and meeting new people. We lived on the edge of town at the foot of Proctor's Hill, which was a great hill in the winter for a boy with a sled, and I made many trips down it.

Hillsdale is a pretty college town with many hills, and many large trees. The college sits on the top of a hill at the north end of town, and provides many cultural advantages to the area. Mother had many happy memories of Hillsdale during her college years, and with four children who needed a college education she saw the benefit of living in a college town. All in all, being offered a teaching job in Hillsdale was a very lucky break for Mother and for us. She was happy to have the job in Hillsdale, but money was always a problem. A woman in those days was always paid less than a man doing exactly the same job.

A young man later came directly from college to teach in Hillsdale, and was paid more than my mother, who by that time had been teaching there for several years. When Mother asked to be paid at least an equal amount she was told the young man was paid more because he was the head of a family. Mother pointed out that she, too, was the head of the family, but a member of the Board of Education responded that if she didn't like it she should go somewhere else. The new teacher's "family" consisted of a wife and no children.

Teachers felt lucky to have a job. They didn't have the job security teachers have now, and did whatever was asked of them. Mother taught English, managed the library, and served as study hall teacher. As librarian she bought new books and catalogued them with cross-references, rebound the old worn books, etc. She was also the debate coach, and spent many after school hours with her debaters researching topics, preparing arguments, and driving to debates. This was often done on Saturdays or during weekday evenings on snowy roads. School boards got their money's worth from teachers in those days.

As if all of this wasn't enough, Mother also accepted the position of librarian for the city library. I don't know what she was paid, but I suppose she thought that every little bit helped. She worked there in the evenings and on Saturdays, as well as afternoons after school. I wonder how she was able to do all the jobs she had while still keeping her household together and rearing four children. One of President Roosevelt's first acts as president was to close all banks until banking policies could be revised. People who had money or valuables in the bank had no access to them. No one knew how long they would be closed, or whether people would ever get their money. As it turned out the banks reopened after a while, but it was an uncertain time for everyone. During the worst of the depression the school board in Hillsdale didn't have enough money to pay their teachers, so they made payments in script. Script was just a promise to pay when the money became available, but most merchants accepted it because they genuinely wanted to help those who were being paid in script, and they were struggling to survive themselves. Anything was better than nothing.

We children all had to assume certain duties. Margaret was only ten years old when we moved to Hillsdale, but she soon learned to iron and do the grocery shopping for the family. At mealtime we all had jobs, such as setting the table, washing and drying the dishes, and sweeping the floor. Bob and I did the family laundry every Friday, but this was not with the automatic washing machines we have today. Our washing machine washed the clothes, but it didn't rinse or spin them dry. This was a big improvement over the machine Mother had earlier that had a handle on the side that she had to push and pull back and forth to agitate the clothes. Our washing machine in Hillsdale had two tubs of rinse water, one for the first rinse and the other for the final rinse. These two tubs sat on a bench by the washing machine along with the wringer. The wringer had two rollers that could be engaged electrically so wet clothes could be fed between the rollers to squeeze the water out. This was done first from the wash water into the first rinse, then from the first rinse to the second, and finally from the second into a basket. We lifted the clothes up and down in the rinse water to get the soap out, and fed them through the rollers which were under considerable pressure.

One day Bob was bent over the tub sudsing the clothes up and down. He had thick wavy hair, and as he bent over his hair fell forward and into the wringer. I was standing there watching as the wringer pulled him forward until his head hit the rollers. As his head hit the wringer Bob pulled back in a kind of jerky motion until he was perhaps three or four inches away, at which time the wringer got the best of him again and yanked him back against the wringer. The process repeated four or five times. Each time he pulled back almost enough to free himself, but then the whole procedure would start all over again. I finally realized he was at the mercy of the wringer, and hit the panic lever to take the pressure off the rollers. When it released he was able to stand up and stagger back. The whole procedure took only a few seconds. It was funny, but I kept from laughing because Bob at that age had a short temper, and I knew he wasn't going to be in a laughing mood after that experience.

Sometime later Bob had to change a tire on a car that he owned. Today motorists change wheels when they have tire problems, but in those days we removed the tire from the wheel. This was done with tire irons, flat iron bars about eighteen inches long that were forced between the tire and the rim of the wheel so the tire could be pried from the rim. We pried part of the tire up and over the rim, left the tire iron there, then did the same with another tire iron close to the first, gradually working around the wheel. Bob had been working with those tire irons for a while, and they were under a fair amount of pressure. I was my usual helpful self, observing from my perch on the front fender of the car. After all, it was pretty much a one-man job, it was <u>his</u> car, and, besides, everyone likes to watch somebody else work. Suddenly one of the tire irons popped free of the rim, made a couple of turns in the air, and cracked Bob in the throat. He immediately grabbed his throat, and began to gag. I soon realized that he was all right, and at that point I could see the humor in the situation as Bob began to dance around. However, I didn't laugh until Bob dropped his tire iron, and I got a safe distance away. I thought this was at least as funny as the times he fed me the fly and the horse apple.

We all had jobs to help keep the household running. Two of us would wash the dishes after each meal, on a rotating basis. For some reason we found the job of drying the dishes more desirable than washing the dishes, so naturally there had to be some way to decide who would get which job. When Margaret was my partner I could usually get her to flip a coin. That was over sixty years ago, and she is still whining about my unbelievable luck in always winning those coin tosses. Of course if she won I could usually get her to make it the best two out of three, or three out of five.

I knew Mother was working hard and had great responsibility and worry, but I didn't fully realize just how hard things were for her, or her longing for my father. It wasn't until I had a family of my own, with five children, a big farm house, an orchard with two hundred fruit trees, and a full-time job as a high school principal that I began to have some idea of the task she faced by herself. I had Marge, but I could imagine myself alone, and my understanding of what my mother faced grew greatly.

Saturday morning was house cleaning time. Mother rousted us out of bed at six o'clock so we could get all the dusting and vacuuming done before she went to the public library. I remember how badly I wanted to sleep in on Saturday, because we had to get up early every school day and on Sunday to go to Sunday school. We all helped with the running of the house, but it was Mother who had the responsibility and the worry.

On Sundays we attended church at the College Baptist Church. This was the same church where my Grandfather Henry had been the pastor from 1919 to 1923. Reverend Burt Bouwman was the pastor there when we attended, and he liked to relate fundamental Christian concepts to current affairs. He was in that position for several years, and my mother attended church every Sunday, so she eventually became weary of hearing the same sermon week after week. Always willing to express herself, she finally told Reverend Bouwman after one of his sermons, "You have only one string on your violin, but you play it very well."

I started school at Hillsdale High School in September, 1931, and I remember standing outside the school with a crowd of other students waiting for the doors to open. Over the entrance of one door were the words, "Enter to Learn," and over the other door the words, "Go Forth to Serve." I was a stranger there. The other kids knew each other and talked and laughed, but I don't remember having any particular feelings about being an outsider. The kids were friendly when I met them, and I soon felt included.

My first day at Hillsdale High School was a shock. In one of my classes I found myself sitting next to two Negro girls. This was a strange situation for me, as I had never known a black student to attend school with white students. I remember thinking I would change my seat the next day when I went to that class, but the next day they were gone, and I never saw another black student during my four years there. I had grown up in Texas as a product of segregation. My reaction to those two little black girls was the result of observing black people having separate public drinking fountains and rest rooms, having to sit on the very back seat of the bus, and having to stand if those rear seats were filled even though other seats were empty. There were black theaters in Wichita Falls, although some white theaters would allow black people to sit in the balcony. Blacks were expected to step aside when meeting white people coming the opposite way on a sidewalk, and black people were expected to go to the back door of a white person's home. They most certainly could not stay at hotels, or eat in restaurants unless those places were specifically designed for black people. It seems impossible now that there was such insensitivity, but there was, and I was a product of it as a child. Even in the 1950s, when I was the principal of Saline High School in Michigan, our black students could not stay at the same hotel as the white students when we took our seniors to Washington, D.C. They had to be housed at Howard University, a black university. We had only one black family in Saline, a family named Woods, and they were a lovely family with the nicest children. One of their sons, Allie, was president of his senior class, and was liked and respected by everyone, and he stayed at Howard University on his senior trip.

When I started high school in 1931 Bob was a freshman at Hillsdale College where it seems every Ford who ever lived attended. Bob was sixteen, Margaret was ten, and Bill starting first grade at Bacon Street School just a couple of blocks from our house. We had always called him Buddy, but Mother thought he should take his real name, so she asked him what he would like to be called in school. His name was William Edwin Ford, so he had several choices: William, Will, Billy, Bill, Edwin, Eddie, or Ned. He quickly chose Bill.

We hurried each morning to get dressed, eat breakfast, clean up the kitchen, and start off to school on time. Mother frequently cooked Ralstons (a hot cereal) for breakfast, and put the leftovers in the refrigerator where they became quite firm. Then she sliced it and fried it that night for supper, which we ate with syrup. Every day I walked past Bill's elementary school on my way to the high school. I felt something of a protector for Bill, although he now says he really needed protection from me. One fall morning as I approached Bacon Street Elementary School I saw a crowd of kids in a semi circle near the west wall of the school. As I got closer I saw that the crowd was surrounding two boys. A small boy had his back to the wall, facing a larger fat boy who was threatening him with a doubled up fist. I soon realized the smaller boy was Bill. The larger boy didn't see me come up behind him, so when I grabbed him by the collar and spun him around he was suddenly looking at someone much larger than he was. I held my fist under his nose and told him if he ever bothered my brother again I would beat him up. I wonder if he had turned and run would I have yelled, "Yeah, you big sissy, you big coward." For several weeks after that I asked Bill if the big kid ever bothered him again, but he never did.

Mother used some of the insurance money from my dad's life insurance policy to help Bob through college. He understood that after he graduated he was responsible for paying back what Mother had lent him so she could help me. I paid her back when I graduated so she could help Margaret, and Margaret helped Bill. Mother carefully budgeted her insurance money to be used only when absolutely necessary to supplement her salary. When Bob and I attended college we worked for the college maintenance department from the time school was out in the spring until school began again in the fall. We earned thirty five cents an hour, but never saw a penny of the money. It was all applied toward our tuition. It was never enough to meet all of our tuition, hence the need for Mother's help.

When Bob graduated from college he borrowed more money from Mother to work on a Masters Degree in chemistry at the University of Michigan. After getting his Masters he got a job teaching chemistry and science in the Hanover-Horton High School just north of Hillsdale at a salary of eight hundred and fifty dollars a year. Times were hard, jobs were scarce, and so was money. When I graduated I found a teaching job in Pittsford, Michigan for one thousand dollars a year. From that I was able to pay Mother back what I owed her, and save enough money to study voice at the American Conservatory of Music in Chicago the next summer.

Things quickly fell into a routine after school got underway in Hillsdale. Dad was often in my thoughts, but one has to accept what is. Life went on, and we managed to adjust. School and our day-to-day routine occupied our thoughts and our time and our energies. I met my new classmates, and soon had a circle of friends. That first fall was a new experience for us when the evenings became chilly, and we found ourselves needing winter clothing. Mother took us to the College for a home football game one Saturday afternoon, and we enjoyed the crowd and the game and the excitement. The players had old leather helmets and distinctive jerseys with blue and white stripes. The stripes ran horizontally around the body and lengthwise down the arms. Bob thought that was so they would look bigger in the body and longer in the arms. The other thing I remember from that first football game was that we nearly froze, so Mother took us down to the Penney store and bought long winter underwear. It felt good, but I still didn't realize how cold the winters could be.

Fall is the best time of year in Michigan, with the smell of leaves burning, and the colors of the trees. On crisp fall evenings my friends and I bundled up in sweaters and jackets, roasted hot dogs and marshmallows over a fire of burning leaves, visited, and sang songs. Without television our entertainment was what we could provide for ourselves. In the winter we had sledding and skating parties at Cold Springs, a spring-fed pond. We enjoyed the simple pleasures because that was all we had. Occasionally someone might plan a party, and then we'd roll back the rug and dance to records played on a wind up Victrola while we drank apple cider and ate popcorn.

One snowy evening I was walking towards town, and as I passed by a house I heard beautiful music coming from a radio inside. It was so beautiful and so new to me that I stopped outside in the cold and snow just to listen. Most families eventually had a radio, and we got ours during my junior year in high school. Mother bought it from relatives who owned a music store in Hancock, Michigan, and I remember how excited we were that it had a shortwave band as well as the regular AM band. Bob spent half the first night listening to shortwave stations from around the world.

I was something of a novelty during my first year in high school. My Texas twang set me apart, as did my dark suntan, and of course any new kid in school is a novelty. Since I was from Texas they assumed I had been a cowboy who lived on a ranch and rode horses, and I was willing to let them believe that. But by my sophomore year the novelty of a new boy from Texas had long since worn off, and they discovered that I was no more cowboy than they were. Fame is fleeting. I took Latin that first year, and the other kids were amused when I was called on to read, because I spoke Latin the same way I spoke English, with a strong Texas accent. That fall a classmate named Norma Sperbeck invited me to a party one Friday evening with three other boys and an equal number of ninth grade girls. After some cider and donuts Norma turned the lights down and suggested we play Post Office. I had no idea what Post Office was, but everyone else seemed enthusiastic.

Times have changed from the years when I was an adolescent. I never saw a cowboy movie where the cowboy kissed the girl . . . his horse, maybe, but certainly nothing as risqué as kissing the girl. An organization known as The Hays Office controlled the movie industry, and could approve or disapprove a film based on morality. A married couple could not be shown in the same bed together, and profanity was forbidden. Gone With The Wind was nearly banned because Rhett Butler said to Scarlett O'Hara,

"Frankly my dear, I don't give a damn." Now little is left to the imagination, but in 1931 Post Office was about as much excitement as a thirteen-year-old could stand. The girls took turns being the post mistress in a little alcove that served as the post office, and one of the boys would go into the post office to mail a letter. His letter had to have a stamp, and the stamp was the kiss he gave the postmistress. I suppose I have forgotten some of the details, but I do remember thinking it was a game I thoroughly liked.

To add a little variety we next played Spin the Bottle. We all sat in a circle with a glass milk bottle in the center, and each person got to spin the bottle until it came to rest pointing at someone of the opposite sex. The spinner and the one it pointed at then went into the private alcove and kissed. This may not seem like much now, but in 1931 it was a big deal. I was being introduced to the world of sin. At the fiftieth reunion of our high school class I reminded Norma Sperbeck of that wonderful party, and she told me that I was the reason for the party. I was flattered, but I couldn't help but wish I had known of my popularity at the time.

During the Depression there may have been some kids with an allowance, but I didn't know any. The only money I had was what I earned. My first job was mowing Cousin Edna's lawn. The next one was delivering handbills advertising coming attractions at a local movie theater. I didn't get any money for that job, but I did get to see all the movies for free. My biggest money making venture occurred during the Christmas holidays. Every year Grandpa Patton sent me a hundred-pound bag of pecans and a big box of mistletoe. This was a gift, so everything I earned was profit. I bought bags from the grocery store, and packaged the pecans in one pound amounts. Some bags had plain unshelled pecans, some had cracked pecans so people could easily shell their own, and some had shelled pecan meats. I would put a load of these pecans on my sled along with sprigs of mistletoe. I sold the regular pecans for twenty five cents. The cracked pecans and the shelled pecans were a little more.

I packaged the pecans during the week and went out Saturday morning to sell. I started about nine o'clock, and by noon I would be back home. Bob worked Saturdays at the local J.C. Penney store from eight o'clock in the morning until ten o'clock in the evening for two dollars. On my way home at noon I would stop by the store where Bob was working to show him the several dollars I had made in only three hours. It probably galled him, but he hated the thought of selling door to door. We had a nutcracker that could crack one nut at a time from both ends of the pecan, and I spent hours each week cracking pecans and picking out the pecan meats to sell on Saturday. It was slow tedious work, and I suppose if I included the hours I spent during the week I really worked more hours than Bob. I finally hired a neighbor boy to crack and shell the pecans for me. I don't remember what I paid him, but he worked for a couple of weeks, and then decided it wasn't worth it, so I was back doing my own cracking and picking.

I quickly learned that I had a moneymaker selling mistletoe at the sorority houses at the college. The girls really bought up my mistletoe, much more so than at the fraternity houses. Grandpa Patton was generous to send me the pecans and the mistletoe every year, so I could earn some spending money that I wouldn't have had otherwise. Grandpa was giving me the opportunity to earn money rather than just giving me money. When I lived in Wichita Falls Grandma would never give me ten cents to see a movie, but she would let me earn it by watering her lawn.

During my senior year in high school I used most of the money I made to buy a new blue serge suit. I inherited my previous suit from my brother, Bob, who had inherited it from a family friend in Indiana. When it was my turn for the suit the seat of the trousers had worn through, and been patched as well as Mother could patch it. It was a light gray wool suit and I wore it to the occasional party and dance at the high school until I bought the new suit during my senior year. The old one looked good so long as I remembered not to put my hands in my pockets. That would raise the coat in the back to expose the patch job on the trousers. If I wanted to look casual and nonchalant I could put my hands in my pockets, but I had to remember to keep my back to the wall. With my new suit I could forget all about the techniques I had mastered with our old gray standby.

Between my junior and senior years in high school I bought a paper route from a friend who was moving away. He had no right to sell it, but it was a routine practice, and his recommendation to the manager of the newspaper was all that was needed. The route was three miles long, and I delivered a variety of papers, including <u>The Detroit</u>

News, Detroit Times, Jackson Patriot, and Toledo Blade. I can still drive by the route and remember some of the houses, and which paper they took. It was a long route, so I needed a bicycle. A new bike cost about twenty five dollars, and I arranged a loan from Cousin Edna which I repaid each week until the bike was paid off. This took some time. Each paper cost me twelve cents. The customer paid me fifteen cents, which meant that I delivered a paper six days a week for three cents profit. I had seventy customers, so I cleared two dollars and ten cents a week. It wasn't a handsome amount, but it was something.

I also had to go through the entire route on Saturday morning to collect for the papers, and that usually took me about three hours. In some cases a customer might have his paper stolen, or on a rare occasion I might miss a delivery, and the customer would then deduct three cents, which meant that I had delivered his paper for a week for free. The paper had the price printed on the top of the front page and it read, "3 cents." Therefore, if they didn't get a paper it must mean they were entitled to reduce their payment by three cents. Of course they were getting six papers a week, not for eighteen cents, but for fifteen cents. Anyway, I lost out a few times. And then there were people who were either never home when I collected, or didn't have the money. I remember carrying one customer for over a month, and when I finally stopped delivering his paper it made him mad. One customer couldn't pay his bill, and offered to give me a haircut as payment for his paper. I needed a haircut, so I took it. He wasn't a barber, but it wasn't a bad haircut.

In my senior year I acquired a morning paper route delivering the *Detroit Free Press*. This was in addition to my afternoon route, but now I was getting up at five o'clock every morning to ride my bike to the paper office to get my papers, fold them, deliver a three mile route, and get back home in time for school. I recall some awfully cold snowy mornings when I had to get out and deliver papers. Like the post office I delivered in all kinds of weather, hot, cold, rainy, and snowy. An afternoon route for the *Hillsdale Daily News* eventually became available, so I took that and dropped my other afternoon routes, but I still kept my morning route. My new afternoon route was Route #1, which was the best route of that paper. It went straight south on Howell Street (the main street of town) for seven blocks. I went down one side of the street and came back on the other, finishing just one block from home. I was now making five dollars a week, and felt pretty well to do compared to what I had been making. I was careful with my money, and didn't spend it without giving any purchase considerable thought. I didn't buy anything I didn't really need, except, of course, malted milks, which were ten cents. The local Jack Frost ice cream store occasionally had a one-cent sale where I could get one malted milk for ten cents, and a second one for one cent more. I would take Bill with me, and we could both get a thick malted milk for a total of eleven cents. It's hard to accept paying two dollars and fifty cents for a malted milk these days.

In Hillsdale there was a clothing factory known as The Pants Factory which sold pants, shirts, jackets, hats, and gloves. Many people outfitted their families from the "seconds" sold in their outlet store. I could buy a pair of pants that were marked as "seconds" for twenty-five cents. The imperfections often could not be seen, so that is where I bought all my pants. People can find many ways to economize when they have to. People today would be shocked if they suddenly found themselves as destitute as so many people were in the 1930s. We repaired worn out shoes by gluing on rubber soles from the five and ten cent store. Most boys got home haircuts. We all wore hand-me-down clothes and homemade clothes. There were kits women could use to repair runs in their silk stockings, and when Marge's grandmother made an apple pie she saved the apple peelings to make apple jelly. I remember seeing a wash cloth that she had patched with a piece of worn out bath towel, and more than once I cut a piece of cardboard to cover a hole in my shoe until I could repair it with a rubber sole.

When a parent was out of a job there was no money coming in at all, so there were many desperate families. I had classmates who dropped out of school because their families simply could not support them. Some kids hopped a freight train to bum their way to California, hoping they might find something to do there. On every freight train we would see people riding on top of the train, or in empty boxcars, or underneath on what were called the "rods." People went somewhere, anywhere, to try to find something better than they had at home. The unemployed father of the valedictorian of the class ahead of me was arrested in a grocery store one night in

Hillsdale while stealing food for his family. Fiorello LaGuardia, later mayor of New York City, was once a judge hearing a case against a man who was arrested for stealing a loaf of bread from a grocery store to feed his family. After hearing the case, Judge LaGuardia fined everyone in the courtroom one dollar, "for living in a country where a man had to steal to feed his family." I lived in those times. The protection people have today to help them survive in times of trouble is a wonderful thing. We can only imagine the hopelessness and desperation so many people experienced in those terrible years.

I always liked music. As a little child we had a record titled "Humoresque" that had a bouncy rhythm, and I called it "Dootsy Dootsy." I would often ask my parents to play Dootsy Dootsy for me. I remember my elementary music teacher (before the spit ball incident) asking me to sing a song we were practicing, and my dad had me sing a song from the church hymnal for a Sunday evening service. To encourage my interest in music they had me take piano lessons from our church organist. I was not a child prodigy on the piano, but still I continued. Later my Grandma Patton bought a violin that needed repairing. My folks had it repaired, and suddenly I was a violinist. My skill and dedication for the violin were equal to my skill and dedication for the piano, but still I continued. I loved music, but I wanted the skill to make beautiful music without having to work for it. I played both instruments as well as my mother's constant prodding enabled me. I played both the violin and the piano in recitals, but success required more dedication than I was willing to give.

After we moved to Hillsdale my mother gave up any plans she had for me with the piano, but she still had hope for the violin, and arranged for me to take violin lessons from the high school band teacher who was an accomplished violinist. I had lessons every Saturday morning, but my poor mother had neither the energy nor the time to keep after me to practice, and my progress showed it. A violin played by an artist produces a beautiful sound, but hardly anything sounds worse when played by a beginner. I was sufficiently musical to realize the sound coming from my violin was an affront to the ears of anyone who had an appreciation for music. The only time I played it was just before and during my lesson every Saturday morning. I didn't have the call, and Mother wisely soon gave up on this fruitless effort.

I played the violin well enough to play in the high school orchestra for a couple of years, probably because I owned a violin, and the orchestra director, who was twice the size of any other teacher in that school, needed violins in her orchestra. Our practice room had a stage at one end that stood about eighteen inches above the level of the floor. By that time I was really more actor than violinist, because I had perfected some moves to convince an audience that I was a violinist of some skill. During a practice session one day I was playing with obvious emotion, and unknowingly inched my chair closer and closer to the edge of the stage. I finally reached the edge of the stage, and suddenly felt myself going backwards. I was able to hold my violin in front of me to prevent it from being damaged as I landed unhurt on my back, and I later thought about the opportunity I had missed. If I could have just managed to slide that violin around behind me my violin days would have mercifully ended.

I was once talked into playing a duet with a girl who also played the violin (the word "also" gives me more credit than I deserve) at the College Baptist Church on Sunday morning. We practiced once or twice, but I knew on that Sunday morning that I was totally unprepared. I can't understand why I hadn't practiced more, knowing I was going to appear before an audience, but I hadn't, and I knew it was going to be awful. I was wishing something, anything, would happen to remove me from the prospect of what I knew was going to be a disaster. About an hour before my crucifixion, when one might think I would be practicing my part, I was playing with a broken B.B. gun that belonged to Bill. When I pulled the trigger part of the broken gun cut the middle finger of my right hand in two places. All I could think of was, "Thank you, God, thank you, thank you!" Since the cut was on my bowing hand I could have still performed, but fortunately no one seemed to think of that, and I wrapped the finger in a much larger bandage than I really needed. I gave a convincing performance of pain and suffering, and the congregation was spared what would have been an unforgettable experience. It really would have been awful.

While I had little enthusiasm for the piano or the violin, I did enjoy singing. My first performance was in our high school operetta, playing the part of an Indian Chief, Wokomis, in a production of Lelawala, Maid of the Falling Waters. A classmate with a truly lovely voice played the title role. Barbara Crume had a beautiful mature voice, and at graduation she and I sang a duet. Barbara was our valedictorian and also a talented actress. After graduation she went to Hollywood to do voice dubbing in the movies. I enjoyed singing as much as I had disliked practicing the piano and the violin, and Mother, still not giving up on me, started me on voice lessons with the voice professor at the college, Aubry Martin.

During the summers of 1932 and 1933 Mother studied at Syracuse University, and needed to find a place for Margaret, Bill, and me to stay. Bob stayed at home to work at the college. Bill and I stayed with Mother's Aunt Berti. Aunt Berti and Uncle Will owned a farm near Goodland, Indiana. The farm had a large pasture with many trees. The house is gone now, but in my memory it is still there. Uncle Will was in his upper sixties at that time, but he was still young at heart. It was a generous thing they did at their age to take two young boys into their home for two months. Bill and I had a wonderful time, but we didn't fully understand what they were giving us. We didn't have any chores to do except to help Aunt Bertie with the dishes after each meal, and we had the most carefree existence one could imagine. It may be true that "all work and no play makes Jack a dull boy," but the reverse isn't true. For those two summers Bill and I experienced all play and no work, and there was nothing dull about it.

Uncle Will had a Shetland pony named Toots that Bill rode, and three horses, Nig, Star, and a strawberry roan named Jack. Uncle Will said if I could break Jack to ride, I could ride him whenever he wasn't working, but I was no cowboy who could throw a saddle on a wild horse and ride him to a standstill. I thought a gentler approach would be easier on both me and the horse, so I spent a week talking to that horse in his stall, and touching him, and gradually putting my weight on his back until I was finally able to sit on him. Now I had a horse to ride. He was a big old farm horse, and I had to ride him bareback, but he was mine to ride. I got on his back by putting my bare foot on the knee of his left front leg and pushing myself onto his back, but I never got on that horse that he didn't try to bite me. I had to keep the right rein tight so he couldn't turn his head to get at me, but he never stopped trying. I think Uncle Will gave Jack to me because the horse was just about useless for farm work. He either wouldn't pull his share, or he would jump and shy away from the noisy farm machinery. When I rode him he always panicked and tried to bolt whenever a car came by.

Outside the back door of the farm was a windmill powered well that pumped ice cold water. North of the barn ran a stream, and beyond the stream was a pasture with large trees. Bill and I knew every inch of that pasture, and tramped and rode our horses over it nearly every day. Two hundred yards east of the barn was a wide spot in the stream that formed a pool six feet wide and four feet deep. We spent several days getting all the rocks and debris out of the pool, and when we finished we had a pretty good fishing and swimming hole. Aunt Bertie didn't let us use her bathrooms for baths, but gave us a washcloth to go bathe in the creek. We took soap down to the swimming hole, used the washcloth to take our baths, and then dried ourselves in the sun. We had the run of the farm to do whatever struck our fancy. Those were dream summers for us. We didn't realize how lucky we were.

Uncle Will had a hired man named John House who was thirty-five years old, lanky and good-natured. His dark hair hung down over his forehead, making him look like Will Rogers. John was always willing to take us with him during his chores, or when he hitched Star and Nig to the wagon to go into town to get buttermilk to feed to the hogs. He was laughing at us or with us most of the time.

The day that Bill and I arrived at Uncle Will's farm I was standing with Uncle Will and John House when a woman I had never seen before came up and talked to us. She had red hair, a lined suntanned face, and many freckles. When she left I said, "I think that's the ugliest woman I ever saw." John House simply responded, "That's my wife." I wished I could die on the spot, but John never mentioned it again, and never seemed to hold the remark against me. I hope he just considered it an ignorant comment from a fourteen year old kid. It was a terrible thing to say, and at the very least I might have thought to find out who she was before making such a stupid remark. Actually, John's wife, Ethyl, wasn't ugly. She wasn't a movie beauty, but she really wasn't homely, and as

I came to know her I realized she was so pleasant and friendly that I thought of her in terms of her personality rather than her appearance. Ethyl may not have been a model, but she was a beautiful person, and I became very fond of her.

Uncle Will was a successful farmer who farmed his own farm, and managed several others on a fee basis. Uncle Will and Aunt Bertie were frugal, and spent their money wisely. They were very well off financially, but one would never have guessed it. They lived modestly, dressed respectably but not fashionably, and drove an old car. They had several hundred thousand dollars at their deaths, which in those days was a sizeable estate.

Uncle Will enjoyed kids. He would tease and joke with us, and his eyes crinkled when he laughed. The first year we were there he said one morning, "Let's build a tree house." He had already selected a large tree on the north side of the creek for this project, so we went to the lumberyard for lumber and nails, and then came home to start to work. Uncle Will had a plan in mind to build an eight-sided house around the trunk of the tree, about fifteen feet above the ground. He put in two windows that could be moved sideways to open or close, and a section of the roof that could be opened. Next he made a rope ladder that we could pull up through a trap door after we got in the house. We filled gunnysacks with straw for a mattress, and after that slept there most nights. The tree house served as our place for the two years we spent there, and we enjoyed going up there after swimming, fishing, hunting, or just exploring.

The second summer we were there Uncle Will again surprised us by saying, "I think we should build a log cabin." He went out to the pasture with us and picked a spot just up the hill from our swimming hole. We decided to have it face south with a stone fireplace on the north side. Uncle Will envisioned having it available for Boy Scouts, Girl Scouts, and other groups to use for hot dog roasts and other events. We cut logs from the pasture and hauled them to our site with the horses. We next gathered large rocks for the chimney and made that our first project. Uncle Will, of course, was the brains and director of this effort, and he soon had a chimney built. We then moved the logs into position, placing the bigger logs on the bottom, and smaller logs on top to form the walls. We got the two ends and the north wall finished, but the south wall was left only about three feet high with a doorway. This was as far as we got before we left that summer, and I don't know how Uncle Will planned to do the roof. As it turned out, we didn't come back for a third summer, so the cabin remained unfinished.

When Bill and I got tired of working on the cabin Uncle Will would say, "OK, let's rest." A few seconds later he would say, "While we're resting let's do . . ." and then he would name something that was going to be at least as hard as what we had been doing. That was his joke, and we laughed every time it happened. He was just great with us those summers. He knew what would interest us and he had fun, too. Uncle Will was always coming up with something new. I remember he showed us how to sharpen one end of a slender willow branch, and put a corn cob on it. We would then swing it around and give it a snap that would send the corncob flying a great distance. It was amazing how far we could fling a corncob, and it was one more thing we could do if things got a little dull. Uncle Will also made Bill a chariot out of some large farm machinery wheels, and then made a harness for Toots so she could pull us around the farm. I remember Uncle Will laughing as he watched us. He was a great uncle. Every kid should be so lucky.

After World War II Bill and I drove down to see Uncle Will and Aunt Bertie and the farm where we had such wonderful times. Uncle Will must have been in his early eighties then, but he still had that wonderful laugh. He told us that one summer evening in the early 1940s three boys knocked on his door to tell him that the log cabin was on fire. They then asked Uncle Will what he would pay them to put the fire out. Uncle Will suspected the boys had set the fire, and he told them, "If that log cabin doesn't mean any more to you than that, let it burn." Those boys didn't know Uncle Will like I knew him. When Bill and I went to the cabin site all that remained was the stone fireplace.

Bill and I hunted rabbits, squirrels, and pigeons, and were usually successful. Aunt Bertie would cook them for us after we cleaned and dressed them. I remember once shooting a possum, but when Aunt Bertie cooked it the thing was so greasy I couldn't eat it. We finally took it out in the back and buried it. We always had rabbits when the oats were being cut. Bill and I followed the machine that cut the oats, waiting for rabbits to explode from their hiding place. When they did Bill and I would be after them in a flash. I can't imagine doing it now, but we could actually run the rabbits down and catch them in our hands by diving at them as we got near.

Those were two wonderful summers. We rode horses, swam, fished, hunted, took part in the harvesting, and enjoyed wonderful harvesting dinners the wives prepared. Uncle Will and Aunt Bertie gave us unforgettable memories that I treasure more with each year that passes.

Bill and I were always with Uncle Will and John House when something was going on. One hot summer day Uncle Will and John and John's brother-in-law were shocking oats, and at noon went to Uncle Will's house for lunch. After lunch we all lay down on the floor for a fifteen minute nap before returning to the field. By the middle of the afternoon everyone was hot and tired, so Uncle Will gave me a five-dollar bill and told me to walk into town to buy a carton of ice cream for each of us. I took off running and brought back five QUARTS of ice cream. Uncle Will expected five Dixie cups of ice cream at about ten cents each, but cartons meant quarts to me. Ice cream was always hand packed in those days, and we couldn't take them back, so there was nothing to do except eat. I cleaned mine up with no trouble, and I think Bill did well with his, but the men all got sick and had to go home. Uncle Will never complained about the five quarts of ice cream or the lost day's work. I guess he saw the humor in my mistake, but considering what five dollars could buy in 1932 it was a costly mistake.

Automobile safety was almost unknown in the 1930s. There were few safety features in cars, and no laws concerning passenger safety, so some of the things we did back then now seem appalling. The car's front fenders ran from the bottom of the hood up and over the front wheels. This created a valley between the fender and the hood, and Uncle Will always let Bill and me lie in this valley as he drove down the highway. We rode there and loved it, never thinking about what would happen in the event of an accident.

I would love to return to that farm and see it just as it was, but things change. Uncle Will and Aunt Bertie are gone, the house and barn are gone, and the pasture with all the big trees is now a cornfield. I hope there is a life after death when I can meet all those dear people again, and have a chance to tell them how much I appreciate what they gave to us, and how much I love them for it. We visited Uncle Will and Aunt Bertie occasionally after that, but usually only for a weekend. Our happy carefree days were a thing of the past.

I graduated from high school in June 1935, and immediately started working for the maintenance department at the college. The money I earned was applied towards my tuition in the fall. The head of the maintenance department took one look at me, and decided it would be good for that skinny kid to be outside in the sunshine, so for the next four summers I mowed every lawn on campus, including all of the college fraternity and sorority houses. I never had to be told what to do on a given day, because as soon as I had mowed every lawn I simply started over again. I knew every inch of those lawns by the time I graduated. I used to envy the fellows who painted, because they at least had company, and weren't sweating in the hot sun all day. I was given other jobs on a couple of occasions. Once I washed walls in a sorority house, which wasn't a bad job. I had someone to visit with, and it made the time go faster. Later, however, I came to appreciate my mowing job when I was assigned to shovel coal out of the basement of a fraternity house. A few minutes into that job I realized there were worse things than mowing lawns.

One summer I stripped wallpaper from what had been the ATO fraternity house when my dad was a student. In the front hall near the telephone I pulled a piece of wallpaper from the wall, and there, written on the wall underneath the wallpaper was my dad's name in his own handwriting.

I started college in the fall of 1935. My Grandfather Henry and Grandmother Sarah had attended Hillsdale College, as had my parents. I went there because I could live at home and work off part of my tuition, but I was also glad to be following in the footsteps of my parents and grandparents. In the 1930's there were only five hundred students, so everyone knew everyone else. My dad had been a member of the ATO fraternity, so when I was invited to join I accepted largely for sentimental reasons. If I had lived on campus instead of at home I might have enjoyed the fraternity experience more, but I didn't like the drinking, or some of the behavior. I went on inactive status my senior year because of financial hardship, but it was more because I just didn't like what I saw in the fraternity.

There was much that I enjoyed at Hillsdale College, but what gave me the greatest pleasure was music, specifically my voice training. During my last three years in college I had wonderful musical experiences, playing Captain Corchran in Gilbert and Sullivan's H.M.S. Pinafore, and Brom Brock, the romantic lead in Maxwell Anderson and Kurt Weill's Knickerbocker Holiday. We performed the first amateur production of that musical in the United States. It was a story of New Amsterdam in the days of Peter Stuyvesant. It was a wonderful show, and I had more fun doing that production than any I have done before or since. I also sang the baritone solos of Handel's Messiah in Hillsdale and in Jackson, Michigan, and the baritone solos in the Seven Last Words at Easter. My musical experiences at Hillsdale were the highlight of my college education, and gave me my fondest memories.

My first voice teacher died suddenly during my freshman year, and was replaced by Jay Paul Hinshaw. When World War II began Jay was too old for the draft, but he felt guilty not being a part of the national effort, and voluntarily joined the service. After the war his wife was the head of the cosmetics department for a large department store in Chicago. She frequently made trips to Europe as their buyer, and Jay often accompanied her. During one trip they went to Rome. When they got off the plane they took a taxi to their hotel, and along the way discussed what they would like to see while they were there. The driver overheard them, and when they got to the hotel he said he would drive them on their sightseeing tour. They stayed in Rome for three days, and the driver was there for them every morning. At the end of the third day, when Jay offered to pay him, the driver said, "You don't remember me, but I remember you. I was in a prisoner of war camp during the war. You were an officer there, and you were so kind to me that I won't accept any money from you for these past three days." It was his way to partially repay Jay for his kindness.

Jay also directed the College Church choir, and I sang many solos there and in most of the other churches in Hillsdale. In my senior year I was the paid soloist for the Christian Science Church every Sunday, and I occasionally was hired to sing at weddings. One of my most satisfying experiences after college was when I sang a solo in the church in Wichita Falls where my dad had sung so many solos. My Grandfather Patton was there, and afterwards said he was struck by the resemblance I had to my dad when I sang.

I wanted to sing professionally, but to be a success in any of the arts requires both talent and a great measure of luck. You have to be at the right place at the right time when those rare opportunities present themselves. My voice coach at the American Conservatory of Music in Chicago told me that I didn't have a great voice, but I had a voice that would offer me opportunities in light opera and Broadway musicals. He then added, "If you want that don't get married," implying that I couldn't support a wife and family while knocking around and looking for work. That advice came a little late, as I had already met the girl who pushed singing into second place in my priorities. By the time the war was over I had a wife and a little boy and another on the way. I would have loved to perform on Broadway, but who knows if I would ever have had the lucky break that I needed. On reflection I think it all turned out for the best. I wouldn't trade the life I've had with my wife and children for any musical success I might have known.

Few singers keep the vibrancy and flexibility of their voices late in life. Most of us eventually lose our ability to sing as we age. My singing voice is totally gone now, and, for me, not being able to sing is almost like losing my eyesight. I hear the music, and I know how I should sing it, but when I try the sound is painful for me to hear. When we're young we can't imagine that things aren't always going to be just as they are, the way we feel and the things we can do. It reminds me of the song lyrics, "Those were the days, my friend. We thought they'd never end. We'd sing and dance forever and a day."

When I graduated from Hillsdale College in 1939 Mother gave me a suitcase for a present, quite a common gift in those days. It seems like, "Here's your hat, what's your hurry," but that wasn't her intent. I didn't have a suitcase, and it was much appreciated. She also gave me a Webster's Dictionary which I still have and cherish. I graduated with a teaching certificate, a major in music, and minors in English and history. Now it was job hunting time, and jobs weren't plentiful. Those that were available didn't pay much. The Teacher Placement Bureau at the college told me of a teaching vacancy in Pittsford, Michigan, ten miles east of Hillsdale, so I borrowed Mother's car and drove there for an interview. After the interview the superintendent, Elbert Van Aken, offered me a job teaching band, choir, English, history and study hall for one thousand dollars a year. Shortly after I took the job Cousin Edna told me that when she taught school Elbert Van Aken was one of her students. That may have been a factor, but he never mentioned it.

After landing this job I saw an ad in a magazine seeking someone to work as a summer receptionist and handyman at a resort hotel in South Haven, Michigan. It was called the Webster. My pay included a small room with no windows in a storage area away from the guestrooms. I also got my meals at one of their restaurants. But there didn't seem to be much business coming to that hotel, and I was not surprised when after three weeks the manager said she had to let me go. I can't remember what my salary was, but I spent very little, and at the end of three weeks I had a small amount of cash and a check for over thirty dollars. I didn't know it at the time, but my future wife was then a sixteen-year-old girl living just eight miles south of where I worked that summer. As we look back on our lives, it is amazing how our paths seem to cross, and cross again, and cross yet again.

Since I didn't have a job to tie me down I decided it would be fun to hitchhike to Texas. It wasn't one of my better ideas, but I did get there, and back. I first hitchhiked from South Haven to Hillsdale, where I packed my suitcase, and then hitchhiked to Goodland, Indiana where Bill was spending another summer with Uncle Will and Aunt Bertie. I was footloose and fancy free, and visiting my childhood home seemed like a great idea. Both of my grandparents were still living in Wichita Falls, along with my Aunt Lavern and Uncle Walden, so I knew I would have a place to stay, and they, of course, would be delighted to have me. It never occurred to me that I might be an inconvenience.

I stayed a day or two with Aunt Bertie and Uncle Will before asking Aunt Bertie to drive me to Kentland where I would start hitchhiking to Texas. When I got out of the car I saw that Bill had tears in his eyes. I asked him if he would like to go with me, and he nodded yes. Bill was staying with Uncle Will and Aunt Bertie while Mother was taking classes for her graduate work. I doubt she would have approved of me taking Bill on such an adventure, but that didn't cross my mind then. So Aunt Bertie drove us back to Goodland, we packed Bill's suitcase, returned to Kentland, and started out. It took us four days to get to Wichita Falls, sleeping in tourist homes, a railroad yard in Tulsa, and a hotel in Oklahoma City. The third day we got a ride from St. Louis to Tulsa, and after riding for some time I learned we were being charged one cent a mile for each of us. I hadn't heard the driver say that when he picked us up, but Bill said he did and I quickly began to calculate how much money I was going to have left after paying the fare. Hitchhiking is unpredictable, and our hitchhiking had been a little slow, actually a lot slow. I didn't want to be put out by the side of the road in the middle of nowhere, so I kept quiet. Any ride to Tulsa seemed pretty good at that moment.

We arrived in Tulsa, paid our fare, and began to look for a place to spend the night. After the expense of the ride I thought we might camp out under the stars, and the railroad yard looked like an ideal spot. It was out of the way, it was dark, and we were alone. What more could we want? All my life I had worn pajamas when I went to bed, so I put on pajamas there in the railroad yard to sleep on the ground. It seems stupid now, but old habits are hard to break. We awoke early the next morning, got dressed, and wondered if we might find a freight going our way. We had no idea where the trains were going, but I picked out one that was going somewhere, and we tried to hop on. I thought somewhere is better than nowhere, a very poor deduction. I was able to jump through an open boxcar door, but Bill was too small to keep up with the moving train, so I had no choice but to jump back off, and soon we found ourselves back on the highway to Oklahoma City. We caught a short ride to Sapulpa, Oklahoma, between Tulsa and Oklahoma City, and stood in that little town so long I thought we might take root there. We waited there with our thumbs out from early in the morning until late in the afternoon. I had just about decided that Sapulpa was going to be our permanent address when some kind soul picked us up and took us to Oklahoma City.

I still had my thirty dollar check from the Webster Hotel in South Haven, but I was just about out of cash. During the Depression there was an organization known as the Travelers Bureau where drivers and riders could get together at a cost of one cent per mile, and that organization helped us find a ride to Wichita Falls the next morning. I had enough money to pay for the ride with fifty-five cents left over. After sleeping on the ground the night before, I was ready for a bath and a real bed, so I went to the desk clerk of a modest hotel, and asked him how much a room would cost. I found it was more than I had, so I told Bill we would have to sit up for the night. After we had been there a little while the desk clerk called me over to him and asked how much I could spend. I told him all I had was fifty cents, and he said there was a room we could have for that. Bill was only thirteen, and I think the clerk felt sorry for him, so we both had a bath and a bed for the night. We didn't have any money for breakfast, but I figured we could eat when we got to Wichita Falls. I had one nickel left the next morning after we paid two girls for our ride to Wichita Falls. When they stopped for a coke (a coke cost a nickel in those days) I said that I didn't want one, but I bought one for Bill. When we arrived in Wichita Falls I had no cash, but I still had that thirty-dollar check.

Our relatives housed us and fed us, so I was able to keep most of the thirty dollars I had been carrying around with me all the way from Michigan. I knew I would need another suit when I started teaching in September, and found a pretty suit and a pair of shoes on sale, and still had enough money to get home, almost. I can't speak for our grandparents or our aunt and uncle, but Bill and I had a wonderful time.

When it was time to head back to Michigan Aunt Lavern arranged for us to ride with a friend to Oklahoma City. I had hitchhiked in Michigan many times with good success, but in this relatively unpopulated part of the country people were hesitant to pick up two kids with suitcases, so when we got to Oklahoma City I didn't even consider hitchhiking. Our ride dropped us off at the Travelers Bureau and I arranged for a ride from Oklahoma to St. Louis for the usual penny a mile for each of us. I was running low on money, but this would get us through the most barren part of our trip, and I thought we could hitchhike from there. We got into St. Louis in the evening, took a streetcar to the eastern outskirts of the city, and found a tourist home. I bargained with the lady to let us have a room for fifty cents, telling her it was all I could afford. When I paid her with a five-dollar bill I had to explain that five dollars was all I had, and we still had a long way to go.

The next morning we weren't having any luck getting a ride, and I learned from another hitchhiker that there was a place nearby that had great malted milks. Although we didn't have much money this seemed like an emergency, so we found our way there and had malted milks. Then we finally found a ride that took us to Terra Haute, Indiana, where we spent the night. The next morning a fellow traveler told us that hitchhiking was illegal in the city limits of Terra Haute, and that the police would throw us in jail if we tried. That got my attention. I didn't think the city jail was any place I really wanted to visit, and I was certainly tired of hitchhiking, so I walked to the Western Union Telegraph office and wired Uncle Will, asking him to send us seven dollars for bus fare to Goodland. I spent the last of our money for a breakfast of greasy eggs while I waited for Uncle Will's response. He sent the money, which we picked up at the telegraph office, and that evening after dark we stepped off the bus in front of their house, more than happy to be back. I repaid Uncle Will from my first check when I started teaching in the fall.

Pittsford was a small town. The old three story school stood on the south side of a highway that separated most of the town from the school. When I arrived in Pittsford I learned that a new school was being built across the highway, but it wouldn't be finished until Christmas, so I started in the old school. That was fifty-eight years ago, but the original school building still stands. I rented a room from Etta and George Hackett who owned a home a half a mile west of the new school. The price was six dollars a week, including meals. I was paid twenty-five dollars a week, but I didn't get paid during the summer or during Christmas vacation. George and Etta were in their late sixties, and had no children, so Etta adopted me. I lived with them the two years I taught at Pittsford, and have affectionate memories of those two nice people.

The first morning I had what became my usual breakfast of grapefruit, egg on homemade toast, and milk. I then started walking to school to meet the students and make my grand entrance. I was wearing the new suit I had bought in Wichita Falls, but just before reaching the school I made the startling discovery that my pants were unzipped. I quickly corrected that problem, but it was almost a very embarrassing first impression.

I was twenty-one, probably not very mature, and I was expected to be an authority figure for some large farm boys who were only three or four years younger than I was. Pittsford was a farming community of solid citizens, and most of the students were nice kids from good homes, but there are always characters in every school, and I'm sure it was a temptation for some of the older students to try me. Through thirty-six years of teaching I have seen students test every new teacher, regardless of age or maturity or experience.

The problems I had my first year were the result of immaturity and lack of experience. There were two incidents I should have been able to avoid if I had known how to handle them wisely. In the first I was supervising an overflow study hall during the last period of the day on Friday. During the class I left the room for a few minutes, something a teacher should never do. When I returned a girl was out in the hall saying Dick Smith had said something offensive to her. I should have handled it privately with the two students, but I let my irritation lead me to meet the problem head on. When I entered the room Dick was sitting in his chair, tipped back on its two back legs. As I walked past him I intended to put his chair down on all four legs, but instead the chair fell over with him in it. It was still not a serious problem until another student, Ray Poulson, said, "I bet you wish you had a couple of extra years on you, don't you, Dick?" I thought I had to meet every challenge directly, so I walked over to Ray and said, "Well, you have a couple of extra years on you, if you want to whet your horn." Ray immediately stood up and hit me with his fist. Without thinking I began to whack away at Ray, knocking him backwards over his seat. I quickly grabbed him by his shirtfront, pulled him up straight, and pushed him down hard in his seat, as I said, "Sit down!" I had learned something since the fight I had at the Fannin School, and I didn't say anything about being a big sissy or a big coward. I later heard that Ray's father went to the superintendent to complain that Ray had come home with bruises, but nothing was said to me after I filed my report on the incident.

Things were a little tense with some of Ray's friends for a few days after that, but the next week I met Ray in the hall, grinned at him, and said, "Hi." Ray smiled back and said, "Hello." Through the years I have seen girls have spats with other girls, and they not only hold hard feelings for weeks or even years, but they get all of their friends involved too. Boys on the other hand can have a fight, but when it's over, it's over, and they may even end up good friends. My confrontation with Paulson was a prime example.

I was twenty-one when I went to Pittsford, brand new in the field of teaching, and very much in awe of the superintendent, Elbert Van Aiken. Years later, when I was the high school principal in Belleville, I made numerous trips to the University of Michigan Placement Bureau to look for new teachers, and found that the assistant director of the Bureau was the same Elbert Van Aken. I became well acquainted with him, and found him to be a warm and pleasant old friend. I once reminded him of my experience with Ray Poulson, and said that it was my fault, and that I had handled it badly. Elbert said that Ray Poulson was now the president of the Pittsford school board, and that Ray insisted the incident was his fault. I intended to drive to Pittsford someday to see Ray, but it was never convenient to make the trip, and so the years went by. Finally, fifty-five years later, I did take the time to drive to Pittsford to see Ray, and to laugh over the incident that happened so many years before, but I discovered that I had waited too long. Ray had died just a few months earlier.

Six weeks into the school year there was a school affair on a Friday evening so parents could meet the new teachers. The custom, which should not have been allowed, was for the students to initiate the new teachers. Some high school boys threatened to take me for a ride out in the country that evening, and, I told them that it wasn't going to happen. Of course that amounted to a challenge. Another young teacher just ignored them, and on the night of the affair he was left alone, but a group of junior and senior boys did get me in a Model A Ford. I was in the middle of the front seat with a boy on either side of me. They drove around the countryside trying to get me lost, but I was familiar with that part of Hillsdale County, and knew where we were all the time.

Around eleven o'clock at night they stopped at a crossroads between Pittsford and Hillsdale, planning to let me find my way back on foot while they drove off laughing and joking. But I not only was familiar with this part of the country, I was also familiar with Model A Fords and their ignition switches. The Model A had an ignition switch that popped out half an inch when the key was turned to the "on" position. It was possible to remove the key without turning off the switch, and the car would still run, but if the ignition button was pushed in the car would stop, and you needed a key to get it restarted. I had quietly removed the key when it appeared they were going to stop at that crossroad. When I got out I pushed the switch button in, stopping the engine, and made a throwing motion as if I were throwing the key into the ditch. I actually had put the key in my sock before we stopped. My parting comment was, "If I walk, you walk."

The boys began looking in the ditch for the key while I walked to a nearby farmhouse. When the farmer answered the door I told him the situation and asked him to drive me into Hillsdale. He drove me to my mother's house where I gave him the key to the boy's car, and asked him to return it to them. I then borrowed Mother's car, drove back to Pittsford, and went to bed. In the meantime the boys had given up trying to find the key, and decided they would try to hot wire the ignition. They got everything apart, but couldn't figure out how to cross the wires, so when the key was returned to them they couldn't use it. I don't know what time they got home, but I know I was in bed long before they were, and it was satisfying to beat those kids at their own game, especially when the story appeared in the school newspaper.

All this happened while we were at the old school house. Sometime before Christmas we all gathered our belongings, teachers and students alike, and walked as a group over to a beautiful new school. Having grown accustomed to the old school, everyone enjoyed and appreciated this attractive new building, and the students took good care of it.

In those years teachers had restrictions that present day teachers would find hard to believe. Some schools required teachers to remain in town on weekends. They were also expected to live in the town, and to attend church every Sunday. Women teachers could be fired if they smoked, even in the privacy of their own rooms, and men were not allowed to smoke except in the privacy of their homes. Any use of alcohol was strictly forbidden. Town people could smoke and drink, but teachers were held to higher standards. I worked at athletic events and directed plays without any extra pay.

I even came back for two or three days during Christmas vacation (during which we were not being paid) to process books that had been given to the school by the Kellogg Foundation. I didn't feel misused, because this was typical, and in this little town there wasn't much to do anyway. I was single, with no car, and these activities were a change from the routine. For recreation I enjoyed spear fishing in the fall, and playing sports after school in the gym with another first year teacher and the high school principal. I have many happy memories of my time in Pittsford.

School ended in early June, and so did my salary until the following September. My brother Bob was teaching in the little town of Covert near Lake Michigan, and I decided to visit Bob to see his school. In Pittsford I was teaching choir, and since Covert High School was still in session I decided to visit their choir class in the hope I might hear something I could use. The teacher welcomed me to her class and mentioned that her accompanist was out ill that day, so they would be singing without accompaniment. The fact that her accompanist was absent didn't mean much to me then, but it surely would have if I had known that her accompanist was the girl who would be my future wife.

I was still studying voice under Jay Paul Hinshaw, and he encouraged me to attend the American Conservatory of Music in Chicago over the summer. I had sung the operatic aria, Di Provenza, at the commencement concert in 1939, and sang it again for my application for a scholarship at the American Conservatory that summer. I won a scholarship with a guest voice teacher that year, Barre Hill, who was the voice professor at the University of Oklahoma. Barre was originally from near Hillsdale, studied voice, and toured Europe with a well-known operatic soprano, Mary Garden. I gave my whole attention to my music that summer, practiced religiously, and became a much more accomplished singer. I couldn't manage the expense of summer school, even with my scholarship, so I found a job working in a Hardings Restaurant as a bus boy. I made a little money and got my dinner there, so it was enough to see me through the summer.

When my first year of teaching ended I came home to Mother's for a couple of weeks before leaving for Chicago. During that time Bob and his wife, Jane, came to visit for a few days so they could be there when a Covert student and her parents came to Hillsdale to look at the college. Bob and Jane had suggested that Covert's valedictorian come to visit the College campus, and Bob asked Mother if they could invite the girl and her parents for dinner. When they arrived I discovered that her father had lost both of his hands in a boyhood accident on a train track. I was amazed at his ability to do anything anyone else could do. He drove his own car, his hand writing, done by holding a pen between his two arms, was beautiful, and he fed himself at the table so naturally that one almost forgot his lack of hands. He had an outgoing personality, and through the years I came to admire him for his cheerful outlook on life. He had been a boy who loved sports, and at age fifteen that was taken from him, but I never heard him complain. He was one of the most unusual people I have known.

I was impressed with the mother and father, but what really got my full attention was their daughter. I was introduced to Margery Blaney, later learning her nickname was Peachie, and that she was the chorus accompanist who was ill the day I visited Covert. She was seventeen years old when I met her in June, 1940, and I was totally taken with her. She was a slim brunette with blue eyes and blond streaks around her face. I didn't think I had ever seen a prettier girl, and it was just about all I could do to keep from grabbing her to tell her she was mine. She sat across from me on the couch in the living room, and I can still see her sitting there with her feet together and with her sunglasses on. She also sat across from me at the dining room table while I tried to be my most charming self.

At the end of the meal Mother asked me to start a fire in the basement stove that heated our water. I hurried down to do that, thinking that when I came back up from the basement I would ask Peachie to go to a movie with me, but when I returned I discovered that she had left to return to Covert. I was disappointed, and hoped I could see her again. I later learned from Bob and Jane that she decided to come to Hillsdale the next fall, and I assumed there would be other fellows at Hillsdale who would think she was as special as I did. As General Sherman said about war, the winner is the one who gets there firstest with the mostest, so before I left for Chicago I sent her a letter telling her I was sorry to have missed saying goodbye when she left, and offering to show her around Hillsdale in the fall. She told me later that she believed that line, and thought how nice I was to want to welcome her to Hillsdale. I'm glad she was only seventeen, and took everything at face value. I met her in the fall, and from that moment on tried to keep her dated up so far in advance that no one else had a chance. It apparently worked, because two years later she married me. She has been as special as she is pretty, and she has been a wonderful wife and a wonderful mother. I often wonder how I could have been so lucky. She has always made me proud of her, and I consider her my greatest asset. My mother always said that the best thing that can happen to a boy is to meet a nice girl, and I met the nicest.

Margery's father, Frank Blaney, was from an Irish family on the south side of Chicago. He would sometimes hop a train to take him in and out of the city, and when he was fifteen he often rode the train home from a sports facility. His routine was to jump off when the train slowed down at a crossing near his home, but one evening he slipped and fell under the train. When he regained consciousness he found his hands hanging by skin just above the wrists. He climbed across a barbed wire fence, got his hands caught in the barbs, worked them free, and then went to a nearby house where he kicked on the door. When the lady came to the door she promptly fainted. He then walked to the next house, and was taken to the hospital where his hands were amputated. I can only imagine the trauma he must have suffered, and it makes his optimistic outlook on life even more admirable. Frank married a pretty girl, Marjorie (Midge) Cox, who was a special person to look past his handicap to see his character. I couldn't have had a better mother-in-law. I once asked her if she ever had any reservations about marrying Frank because of his handicap, and she quickly replied, "Never once."

There weren't many jobs available for a man with no hands in the 1920s and 1930s, so Frank did the only thing he could do. He traveled the country selling products door-to-door. He was embarrassed to do this to support his family, but he had no choice. He started by buying bars of soap, and selling them at a small profit. A friend then advised him to buy needles from a Chicago wholesale house, because they would be smaller, easier to carry, and would sell better than soap. After that Frank sold needles. Every fall he and Midge packed up their two daughters and headed out, deciding on the way where to go for the winter. Their two girls missed school, but they didn't miss their education, because Frank held classes every day with lessons and assignments. He had not graduated from high school himself, but he valued education. When they were in Florida or California the girls would enter public school, but Marge never completed a full year of school until she entered the seventh grade in Michigan. They led a gypsy life, traveling back and forth across the country, living out of a tent.

I taught at Pittsford again the next year, but spent every weekend and some evenings in Hillsdale with Marge. I earned the same salary as the year before, but now I had a new way to spend it. The money I used the previous year to pay off my college debt I now spent on Marge, so I didn't save much, but I was having fun. Most of us have a mental concept of the kind of mate we want to find, but I suspect some settle for less. When I met Marge I had dated enough to have a pretty good concept of my ideal girl, and after we had dated for a few months I thought she was the girl I had been looking for. Now, fifty-seven years later, I know she was the right girl for me. She had intelligence, high standards, a wonderful sense of humor, and, as an added bonus, she was beautiful. We shared a love of the arts, and we were both charmed by children. I couldn't have found a better life's partner or a better mother for our children. There was no pretense about her; what you saw was what you got. She was even-tempered, fun to be with, and she had the best sense of humor of any girl I had known. After we were married she told me that I had the best sense of humor of any boy she had dated. I still love her laugh.

Shortly after we started dating she was eating an apple, and I asked her how close to the core she was going to eat it. Without batting an eye she said, "I eat the whole apple."

I asked, "The core too?"

She said, "Yes, and even the seeds, too." I didn't believe her until I saw her eat the entire apple, the core, and the seeds, and she carried it off with a straight face. Many years later when our children were carrying their lunch to school she put a piece of cardboard under the meat in their sandwiches on April Fools Day. Life with her has been interesting.

At the end of the second year in Pittsford I again studied voice in Chicago with the leading voice teacher there, Theodore Harrison. The previous year all my attention was directed towards my vocal study, but this year the girl I left behind was a real distraction. While I studied music she was traveling out west with her parents. Some family friends from Chicago were driving out to Yellowstone National Park to meet the Blaneys about the time my summer school was ending, and Marge made arrangements for me to ride with them.

I had never been out west except for the trip to Colorado in 1928, and I hadn't seen Marge since June, so I was eager to go. We met them after three days on the road, and I found that Marge looked just as good to me then as she had when I last saw her in June. I had a wonderful time in Yellowstone and in Colorado where we drove after leaving Yellowstone. Marge's folks had their trailer with them, but I shared a bed with Frank in the back of their Oldsmobile. One night in Yellowstone I got up to use the restroom, and was on my way back to the car when I heard a camper yell, "Get out of here," and then realized that a bear was rushing towards me. There was no place to go for safety except a nearby car, so I jumped on the top of it. The next morning two old maid school teachers who were sleeping in that car joked that they thought it was their lucky night . . . a young bachelor right there on top of their car.

In 1940 the Second World War was raging in Europe, and the United States began to prepare itself for possible involvement by instituting the draft. That winter I received my draft notice classifying me as "1-A," meaning I was a prime candidate. I had not yet been ordered to appear for a physical, so I continued my life as usual, teaching during the week and seeing Marge every weekend. I understood they shoot at people in wars, and I was in no hurry to volunteer.

At the end of my second year at Pittsford I found a teaching position in the Hoover School District in Flint, Michigan that paid fifteen hundred dollars a year, a fifty percent raise, but now I needed a car to return to Hillsdale on the weekends, and to get to school every day. Bob was then working in Detroit, and didn't need a car, so he agreed to sell me his car on credit. I had the car for about four months, but even with a fifty percent raise I had less money than I had at Pittsford because the repairs and operating costs of the car and my weekly trips to Hillsdale kept me poor. My intention to pay Bob was honorable, but as crusty old Colonel Baxter said to me on one occasion, "The road to hell is paved with good intentions, Lieutenant." At any rate, I returned the car to Bob when I left for flight training in January 1942. I hate to confess that the car had a bent front fender which occurred when I was looking at an attractive girl walking down the street in Flint, and the car in front of me stopped suddenly. I hate even more to admit that Marge was in the car with me at the time. Even though Bob got a bent car back, I put a heater in it, and replaced two cylinder heads to stop the car from over-heating every time I drove it, and Bob never complained about not getting paid. I suppose he hated to complain to a guy who was going into the army at the beginning of a world war.

Early in the fall of 1941 I received the same letter so many other young men received that year. It began, "Greetings", and was signed by President Roosevelt. It directed me to report for the first of two physical exams that were given before being inducted into the army. Knowing that I would soon be inducted I decided to apply for pilot training, having read about fliers in the First World War. They didn't live in mud filled trenches, were commissioned officers, wore silver wings, and received more pay. If I could get into pilot training I could earn a commission, get those coveted silver wings, and receive seventy-five dollars a month while in training instead of the twenty-one dollars a private made. After being commissioned, flying officers were paid a fifty percent bonus for flight pay, so there were some real incentives to try to get into the flight program.

During my first semester in Flint I developed a hernia on my left side, but it was small. When I visited a recruiting office in Chicago I told them I had a hernia, and was told that the Army Air Corps would not accept me, so I returned to Flint and taught until I took the first physical for the draft. The doctors there did not notice the hernia, so I thought that if those doctors didn't find it maybe the doctors giving me a physical for the Air Corps wouldn't find it either. A few days later the Japanese bombed Pearl Harbor and we were at war for the second time in twenty-four years.

I knew I would soon be called into the service, so I took a day off from school and went to the Federal Building in Detroit to volunteer for the Army Air Corps Cadet Flight Program. We were all lined up for a number of procedures, including a physical. As I had hoped, the doctor didn't discover the hernia, and declared me fit for the program. Air Corps Cadets had to pass the physical, have a minimum of two years of college, and be single. In 1941 there were no aptitude tests as there are now. Anyone wanting to become a pilot would be accepted if he met the qualifications and passed the physical. If he later washed out of pilot training he would be placed in a program to become a bombardier or navigator. If he refused that assignment he could be drafted into the Army as a private.

A young man ahead of me in line for the physical told an officer that he already had his second physical for the draft, and wondered if that would matter. He was taken out of the line, and told that they could not accept him until he had a written release from his draft board. Draft boards did not like to give releases, because they had quotas to fill, so I learned from his mistake, and when I passed that officer I said nothing. He didn't ask and I didn't tell. As far as I was concerned my draft board could find out later where I was, and by the time they did I'd already be sworn in and in training.

After passing the physical we were lined up before an Army captain who swore us into the army. He told us we had a fourteen day leave to take care of any personal business, but we should understand that we were in the Army, subject to Army regulations or even a court-martial. We were to report back on January 21st to go to the Aviation Cadet Reception Center in San Antonio (now known as Lackland Air Force Base). Our son Jim entered pilot training there in 1968, and our son Bruce entered pilot training there in 1980. It is strange how our paths cross and cross again. The captain who swore me in was Ward Estes. He later became the principal of Redford Union High School when I was the principal of Belleville High School, and our schools competed against each other in athletics. Ward became a good friend, but he had to put up with frequent complaints about how he terrorized me, and how he was personally responsible for me having to spend four years in the army.

When I returned to Flint I notified my superintendent that I was off to win the war. I finished out the week, and then moved back to Hillsdale to spend as much time as possible with Mother and Marge. Marge accepted a <u>small</u> diamond ring from me on Christmas Day, 1941, and I was glad to have her "sewed up" before I left. Fortunately for me, most of the other young men were also entering military service, so I didn't feel I was leaving her to the wolves, at least not too many wolves. It was a sad parting when I told her goodbye on the porch of Mother's house, and left to stay overnight with friends in Dearborn. I got up early the next morning to catch a bus into Detroit to report to the Army at seven o'clock. I was starting what would be the most memorable four years of my life.

The War Years
1942-1945

I left Hillsdale on a Sunday night in January 1942 for an unknown future. I told Mother and Margaret and Bill goodbye, and then talked to Marge alone on the front porch of Mother's apartment. In December I had given her a small engagement ring in a kitchen full of dirty dishes. I suppose I could have found a more romantic setting, but my focus was just on getting the ring on her finger. She cried as we said goodbye, and it was hard to leave her. All during my flight training she was foremost in my thoughts. Flying took second place.

Thus began the most exciting years of my life. But on that night it seemed a sad and scary start to an uncertain future in a world at war. Would I survive the war? If not, where and how would I die? Would I ever again see my family and the girl I so dearly loved? It was a lonely feeling. Mother had lived through World War I, and knew that many young men did not return, so it must have been with a heavy and worried heart that she watched me leave. I know how I felt when my own sons became military pilots, especially Jim who entered the Air Force during the Vietnam War, and spent a year flying combat missions in Vietnam and Laos.

I had orders to report at 7:00 a.m. on Monday, so I was up early to catch the bus to the Detroit Federal Building. I arrived a little before seven with the suitcase Mother had given me when I graduated from college. There I met a young man who had been sworn in with me in Detroit two weeks earlier. Howard Heym was a tall blond young man from Oregon who had been working in Detroit. We went through pre-flight, primary, and basic flight training together, and then Howard was sent to twin engine advanced while I went into advanced single engine training. When we reported to the sergeant that morning we were told there had been a mistake, and that we should report at seven o'clock that night. So we killed the day by sight seeing and watching Glenn Miller perform at a local theater.

That evening we reported again at seven o'clock, and boarded a train known as The Wabash Cannon Ball which took us from Detroit to St. Louis. It was January, and when we left Detroit it was already dark. Except for Howard Heym and one other young man, I knew no one. I was alone with thoughts of my family and Marge as I looked at the lights of the farmhouses and listened to the mournful wail of the steam engine's whistle. I sat on the left side of the train as we headed west so I must have seen the lights of a farmhouse where Marge and I would raise our five children many years later. This beautiful old home is on the northwest corner of Elwell and Hull Roads near Belleville, Michigan. Unaware that I was passing a large part of my future life, I rode on into the night deep in my thoughts.

We arrived in St. Louis the next morning, and were put in a hotel for the day before shipping out again on another train to San Antonio. We arrived in San Antonio in late January, and I remember one man saying, "Jeez fellas, look, there's an orange tree!" It was the first orange tree most of us had ever seen. We were met by two Army trucks, and were told to load our suitcases in the back of the truck and to get in and sit on the benches. At this point I had the most sinking feeling of my life. I knew with finality that I was in the army, and it was not a good feeling. Up until that time there had always been a way to avoid trouble if it got too unpleasant. But now there was a war on, I was a member of the cast, and I wasn't going to be a civilian again until the war was over. If I quit the flight program I would be transferred to the marching army, and that seemed worse. I'd read many stories about the infantry in WWI, so I braced myself for whatever lay ahead.

When we arrived at the Aviation Cadet Reception Center we were assigned to a building where we slept the first night. The private who drove our truck from the train station ordered us, in a very authoritarian voice, to come out and unload his truck. We fell to that task with vigor, as we knew that anybody in a uniform outranked us. At five a.m. the next morning we were rudely awakened by a bugle playing reveille over a loudspeaker right outside our building. We all got dressed, stumbled out into formation, and then marched (I use the term loosely) across a field to the mess hall. When we were seated our sergeant addressed us with an air of military authority, and we believed every word he said. "Misters," he said, "you're in the army; you hear what I'm telling you? I'll talk to you later about other things, but right now you're here to eat breakfast. You can have all you want to eat, but whatever you put on your tray, you're going to eat, and that goes double for butter! You put it on your tray, you're going to eat it."

We were given uniforms after marching around in civilian clothes for a few days, and were glad to get them because they let us fade into the crowd instead of standing out in our civilian dress. The first day some cadets from advanced training at Kelly Field drove by as we were standing in formation, and called out, "You'll be s-o-r-r-y." They knew what they were talking about. The bugle played reveille at five o'clock every morning, and never got any more pleasant than it was the first time we heard it. We had five minutes to get dressed for roll call, and then ran back into the barracks to make our bunks, wash, shave and fall out again to run to breakfast. Most of the fellows were pretty much in a fog when they first got up, and it took them awhile to come to life, but I was always wide awake the minute my eyes opened, and I had more pep and humor then than at any other time of the day. The minute the bugle woke us I was up laughing and joking. Finally one morning a fellow cadet looked at me sourly and said, "Ford, how can you be so cheerful this early in the morning?"

We lined up the first morning, went through the food line, put what we wanted on metal trays that served as dishes, and then ate it, all of it. We hadn't questioned the private the day before when he ordered us to unload his truck, and we sure weren't going to question this sergeant with all those stripes on his sleeve. The second lieutenant we met a day or two later might as well have been a general.

We were assigned to two story wooden barracks with a sidewalk made of wood slats. There was absolutely no grass anywhere that I ever saw while I was there, either around the barracks buildings or on the parade ground. This military facility had been hurriedly built, and the only objective was to make it functional. The barracks were long open buildings except for two small rooms at one end. An enlisted man in charge of the barracks roomed in one, and the other was used as a storage room for the civilian clothes we no longer needed. There were bunks every three feet along both sides of the room, and the bunks were made up with every other bunk having its pillow at the opposite end. Thus the head of one bunk was next to the foot of its neighbor.

We arrived on Saturday afternoon, and it was Tuesday or Wednesday when we finally received our uniforms, two olive drab wool shirts, two pairs of matching pants, two tan neck ties, six pairs of olive drab wool socks that shrank to half their size after the first washing, an overseas cap, a garrison cap with a brown leather visor and a blue band that went around the body of the cap with a set of gold wings and propeller for a hat emblem, two pairs of brown shoes, and a belt with a solid brass buckle which had to be kept highly shined at all times. We were also issued fatigues, a footlocker, two blue barracks bags (like a duffel bag), a helmet, and a gas mask. We then marched back to our barracks to put on our new uniforms, pack our civilian clothes, and fill out a home address tag where they were to be sent. That was the last contact we were going to have with civilian life until the war was over. We then marched to the post barbershop for a military haircut. It took longer to sign for the haircut than it took the barber to cut our hair. The barbers enjoyed asking the first victim of the day how he would like it cut. "Do you want the sides left a little long? Do you want any off the top?" The barber then started at the back with his electric clippers, and kept going until he reached the eyebrows. We had perhaps an eighth of an inch left when they finished.

We spent four weeks at the Aviation Cadet Reception Center where we learned marching, saluting, military customs, and the three acceptable military responses, "yes sir, no sir, and no excuse sir." After a few days we began to feel a little less intimidated, and learned what soldiers throughout history have learned, how to avoid unpleasant duties and situations; in other words, how to beat the system.

Every time we transferred to a new military facility we were confined to the post for two weeks. After two weeks at the Cadet Reception Center we were allowed to go into San Antonio on Saturday and Sunday during the day. We enjoyed walking the streets, visiting the Alamo, sitting at a soda bar for a coke or ice cream, and eating in a restaurant. Military personnel were required to be in uniform at all times except when engaging in some activity that required special clothing. It was unusual to see men on the street out of uniform, and it always prompted the question, "Why isn't he in the service?" Marge's birthday was February 28, and we were soon to be shipped out to primary flying school for our first flight training, so on our last weekend there I went into San Antonio and bought Marge a pretty black pleated skirt and a white blouse. In those days it was considered quite improper for a girl to accept a gift of clothing from a man to whom she was not married, and since she was living in the home of an elderly lady during her second year in college she had to keep the giver of that gift a secret.

On February 24, 1942, we packed up all of our gear and reported to the parade ground to be trucked to the train station for the trip to Parks Air College in East St. Louis, Illinois where we received our first flight instruction in the Fairchild PT-19, a low winged monoplane with a 175 HP engine. It had a blue body, yellow wings, and an identifying number on each side, a fact I regretted a short time later. To start this plane a cadet stood on the left wing and turned a crank fifteen to twenty turns to store enough energy to turn the engine over when the cadet in the cockpit engaged the starter. It took both hands and a good deal of energy to turn that crank. Then if the cadet in the cockpit didn't get the engine started, you had to do it all over again. Sometimes it might take three or four attempts for some dumbbell to get his engine started, and each time we would pray that he would get it started this time, and curse him a little under our breath when he didn't.

Parks Air College was a civilian flying school that had a contract to train Army Air Corps Cadets. In addition to teaching the primary phase of flight training, they also taught classes in navigation, meteorology, theory of flight, and aircraft engines. While these programs were under the direction of military officers, the pilot instructors were civilians. My instructor was Ned Dolan, a man in his thirties. Dolan was a patient instructor, and I have always felt lucky that he introduced me to flying. I don't know why I didn't keep in touch with more of the people who were important in my life, but often I didn't, and I never wrote him or tried to get in touch with him after I left Parks. I returned to Parks Air College in the early 1960's and talked to some old pilot instructors who had known Ned Dolan, but no one knew where he had gone. Twenty years later I located my basic flight instructor, Carroll V. Glines. He didn't know Ned Dolan, but he knew a young airline pilot by that name, and when I located him I discovered that he was my old instructor's son. He told me his father had been an airport manager in Pennsylvania, but died several years earlier. I had driven through Pennsylvania any number of times, and would have loved to have seen Ned Dolan again.

We traveled by train from San Antonio to Parks Air College on a gray chilly day in late February. Our rooms were in attractive brick buildings, and were a long step up from the wooden barracks we had back in Texas. I had three roommates there, a short chunky kid from Texas named James Robert Ewing McKinney, another kid from Texas named Rufus Gladstone Thompson, and a big blond kid from Michigan whose last name was Patton. Rufus Thompson saw McKinney's names, promptly named him E-wing, and the name stuck. Rufus Thompson and I went through all three phases, primary, basic, and single-engine advanced at the same flying schools, while E-wing left us after basic and was sent to twin engine advanced training. I have no idea what happened to Patton, or Rufus Thompson, but I did find McKinney many years after the war, and learned he had made a career of it, retiring as a colonel.

The first five weeks at Parks were different from anything I had experienced before. Every class had a designation, and ours was 42-H. We were the under class, while the class just ahead of us, 42-G, was the upper class. They had just finished five weeks as underclassmen, and now as upperclassmen it was get even time, even though we had not been the cause of their misery. It was immediately obvious that our upperclassmen felt they had been put on earth to make our lives as miserable as possible, and their imagination and creativeness were impressive. The instant an upperclassman entered our room we had to jump to attention and yell in unison, "42-H, attention" as we hit a brace. A brace is an exaggerated position of attention. We stood as rigidly as possible with our chests stuck out, our stomachs sucked in, our backsides pulled in, our heads pulled back, and our chins pulled down to create as many wrinkles as possible. While we struggled to get into this impossible position the upperclassmen would stick their faces in front of ours and yell at the top of their voices, "Get those shoulders back, get that knob (head) back, get that chin down, suck in that raunchy gut, get your eyes on a point, let's see some wrinkles," etc. We were expected to "hold tea cups," which meant holding our hands tight against our sides with the thumb and index finger together. As a final touch, we had to hold our breath until we turned red. If the veins in our neck bulged out, so much the better.

A favorite trick of the upperclassmen was to come to our room after the evening meal, and stand in the doorway with the toes of their shoes just at the line that separated the hallway from our room. Theoretically we could relax while we were in our room, but there was no relaxing while an upperclassman was standing at the doorway, and we watched him as a mouse watches a cat. We had to be ready to jump to attention and yell, "42-H, attention," when his toe suddenly slid across the line, as we knew it would. They were not allowed to touch us, but they could make our lives miserable in a hundred different ways. Having just been freed from their role as underclassman, they took delight in seeing that we weren't deprived of that unique experience.

We couldn't just ignore them. There was a war on, and we were going to be part of it in some capacity. We chose this route because we wanted to fly, and the hazing was considered a test to see if we could stand up under pressure. If we refused we would be washed out of the program and put in the infantry. For the most part the hazing was done in good humor, and we accepted it in good humor. I've since had men from other branches of the service tell me they would not have stood for it, but they would not have been pilots, and wouldn't have worn those cherished silver wings. One cadet in our class, a fat kid named Collins, decided he had all the hazing he was going to take, and simply refused to do what he was told. Within a day or two Mr. Collins was gone, most likely as a private in the infantry.

There were rules for literally everything we did. Clothes were hung on hangers in a prescribed manner, shirts and jackets were put on hangers so the buttons faced out, all buttons had to be buttoned, all hangers faced the same way in the closet, and shoes were shined with the laces tied, and then neatly placed on the closet floor. Our blue barracks bag was tied to the foot of our bunk, and our dirty clothes and anything else that needed to be kept out of sight were put in the barracks bag. Bunks were made with military corners of forty-five degrees, and the upperclassmen would measure the angle with a protractor. Bunks had the top sheet folded over the blanket with a six-inch collar, and a six inch space between the top of that collar and the pillow. The upper class had a ruler to measure that, too.

The bunks sagged a little in the middle, and we had to pull the blanket so tight that if an upperclassman quickly moved his hand over the blanket the breeze would make the blanket ripple. A bed simply had to ripple, and if it didn't ripple the offending cadet had to find the ripple. He would crawl head first under the blanket to the foot of the bunk, then turn and come back under the top sheet, turn again and go the length of the bunk under the bottom sheet, and then under the mattress pad, where he would stand up holding the imaginary ripple between his hands as he tried to control its imaginary thrashing around while he stood at attention. He then had a minute or less to remake his bunk, with a ripple! The rest of us stood at attention as we watched that poor soul try to remake his bunk in one minute so it would pass inspection. If we laughed or even smiled we found ourselves looking for a ripple in our own bunk.

Frequently in the evening the upperclassmen would call out, "42-H front and center." When we heard that we had to rush out and stand at attention with our backs against the wall. Their next order was, "Pee pad inspection in ten seconds." We then ran back into our rooms, tore our beds apart to get the mattress pad, and ran back into the hall to stand at attention against the wall with the pad held up in front of us for their inspection. After that inspection the upperclassmen would say, "42-H, bed inspection in one minute!" Then they would be in there with their rulers and protractors, knowing full well they could find some poor soul to haze. If we smiled or laughed we were ordered to, "Wipe that smile off your face, mister." Then we had to get down in a squatting position, place our hands on the floor and balance in such a way that we could lift our feet and rub our nose on the floor. We then returned to a position of attention without the smile.

One Saturday morning, when several of us were getting ready to take the bus into town, some upper class cadets gave two of us special attention. We had to face each other, nearly nose to nose, and say, "Fuzzy Wuzzy was a bear, Fuzzy Wuzzy had no hair, Fuzzy Wuzzy wasn't fuzzy, was he?" Then one of us would ask, "What was Fuzzy Wuzzy?" and the other would reply, "Fuzzy Wuzzy was a bare bear, sir." It was nearly impossible to keep from smiling, but I knew if I gave even a trace of a smile I would be left there at the mercy of these upper class cadets while my friends were in St. Louis, and that thought kept a smile off my face. The other fellow couldn't keep from smiling, which made my effort doubly hard, but the upper class cadets had a victim to hassle, so they let me go. As we left for St. Louis he was getting down on the floor to wipe the smile off his face.

I wrote to Marge every day, and to Mother at least once a week. But the first week at Parks Air College the upper class was after us constantly, so I literally did not have a minute to write even a post card. From the moment we got up in the morning until we went to bed there was not a single minute when we weren't in class, in formation, or being hazed. The upper class cadets could levy demerits for any kind of infraction, real or imagined, and it was impossible to avoid them. If they wished, they could always find something to penalize, and when the demerits accumulated we had to march them off during the next weekend. The marching area was a cement sidewalk that made a square an eighth of a mile around. We marched in our dress uniform, which consisted of olive drab blouse and pants, tan shirt and tie, and garrison cap. One gray and drizzly Saturday morning I started marching right after breakfast. I had walked for an hour or two when one of our upperclassmen appeared accompanied by two girls. Every time I passed him he would make funny remarks for both my benefit and the benefit of the girls with him. I later learned his name was Howard Lorence from Eugene, Oregon. He became ill at Parks, and was held back a class, so we went through all three phases of flight training together. I became well acquainted with Howard when we were both sent to Goodfellow Field in San Angelo, Texas as flight instructors. Howard and I became dear friends there, and kept in touch through the years even after he returned to Oregon and I returned to Michigan. We maintained a close friendship until his death many years later.

Meals were a frantic time for under class cadets at Parks, but I later discovered that mealtime at Basic flight training was even worse. At Parks we marched to the dining facility, and stood in line outside the cafeteria while the upper class went to the front of the line. The first day we went to the cafeteria to eat before going to the field to meet our flight instructors. When I finally got through the line I had a good lunch, and sat down at a table to eat in peace and quiet. I took just one bite when the upperclassmen called out, "42-H, fall out for the flight line." I quickly stuffed food in my mouth, grabbed an apple, and ran for the bus. For the five weeks I spent as an under class cadet at Parks that was typical of the amount of time I had for lunch. The evening meal was a little more leisurely, but my habits were formed, and I continued to eat at the same speed, rushed or not. When Marge and Mother came down to visit they were amazed at how fast I ate.

I was lucky to have Ned Dolan as my instructor at Parks. Some of my classmates had instructors who yelled at them, and whipped the joy stick from side to side to whack their knees when they did something wrong. One student, named Shorty Glidden, was so short his undershorts came down to his knees. His instructor gave him some instructions, and finished by saying, "Now, I don't want you to remember this. I want to have to tell you every day!" Whether a student made it in the program or washed out was based on the judgment of the instructor, and some cadets who washed out of the program here in the United States then entered the Canadian program and became eminently successful pilots. When I became an instructor myself I understood how flying instructors can become impatient and short tempered after seeing the same mistakes made by class after class after class. It happened to me after I instructed for two years in the backseat of a BT-13.

On my first flight with Ned Dolan I rode in the front seat of the PT-19 while Ned got in the back seat and flew around the area pointing out landmarks such as the huge Skokie smoke stacks, the Mississippi River, and the city of St. Louis. I had been in an airplane only once before when Bob and I paid fifty cents for a ten minute ride around Hillsdale, so I was a complete novice when it came to flying. For some reason the scrap wood airplanes suspended with ropes that Bob made in Texas hadn't done much to train me as a pilot. After orienting me to the area, Dolan demonstrated a stall by reducing the power and pulling the stick back to put the plane in a nose high position. As we lost flying speed the plane shuddered and then dropped out from under us. I didn't know anything about flying, but I could tell that we weren't flying anymore; we were falling! I grabbed the metal frame of the airplane and hung on for dear life as Dolan showed me that there was nothing to fear. All we needed to do was to pop the stick forward and give the engine power, and we were flying once again.

The first spin was even more exciting. He put the airplane in a stall, but instead of recovering he kicked full right rudder, and pulled the stick back into his lap. The plane was really falling now, obviously there was no way to recover, and in a minute or two we were both going to die. The plane was spinning to the right, or the world was spinning to the left, I couldn't tell which, and soon it wasn't going to make any difference anyway. Then Dolan jammed full left rudder, waited two or three seconds, pushed the stick full forward, and, voila, with a little throttle we were saved. He had me do some stalls and spins and I was able to recover from them, but Dolan in the back seat was my security blanket. After eight and half hours of dual instruction Dolan said, "I'm going to solo you now. I want you to go west of the field and do a couple of spins. I'll stay here and watch you." I felt comfortable with stalls, but doing a spin without Ned Dolan in the back was unnerving, and I was not a confident pilot that afternoon. I took off, said a little prayer, and put the plane into a two-turn spin to the right. I recovered without a hitch, climbed back up to altitude and did a couple more, gaining confidence each time. When I landed I knew I was a pilot, not much of one yet, but a pilot.

Each new cadet who soloed had to get under an ice cold shower and recite, "I am no longer a dumb dumb dodo bird, I am now an Aviation Cadet!" We had to repeat that once for every hour of instruction that it took us to solo. After three or four times I became so cold I couldn't enunciate the words, and it became an unintelligible jabber. When I completed eight efforts they turned on the hot water to warm me up, and then wrapped me in a blanket.

Half way through my time at Parks I nearly ended my flying career. After practicing stalls and spins I was ready to return to the field, when I saw several boats down below me in the Mississippi River. The rules required us to stay above one thousand feet in that area, but the real sensation of speed is down near the ground. That is where the fun is, so I dropped down to about five hundred feet and flew at that altitude for two or three minutes looking at the boats below me. I was starting my climb back up to a thousand feet when I noticed another plane approaching me. I turned away from him only to see him turn inside me to cut me off. I assumed it was another student who hadn't seen me, so I turned the opposite way and saw him again turn inside me. It was obvious then that the other plane was trying to get close to me, and there was no way to avoid him, so I turned back to the field. It didn't seem like such a terrible crime. Five hundred feet is hardly buzzing or hedge hopping, but it was against the rules, and when I landed I was told to report to Lt. Longino who grounded me pending a check ride with the much feared Lt. Wright. I thought I would have a better chance in front of a firing squad.

Lt. Wright was the military commander of Parks Air College Cadet Training Program, and he was reported to have said, "For an officer to be a good officer, his men should hate him." I don't know if this was his philosophy, but none of us wanted to find out, and we all tried to keep as much distance between ourselves and Lt. Wright as possible. Now I was destined to take a check ride with him, and I was afraid the outcome was preordained even before we took off.

The names of the cadets who were still flying were listed on a board under the name of their instructor. While I was grounded my name was still on the board, and for two or three days I waited for the call to fly with Lt. Wright. While I was waiting Marge and Mother came down to see me. It was wonderful seeing them, but my joy was dampened by the prospect of flying with Lt. Wright, and the possibility that my flying days might be over. Breaking flying regulations was an almost guaranteed way to get washed out, and the future looked grim. After the weekend Marge and Mother returned to Hillsdale, and on Monday I reported to Lt. Wright for my check ride.

By this time I was as comfortable in the airplane as I was driving a car. I was smooth and coordinated on the controls, and landings always seemed easy for me. Maybe I thought I was better than I really was, but I was not apprehensive about my flying ability when I reported to Lt. Wright. We climbed into the plane to take off, and I tried to remember everything I had thought about as I anticipated this ride. He asked me to do a few stalls and spins, and gave me some forced landings, which I thought went well. He then asked me to do a chandelle, which is a 180 degree maximum climbing turn. I had never done one and told him so, but he asked me to try it anyway. I don't know how good my chandelle was, but I made the 180 degree turn without stalling. He finally said, "Let's go home," and I headed for the field. I had been cautioned by Ned Dolan to check the landing tee to be sure the landing pattern hadn't changed while we were up, because if there was a wind change we might not land in the same direction that we took off. A check pilot always watched to see if the student checked the tee before landing. I remembered that advice, and flew over the field making an exaggerated effort to check the tee so Lt. Wright couldn't help but notice. I then went out a short distance to enter the traffic pattern. On the final approach to the field Lt. Wright shook the stick and said, "Check the tee!" After I had made my big show of checking the tee somebody had changed it.

I landed, parked the plane, and stood at attention until Lt. Wright dismissed me. He went over several things about the flight that I can no longer recall, and ended his comments by saying, "That's why I consider this an unsatisfactory ride." He then asked, "Do you have any questions?" I badly wanted to know if I was eliminated from the flight program, but something just told me it would be better if I didn't ask the question, so I answered, "No sir," saluted, and marched off. I didn't want him to make a decision on the spot, hoping he might make a decision I liked better if he had time to consider it. For the next three days the flight board showed me as being grounded, but my name was still there, so I hadn't been washed out yet, at least not officially. Dolan could have contacted Lt. Wright to ask if I was eliminated, but instead he told me, "If your name is still there tomorrow I'm going to start flying you again." Dolan said he didn't know if Lt. Wright meant to leave me on flying, if he forgot to notify the flight line that I was eliminated, if someone there had forgotten to remove my name, or if Lt. Wright was simply making a distinction between an unsatisfactory ride and a failure. In any event, I started flying the next day and I viewed the Mississippi River from above one thousand feet for the rest of the time I was at Parks. The last five weeks we perfected our basic flying skills, took a short cross-country flight, and finally were introduced to chandelles and lazy eights. Of the group that came to Parks in our class nearly seventy-five percent washed out.

When we became upperclassmen we anticipated with some relish our chance to indoctrinate the new under class with the facts of life at Parks, so you can imagine our disappointment when the order came down that there would be no hazing of the new under class. It was a mixed disappointment, however, because this should mean we would not have to endure hazing when we got to Basic flight school. We had been hazed by experts when we were the under class at Parks. At the flying field we were free of hazing, except on foggy days when the upperclassmen would sometimes line us up at the edge of the field and order us to blow as hard as we could to blow the fog away. Back at our rooms, however, it was a different story.

Our rooms were subject to informal inspection at any time. Every Saturday morning there was an official inspection by the upper class and our Commandant of Cadets, Lt. Payne. These inspections were white glove inspections, so we made our bunks more carefully than ever, organized our closets, shined, laced, and neatly placed our shoes on the floor, and washed and dusted everything in our room. The inspection team used white gloves to wipe everything, the desks, the chairs, the bars in the closet, the undersides of closet shelves, the wood strips the shelves rested on, and even the floor. To prepare, we scrubbed the floors, then waxed and polished them, and as a last effort we took a white undershirt and wiped the floor as we backed our way to the foot of our bunks. We then turned without moving our feet, and put the white undershirt in the barracks bag. There was a hole on the underside of our bunks and the inspectors would stick a finger into that hole to see if they could find dirt. They even checked the soles of our shoes. One weekend when family and friends were invited to visit we had a formation for them in the early afternoon, after which there was an inspection. The cadets were divided into two groups, and the winners of the inspection were allowed to go into St. Louis with their families or girl friends. There were no wives there, because married men were not accepted into the flight program. The team that lost the inspection that day lost because a single thread was found on the floor of the closet in one room.

Marge came down to Parks again for the weekend after I completed my training. We went into St. Louis for dinner and a dance, and it was wonderful to see her again. I had three days until I had to report to Enid Army Airfield in Oklahoma for Basic Flight Training, so on Monday we caught the same train that I had taken nearly three months earlier from Detroit to St. Louis, the Wabash Cannon Ball. My brother Bob met us in Adrian, and drove us to Hillsdale. It seemed so good to be home again without the routine of army life. I enjoyed being in Hillsdale, and having time with my family and Marge. She was the most important thing in my life, and I missed her when we were apart.

At the end of three days I made another sad goodbye, and took a bus from Jonesville to Chicago to catch a plane to Oklahoma City. Servicemen were well treated by nearly everyone, and public transportation was generally free to men in uniform, as was admission to the theaters. The postal service delivered our mail free if we wrote our name and rank and address in the upper left hand corner of the envelope, and when I arrived in Chicago I had free transportation to the airport. It was still early in the war, and the government didn't quite know what to expect, so when a plane took off the curtains had to be drawn over the windows to prevent enemy agents from taking pictures of our airports and cities. It seems funny now, but at the time no one knew what to expect. We took off after dark that night in a DC-3 and landed in Oklahoma City well after midnight. The DC-3 was the workhorse of the airlines, and had been for years. Thirty years later our son Jim flew the military version, the C-47, in Laos and Vietnam for electronic surveillance during the Vietnam War.

When I arrived in Oklahoma City there were soldiers and other military personnel everywhere, either waiting for another flight out, or for bus transportation to a nearby base. I didn't see anyone there from Parks, so I waited until morning to catch the bus to Enid Army Airfield. There were cadets there from other primary schools, and we all boarded the bus about seven o'clock in the morning for a ride through bleak country under gray skies.

Parks Air College had permanent brick buildings, lawns, and cement sidewalks. In short, it was pretty civilized. As we neared Enid the first thing I saw was the water tower that stood high above the landscape, and as we got closer I could see wooden barracks on a desolate plain with no trees, no grass, and the familiar wood sidewalks we had known in San Antonio. When we entered the main gate I had the same sinking feeling I had experienced when we boarded the buses in San Antonio, but I was at least grateful that we would be spared the hazing we had endured at Parks.

Even though we knew there would be no more hazing we were still a little apprehensive until some cadets in garrison caps waved to us as we got off the bus, and called, "C'mon over here fellas." We looked at each other and said, "They called us fellas," and thought, "What a change from our greeting at Parks." We picked up our suitcases and struggled over to them, all smiles for our new found friends. When we reached them we were met with screams of, "DROP THOSE BAGS AND BRACE, MISTER!" The bags hit the ground, and once again we were straining in a brace as we thought, "God, not again!" Either these guys hadn't heard that there was to be no more hazing, or they just didn't care. Whichever it was, we had five weeks of hell ahead of us.

They assigned three cadets to a room, and then ordered us to fall out to a large black topped area. We started at nine in the morning, and were given close order drill until noon. The orders were forward march, to the rear march, by the right flank march, by the left flank march, etc. There was a sharp wind when we first arrived, and it got stronger by the hour until eventually we were leaning into it to keep from being blown over. After drill we marched to the mess hall, and remained standing until some officers came in and sat at the head table. Then they gave the command "Gentlemen, be seated." The class of 42-H collapsed in our chairs after an exhausting morning, grateful for a break from the marching and hazing. As we did so there was an explosion of voices as every upperclassman started screaming at the top of his lungs to, "Sit up straight, sit on the front three inches of your chair, stop looking around, get your eyes on a point, you're not going to buy this place, get those shoulders back, pull your chin down and, sound off." You can't appreciate that moment unless you were there. We were momentarily frozen by the unexpected and overpowering attack. After a few days we were prepared for it, because it happened every meal, so the shock value dissipated a little, but when an upperclassman spoke he had our undivided attention.

When we were told to sound off we immediately gave the following information in this exact order, name, rank, serial number, hometown, college, and fraternity. My response was, "John P. Ford, Aviation Cadet, 16059305, Hillsdale, Michigan, Hillsdale College, Alpha Tau Omega, sir!" This was given sitting at attention on the front three inches of my chair with my head back, my chin down, and my eyes on a point.

When the food was brought to our table it was first passed to the upperclassmen who took what they wanted before passing it back our way. The upperclassmen usually cleaned the serving dish the first time around, and frequently the second time around. When the third serving arrived we got what the upperclassmen didn't want. The underclass cadet sitting at the end of the table was called the gunner. It was his job to hold his hand up to signify to the civilian servers that we needed a refill. We were not allowed to look around the room, or even around our own table, but we had better know when the upperclassmen needed food, and see that it was immediately passed down the table to them.

If we were caught glancing anywhere but straight ahead we were given tasks to do while everyone else was eating. It was always preceded by the question, "Do you want to buy this place?" One punishment was to have the offender eat a "square meal," which meant that our fork had to move from our plate to our mouth and back to our plate in a square pattern, while our eyes were focused on some point in the distance. We could not look at our plate, and had to guess where our fork was going. Another option was to have the offending cadet count the window panes in the room. We couldn't bluff, because the upper class cadet knew how many panes there were; he had counted them when he was an underclassman. After dinner they asked, "Do you want dessert, mister?" Of course we always wanted dessert, and the upperclassman would ask, "Are you famous?" The answer had to be, "Yes sir." We had to be famous for something, so we might say, "I'm famous for a joke, sir", or "I'm famous for a limerick, sir" to which the upperclassman responded, "Elucidate, mister." Then we would tell a joke or recite a limerick and would be given permission to eat dessert.

The upperclassmen occasionally had us exchange tables with other cadets so they could hear some new jokes or limericks. As we stood in line outside the mess hall, waiting to be admitted, we exchanged jokes and limericks with others so we would have something new to offer. One cadet said he was famous for cutting toilet seats in half for half-assed upperclassmen. We could get away with insulting the upperclassmen if it was funny enough. I had a classmate by the name of Gefvert who was particularly hard on the underclassmen when we were upperclassmen. He once asked an underclassman why he was famous and the cadet said, "Sir, I'm famous for a saying." Gefvert responded, "Elucidate mister," and the cadet said, "Sir, if my dog had a face like yours I'd shave his ass and make him walk backwards." Gefvert was apoplectic, and told the cadet he'd better be famous for something else, at which time the cadet gave an even worse answer that I can't put on paper. Gefvert would have killed him if the other upperclassmen hadn't laughed him down.

There was a lot of foolishness in the training program, but it did teach us to tolerate things that were stressful, unpleasant, or even unreasonable. We were never physically hurt by our upperclassmen, and if they even wished to remove a thread from our uniform they had to ask, "May I touch you?" We accepted their authority, but at the same time we recognized that it was all just a game, and anyone who couldn't take the hazing was eliminated from the program. We had endured this for five weeks at Parks, and we could survive five weeks here too.

The second day at Enid we were given rifles that were covered inside and out with a brown gooey substance called Cosmoline that protected the rifles from rust. We were told to go to our barracks and clean those rifles so they could pass a white glove inspection. It looked like an impossible job, but we set to it. I had barely begun when I was ordered to report to the post band. They noticed from my records that I had been a band director, and they hoped they had found a real asset. I had to tell them that I was a music major, but I didn't play an instrument. My instrument was my voice. That didn't deter them, so I agreed to play the cymbals. I was delighted to join the band, and immediately returned the rifle to the place where I had gotten it. We played Retreat every afternoon at five o'clock as the post's flag was lowered in a ceremony attended by all cadets. It was a sorry band, but we were happy with our lot because we escaped rifle inspection during the whole time we were at Enid. There was a little kid named Adrian J. Seymore who marched next to me every day. He wasn't much over five feet tall, and I always felt a little guilty as A.J. struggled under a big base drum while I bounced along with my cymbals. When we became upperclassmen a new band of underclassmen was drafted to do the honors. The new under class took over the rifle responsibilities, too.

We weren't hazed in our rooms as we had been at Parks, but if we were in the hall when an upper class cadet appeared we had to slam ourselves against the wall, with our heels banging against the baseboard, and remain in this position of hard attention until the upperclassman passed out of sight or said, "As you were." For the first week we were not allowed to leave the barracks, so we had to appeal to some kind upperclassman to buy whatever we needed from the Post Exchange. Surprisingly, they were pretty good about doing that for us. After the first week we could go ourselves, but until we soloed in our new airplane, the BT-13, we had to go dual, which meant we had to find a classmate to go with us, and we had to run everywhere we went. After we soloed we were free to go by ourselves.

After a few days at Enid we marched over to the flight line to meet our instructors. My instructor was a short slender young man named C.V. Glines. I later learned that the "C" stood for Carroll. Lt. Glines was my instructor for ten weeks, and I don't think I ever once saw him smile. He was, however, patient and calm, if not oozing with warmth and charm. Twenty years later I saw his name in an Air Force directory, and learned he was stationed at the Pentagon in Washington. Later that year I accompanied a class of senior students on their senior trip, and when we were in Washington I went to the Pentagon and talked to him. After retiring from the Air Force he became a prolific writer of books about World War II. He wrote several books about the Jimmy Doolittle Raid on Tokyo, and was made an honorary member of that group. He also wrote several books on the DC-3, and a book on the shooting down of Admiral Yamamoto near the end of the war. He didn't remember me, but he appreciated my visit, and I discovered that C.V. Glines does smile, a lot.

When we got to the flight line Lt. Glines showed us our new airplane, the BT-13, and it looked like a big plane to me. The PT-19 at Parks was smaller and slower, with a one hundred and seventy five horsepower engine. The BT-13 had a four hundred and fifty horsepower engine, and it took some time before I felt at ease with it. It also had a few more gadgets to deal with, such as a two position prop. When taking off or landing we used low pitch, while all other flying was done in high pitch. We had to follow a precise procedure to change pitch, and these new procedures made the BT-13 a challenge for a young pilot. In primary we just learned to fly the airplane. In basic we added formation flying, night flying, instrument flying, aerobatics, extended cross country, and night cross country flying.

I flew mechanically at first, without much feel for the plane. After ten hours I took my first check ride with a Lt. Unruh. Lt. Unruh then gave his evaluation to Lt. Glines who told me, "You certainly impressed Lt. Unruh with that ride." After a dramatic pause he added, "With the horribleness of it." I'm sure that was a fair description, but Lt. Glines had the patience to stay with me, and I soon developed a feel for the plane.

There was an area near Enid Army Airfield called The Salt Flats that was used as an auxiliary field to reduce the traffic at Enid. It was also used for night flight training, as it was a hard flat surface, and there was plenty of room for young pilots who might overshoot or land short. When we were scheduled for night flying we had flying in the morning, ground school and physical training in the afternoon, and then returned to the flight line that night. We got back to our rooms about two o'clock in the morning only to be rousted out again at five-thirty by Reveille. We must have been young and tough. I had the same schedule when I was an instructor at Goodfellow Field until someone had the great idea of having us fly in the afternoon after night flying so we could sleep in the next day.

One night we were at the Salt Flats shortly after our first solo in night flying. We had not yet received any instrument training, so when fog moved in we were told to fly back to our home base immediately. I flew back with a fellow cadet named Tucker, and as we flew towards Enid the fog got thicker and thicker until we couldn't see the ground. We could see the lights of the field glowing up through the clouds, so we knew where we were, but without instrument flight training we weren't capable of safely letting down through the fog. We were wondering what we were going to do, when we saw an opening in the fog, and dove through it to our landing field below. Everyone returned safely that night, but the potential for tragedy was there. Tucker was nicknamed Judge because his favorite saying was, "Don't worry 'bout nuthin' judge," and that night he kept saying it all the way home.

Our training included a solo cross-country night flight. It was a three cornered flight between Enid, Oklahoma City, and Tulsa. We started in the early evening when it was still light, and I flew over Sapulpa, Oklahoma, where Bill and I had spent so many hours trying to thumb a ride to Oklahoma City just three years earlier. I could see the place where our ride from Tulsa dropped us off, and the route we walked to the intersection where we stood for so long. When Bill and I were there I never dreamed I would be flying over that same little town three years later on my way to becoming a military pilot.

As the sun sank lower and lower the ground below us darkened. Things on the ground became less well defined, and I began to see lights here and there from houses and cars and businesses. Eventually I could see only lights as night fell completely. The lights below blinked and sparkled from farmhouses and from cars driving along the darkened highways, and the small towns were aglow with multicolored lights. I always loved flying at night. It really is a magical fairyland.

We were flying under visual flight rules, which means we navigated by looking at the ground, or at least the lights on the ground. Flight navigation now is quite sophisticated compared to what we had in 1942. That night we flew from rotating beacon to rotating beacon, which were about fifty miles apart. If the beacon was located at a landing field it showed a green light after the flashing white light. If there was no landing field it flashed a red light. It seems primitive now. Before we took off from

Enid we determined the compass headings to take from one beacon to the next, and as we started on a given heading we could see the next rotating beacon up ahead of us.

Halfway through this cross-country I realized I had unconsciously pushed the throttle forward until I was at full throttle, but I was still below cruising speed and unable to hold my altitude. This happened so slowly I hadn't been aware of it, and now I couldn't imagine what the trouble was. It was night, I was an inexperienced pilot, and I didn't know what was wrong, so of course I didn't know what to do about it. I saw a rotating beacon down below me with a green light, so I knew there was landing field there, and I thought, "If all else fails (and it was beginning to look that way to me) I might land there." There were no runway lights that I could see, but I knew if I flashed my landing lights they were supposed to turn their lights on for me. But I had no idea whether they had runway lights, or if there was anyone there to turn them on. As a last resort I decided that I wouldn't jump out of the plane, but would take my chances landing blind in the dark if necessary. That was the worst of all the possible choices I might have made that night, so naturally it was the one I made. First I tried to turn on my landing lights, but a fuse must have burned out, because my landing lights went out and never came on again. My situation was getting worse by the minute, and my options were getting fewer. Jumping out didn't appeal to me, but it would have been the best decision, because landing in the dark without landing lights is usually a fatal mistake.

I've heard the expression, "God spoke to me," and that night my own personal angel must have whispered in my ear, because I suddenly remembered a remark a classroom instructor had made about carburetor icing, which can occur even at temperatures above freezing under certain conditions. It happens when moisture in the carburetor begins to freeze, gradually cutting off the flow of gas to the engine. He then continued, "Your carburetor deicing equipment must be used before icing occurs. If all else fails, push your throttle all the way forward, then pull your mixture control all the way off. Lastly, push the mixture control all the way forward. This should cause the engine to backfire, blowing the ice out of the carburetor. It may also blow your carburetor off."

I never would have thought of that advice if I had been asked at any other time, but it came to me at that moment on a dark night in a lonely cockpit with an engine that was failing. Throughout my life it seems that I have had someone looking out for me, and guiding me in the right direction. Could it be my dad, my Grandmother Patton, or my Grandmother Sarah? At any rate I already had the throttle full forward, so I pulled the mixture control all the way back, and waited a second or two before pushing it full forward. There was a tremendous backfire, and my engine suddenly came to life. I thought, "If once is good, twice must be better," so I repeated the operation. Again I got a tremendous backfire, but I really think the second time wasn't needed.

I returned to Enid that night with no further problems, but many other students experienced the same trouble I had with carburetor icing. They continuously lost altitude, even with full throttle, just managing to maintain flying speed low to the ground. Some came back with tree branches in their engine nacelles, and one came back with a telephone wire hanging from his landing gear. A cadet named Marvin Moore landed, got out of his plane, and kissed the ground.

After two weeks at Enid we were allowed to go into town on Saturday, but had to return to the field for bed check at night. We enjoyed getting away from the military atmosphere, and especially from our upperclassmen. After five weeks we were allowed to stay in town overnight, and several times we rented a room at the Youngblood Hotel. We slept three to the bed by lying crosswise, and we usually had some friends who slept on the floor. Our rooms at the Field would have been more comfortable, but it was such a treat to be free, even just for a night, that it seemed well worth the inconvenience.

Earning silver wings was important to us all, but I saw it mainly as something I needed to accomplish to marry Marge. I needed to finish the flight program to earn my commission and my wings to have the money to support us. She was my top priority, and I anticipated marriage by saving every cent I could. I earned seventy five dollars a month as a cadet, and except for haircuts and laundry expenses I spent little. The friends I went into Enid with on weekends had no such motivation. They spent all their money having a good time, and then wanted to borrow from me. I didn't want to dip into my savings, so I would hock my watch with some pawnbroker, and then retrieve it when my friends repaid me. In the meantime I was without a watch. Near the end of the next pay period they would be broke again, and want to borrow again. I hocked my watch three times, grew tired of the process, and finally refused to lend them any more money, which made them angry. They thought our previous arrangement had worked just fine.

When we became upperclassmen at Enid we decided that what was good enough for us was good enough for the new underclassmen. I don't remember doing much hazing, except for occasionally giving them close order drill for the amusement of my classmates. One day as I was collecting my drill victims after lunch I heard a voice ask, "Are you Jack Ford?" It was an underclassman who introduced himself as Johnny Proctor. This was the same Johnny Proctor who had been in my Boy Scout Troop in Wichita Falls, and who had traded his pigeons for my ducks. My drill team escaped that day as I dismissed them to reminisce with Johnny. Four months later he was killed in a training accident at Foster Field.

Ten weeks after arriving in Enid our class was sent to a variety of advanced flying schools. Some went to multi-engine to prepare for bomber squadrons, while others went to single engine to fly pursuit planes (now called fighters). Lt. Glines recommended me for single engine, and I went to Foster Field at Victoria, Texas. When I later became a flight instructor I recommended my best students for single engine, as I think a fighter pilot must have a feel for the plane almost as if it is an extension of his own body. Multi-engine pilots can fly more mechanically. So I was pleased to be sent to single engine, especially in view of Lt. Gline's assessment of my first check ride with Lt. Unruh.

It was a hot June day when we packed up our gear at Enid and headed to the train station where we boarded old passenger cars pulled by a coal-burning locomotive. As the train pulled out of the station I walked to the back of the train, stood in the open doorway, and watched the black and orange checkered water tower get smaller and smaller until it disappeared. I hoped to never see that miserable place again, but I saw worse later.

The weather was hot, and the cars were hot and stuffy, so we opened all the windows to get a little breeze, loosened our ties, and unbuttoned our collars. We wore summer uniforms, but they were made of very heavy khaki with long sleeves. They were a little better than our winter wool uniforms, but they weren't lightweight, and we rode all day and all night sitting up as the soot from the coal burning locomotive drifted in through open windows. We were a dirty sweaty bunch when we arrived in Victoria. We were bused from the train station to Foster Field, and knew what to expect when we arrived. We were tired and disheveled, and we groaned at the thought of upperclassmen again screaming at us. We stepped off the bus and waited for the inevitable, but . . . nothing! Someone finally appeared and took us to our rooms. The next day we were given schedules, taken to the flight line to meet our instructors, and returned to our rooms.

We could hardly believe that there was no hazing, and no formations. We simply walked to ground school and to the flight line on our own. There were coffee and donuts at the flight line in the morning, and cookies and punch in the afternoon. We could get up for breakfast, or not, as we wished, and we could stop at the mess hall at any time for ice cream. Foster Field was a country club. I never had it so good either before or after.

The plane I flew was the AT-6, called the Harvard. It was later renamed the Texan because so many students learned to fly it in Texas. It was about the same size as the BT-13, but it had a six hundred-horse power engine, retractable landing gear, and was heavier and faster. I did everything I did in Basic, but in addition flew cross country flights at altitudes requiring oxygen, practiced instruments, spent time in the Link trainer, and had my first taste of aerial gunnery.

We were training to be fighter pilots, and learning how to stay behind the plane we were trying to shoot down. We trained by "rat racing." Our instructor would lead us to ten thousand feet, and then he would dive and climb, and loop and roll while we tried to stay with him. It was the most fun I had during training, and we all looked forward to those sessions. We also flew night formation and cross-country flights, which, as I was now familiar with carburetor icing, were not nearly as exciting as my first night cross-country flight at Enid.

We expected to be assigned to a fighter squadron, so aerial gunnery and strafing were an important part of our training. For aerial gunnery training we shot at a target pulled by a tow plane at the end of a long cable. Pulling a target was just one step up from combat, because inexperienced pilots were firing at it with real thirty caliber machine guns. I'm sure the pilots of the tow planes didn't think the cables were nearly long enough. We couldn't come at the target directly from behind, because this would put the tow plane directly in the line of fire, so we started firing as we approached at a forty five-degree angle, and stopped firing before we got directly behind the target. I can remember the pilots of those planes making some pithy suggestions to cadets who seemed to forget there were real live pilots in the tow planes who wanted to remain real live pilots.

Foster Field is located southwest of Houston near the Gulf of Mexico, and in July and August it is both hot and humid. Everything else at Foster Field was wonderful, the flying, the training, and the daily routine, but the weather was awful. We were wet with perspiration most of the time. Our summer uniforms were heavy khaki with long sleeves, and we had to wear a tie. The planes had a Plexiglas canopy over the cockpit, and when we were below three thousand feet, especially when we were sitting on the runway, it was like being in a greenhouse. The humidity was so high that after taking a shower we were wet with perspiration before we could even towel off. One Sunday afternoon I took a metal chair into the shower, and just sat on it to let the cool water run over me.

One of my roommates at Foster Field was a cadet named Pappy Jackson. He was called Pappy because he was a little older than the rest of us. He was a crop duster pilot before entering the army flight program, so he was an experienced and accomplished pilot before he started our flight training. Pappy would fly with our flight instructors, and show them things he could do in an airplane that were new to them. Pappy was a good pilot, but his personal grooming left a lot to be desired. He had a chunky build, with a head that seemed to sit on his shoulders without a neck, his face was puffy, which made his eyes mere slits, and he refused to take a shower. The smell was almost more than I could stand. We would say, "Pappy, go take a shower," but he just ignored us. One Sunday while I was in Victoria some of the other cadets dragged Pappy down to the showers, pulled his clothes off, put him in the shower, and scrubbed him with a stiff scrub brush used to clean the toilets and floors. It must have been pretty hard on Pappy, but it didn't improve the smell much, because he just put his dirty clothes back on after the shower. After five weeks we were assigned new roommates, and I was spared having to spend any more time with Pappy. Stinky would have been a better name for him.

All through flight training I kept in close touch with Marge, both by letter and by phone. We planned to be married after I received my wings on September 6, 1942. Our plan was to be married in Covert, Michigan at the Congregational Church. I expected to get my orders on the day I got my commission, leave immediately, and be in Covert in time for our wedding on September 8, the wedding anniversary of my Grandmother Sarah and Grandfather Henry. Marge was going to wear my grandmother's wedding dress, and my Grandfather Henry was going to marry us.

When September 6 finally arrived we had a brief ceremony at the base chapel, and then marched to the flight line to receive our gold bars and those coveted silver wings. There was, however, one important thing missing, our orders. Without them I could not leave Foster Field. I could not go to Michigan. I could not get married in Covert. We were stuck there until our orders came. I immediately called Marge and told her the orders might come the next day, and I could try to get home by driving all day and all night with some other cadets.

We had turned in all of our government issue, expecting to leave immediately after the ceremony, so we were now without towels or bedding. The orders did not arrive that afternoon, so we were also homeless, or almost so. Our rooms were still there, but we had no sheets or blankets. There was nothing to do but go to our rooms and lie down on the bare mattresses. It wasn't much, but it was better than nothing. I hoped for orders the next day, but the next day came and went, and still no orders. I called Marge to tell her I could not get home for the wedding, and we made plans for her to fly from Chicago to Houston via Dallas so we could get married at Foster Field. This all happened so quickly there wasn't time to notify guests of the cancellation. The church was decorated, the food had been prepared, a horse and wagon had been arranged, and some guests actually arrived.

As I look back on it, flying Marge to Texas was an impetuous thing to do. I had no idea where I might be sent, if there would be any place for us to live together, or how long it would be before I might be sent overseas. Maybe impetuous is a little generous. Stupid might be more appropriate, but the angel who was with me on my cross-country flight in Enid was still on the job, and we were able to live together throughout the whole war. I was in love with this wonderful girl, and being married to her was the only thought on my mind. Young people think they can meet any situation and work their way through any problem, and usually they can. At least we did.

Marge's father drove her to Chicago where she caught a plane to Houston by way of Dallas. While she was in the air between Chicago and Dallas my orders came, and I had to leave within the hour. I was originally scheduled to go to March Field in California to train in the P-38, a plane I would have loved to fly, but before we left my orders changed, and I was sent to Goodfellow Field in San Angelo, Texas to become an instructor in the BT-13, the same plane I had flown at Enid with Lt. Glines. I asked a roommate who had grown up in San Angelo for the name of a nice hotel, and he suggested the Cactus Hotel. The name doesn't sound like much, but it really was a very nice hotel, and certainly the best one in town. Then I called the Dallas Airport and asked them to page Marge when she arrived to tell her to meet me in San Angelo. I wonder what went through her mind when she received a message sending her to the Cactus Hotel.

In the meantime Marge had her own problems. She received my message at the Dallas Airport, but there were no flights from Dallas to San Angelo. The airline clerk suggested she take the train from Ft. Worth to San Angelo, but she first had to get to Fort Worth. She was nineteen years old, and had never been on her own, so this was a new experience, and I'm sure she wished for someone to take over for her at that moment.

She found a bus to Fort Worth, but the train to San Angelo didn't leave until that evening, so she spent the entire day sitting in the bus station. She then traveled all night on a coach seat, and arrived in San Angelo at nine thirty the next morning. While she collected her luggage all the experienced travelers hailed the few available taxis, and when she finally got everything together the parking area around the station was deserted. She was in a wool suit, the temperature was hot, there were dust and tumbleweeds blowing, and she wondered how she could get to the Cactus Hotel. This was her introduction to West Texas. Eventually a cab came and took her to the Cactus Hotel, and she was given room 922. She was timid in strange situations, and sat in her room the entire day, not going out to look the town over, or even to get something to eat. When I arrived in San Angelo it was two thirty in the morning. I made my way to her room at the Cactus Hotel, and when she opened the door she was dressed in the outfit I had bought nine months earlier for her birthday, a black pleated skirt and a pretty white blouse. She was tired and hungry, but she looked beautiful to me, as pretty as I remembered her.

When I arrived at the hotel I asked the desk clerk if there was a room I could rent for the night, and learned they were full. I told Marge about the room situation, and asked if I could sleep on her floor for the rest of the night, but she was an old fashioned girl, and there was no way she was going to let me spend the night in her room until we were married, even under these circumstances. I loved her because she was pretty, she was bright, and she had a wonderful sense of humor, but also because she had good moral values. I admired her for it, but it did seem a little hard refusing me a place on the floor under those circumstances. But knowing defeat when I saw it, I said goodnight, picked up my suitcase, and headed for the only other hotel in town, the St. Angelus.

I met her for breakfast the next morning, and then reported to Goodfellow Field for indoctrination. During a break that morning I asked if I could have a ten day leave to go home for my wedding. I thought we might salvage some of our plans, but the request was refused. The training command was being expanded, and they needed all the instructors they could find, so I called Marge to tell her I couldn't get a leave, and we made plans for a wedding that night at the post chapel. I contacted the chaplain,

Captain Archie Manes, to set the time, and asked a friend of mine, Claude Phillips, to be my best man. Claude assured me he would be there for the eight o'clock wedding. I went back to the Cactus Hotel after finishing work at Goodfellow that afternoon, and was admitted (!) to room 922 to take a shower and get dressed for the wedding. I wonder what it was that made me persona non grata after the sun went down.

I called a taxi to take us to the chapel where the minister and his wife and their children had already arrived. He had arranged for an organist, but there was no Claude Phillips. My "friend" Claude never showed, and I had to go out behind the church to find a cadet who was walking off demerits to be my best man. I'm sure he was delighted to have an officer relieve him from walking tours for a few minutes. I had no idea who he was, and to this day don't know his name. He and the minister must have done a good job, though, because it is now fifty-five years later and our marriage is still intact. We had a double ring ceremony, with rings I bought in Victoria. I had no trouble putting the ring on Marge's finger, but when she tried to put the ring on my finger my hand shook so much that she had to hold my hand with her left hand in order to get the ring on my finger. Through the years I have been reminded of that many times. My story is that when I heard she was coming to Houston I slipped out of Victoria in the middle of the night and went to San Angelo, only to find her waiting for me when I arrived in the wee small hours of the morning. I then knew that it was hopeless, so I married her.

Since we didn't have a car we begged a ride into town with the chaplain and his family. We ate at the hotel, and had a dinner of enchiladas with lots of onions. We bought some mints after dinner, but I doubt it did much to smother the onions. Goodfellow Field was a training base for young fliers, and that night they were night flying. I remember sitting in the room, looking out the ninth floor window, and watching the planes with their red and green running lights. We have been back to San Angelo several times, but Goodfellow is no longer a flying school, and the skies are now empty. It doesn't seem right not to see those Vultee BT-13s roaming the skies. We always want to return to our past, hoping to find things just as they were so many years ago. I would love to look up one more time to see the sky full of planes, and all of us young again. It is beautiful flying at night, and it is beautiful watching planes fly at night.

Early the next morning Marge and I had breakfast, and then I returned to Goodfellow Field to discover that we were all being given a nine day leave. Such is life in the military. I hadn't been home in nearly four months, so I wanted to go home for the nine days, and Marge, who had just made the trip down from Chicago, was agreeable. We caught the overnight train from San Angelo to Fort Worth, arriving in the early morning and made a rail connection to Chicago.

We didn't have much money between us, just the money I had been able to save from my cadet pay, plus a hundred and fifty dollars I borrowed at the time of my graduation. Marge had a little money from what she earned working that summer at the Chicago Club in Charlevoix, Michigan. We rode in coach, spending three nights in a train filled with servicemen, as all trains were in those war years. Many of the servicemen sat on suitcases in the aisle the whole trip. It wasn't much of a honeymoon, but we didn't have money for anything better. It wasn't until ten years later that we took a trip that might, with some stretch of the imagination, be called a honeymoon, and by that time we had four children.

Marge had just left home to come to Texas, so it wasn't a treat for her to return home so soon, but I enjoyed seeing my family. I was proud of my new officer's uniform with gold bars and silver wings, and I enjoyed showing them off. Marge's folks offered us their house trailer to use at Goodfellow Field, and it required some repairs, so near the end of the nine days I caught a bus to Chicago to board a train to San Angelo while Marge stayed behind to get the trailer ready.

I arrived back in San Angelo, and checked into the Cactus Hotel while I waited for Marge and her dad to come down with the trailer. During the next week I looked for a place to put the trailer, both from the air and on the ground, but couldn't find any place that looked desirable. In the meantime Marge and her dad hooked up the trailer and started south. This was wartime, and many items were simply not available to civilians or to military personnel unless it could be shown they were important to the war effort. Tires were one such item. The tires on the trailer were old, and they had one disaster after another as the tires took turns blowing out. Marge's dad had them vulcanized, but finally they had to give up and limp back home. Marge then called me to say it was impossible to get the trailer to San Angelo, so I stopped looking for a place for the trailer, and started looking for an apartment.

Howard Lorence and I often flew together, and until Marge said they weren't coming with the trailer we would fly up and down the roads leading to San Angelo to look for them. It was then that Howard and I became such close friends. We remained close friends through the years even though we lived almost a continent apart. It was Howard who had stood by the quadrangle with two girls and razzed me as I was walking off demerits at Parks. Howard was a delight, and I felt a real kinship with him. He was fun to be with, and I enjoyed his humor, but a year and a half later Howard left to fly the new B-29. After the war we saw Howard and his wife occasionally when they flew to Michigan to buy a new car, and we always looked forward to seeing them. Howard died in his middle sixties from Alzheimer's disease, as had his father before him. We lost a dear friend, and I miss him.

I looked in the local paper, and saw an ad for an apartment at 16 North Jefferson Street. I took a city bus to Jefferson Street on Saturday morning, walked two blocks to the little white house, and met the owner, Mrs. Hunter. I paid her a month's rent of sixty dollars in advance, and we had a place to live. I was paid a housing allowance of sixty dollars, so I felt I could afford it. We slept in the dining room, and shared a kitchen and a bathroom with the Hunters who lived in the back of the house. It was a minimally satisfactory arrangement, as the Hunters felt free to come into our part of the house at will, but with the shortage of housing we were glad to have it.

Our bed had slats that were just a little too short, and if we took a deep breath or rolled over, the mattress and springs would come down with a crash that could be heard throughout the house. I don't know how many times in the middle of the night we suddenly found ourselves crashing to the floor, but I know we must have been credited for a lot of activity that we didn't deserve. The one phone in the house was in our bedroom, so any time there was a call for the Hunters they had to come into the bedroom to take the call. The Hunters also had a teen-age son named Haskell, and his friends occasionally called him after we had gone to bed. I would answer the phone and then call Haskell to come take the call, and we would be there lying in bed as Haskell chatted. In spite of the inconveniences we genuinely like the Hunters, and enjoyed our time with them.

Life was good for us during the war. I was married to a girl I truly loved, and I had found my way into an elite organization that was held in high esteem. Pilot's wings conveyed a romantic image, and there were movies and songs about us, such as "He Wore a Pair of Silver Wings," and "Johnny Got a Zero." Marge told me that when she went into a store alone she felt invisible, but when I was with her in uniform the clerks fell all over her.

In addition, pilots were paid fifty percent more than non-flying personnel. The difference in pay seems unfair, because there is hazard in flying, but not as much as an infantryman experiences in combat, or a sailor in seas full of mines and torpedoes. I flew as an instructor pilot in friendly country, and no one was shooting at me, although sometimes my students seemed bent on killing us both. I didn't think of the inequity at the time, and gratefully accepted the fifty percent extra pay each month. I didn't fully appreciate my life as a military pilot then, and feel a little ashamed of my complaints about an army life that gave me so much. I really had much to be grateful for, and little to complain about.

In the early days of our marriage we didn't have a car, as I was still trying to pay off the one hundred and fifty dollar loan I had taken out when I graduated from Foster Field. I usually rode the city bus to and from Goodfellow Field, as it stopped about a block and a half from our apartment. Frequently, however, I found a ride with other pilots who lived nearby. One day I rode home with a pilot who told me he had bought a collie pup. I always had a special attachment to collies. They are a gentle intelligent dog, and as a little boy I always wished I could have one. A block from our house in Wichita Falls there was a collie in a fenced-in yard, and every Sunday as I walked to Sunday school I would stop and pet that dog. I also read every book that Albert Payson Terhune ever wrote about his collies, Lad, a Dog, Treve, Bruce, etc. So I suggested to Marge that we walk over to the house where the pup came from.

Marge always wanted a wire haired terrier that she had seen in a movie called The Thin Man. They are cute dogs, but I was in love with collies. When we got there it was a cloudy drizzly day, and one little fellow came over and began biting at my shoe. I picked him up and knew I had found my collie. As I "just happened" to have my check book with me, I wrote a check for twenty five dollars, bundled the puppy in some old cloth, put him under my coat, and took him home. Marge said he should have a good Scottish name, and suggested Robbie after the Scottish poet, Robert Burns. We put some rags in a cardboard box to make a bed, and Robbie came to know that as his box. The first night I had to be at the field all night as Airdrome Officer, so Marge put his box by her bed, but he missed his mother and the other pups, and cried all night. Marge put her hand down in his box so he knew he wasn't alone, and he chewed on her hand with his sharp little puppy teeth until she had to take her hand out before he chewed it off. He soon adapted to being alone, and slept in his box in a corner of the kitchen every night.

When he was small we punished him by saying, "Go get in your box," and he would dutifully run and get in his box. When he was too big to get in the box, if we ordered him to, "Go get in your box," he would go to the kitchen and sit by his box with his head in it. He was a wonderful friend, and I loved him. He grew into a large collie, and was a gentle, intelligent, and playful dog. He was also good with the children in the neighborhood.

America was at war, and I spent nearly four years in military service, but I was not in the war as many young men were. I recognized my extreme good fortune in having married someone I dearly loved, and being able to live a normal life with her. I went to work in the morning and returned home in the afternoon just as one would in peacetime. We also experienced a standard of living we hadn't known before. The early years of marriage should have some sense of magic to them, and ours certainly did. I knew how lucky I was to be in San Angelo at Goodfellow Field.

I wasn't flying the fighter planes I would have liked, but I didn't have anyone shooting at me either. Flying as an instructor pilot was interesting at first, but as the months went by I became weary. Every student, class after class, made the same mistakes as the students before him. Unconsciously I began to think, "Don't they ever learn? They're still making the same mistakes they made a year ago." It's easy to forget that the student you're flying with today isn't the same student you flew with a year ago. Instructors were assigned four or five students who came from primary flight school with about seventy hours flying time. I should have remembered my own problems when I began flying the BT-13. I flew with them for ten weeks, and by the end they would become fairly proficient. Then in came a batch of four or five new students, and I knew before we ever got in the airplane just what mistakes they were going to make. After two years in the back seat of that airplane doing stalls and spins and aerobatics for five hours a day I was weary of it.

My students at Goodfellow were all young men who wanted to do well, and I liked them personally. Russell B. Thayer III was an especially good formation pilot. At the end of each class we had a contest in events such as acrobatics, short field landing over a hurdle, and formation flying, and Russell Thayer won the formation event. Another student was a big blond kid named Boyd Welborn from Houston, Texas. He was an affable kid, and I enjoyed him. I still occasionally think of them, and wonder if they survived the war, and where they are now.

I also remember some students I probably shouldn't have passed. A student in the first class I instructed, named Farenbach, looked for all the world like a dopey cartoon character in the The Saturday Evening Post. He wasn't as dopey as he looked, but he was no rocket scientist either. He flew well enough to get through, and he ultimately returned to Goodfellow Field as an instructor. The students I had misgivings about were all checked several times by check pilots, so I guess I don't have to take all the blame. I remember one student in particular, named Korpac, who was a very poor pilot. Korpac was from Texas, and once asked if he could fly in his cowboy boots, as he thought maybe he could fly better if he could wear them. I told him he was going to have to learn to fly in the same kind of shoes as everyone else.

Students always flew in the front cockpit of the BT-13, except when they were flying instruments "under the hood." Then the instructor was in the front cockpit to act as an observer. Instructors became so accustomed to flying from the rear cockpit that we did as well there as from the front. Since I was usually in the rear cockpit I was always looking at the back of the student's head. The student was expected to keep his head moving as he looked for other planes, because there were many other students and instructors in that same area. Korpac knew I was back there rating his work, and he kept his head moving, looking for other planes, but as he turned his head from side to side I could see him rolling his eyes as far around as possible to try to see what I was doing. He was giving more attention trying to see me than he was watching for other airplanes. I once told him to stop looking at me. I wasn't going to jump out, and he should concentrate on looking for other planes.

Korpac's coup de grace came the night we engaged in night flying from an auxiliary field. I sent him around the pattern solo to shoot night landings while I sat on the ground and watched him. We had two way radios, and I suddenly heard Korpac calling the radio control to say he was lost. I thought, "How in the world can somebody get lost in the traffic pattern?" It soon came to light that he had gotten lost on the ground. He had his plane at a far corner of the field with the nose of the airplane up against a fence. There was no way to back up, so he had to shut the engine off so he could be turned around and headed in the right direction. I don't know who was the bigger dullard, Korpac for his lack of judgment, or me for not washing him out. He was a poor cadet, and was never going to command respect from anyone.

Another cadet was a boy named Roman. He was a nice kid who flew pretty well, but he became helpless in one situation. When I asked Roman to do a two-turn spin to the right or left he would do it perfectly. But he had trouble with snap rolls, and often fell out of them into a spin. When this happened he simply couldn't recover. I tried to talk him out of the spin, but I always ended up having to recover for him. I told him to give full opposite rudder, then neutralize the rudders and pop the stick forward. Roman knew that, but he panicked when he fell into a spin unexpectedly. He should have been washed out, and I was wrong in not doing so. Instead, I made sure he went into multi-engine advanced where he would never have to do another spin. Actually, the BT-13 would recover from a spin all by itself if the pilot gave it a chance. I have taken students up to ten thousand feet, put the plane in a spin, and then taken my hands off the controls. It would make several turns, almost stop turning, start spinning again, and then repeat the process. Every time the spin slowed it would almost recover itself. All the pilot had to do was to start flying when it slowed down.

Several short cross country flights were planned for each class. These cross country flights were usually to two check points, where a couple of instructors acted as the tower so students could check in before they landed. The students would then take off for their next check point. This gave the student experience in navigation, radio communication, and landing at a strange field. Prior to taking off on a solo cross-country the student had to plan the altitude he would fly, the distance of each leg, how long he expected it to take, and the effect wind direction and velocity would have on each leg. We didn't have the navigational aids pilots have now, so the student had to keep track of his position every step of the way. If he began day dreaming or looking at the scenery he could get hopelessly lost.

Once you were lost, it was almost impossible to find out where you were. There are no road signs up there. If a student did get lost the instructor had to fly to wherever the student landed to lead him home. I once got a telephone call from Big Spring Army Air Field at Big Spring, Texas, saying one of my students had gotten lost, and had landed there. This was on a Friday, so I should have had the next day off, but instead I had the pleasure of flying to Big Spring on Saturday to lead him home. Little did I dream that twenty-five years later my son, Jim, would get his Air Force wings at Big Spring.

A classmate of mine at Enid, Adolph Komer, got lost on a daytime cross country flight when he opened his canopy to get some air, and the wind sucked his map out of the cockpit. Hours later we received a telephone call that Adolph was in Dodge City, Kansas. He had stumbled across a military field there and landed. Any cadet who got lost at Enid had to wear a boot around his neck. The boot had a spigot attached to the heel, and the implication was that the wearer was so dumb he couldn't pour water out of a boot. Adolph wore the boot for the next couple of weeks.

There were ways a lost pilot might save himself. One option was to fly low over a railroad station or water tower to read the name of the town. We practiced this with all of our students so they would know how it was done, but we had hundreds of students at Goodfellow Field, and the small towns around us soon complained about pilots flying over their train stations and water towers. After that we simulated the procedure by flying over a windmill away from town to demonstrate how it was done.

Late one morning I demonstrated this procedure, using a windmill that I could see over a little rise. As we crested the rise at treetop level I saw a farmer on a piece of farm equipment being pulled by a team of horses. We were on them in a flash, and as we flew over the horses bolted across the field, raising a huge cloud of dust. The dust hid the farmer, but I could see his hat come spiraling up through the cloud. When the dust cleared the farmer was sitting where his horses had come to a stop up against the corner of the field. I know he couldn't back his equipment out of that predicament, so he must have unhitched his team to get it pulled away from the fence, and I was glad that I couldn't hear all the nice things he was probably saying about me.

Marge and I lived with the Hunters until after the first of the year. In January my flight commander, Jake Greenwell, told me that he was being transferred to fly heavy bombers, and asked, "Ford, would you like to have our apartment? It's a real nice place, and I'm paying only thirty dollars a month." We were paying sixty dollars a month for the room we had, so Jake's offer sounded wonderful. His landlord was a rancher named Marion Balch who also had a feed store in town. Marge and I moved into the small furnished apartment at 613 N. Jefferson in early 1943, and lived there until the end of October 1944. I stopped at the Balch feed store every month to leave our rent check with the clerk, but in all that time I never once saw Marion Balch. To this day I wouldn't know him if I saw him.

We had no car, and either walked or rode the city bus wherever we went, so Howard Lorence came over with his Buick to help us move. I flew every day, and Marge wanted to get a radio so she would have something to listen to while I was gone. The city bus stopped at the corner where the Montgomery Ward store was located, and one day I went in and bought a portable radio. The bus fare was ten cents, and our house was about two miles from that corner, but I was a child of the depression, and knew the value of money, so I walked the two miles to save a dime.

I never saw Jake Greenwell after he left, but forty years later I read a book titled <u>Bomber Pilot</u> by Major General Phillip Ardery. In the book he said that some of his classmates were sent to Goodfellow Field as instructors, Jake Greenwell being one of them. I wrote to Ardery, and asked if he knew where Jake was now, and Ardery wrote back that he was sorry to inform me that Jake was killed on one of his first flights over Germany. I often think of my cadet classmates and war time comrades, and wonder if they survived. I remember them as young and vibrant, but it was fifty-five years ago that we were cadets together, and not many are still alive.

In today's Air Force the planes are more sophisticated. They require more skilled maintenance, and fuel is limited, so pilots only fly missions that are needed for training. Pilots during World War II were blessed, as I think we flew during the best years of aviation. We had high performance airplanes, and were encouraged to fly as much as we wished. We could ask for an airplane anytime for just about any reason.

My brother Bob and his wife lived in San Diego where Bob worked as a chemist for the Consolidated Aircraft Company. We had several days off between our cadet classes, and I had never been to California, so I planned a flight to San Diego during one of our breaks. The BT-13 cruised at one hundred and forty miles per hour, so it was a full day's trip to California, and I took off at seven o'clock in the morning. I first flew north to Sweetwater, Texas, then west to El Paso and Tucson, north to Phoenix, west to Indio and Cochello, and then southwest over the Salten Sea into San Diego. I checked the weather and it looked like the best winds were at fifteen thousand feet, so I climbed to that altitude and headed for Sweetwater.

Between Sweetwater and El Paso I found myself getting very sleepy, so I decided to land at El Paso, lie down in the shade under the wing, and take a short nap. But as I began to let down to land at El Paso I became more awake, and decided I wasn't going to need that nap after all. I did land, but soon took off again for Tucson, climbing back up to fifteen thousand feet. I hadn't flown very long before I began to feel sleepy again, and decided I really would land at Tucson to take that nap. Once again, as I let down for my landing at Tucson I began to feel wide awake, and in no need of rest. At that point I finally realized what was happening. I was experiencing oxygen starvation at fifteen thousand feet, and the plane had no oxygen, so the solution was to get down to where the oxygen was. I dropped down to ten thousand feet and flew the rest of my trip to California and back wide-awake. I was still an inexperienced pilot, and we did all of our instructing at medium altitudes, so I never thought about oxygen. Every day was a learning experience.

I made the trip to San Diego three times while I was a Goodfellow Field, and came to know the route well. I always landed at Lindberg Field in San Diego, which was a Navy airfield. Our third son, David, became a Navy pilot thirty years later, and he frequently landed there also. That field was named after the aviation pioneer, Charles A. Lindberg, who was the first person to fly across the Atlantic Ocean non-stop in 1927. I had a student at Goodfellow named Charles A. Lindberg, who was not the same man, of course, but I have had fun on occasion claiming I taught Charles A. Lindberg how to fly.

At Goodfellow a new instructor had to be accompanied by an experienced pilot on a long cross-country flight before he could go by himself. On my last trip to California in the BT-13 I led a new instructor named Ralph B. Filburn. Fil was a free spirit if there ever was one. He and his wife became close friends of ours, and we had many good times together. As Fil and I were planning our trip, two enlisted men asked if they could fly with us. One was Jesse, a dispatcher in our squadron who rode with Fil. My passenger was from the physical education department. Our route took us directly over Jesse's hometown, so when Jesse asked if we could buzz his home we jumped at the chance. Fil followed behind me as we rolled our planes into a split S, and dove straight down. We flew over Jesse's house, then climbed back up into the sky again, and dove on the house once more. We made three passes in all before heading on to El Paso. We landed at Burbank, where Fil and both passengers were staying, and I went on alone to San Diego. When I returned to Burbank three days later Fil was there and Jesse was there, but my passenger had left a message saying he was taking the train back to Texas. Stalls and spins and aerobatics were our meat, but my passenger obviously didn't share our appetite for thrashing around in the sky. It was so routine for us that I never gave a thought that he might be terrorized by it. I should have remembered how I grabbed the frame of the airplane when Ned Dolan demonstrated a stall on my first flight in primary.

There was one other time that I thoughtlessly upset a passenger. When we introduced students to night flying an instructor was assigned to check for bad weather moving in. I had that assignment one night when there were big white billowy clouds with peaks and valleys and tunnels through them, and a bright full moon overhead. The most fun I had was flying up and over and down into the valleys and through the tunnels in clouds at night by the light of a full moon. It is simply beautiful, as near to being free as a bird as one can get. I checked the weather, and came in to land for a short break, when a young enlisted man approached me and asked if he could have a ride. I said, "Sure, glad to have you," outfitted him with a parachute, and strapped him tightly in the back seat. We took off and went back up to those beautiful clouds where I played tag with them for a little while, then went into a split S, followed by a loop into a slow roll, and finished with a snap roll. I didn't do those maneuvers to impress the passenger. In fact, I hadn't given him a thought. I was just relieving boredom and having fun. I suddenly realized, by the smell, that my passenger had not found that flight fun. I asked him if he was sick, and he just nodded yes, being too sick to talk. I immediately landed, shut down the engine, and apologized to him for not having thought of him when I rolled the plane over, but it hadn't occurred to me at the time that it was anything unusual. I have often wondered if this was his first flight, and if he ever took another.

One night I suffered vertigo and became dizzy while introducing a student to night flying. In a plane that can be fatal, especially to a young pilot. It happened to me that night in the traffic pattern. As I turned on my approach to the runway I looked down in the cockpit, and when I looked up again the world seemed tilted, and I couldn't orient myself. An inexperienced pilot might easily have flown into the ground, but I immediately looked at my instruments and could see that I was in a turn to the left. Now it all made sense. The world was still level; it was I who was in a turn. I had unconsciously begun my turn to the field as I looked down in the cockpit, so when I looked up I felt I was still flying straight and level while the world appeared tilted.

Instructors were required to fly so many hours of night flying, and so many hours of instrument flying each month. Since it was more fun to fly with somebody, Howard Lorence and I met at the field one night, got a plane, and decided we'd take turns flying. Howard flew the first couple of hours, after which we landed and I took the front seat for my turn. Howard was relaxing in the back seat, just keeping me company, and as it got later he fell asleep. I decided to have a little fun with him by turning the fuel selector valve to the off position. When the motor sputtered and died Howard came to life, and was out of his seat like a shot. I could see his wild eyed look in my rearview mirror as he opened his canopy and disconnected his safety belt to jump out. I had to tell him to sit down, and that it was just a joke, as I turned the gas back on to restart the engine. Howard reminded me of that incident every time we got together through the years.

Wichita Falls was an hour's flight from San Angelo, and I flew there occasionally on training flights. One night I was going to fly instruments under the hood, and took Jesse (the same Jesse who had flown with Fil and me to California) as my observer. When practicing instrument flying in clear weather the pilot flew in the back seat under a hood, and had to have an observer in the front seat to watch for other planes. We landed at Sheppard Field in Wichita Falls after dark, stayed only a few minutes, and then took off again to return to San Angelo, but within ten minutes all the lights in the cockpit suddenly went out. I couldn't see the instruments I needed at night, so I turned back towards Sheppard Field.

A few minutes away from the field I turned on my landing lights only to have them come on for a moment and then go out. I tried to call the tower, but the radio was dead as well. I buzzed the tower at eye level, which told them I had no radio and wanted to land. They shot me with a biscuit gun, which is a gun that emits red, green, yellow, or white light. The red light told the pilot not to land, while the green light gave approval to land. We received the green light, but Sheppard Field was still in the process of being built, and they had no runway lights yet, so a jeep was sent out to park at the end of the runway with his headlights shining down the runway to guide us. We made our landing and I called Marge to tell her we would stay there overnight, and would come home the next morning. The plane was in the same condition the next morning, but the engine ran OK, so Jesse and I flew home without lights. On our return we flew over a column of twenty tanks on maneuvers near Abilene. Playing fighter pilot, I rolled the plane into a split S, and dove on the tanks. They immediately went into a circle in some kind of protective formation, as Jesse and I continued to "strafe" them until we were satisfied we had destroyed them all. After our victory we headed home.

In 1943, my Grandfather Patton was still living in Wichita Falls, as was my Aunt Lavern, and one weekend Marge and I decided to visit them. It was a temptation to smuggle Marge in the plane to fly to Wichita Falls, but I could see more trouble down that road than I really wanted to face, so I put Marge on a bus, and then went to the field to fly. When I left I decided to see if I could find her bus. I knew it went east to Ballenger, Texas, and then would head north, so I flew to Ballenger, turned north, and soon saw a single bus on that lonely Texas highway. The average motorist was limited to three and a half gallons of gas per week during the war, so there was almost no other traffic.

It was a typical West Texas summer morning, the passengers had been traveling for a couple of hours by that time, and it was getting hot. I guessed both the passengers and the driver were relaxed and half-asleep. Marge later told me that everyone on the bus was dozing. The temptation was too much. I put the propeller in low pitch for maximum noise, flew just a few feet over the top of the bus, and then pulled up and kept heading north. I had learned something at Parks; don't make a turn that will expose those big numbers on the side of the airplane for all the world to see. Marge said everyone became wide awake as I roared overhead, and were asking who that crazy pilot was as the bus driver swerved over the road for a second or two. Marge, of course, knew who it was, but she wasn't talking. I met her at the bus station in Wichita Falls, and we spent a nice weekend with my aunt. Sunday afternoon I put Marge back on the bus for home, but spared the passengers and their driver the excitement the others had experienced.

Without radar at our training bases we were free to enjoy ourselves once we were out of sight of the field. Many times I taxied out to take off with a student, and saw a friend next to us also waiting to take off. I would hold up my hands as if they were two planes, one behind the other, signaling, "Let's take off in formation," and we'd improvise from there. There were some days when there was absolutely no breeze, and flying the plane was like sitting quietly in a chair. There was no movement of the air at all. In these conditions it was easy to fly formation, and to put the wing of my plane close to the body of the lead plane between his wing and tail. I occasionally put my wing tip under his wheel and lifted his plane, or put my wing tip under his wing tip and nudged him into a turn. It was also fun to fly aerobatics in formation, especially when the skies were calm.

An instructor who graduated with me, named Johnny Bonner, was from Corsicana, Texas, and always declared that when the war was over he was going back to "rodeoing." For a time Johnny lived in the other side of our duplex. One morning Johnny took off as lead, and I took off on his wing. As the day was absolutely quiet I tucked my wing tip in close to his fuselage between his wing and tail. Suddenly, as a joke, Johnny cut his throttle, and I immediately dove to get underneath him, but Johnny also dove. I'll never know how I avoided running into him. The rule in formation flying was to dive underneath the lead plane if you found yourself overrunning the leader. If we pulled up, the lead plane would be underneath our wing and couldn't be seen. By dropping underneath we kept the lead plane in constant view so we could quickly slide up into position again.

When I found myself overrunning Johnny I dove, and when Johnny dove I simply had to keep diving to try to avoid a mid air collision. We did avoid it, but I'll never know how. Johnny told me that he and another instructor one quiet morning taped a six foot string between their planes, wingtip to wingtip, took off and flew around in formation, and landed with the string still attached to both planes. Johnny was no boaster, so I believe him. I do believe that instructing made us better pilots, because we were constantly analyzing our student's flying, and demonstrating how a maneuver should be done. Virtually all of our flying was teaching the basics of flying, stalls, spins, take offs, landings, and instruments, and we became better pilots as a result. Some of my classmates who flew overseas returned with as little as seven hundred and fifty flying hours, while I had twenty-five hundred flying hours in the same amount of time. It had to make a difference.

In the spring of 1943 we still didn't have a car, but I had paid off the loan I took when I had graduated from flying school, so we were free of debt. We were expecting a baby in July, and a car would be a great help to us. So when Mother told us that the local Pontiac dealer in Hillsdale had a 1941 Pontiac in excellent condition, and asked if we would be interested, I happily said we would. The price was $1,050, and three years later I sold it for $1,035. During the war automobile companies only made cars for the military, so to find a recent model car that had low mileage and good tires was a lucky find. Civilians were limited to three and a half gallons of gas a week, and the national speed limit was thirty five miles per hour, even on the highways, so cars weren't driven much. Some professions, such as doctors and ministers, were given a ration card for more gas. Mother bought the car, and with her friend, Amy Betts, drove it down to Wichita Falls where my Grandfather Patton still lived. She was able to get extra gas stamps from the Ration Board because she was bringing a car to a service man.

I borrowed money from a bank in San Angelo to pay Mother when she delivered the car. But I was anxious to see it, so I flew up to Wichita Falls, and met Mother and Amy there, and was delighted with the car. It was a Pontiac Silver Streak, black with red wheels. I kept that car spotless, washing and waxing it every weekend. I flew back down to San Angelo, and drew a picture of it for Marge. Mother came down to San Angelo with Amy in the latter part of June so she could be there when our first child was born.

For over a year and a half I had been flying in skies that had plenty of room in spite of the number of planes around there. I could turn and climb and let down at will. When I got in our car the first time I realized I had forgotten how busy traffic could be, even though there wasn't much of it in San Angelo back then. Now I was suddenly aware of cross streets, on-coming traffic, and stop signs that interfered with getting from point A to point B. It really was a surprise to me, and took some time to get used to again.

When I met Marge she was seventeen, and had never driven a car. After Jack was born I taught Marge to drive so she could get out to shop or visit friends. As with any new driver it took her some time to master the coordination of the gas pedal and clutch. Most beginners make the car jump and jerk until they get the hang of it. Marge practiced with me until she finally became confident or desperate enough to drive by herself. Occasionally I would fly over our house, and look down to see if the car was there. One day I flew over, and saw our car coming up Washington Street towards Caddo, which was just a couple of blocks from our house on Jefferson. As I circled overhead I saw her stop at the intersection, start up with a jerk, and then stop, obviously having killed the engine. She repeated this a couple more times before finally turning the corner and driving into our driveway. That afternoon when I came home I casually asked her what she had done that day, and she told me where she had gone. When I asked if she had had any problems, she said, "No."

I said, "You had a little trouble at the corner of Washington and Caddo, didn't you?"

She looked puzzled, and asked, "How did you know?" I told her I was directly overhead, and had seen the whole exercise. It must have been quite some time before she drove without checking to see if I was up there spying on her.

In late July Marge's folks came down with their trailer, having found some decent used tires. The baby was due to arrive on July 24th, but at 11:00 p.m. we decided it wouldn't arrive that day, and went to bed. Within a half hour she told me her water had broken, and it was time to go to the hospital. Both grandmothers went to the hospital with us, as this was the first grandchild for either of them. Howard Lorence also came to the hospital to give moral support to the expectant father, and he stayed until Jack was born about seven o'clock in the morning, July 25, 1943. Saturday, July 24th had been a hot day, one hundred thirteen degrees. After the baby was born on the 25th I went home to take a shower and change clothes before coming back to see Marge and Jackie. When I returned to the hospital I wore my wool dress uniform, and took some homemade ice cream. When she saw me in my dress uniform she asked why I was wearing such warm clothing, and I told her that it was cool that day, only ninety-eight degrees.

Jack was born feet first, which let him avoid the beet red color so many babies have. When the nurse showed him to me for the first time he had a nicely shaped head with light blond hair. He was a handsome little fellow, and we were delighted to have him, but he forever changed our carefree lives. The first time we decided to see a movie after his birth we got ourselves ready to go, and then suddenly realized, "We can't go. We have a baby!"

Most of our social contacts in San Angelo were with other pilots and their wives, and we frequently had parties at each other's houses. Our only other social activity was the Methodist Church, which we chose because it had the best choir. I sang many solos there on Sundays, including the baritone solos in Handel's Messiah, and The Seven Last Words at Easter. One Sunday a lady walked into the choir room after church and asked if I was the Jack Ford who once lived in Wichita Falls. When I said I was she told me that she was Margaret Vance, my seventh grade math teacher at Zundelowitz Junior High School. She was my all time favorite teacher until she had to share that honor with my own mother and a high school history teacher named Virginia Grommen. Margaret Vance was always warm and kind, and made math class the one I most looked forward to.

I invited her to our duplex, and we took her to the officer's club for Sunday dinner. Then she left to return to Wichita Falls, and I never saw her again. I told her that Sunday that she had been my favorite teacher, and that I had thought of her many times through the years. I also took an art class at Zundelowitz from a teacher who made that class something to look forward to. I made a hot pad for my mother as a Christmas present in that class, drawing a picture of a bucking horse with a cowboy riding him, and then cut it into a square of linoleum and painted it. Forty years later Mother gave it back to me when she moved into a retirement home. The linoleum has cracked, but we still use it.

I flew from San Angelo to Wichita Falls in 1943, and out of nostalgia visited my old schools there. When I went to Zundelowitz I learned that the dour Ms. Dickenson was at that hour supervising a large study hall, so I walked into the study hall in my uniform, and asked if she remembered me. She took a brief look, and said that she didn't. I said, "I thought you'd never forget me, I'm Jack Ford." She looked at me without any change of expression, not a smile or a word, and appeared just as unpleasant as I remembered her. I silently wished her a rotten day and left.

There weren't many garden spots in West Texas, but one day some of us decided to find a place where we could go for a picnic. I flew around looking for a location for our picnic, but had no luck. Then I heard of a place called Ben Ficklin that had a stream and some shade trees. It was out in the country south of town, quite removed from any roads or houses. We decided to go there the next weekend, and all made picnic goodies to share. I made homemade ice cream. We parked and carried our food, and our new baby, until we found a nice area for our picnic. Howard Lorence and his wife, Bobbie, came also. Marge and I have returned to San Angelo several times through the years, and recently found Ben Ficklin again for old time's sake, but what had been a secluded place out in the country is now a city park next to a divided highway.

We were close friends with Howard and Bobbie, and visited each other often. They usually came to us, as we had a baby that restricted our ability to pick up and go, and I used to swear that Howard had some kind of sixth sense, because I never made homemade ice cream that Howard didn't suddenly appear on the scene. Howard would always say, "You crank, J.P., and I'll help." His "help" was to sit on the freezer to hold it still while I cranked. After the ice cream was frozen Howard would "help" eat the ice cream off the dasher, and then have a bowl. There are times of my life I wouldn't want to re-live, but there are also many moments I would dearly love to savor again, and turning the crank with Howard sitting on the freezer "helping" me is one of them.

Shortly after we moved into our duplex a young lieutenant and his pregnant wife moved in next door. He was a bombardier from Concho Field, a training facility for bombardiers on the west side of San Angelo. Most bombardiers were young men who had washed out of pilot training, but he still wished to fly, and was taking flying lessons at the local civilian airport. One afternoon he had an engine failure right after takeoff, and tried to make a one hundred and eighty degree turn back to the field. But he was low and slow, and when he tried to stretch his glide path by pulling back on the stick it caused the plane to stall. In this case it killed him. Ned Dolan taught me at Parks Air College that it's better to fly straight-ahead to an emergency landing instead of trying to turn back to the field. Most accidents are the result of poor judgment, and there was probably a reason why this young lieutenant had washed out of pilot training.

A number of deaths occurred during the two years I was at Goodfellow, and I think every one of them was the result of pilot error. They were all sad, and they all caused broken hearts. One involved a young instructor named King. He was a tall handsome man who hadn't been instructing very long, and he was getting married on a Saturday afternoon. We didn't always fly on Saturday, but if our students got behind in their flying time we had to fly Saturday to catch up. His fiancée and his parents were in San Angelo waiting for him, but on his last flight that morning his student stalled in the landing pattern, and the plane dove into the ground, killing them both. It was a clear case of pilot error. The student made a mistake, and Lt. King wasn't watching him closely enough. It was particularly tragic, and resulted in the needless loss of two lives. When I flew with students I always had my hands on the stick and my feet on the rudders when we were near the ground. I kept my touch light enough that the student didn't feel it, but I was on the controls with my eyes on the airspeed.

After the young bombardier was killed, Johnny Bonner and his wife, Mary Margaret, came to live there. Johnny was a character, a slight kid about five feet four and a hundred and fifteen pounds. Johnny had done some "rodeoin" while in high school and college, and said that after the war he was going back to "rodeoin." He was all Texan, and all cowboy. Every morning we could hear him singing, "Roses pressed in a Bible bring back sweet memories of you," in his Texas twang. Today, over fifty years later, if I call Johnny and start singing, "Roses pressed in a Bible," he will laugh and call me by name. Johnny stayed in San Angelo after the war, and today he looks more like a cowboy than he did during the war, with deep sun and wind induced wrinkles.

Johnny volunteered to go to P-51 training, and ended up in England. I remember him writing, "Don't volunteer for combat flying." I didn't need that experience to know it wasn't as good a deal as I had at Goodfellow. Johnny had been a classmate of mine in cadets, and when he went to England he did so with another classmate, Wendell Beatty. Wendell was shot down over the English Channel, and we assumed it was during a combat mission. Later I heard he was returning from visiting the ladies in Paris, but after all these years I suppose we ought to give him the benefit of the doubt.

After Johnny and his wife left the duplex Bob Jones moved in. He was the chief of surgery at Goodfellow Field Hospital. Bob's brother-in-law was a major named Johnny Saad, who was the Provost Marshall in charge of the military police. Bob didn't like Johnny Saad, and wasn't shy about making it known. Bob once told me he couldn't imagine how Johnny Saad ever got the job of Provost Marshall, because he didn't think Johnny could track an elephant through a three foot snow. Bob also disparaged doctors, saying, "Most of our patients get well in spite of what we do for them rather than because of what we do for them."

Having Bob Jones in the other side of the duplex turned out to be convenient for me, as the hernia the doctors missed when I entered the service had grown much larger. I arranged for a plane to fly out to California to visit my brother, but I knew the hernia was larger, and thought I ought to have it checked. So I walked over to Bob's side of the duplex, and told him I knew I had a hernia, and needed to get it repaired. He took me into his bedroom and checked it for me, saying, "It's as big as a house." He thought I shouldn't fly again until it was fixed, but I told him I was planning to fly to California the next day, and would hate to miss it. He though a minute, then said, "Okay, but if you get in trouble with it, I don't know anything about it." I had been flying with it quite awhile, and figured if I could tolerate stalls and spins and aerobatics, flying straight and level to California shouldn't give me any trouble. I made the trip without incident, and when I returned Bob scheduled the operation.

Hernia surgery in those days required bed rest for fourteen days, and then two months in the hospital. After three weeks it was possible to get an overnight pass to go home, but I had to return the next morning. Every day when Bob made his hospital rounds he told the nurse, "Give Lt. Ford a pass to go home." The next morning I would ride out to the hospital with Bob, put on my hospital pajamas, and stand by my bed waiting for Bob to again send me home. This went on day after day until I was finally released from the hospital.

There was stringent rationing during the War. Tires, gas, sugar, meat, shoes, canned pineapple, and many other items could be had only with stamps from a ration book. Many items that did not require ration stamps were also in short supply, including toilet paper. Toothpaste came in a light metal tube, and you couldn't buy toothpaste unless you brought in your old empty tube to exchange for a new one. Gas was strictly rationed, but those of us who often had to fly at odd hours were given a "B" gas ration status, which gave us extra gas to go to and from the field. By car-pooling we could save enough gas stamps to occasionally take a trip. I didn't smoke, but I bought Camel cigarettes which I could also trade for gas. Sometimes gas station owners would generously give us gas without the stamps because we were in the service.

When I was released from the hospital I was given a nine-day leave, and after counting my gas stamps I figured I could buy enough gas to get us to Michigan and back. I hadn't been home in a long time, and we were both anxious to see our families. Jackie was a year old, and in those days there were no car seats or seat belts, so we put our suitcases on the floor of the back seat, and put blankets over the suitcases to make a level play area for him. Between Dallas and Fort Worth we stopped to get malted milks, and Jackie wanted to taste it, so I gave him a sip. He thought that was the best stuff he had ever tasted, and kept wanting more. I shared mine with him, and when it was gone he lay back in the seat with the most satisfied smile, and the fattest little stomach we had ever seen on him. From that time on he got his share whenever we had ice cream.

The trip to Michigan was uneventful, and we had a nice visit with our families. When we returned to San Angelo we brought my sister, Margaret, and her daughter with us for a visit. I pulled a utility trailer filled with apples and apple cider, and the trip went well until late one evening when the tongue of the trailer broke in the middle of a bridge in Texarkana. It was black out there, and I could hear the apples squish as cars ran over them. Just as things really looked hopeless a carload of young men stopped to help. They had obviously been drinking, but all the sober people had passed me by.

They put the trailer on a flatbed truck, and took it to a shop where I was able to repair it the next morning.

I was supposed to sign in at headquarters before midnight that night, but there was no way I could get there after the trailer broke down. We had supper in Dallas, and I called Fil to ask him to go to Headquarters to sign me in. He did, and we rolled into San Angelo in the wee hours of the morning. I don't know how many times Fil and I did that for each other, but it was several. The last time was twenty-five years later when Fil was stationed at Selfridge Field in Michigan and I was on a two week tour of duty as a reservist. I went home for the weekend, and didn't want to return on Sunday, so I called Fil and asked if he would sign me in one more time. He did and I showed up early Monday morning.

Two months after the hernia operation I received a return to flying form from the flight surgeon, which I took to the director of flying. As I handed it to him, I said, "I have something for you." He looked at it and handed me a sheet of paper saying, "I have something for you, too." It ordered Goodfellow Field to provide fifteen of their most experienced pilots to report to Laughlin Field in Del Rio, Texas to transition into the B-26 Martin Marauder. Fil and I were both on the list. We were supposed to leave San Angelo and report to Del Rio that same day. I called Marge to tell her the bad news, and began to process out of Goodfellow, but there wasn't enough time to complete everything that day, so we finished the next morning. That afternoon we said goodbye to our families, and headed for Del Rio in Fil's bright blue Plymouth.

I thought the barracks at Enid were bad, but the buildings at Del Rio were thrown up hurriedly early in the war, and three years later were still as primitive as when they were built. There were no finished walls, so the two by four studs were what we saw from the inside. The walls were plywood sheets nailed to the outside of the studs, which were covered by black tar paper. We had two bunks, with a table and two chairs between the bunks, and an open closet for our clothes. We kept underwear and socks in footlockers. Fil was a fun guy to live with, and he amused me with his bravado. We both missed our wives, and most evenings we would sit at the table and write to them. In elementary school I was taught penmanship by the Palmer Method, which uses the entire arm to write. It makes for better penmanship than the pinched writing that comes from using just the hand, but moving my entire arm caused the table to shake. After a few nights of sharing the same table Fil finally put his pen down, looked at me, and said, "You and your Goddamned Palmer method!" Through the years Marge has expressed the same complaint, but in a gentler way.

Fil could be blustery and loud, but it was just an act. A young lieutenant named Horsefall had the room next to us. One evening he came over as Fil and I were writing to our wives. Marge had sent me some cookies that were sitting in an open box on my bunk, and Fil suddenly put his pen down and said, "Give me some cookies." Without looking up I said, "No, I'm not giving you any of my cookies." Then Fil demanded, even louder, "Give me the damn cookies or I'll take them." When I told Fil something to the effect that he would pay hell trying he jumped up, knocked his chair over, and the battle was on. We were soon down on the floor wrestling with each other, and the box of cookies ended up in pieces. Only when we began to laugh did Horsefall realize that we weren't serious. Sometime later Fil heard a new lieutenant out in the hall boasting, "I can whip any man in this building." He must have been another free spirit, but Fil was up to the challenge. He walked out into the hall and told the newcomer, "If you'll start with me I'll save you a lot of time." Fil was a character.

Wichita Falls and San Angelo were barren, but they seemed lush compared to Del Rio. It was a dusty little town in a part of Texas not fit for even the sheep and goats they raised there. The temperature often exceeded one hundred degrees, and summer temperatures of one hundred and ten to one hundred and thirteen degrees were typical. No cars had air conditioning, and it was rare to hear of a home being air conditioned. But our summer uniforms were still long sleeved heavy wool shirts and pants plus a neck tie. On hot days it was a toss up whether it was better to drive with the windows down, and get hit by a hot blast of air, or keep them closed and get baked in an oven. I often alternated opening and closing the car windows, and couldn't get even minimally comfortable either way.

About the time we finished our training Marge's dad came to San Angelo by train, helped her pack our stuff in the utility trailer, and drove Jackie and Marge back to

Michigan. There were few places to rent in Del Rio, so I asked the ration board for some good tires for the small house trailer that Marge's dad owned. My request was granted, and I mailed the tire certificate to Marge who put new tires on the trailer. Frank then turned around and drove Marge and Jackie back to Texas, pulling the trailer. They arrived December 26, 1944. I spent Christmas alone, and I was very glad to see them the next day. Frank then had another long train trip back to Michigan. It just goes to show what we will do for our kids.

For Christmas I bought Marge a pretty cameo locket that had a small diamond. It was the first piece of nice jewelry that I bought for her except for her engagement ring, which had an even smaller diamond. I still had a few more days of training in the B-26, and we didn't know where I might be going from there. It was unlikely that I would remain in Del Rio, so I don't know why I dragged my family and Frank all the way down there, but I did. My future was uncertain, but as luck would have it I was one of three pilots out of two hundred who stayed in Del Rio to instruct new students transitioning into the B-26.

The B-26 was a twin engine cigar shaped bomber made by the Glenn Martin Company in Baltimore. Each engine produced two thousand horsepower, and it cruised at 225 miles per hour. It had a short wing, which required it to land at a high speed. The B-25 of the Dolittle Tokyo Raid landed at 90 mph, while the B-26 landed at 150 mph. The B-26 was a difficult plane for inexperienced pilots, and had a high crash rate in the early years of the war. It was called the Martin Marauder, but it had several other nicknames, such as "The Baltimore Whore" (no visible means of support), "The Flying Coffin," and "The Widow Maker."

McDill Field in Tampa, Florida was a B-26 training field, and they had so many accidents that there was a saying, "One a Day in Tampa Bay." Some of my cadet classmates later lost their lives in B-26 crashes at McDill. Senator Truman, later President Truman, headed a commission to investigate the high number of B-26 crashes, and considered a proposal to ground them all permanently, but General Jimmy Doolittle conducted his own investigation and concluded that with an experienced pilot the B-26 was a sound airplane. It was not a plane for young pilots with only a few flying hours.

The B-26 carried a six-man crew, pilot, co-pilot, bombardier, navigator, radio operator, and crew chief. The crew chief was responsible for the maintenance of the plane, and any time the plane flew he was in it. We all thought this was a good system, because if the crew chief had to ride in the plane he would be highly motivated to keep it in perfect flying condition. The noise from the engines was deafening during flight. The pilot and co-pilot sat side by side in the cockpit, but when we spoke to each other we had to lean over and shout. It was a noisy beast. I enjoyed flitting around the sky in the BT-13, but I also enjoyed the B-26. It was a high performance combat airplane, a challenge to fly, and it gave me a real sense of accomplishment.

My instructor at Del Rio was Dick Vaile. Dick was so somber that one day when we were alone, I said, "You know, your students have given you a nickname." When he asked what it was, I said, "It's laughing boy, because they've never seen you smile." Actually, it was the name I had given him, but after that he made an effort to be friendlier. I came to know Dick better when I stayed there as an instructor myself, and now I write him every Christmas. I also saw him again a few years ago in Oregon. When I first knew Dick he was strict and conservative, but when I saw him in Oregon he had turned into a hippy. It sure seemed out of character for the guy I knew in 1944.

Everyone who flew the B-26 had great respect for the plane, and some had fear. An engine failure on takeoff was pure catastrophe. If an engine quit at that time the windmilling propeller created great drag on one wing while the remaining engine was at full speed on the other. This created an almost uncontrollable yaw as the dead engine pushed its wing back while the good engine pulled its wing forward. The pilot had to immediately feather the dead engine (stop the propeller), give full rudder, adjust the trim tabs, and raise the wheels and flaps to keep the plane from stalling. And all of this had to be done almost instantly; there was no time to think. I said a little prayer before every flight, hoping that this would not be my turn to lose an engine on takeoff.

I never had a single engine on takeoff, but I did see one. The pilot was an instructor named Moose Murdock, who lost his left engine just as he left the ground. He literally stood on the right rudder trying to keep the plane going straight, but even then the plane veered sharply to the left, barely clearing a large hanger before disappearing behind it. We all expected to see black smoke rise up behind the hanger, but in a few minutes we saw him coming back around for a landing. He had the name Moose for a reason. He was a big man, and it took all of his strength on the rudder to control the plane until he could trim it up to fly on one engine. Dick Vaile gave all of his students many simulated single engine takeoffs until we became adept at the emergency procedures, and when I became an instructor I did the same for my students. But some instructors were so afraid of the airplane that they never gave their students single engine practice.

I did lose some engines, but never on takeoff. When I was still in training another student and I had an engine that kept cutting in and out. Finally we just shut it down, and called the tower to say that we were coming in for an emergency landing. They told us to land on the right runway, and as we turned onto final approach I saw the fire engine and the ambulance on the grassy area between the two runways. When we landed I looked to my left, and saw another single engine B-26 landing on the left runway. After I got out of the plane I looked over at the other plane and saw Fil climbing out of it.

The trailer that Marge and her dad brought down to Del Rio was no luxury model. Frank had paid a neighbor in Covert to build it some years before. It was six feet wide inside, and fifteen feet long from the back bumper to the front of the trailer hitch. It was only twelve feet in length inside. At the front of the trailer was a tiny sink with a single faucet, connected by a hose to a nearby water faucet. There were no separate cold and hot faucets. The one faucet provided us with both. The sun heated the water in the hose outside, so the water was hot when we first turned it on, but after we used that little bit of hot water the rest was cool.

There was a countertop around the sink, and a small ice box underneath it. It never kept food cold, but it did cool it somewhat. In front of the sink I built a table that was hinged at the wall so we could put it up at mealtime and let it down flat against the wall afterwards. I built two small boxes for Jackie's toys, and we used them for chairs at mealtime. Directly behind this table was a small closet for hang up clothes on one side, and shelves for folded clothes on the other. Next to the two closets was space for a bed. We bought a couch that could be made into a bed from Montgomery Wards, and somehow got it home. By taking the arms off there was just enough room to fit it into that space, but not without a struggle, and I'm glad I never had to take it back out. We also had a small kerosene space heater that we needed occasionally in the winter months. There was no room for a baby bed, so we put a car seat on the floor next to the table, and that is where Jackie slept. We always found him on the floor beside the bed in the morning.

We first parked our trailer at a motel-trailer park named Val Verde, but in a few days found a small lot on the southeast corner of Avenue D & 6th Street. It had two or three small trees, and was much nicer than Val Verde, but the spots with the trees were already taken, so we were out in the sun. I painted our roof with silver paint to reflect the sun, and ordered some floor tile from Montgomery Wards to replace the worn linoleum on the floor. I soon was notified that the tile was no longer available, and my check was returned, but a week later the tile arrived. I contacted Montgomery Wards, but no one was able to resolve the problem, so I had a new tile floor courtesy of Montgomery Wards. I never heard from them again, and enjoyed my new floor even more knowing it was free.

We fixed up the trailer as best as we could, and moved it to the nicest spot on the lot under a big tree after another couple moved out. We were cramped, but we made the best of it, and we knew it wouldn't be forever, because we were winning the war on both fronts. After moving under the tree we soon realized we had cockroaches, but not the kind we had known in the north. These were huge, almost two inches in length. It was an old trailer, and there were cracks and small openings everywhere. When we turned the lights out at night they would come out from everywhere, including our icebox. I sometimes woke up to feel one crawling across my face. I finally found the source. We were parked right on top of the septic tank, and through a small hole I could look down and see them by the millions. We sprayed and did everything we could think of, but we lived with those disgusting things as long as we were there.

As bad as the cockroaches were, what Marge hated even worse were the large rats that inhabited the bathroom. She is deathly afraid of mice, and there is no scale to measure her fear of rats. We didn't have a bathroom in our trailer, so we had to use the communal shower and toilet, and she lived in fear every time she had to enter that place. By the time we left Del Rio at the end of the war Marge was pregnant with Jimmy, and whenever she needed to use the toilet during the night she would wake me to go out and make sure there were no rats in the bathroom. I often flew at night or had to get up early the next morning, and would tell her, "Just rattle the door before you go in and they'll run away. They're afraid of you." But she couldn't bring herself to go there alone, and she tells me she suffered many a night waiting for morning to use the bathroom. I really regret not getting up for her. She was living in awful conditions without complaint, and it seems to me now that getting up for her was the least I might have done. When we hear of young couples now who feel deprived because they don't have a dishwasher or a separate bedroom for each child we think to ourselves, "You should have to live as we did in Del Rio."

The other people living in the lot were an interesting mix. Jack and Ann Herman lived next to us. Jack was a sergeant who worked as an airplane mechanic. Ann was a pretty blond teenager, and they had a little toddler named Jimmy who was about Jackie's age. Ann was the daughter of a doctor, and had known a good standard of living as she grew up. Jack didn't make much money, and had trouble keeping Ann from spending more than he earned. To curtail her spending he gave Ann one dollar a day for all her expenses, including groceries. Ann couldn't stretch her budget that far, so she often came over to borrow money from Marge, promising that Jack would repay us when he came home. Jack always did pay us back, but I think he felt this kept Ann in check. Jack knew that if he gave Ann two dollars she would spend two dollars, and if he gave her three dollars she would spend three dollars. They loved each other, and were happily married, but I heard them having a big fight one night. The next morning they were both smiling and happy as if nothing had happened. After the war Jack became a dentist, and did extremely well financially, so I'm sure Ann has more than one dollar a day to spend now. They have several beautiful homes, always drive a new Cadillac, and belong to an exclusive country club. We knew them when.

A soldier named Roy Mastin lived with his wife and little boy in another trailer. Roy was a warrant officer who was stationed at Laughlin Field, and they led a quiet and orderly life. He was always home promptly after work, and spent the evening in their trailer. Then Roy's wife left to visit relatives, and we soon realized that Roy was coming home drunk at two-thirty or three every morning. His wife was gone for about two weeks, and we grew accustomed to hearing Roy come staggering home in the wee small hours. But the day his wife returned Roy came home directly after work, and never came in late again.

Towards the end of our training Fil decided he was too hot a pilot to waste his talents in a bomber. He was born to be a fighter pilot! Fil was self-assured, and once said, "What I lack in ability, I more than make up for in self-confidence," so he decided to tell his squadron commander that he was a fighter pilot, and that he wasn't going to fly the B-26 anymore. The squadron commander then sent Fil to the Flight Surgeon, who immediately slapped him in the psychiatric ward. When some of us heard about it we went to the hospital that night to visit him, and laughed uncontrollably. After two or three days Fil conceded that his plan wasn't working, and returned to flying the B-26.

At the beginning of the war Fil was a sergeant in a unit stationed at Fort Custer in Battle Creek, Michigan. One weekend his unit went on a bivouac in the Detroit area. His home was in Detroit, so he asked his commanding officer if he could have a couple hours of leave to visit his parents. His request was refused, but Fil slipped out anyway, and visited his parents, returning later the same evening to find that the unit had packed up and returned to Fort Custer while he was gone. When he got back to Fort Custer the next morning he reported to his commanding officer who simply addressed him as "Private" Filburn. Fil remained in the service after the war, and did eventually get to fly fighters, becoming a squadron commander in Japan. He retired after twenty years, and opened an artist's studio in San Angelo that he operated until his death many years later from heart failure. I have many good memories of Fil, and I miss that unique character. He really was one of a kind.

In spite of the miserable conditions at Del Rio there were some advantages. The little Mexican border town of Via Acuna was just across the Rio Grande, and we could buy things there that we couldn't get in the U.S. Via Acuna was even dustier and dirtier than Del Rio, but it was interesting to go there and buy Mexican arts and crafts. We learned to bargain with the vendors, and could usually get things for about half the asking price. There was no gas rationing in Mexico, so we could buy all the gas we wanted in Via Acuna, but for the outrageous price of thirty cents a gallon. We paid seventeen cents a gallon in Texas. All kinds of leather products were available, including things in short supply that required ration stamps in our country. Meat was also available, but we were afraid to buy it because we could see the beef hanging unrefrigerated in the butcher shop window with flies all over it. Texas grew lots of beef, and while we were supposed to have ration stamps for it, it was easy to get meat either on the base or from friendly butchers. One time when I was flying out to California the butcher at our local grocery store let me buy steaks without meat stamps to take to my brother and his wife, a real treat for them.

When Marge's dad drove Marge and Jackie down with the trailer I saw a bull fight advertised to take place in Via Acuna. Neither Frank nor I had ever seen a bull fight, so we decided to attend that one. We left feeling the bull was at a decided disadvantage, although at this bullring the bulls had a better than average chance, because the bullfighters were obviously beginners. One bull hooked the cape with his horns, and flipped it over the bullfighter's head. The bullfighter frantically tried to pull the cape off of his head, but it had somehow gotten twisted. He couldn't see, and could only imagine what the bull was about to do him. He ran around in circles struggling wildly with his cape while others in the ring rushed to divert the bull's attention. The bullfighter finally got free of his cape, but on the humor scale it rates right up there with the time Bob got his hair caught in the washing machine wringer.

The only fatality we had at Del Rio while I was a student happened when we were night flying. Two young men practicing night landings taxied out to take off, and then started down the runway. They just got into the air when the plane went down off the end of the runway and burned. We never determined the cause. One minute they were alive, with their future ahead of them, and in an instant they were gone. The one boy I remember well, as he was always laughing and joking and happy-go-lucky. One morning he came to the flight line with a nice black eye, and when asked how he got it he said, "Oh, some guy said 'shut up' and I thought he said 'stand up'."

While instructing in the B-26 I once gave a check ride to a pilot who was returning to flying after a long absence. He had been an instructor in the B-26 many months before, but was seriously injured in a crash landing, and spent a long time recovering. We flew around a bit locally, and then came in for our first landing. He flew the plane well enough, but when he turned onto the approach to the runway he suddenly threw his hands in the air, and couldn't complete the landing. I climbed back up to traffic pattern altitude, and then gave the plane back to him to try again. He flew around the pattern until he was on his landing approach when he again threw up his hands. I landed the plane this time, and then taxied back to take off again for one more try. The same thing happened the third time. After I landed I taxied to the line, shut down the engines, and reported that I didn't think he was mentally fit to fly. I never saw him again, and don't know if he ever got back into flying. He must have visualized his crash every time we approached the runway.

One of the fun phases of our training was the low-level cross-country we took with each student. We were supposed to stay above two hundred feet, but it is more fun to be right down on the ground where the sensation of speed is the greatest, and that's where we flew most of the time. West Texas is flat barren country, and I remember pulling up to clear barbwire fences. The purpose of the low level flight was to give the student experience navigating without using reference points such as towns or roads to help him. I had one student who thoroughly enjoyed his flight while he looked at the scenery out of his side window. Ahead of us was a large tree that should have been obvious, because there weren't many trees in that part of the country, but the student gazed out of the right side of the plane and then out of the left side, and never looked straight ahead. At the very last minute I pulled back on the yoke to lift us over the tree. He had no idea why I had grabbed the controls until I made a three hundred and sixty-degree turn to show him what he nearly hit. I know death is inevitable, but I wasn't ready to die just yet, and I didn't want people to wonder how I managed to fly into the only tree in sight.

On another low level cross country I flew down a highway that was nearly deserted because of gas rationing. As I flew over a rise in the road I saw a car coming toward me, and as we converged I dropped my nose so it appeared we were going to meet on the road ahead. He turned right, then left, then right again before finally driving into the ditch, leaving the road to me. The ditch was just a shallow incline off the side of the road, so I know he had no trouble getting back on the highway again. I'm a little ashamed of it now, but I was just having fun, giving him a scare.

On another occasion I had just taken off when I saw a road construction crew operating a road grader on the road that bordered our field. The workmen kept an eye out for planes taking off over their heads, and I could see the driver of this road grader watching me. I blame him for what happened. I cut the power on both engines and started down directly toward him as if my engines had quit. He stopped his grader, and then jumped off and started running. Once he started running I gave power to the engines to resume my climb, but I wonder if he told his wife and friends, and later his children about the day a B-26 lost both engines, and he had to run for his life. Flying was fun in those days.

Many of my students had flown B-17s and B-24s in combat, and then returned to transition into the B-26. They were all capable pilots, easy to instruct, and quick to learn, but they needed instruction and time to learn the procedures. Some, of course, were quicker than others. A second lieutenant named John R. Mattingly was particularly good. He was at ease in the plane immediately, and flew well. When he finished the course I lost track of him. Forty years later I saw a notice in The Retired Officers Magazine regarding a reunion, and the contact person was John R. Mattingly. I wrote to him that I had instructed a John R. Mattingly in the B-26, and I got an immediate reply saying, "I'm the guy." The following summer I met him in Austin, Texas, and finally learned why he had been such an able student in the B-26. He came directly from the B-25, another twin engine bomber, and had five hundred hours in it as an instructor himself.

Matt was on one of my last cross-country flights in the B-26. The war was winding down, and I decided to take some items home to Michigan. We were allotted a certain number of days for these trips, and since the day started at one minute after midnight, that was when we took off. We first flew to Fort Benning, Georgia where my sister Margaret's husband was in officer training. After a short visit with her we flew to Wright Patterson Army Airfield near Dayton, Ohio to refuel, and then flew on to Hillsdale to do what every pilot wants to do, buzz his hometown.

I approached the College Tower from the north at tree top level. The engines made a horrendous noise as I lifted one wing to clear the tower, and headed for the College Baptist Church where the college choir and soloists were rehearsing for a commencement concert that night. I then buzzed the City Hall Tower in the center of town, and made a sweeping left turn over the College Field House, my mother's house, and across the campus in front of Central Hall. Remembering Lt. Longino at Parks, I didn't make a return, as I knew people could get our number and report the infraction. That would have caused me so much trouble I don't even want to think about it now, fifty two years later. I then flew to my Uncle Ned's house where Grandfather Henry lived, and dropped down to roof top level between their house and the barn. I made a wide sweeping turn to the right to repeat the same path, and this time I could see my grandfather standing between the barn and the house waving his straw hat as I barely cleared the barn roof.

I then landed at what is now Detroit Metropolitan Airport, caught a ride to Hillsdale, and that evening attended the commencement concert in the church I had buzzed earlier in the day. One of my music professors told me he was getting a haircut when he heard me fly over, and that everyone up and down Main Street ran out to take a look. I still meet people who remember that day.

I spent only a couple of days at Mother's, as we had to be back in Del Rio the following Monday. I had been lucky so far, and decided to make two more low level passes on my way home. First I swung over Pittsford where I had taught school, stirred up the dust in that little town, and then flew west to Covert where Marge and Jackie were visiting her parents. I flew over their house at tree top level, made a turn to repeat it, and this time saw Marge down below holding Jackie and waving. We then headed for Del Rio. I had three students with me on this flight, and I knew they were capable, especially Matt, so I lay down on the floor between the radio operators and navigator's stations, and fell asleep.

I was awakened by one of my students who said, "Lt. Ford, I'm afraid we're lost." I looked at my watch and knew we should be at Del Rio by that time, so I got in the pilot's seat and discovered they had missed the field and flown across the Rio Grande into Mexico. This was absolutely forbidden. I realized the field was directly behind us and had them fly back to the field and land. When I met Matt in Austin many years later I told him I had wondered for years if they were really lost or if they were just testing me. He assured me they didn't know where they were, but knew they should have reached the field by the time they woke me. Apparently it wasn't a test.

In September 1945, after the war had ended, I took my last flight in a B-26 to Walnut Ridge, Arkansas where planes were cut up and melted down for scrap metal. I saw all kinds of fighters and bombers there, waiting their fate, and I cringe to think of it now. They were beautiful planes, and it's a tragedy that they were destroyed. P-38s and P51s could be bought for three thousand dollars at the end of the war. They are worth a million dollars apiece now, but unfortunately I didn't have three thousand dollars at the end of the war. I don't know what I would have done with a plane if I'd had one, as they were much too expensive to fly, but a profit of a zillion percent seems like a good opportunity missed.

The B-26 had a dangerous reputation, and few were converted for use by corporate executives. They were noisy and expensive to operate, and not a safe, reliable plane for business travel. Soon there were no B-26s flying anywhere in the world. There were a few B-26s in museums, but none were getting off the ground. For years I didn't know that there were any even in museums, until I saw one at the Air Force Museum at Wright Patterson Air Force Base in Ohio. I was excited that one still existed.

Forty years later I read about a B-26 being rebuilt by the Confederate Air Force in Harlingen, Texas, and stopped to see it on a trip to Texas to revisit our old haunts. A few years later Marge and our kids arranged for me to ride in that rebuilt B-26. Jack, who was the instigator of the plan, accompanied me on the flight. The man who planned and pushed the program was the head pilot. His co-pilot was a man who had flown the Constellation, a four engine commercial plane. It was a thrill to be on that flight, but a disappointment that neither Jack nor I had a chance to take the controls. I calculated that I was instructing in the B-26 when both of those men were still in diapers. I had five hundred hours flying that plane, and I'll bet it was more than the two of them had together. It was so expensive to fly that they seldom took it up. But flying that infrequently didn't allow them to ever become really proficient in the plane, especially with the loss of an engine on take off. I thought at the time that it was an accident waiting to happen.

These pilots used two procedures that I thought were dangerous. I didn't want to tell them how to fly their airplane, but I did mention to them the procedures we used so many years ago, and why we used them. Before I arrived at Del Rio there had been an accident caused by a pilot bringing the plane in for landing under considerable power with a long shallow approach. He suddenly lost an engine while he had his wheels and flaps down at low airspeed close to the ground, and the drag of the dead engine, combined with the thrust of the good engine, caused the plane to yaw out of control, killing all on board. A new procedure was then established to hold our traffic altitude until we turned onto the approach, so we could land with power off. With this procedure if an engine quit on approach there was little thrust coming from the good engine, and it was easier for the pilot to maintain control. The pilots of the rebuilt B-26 brought the plane in for a landing from a long way out under considerable power. If they lost an engine they would have to deal with all the problems a single engine can give, and I knew they couldn't do it. Not many could, but especially those two, because they didn't constantly practice single engine emergency procedures the way we did.

The other procedure these men used was shared use of the throttles. When the pilot was landing he had both hands on the yoke instead of one hand on the yoke and the other hand on the throttles. The co-pilot controlled the throttles. When I made a landing I wanted to be in control of both the yoke and the throttles, so if I needed power I could apply it immediately instead of asking the co-pilot. If I needed power I wanted it now, not two seconds from now. A few years later these same two pilots were flying the B-26 with three men from England as passengers when they crashed and burned, killing everyone.

Near the end of the war I flew the Douglas A-26. It was a twin engine plane much like the B-26, but it was a much more stable airplane, and a real joy to fly. It was a single pilot airplane. The man in the right seat was a cannoneer who loaded a cannon mounted in the nose. At the end of World War II the B-26 was retired, and the A-26 was renamed the B-26, which has caused no end of confusion. The original B-26 was the Martin Marauder, while the A-26 was the Douglas Invader. The A-26 was the best plane I ever flew, fast, stable, and fun to fly. It was red lined at 350 mph, and I flew it at that speed.

The War Department released service men based on a point system, with one point for each month he had been in the service, plus extra credit for overseas service. I didn't have any overseas service, but I had been in for nearly four years, which gave me enough points for an early release. They were four wonderful and memorable years, even though I didn't fully appreciate it at the time. I was the first member of my family to fly, and I had the opportunity to fly high performance airplanes, accumulating 2500 hours instructing in stalls, spins, aerobatics, instrument flights, cross country flights, and formation flying. It was a rich experience. I felt great pride at the time in being a military pilot in an elite group, doing what few could do, and I'm still proud today that I was a pilot during World War II.

In October 1945 I received orders to report to Romulus Army Air Field near Detroit to be separated from the service, so Marge and I hitched up our trailer and headed north, putting four years of military life behind us. I wouldn't trade those four years for anything. They enriched our lives. As we left I wondered what the future held.

Darwin in the 1890s

Benjamin and Polly c. 1865

Darwin

Julia

Edwin

Alton

Alton stuck his knife in this cherry stump in 1861, and announced that he was going to war.

The Farm from the west.

The Farm from the north.

The Farm from the southwest.

Henry c. 1890

c. 1900. Henry middle back, next to Ruth and Sarah. Robert is in front, and Caroline is in the rocking chair.

Henry's family c. 1900. From the left: Sarah, Ned, Henry, Robert and Ruth

Henry c. 1920

Sarah c. 1920

Henry at age 91 in 1944

Robert, Ruth and Ned in the 1890s

Robert as a young man at Hillsdale
College, c. 1908

Robert at HIlsdale College in 1906

Robert c. 1913

Leithel c. 1913

Robert and Leithel on their wedding
day

Robert c. 1920

Robert and Leithel c. 1915

John, Margaret, and Bob Jr. in 1922

Robert with Margaret in 1921

Henry, Sarah, and Robert in Wichita Falls,
c. 1923, with Bob Jr., Dad, and Margaret

Robert shortly before he died in 1931

Leithel c. age 70

The Country House in Wichita Falls

Dad and Bill riding "Jack"
on Uncle Will's farm

Dad as a young teacher in 1940

Margaret, Bill, Bob Jr., and Dad c. 1933

Dad as a first lieutenant

Mom at age 19 in 1942

Leithel during the war, wearing Dad's wings

Home in Hillsdale in 1942. From the left: Leithel, Margaret, Bill, Jane (Bob Jr.'s wife), and Mom

Dad and Mom posing for their wedding photographs in 1942. Mom is wearing Sarah's 1880 wedding dress.

Leithel, Margaret holding her infant daughter, and Henry at Ned's farm in 1944.

Dad and Fil Filburn on the day they left San Angelo for Del Rio to fly the B-26

In Saline, 1950. From the left: Dad,
Jack, me, and Johnny Rule

Dad with Robbie in San Angelo

Frank Blaney at his desk as register
of deeds in 1954

Dad at the controls of this B-26 in 1945

My maternal grandparents,
Frank and Midge Blaney, c. 1942

Jack and me, 1949

Jack, Debby and me in 1951 with a neighbor girl (in back).

Dad as principal of Saline High School, c. 1950

Christmas 1946. Mom holding me, and Dad holding Jack

Our house at the Saline Valley Farms

Our Farm House in Belleville

Dad as principal of Belleville High School in 1967

Me in 1953 as the bat boy while Dad played in a softball game behind Saline High School

Me on the front porch of our home in
Saline, 1950

Winter 1952. Dad holding Debby, me,
Mom holding David, and Jack

Me climbing into a T-38 at Webb AFB in 1969

Christmas 1956. From the left: Debby, me, David,
Jack, Mom holding Bruce, and Dad

Dad giving me his favorite wings when I
graduated from pilot training

My last combat mission in the EC-47,
Nakhon Phanom, Thailand in May 1973

Pilot Training at Webb AFB in 1969. From the left:
me, Dick Burk, and Nickey C. Lucas

Ray Martinez's wing tip after taking a direct hit
over our favorite waterfall in southern Laos.

Our wedding in 1975. From the left: Hattie's parents, Willie Alton and Louise Stone, Hattie (wearing Sarah's wedding dress), me, Mom, and Dad

Our family in 1985. From the left: me, Hattie, Mary, Jim Jr., and John

Dad and Bill, c. 1985

Our home in Kalamazoo

Mom and Dad enjoying retirement in 1987

Dad and Mom celebrating their 50th Wedding anniversary in 1992.

Mary's graduation from high school in 1999.
From the left: Hattie, me, Mary, Dad, Mom, and Jim Jr.

Mary's wedding to Michael Keller in 2004. From the left: Jim Jr., Hattie, me, Mary
(wearing Sarah's wedding dress), Mike, Mom, John and his wife, Katie with Henry and Bella

Me dancing with the bride.

Six brides who have worn Sarah's wedding dress. From the left: My cousin Sally, Debby, Mary, Hattie, Mom, and Margaret.

A family photograph with Dad and Mom in 2000.
Standing from the left: David, me, Debby, Bruce and Jack.

John, Mary, and Jim Jr. in 2007

Hattie and me in Scotland in 2004

Hattie and me with our grandchildren in 2007.
From the left: Lucas, Simon, Bella, Henry, and David

Return to Civilian Life
1946-1977

*J*apan surrendered in August 1945, and I began to think of the future. I didn't want to make the military a career, because I had flown so much that it seemed like any other job. Several of my friends flew to Chicago to apply to the airlines, and asked me to go with them, but flying from point A to point B for the rest of my life held no appeal for me then. It did later.

We never know what our lives might have been if we had taken a different path. If I had gone with the airlines our lives would have been easier, and we certainly would have been more comfortable financially. Marge wouldn't have had to finish college while raising five kids and substitute teaching. It was a hard road she was on. I was twenty eight when I left the Army Air Corps, a college graduate with twenty five hundred flying hours, five hundred of them in multi engine aircraft. I could have easily gotten an airline job, and I may have let a golden opportunity slip by, but who can say what might have happened if I had taken a different road.

When the war was finally over we started north, first to San Angelo, and then on to Wichita Falls where we stayed overnight with Aunt Lavern. I feel a certain sadness now as I realize that I was forever leaving the most memorable time of my life. I have many times wished I could turn back the clock and live those years over, knowing what I know now, so I could savor them as I should have then. But in 1945 these events were all too recent to appreciate, and as we headed home our thoughts were on other things.

An hour out of Del Rio we drove through a cold front, and the temperature dropped thirty degrees. For the rest of the way back to Michigan we used our car heater. It was a warning of things to come.

A dentist at Laughlin Field encouraged me to go to dental school, but first I had to return to college to take pre-dental classes in physics and chemistry. That would add a year to the three years of dental school, but it didn't deter me, and we made plans to return to Hillsdale College. We had one child, with a second due in March, no job, fifteen hundred dollars in Savings Bonds, no home of our own, and a four year dental course ahead of me. The G.I. Bill paid the school costs of ex-servicemen, plus a small cost of living allotment, but I couldn't live on that. Marge wanted to find an apartment of our own, and we should have, but to save money I moved my family into my mother's house, and everything about it was wrong. It wasn't fair to Marge or to Mother, who still had Bill in College, or to my sister, Margaret, who was living there with her daughter. And I was not academically bent. My grades were good, but school was not something I enjoyed or found easy. I had to work at studying, unlike some who seem to easily absorb the material, and I should have known that I was in the wrong cage. In addition, when price controls were lifted the cost of things nearly doubled overnight.

But I was tenacious if nothing else. I finished my classes at Hillsdale and was accepted into Dental school at both Stanford in California and at the University of Michigan. Stanford interested us, but the cost of trying to live out there was daunting. Ann Arbor was close, and seemed more realistic, so that is where we went.

During the year at Hillsdale a new baby boy was born to us on March 10, 1946. Jackie was blond, but this little boy was olive skinned, and had brown hair. One afternoon in Wichita Falls, when I was just a small boy myself, a friend brought his little brother with him to play. He was two or three years old, with big brown eyes, and was a shy little fellow. I was charmed by that little boy. I never saw him again, but I remember where I was when I saw him. Jimmy was like that little boy, with a dark complexion and big brown eyes. While Jackie was a happy outgoing child, Jimmy was solemn and serious, and seldom smiled. The only way we could get him to laugh was to ask Jackie to, "Make Jimmy laugh." Then he would go play with Jimmy, and Jimmy would give a deep husky laugh.

Jimmy was a daddy's boy, and seemed to prefer me to his mother, a definite advantage to her when Jimmy needed feeding or comforting during the night. After we moved to Ann Arbor we sometimes went to Mother's for the weekend, and if Jim woke up in the night Marge couldn't quiet him, but the minute I took him he would cuddle on my shoulder and quiet down. I finally started sleeping with Jimmy when we visited Mother so if he woke up in the night he could see that I was there, and would go right back to sleep without a sound. Jimmy was a particularly bright little boy who talked in complete sentences when he was eighteen months old. We didn't appreciate his ability, but our parents did.

At the end of the year in Hillsdale I drove to Ann Arbor to look for a place for us to live while I went to dental school. I knew less than nothing about real estate, and bought an absolute disaster of a house at 1334 Harpst Street without Marge ever having seen it. I think either Jack or Jim would have known better. It was a prefabricated house purchased from Sears and Roebuck, and I quickly learned that all houses are not alike. I bought it because it met my basic criterion, it was cheap, but that is the only good thing I can say about it. The front porch had screens that were rusted and torn. The floors needed to be sanded, the walls badly needed painting, the only toilet in the house was so plugged with rust that it barely flushed, and the kitchen had an ancient sink, limited cupboard space, and a worn linoleum floor. In addition to all this the place was filthy dirty, and full of all the junky furniture that the former owners left behind.

I wonder what Marge must have thought when she first saw that disaster. She should have recognized the mistake she made when she flew to Texas to marry me, cut her losses, and run. Before we could move in we had to remove all the junk, and then clean that pig pen. I can't remember how many trailer loads of stuff I hauled off to the dump, and after we finally did get the place cleared we could see weeks of work ahead of us to make the house livable, and I was supposed to start dental school that summer.

In Hillsdale we went to every auction we could to buy things we needed for the house, and in early June we hired a mover to haul our furniture to Ann Arbor. Then we washed and scrubbed the place, and were ready to have our newly acquired auction furniture moved in when the movers arrived. The first night we got Jackie and Jimmy to bed, and retired after a tiring day. We were just drifting off to sleep when I heard a terrible racket coming from the basement. I sat up in bed and said, "What the hell is that?"

Marge answered, "It sounds like a water pump to me."

I said, "A water pump? Don't we have city water?" A quick trip to the basement confirmed that it was indeed a water pump, and no, we didn't have city water. The pump was the darndest looking thing I had ever seen. It had a small centrifugal pump that pumped water into an upright metal tank perched on cement blocks. The noise we heard upstairs came from the tank bouncing around on those cement blocks.

I also discovered that we didn't have city sewer. We had a septic tank. A short time after we moved in our drains began to get sluggish, and then stopped up completely. We called a septic tank cleaner who emptied our tank and told us that the former owners had thrown bottles and cans and ashes into the septic tank. He said it was the worst mess he had ever seen.

Shortly after fixing the septic tank the water pump died. Even though the war had been over for a year civilian goods were still in short supply. While we waited for the new pump to arrive we were without water, except for what we could get from the neighbor across the street. For three weeks we hauled water by the bucket for drinking, bathing, and flushing toilets. The day the pump arrived I installed it, primed the pump, and we had water again. What a luxury.

My first job was to use muriatic acid to clear the rust that clogged the toilet. We then sanded the floors and cleaned out the fireplace. I asked Marge to go to the basement while I cleaned the fireplace, so she could tell me when I had knocked the ashes loose. I opened the trap door in the basement so she could see when the ashes started to fall, and then used a stick to poke at the trap door in the back of the fireplace. Suddenly I heard her yell, and could see that the ashes had broken free and dropped to the bottom of the chimney. On my way down to the basement I met her coming up, absolutely covered with soot. When the ashes broke loose they fell with a rush, and the dust blew out of the trap door, covering her from head to toe. It was in her hair, her eyebrows, her ears, and her clothes, and she had lots of unkind things to say to me.

We next wallpapered our bedroom, something neither of us had ever attempted before. We didn't have any money to hire it done, so we had to do it ourselves. Anyway, wallpapering shouldn't be too hard; we had both gone to college, and I had learned to fly the B-26. I should be able to wallpaper a small room. We bought the cheapest paper we could find, and brought it home with wallpaper paste and some wallpapering equipment. We were ready. Of course the paper, being the cheapest we could find, was thin and flimsy, and tore easily.

It seemed like a good idea to start by wallpapering the ceiling, because that was what people were doing in the magazines we read. We didn't buy anything that wasn't absolutely necessary, so the fact that I didn't have any ladders meant I had to improvise. I stood on our bed, started the paper at the edge of the wall, and then walked down the length of the bed, gluing the paper to the ceiling as I went. I started at the head of the bed, which was against the wall, and then walked towards the foot of the bed, but I quickly discovered that I bounced with each step, and in the center of the bed my bouncing became more pronounced. I had to stick the paper to the ceiling on my way up, because I couldn't reach the ceiling on the way down. By then the paper I stuck to the ceiling at the beginning of this performance had come loose, and was following me down the length of the bed, finally enveloping me. After several increasingly frustrating attempts Marge suggested that she follow me with a broom to hold the paper against the ceiling. It worked, and we finally got the ceiling papered, while liberally pasting ourselves, and making frequent repairs to tears in the cheap paper.

We then sanded and refinished the floors, painted the walls, and bought some unassembled kitchen cupboards that we installed after tearing out the old cupboards. We painted them a colonial gray, and put down new yellow linoleum on the floor. It was a pretty kitchen when we finished, but virtually all of the work had to be done after we put the boys to bed. We usually finished for the night at 2:30 or 3:00 in the morning.

I don't know how we stood the pace, except we were young. We also replaced the rusted porch screen with new copper screen.

At the end of the summer I passed my courses, but I realized that I had bitten off more than I could chew, and withdrew from the dental program. The airlines were beginning to look awfully good to me, but the country was in a recession. My friends who had gone with the airlines had all been laid off, and I needed a job now to support my family. Since I had taught before the war I registered with schools in the Ann Arbor area for substitute teaching, and I found myself doing what my dad had done seventeen years earlier, walking the streets looking for a job. I found one at Montgomery Wards as head of their shoe department. I had worked at Schmidt's Shoe Store in Hillsdale when I was in college, and really disliked it. I didn't like it any better in Ann Arbor, but it was a job, and I brought home forty dollars a week, which would at least buy groceries.

During my hunt for substitute teaching I went to Saline, and talked with the superintendent of schools, Leo Jensen. He had little need for substitutes, but in the spring he came to me at Montgomery Wards and asked if I would be interested in coming to Saline to be the band director and high school principal. I had taught band in both Pittsford and at the Hoover School in Flint before the war, but I felt like a fish out of water, because the only instrument I had ever played was the violin. Fortunately, the superintendents who hired me assumed that a music major could teach anything, and I needed a job badly enough that I was willing to let them believe that. I had decided that I didn't want to return to teaching, but the offer from Leo Jensen was far better than selling shoes, so I readily accepted.

All through the winter I had diligently looked for work. At the end of World War II the government established the Veteran's Administration to provide assistance to the millions of servicemen enrolling in college, so I applied for a job at the Veteran's Administration. About the time I was offered the job in Saline the Veteran's Administration offered me a job at twenty eight hundred dollars per year. Saline offered me three thousand dollars per year. I was afraid the Veteran's Administration might only be temporary, while I knew the Saline schools were always going to be there, so that, plus the extra two hundred dollars per year, found me in Saline in the fall.

Before I was offered the job in Saline a friend from Hillsdale College became a Special Agent with the FBI, and suggested I apply. I had my interview, and my personal investigation, but before I could be hired the FBI instituted a requirement that all agents have either a CPA or a law degree, and that job possibility disappeared. It was a real disappointment, because we had been looking forward to a letter from the FBI telling me when to report. When the letter came saying I couldn't be considered because of their requirements I was not home, and Marge, knowing how disappointed I would be, hid the letter until she could break the news to me herself. I love her for many reasons, and her kindness in situations such as this is one of them. No man ever had a better life's partner.

I was twenty-nine when school started in Saline, and hardly knew what was expected of a school principal, but I gradually learned the job and tried to establish myself with the teachers and the community. Saline was a small school, with seven or eight teachers in grades seven through twelve, and there were only forty students in the entire senior class. A couple of the teachers had wanted the principal's job themselves, and were disappointed when they didn't get it, so I met resistance from them and from some of the teachers who sensed my inexperience. It is hard to lead when you don't have any idea what direction you're supposed to be going.

The principal in a small school is a lonely person. Teachers see the principal as an authority figure, and are reluctant to include him in social affairs. The superintendent and the school board aren't part of the school staff, so the principal is in no man's land. This is especially true if there is no assistant principal to commiserate with. Although the teachers in Saline did not accept me at first, I was popular with the students and parents. I taught band and American History, and I enjoyed my students. I was really a part-time principal. It was a great job, because I had the fun of being in the classroom, and also some freedom as principal. And I was only twelve years older than most of the seniors, so my youth helped me relate with the students in a positive way.

We lived in Ann Arbor during my first year in Saline, and I drove back and forth each day, returning some evenings for school activities such as football games, concerts, and PTA meetings. I wanted to avoid that drive, and to live in the community where I worked, so we put our house up for sale. I told our friends I was moving to stay alive. The man in the house on our left died of a heart attack. The man on our right committed suicide. The man on his right died of cancer. The man across the street died of a heart attack, and the man directly behind us died. It was time to find a safer place to live.

We made a profit of fifteen hundred dollars when we sold our house in Ann Arbor, and until the equity was paid off I drove to the house every month to collect a payment of thirty-nine dollars. Jimmy was two years old at the time, and the second month I went to collect our payment I took Jimmy with me. He didn't realize where we were going, but when I drove into the driveway his face brightened, and he said, "I be glad to be home, Daddy." He must have missed the only home he had known, but I had to tell him that we didn't live there anymore, and that we couldn't stay.

The job in Saline paid three thousand dollars for the school year from September through June, and I needed to save enough from those nine monthly paychecks to get us through the summer. I understood the idea, but it was like trying to feed the multitude with two loaves of bread. Jesus could do it, but not me. The most we ever had left for the summer after the June paycheck was two hundred dollars. Usually it was less than that.

In the fall of 1947 Marge called me at school to tell me that Robbie, our collie, had been hit by a car in front of our house. He never recognized cars as a danger, and would blissfully trot out into the street, oblivious to the cars coming towards him. I came home after Marge's call, and found that one of his front legs was badly injured. He dragged it on the ground as he walked, which quickly made the foot raw. I tried to tape his foot to keep the foot from dragging on the ground, but whatever I invented was as troublesome to him as his foot dragging. He had been a healthy energetic dog, but now he grew frail, with a coat that was thin and sparse. We finally took Robbie to a vet who told me what I already knew. He had nerve damage that would never heal, and the vet felt we should put him down.

As Marge and I waited for the vet to give him a shot that would end his life, Robbie came to me and to Marge and put his head in our laps. We loved him, and could hardly bear the thought of losing him. The vet said, "Why don't you wait here while I take him into my office and give him the shot." I heard Robbie's jaws snap three or four times, and then the vet came to tell us it was done. It was after dark when I picked Robbie up and carried him out to our car to drive him home. When we got home I wrapped him in a lightweight blanket, dug a grave in the back of the house, told him goodbye, and buried him. Marge and I went to bed that night in tears as we lay there in the dark, and thought of that beautiful dog. Even now, writing about him brings a lump to my throat.

When we left Ann Arbor we couldn't afford to buy a house, and we hated to use our $1500 in government bonds until they had matured, so we searched for a place to rent. During the war Henry Ford had built inexpensive housing in Ypsilanti for workers who came up from the south to work in the Willow Run Bomber Plant. When the war was over the workers dispersed, and most of the homes were vacant. The University of Michigan purchased the houses after the war to use as student housing for the many young servicemen who were returning to school. We qualified to live there because I was getting my masters degree on weekends. The units were row houses, each one connected to the one next to it by a common wall made of fiberboard, and the walls were so thin we could hear our neighbors' conversations. We all had much in common. We were all young, we all had families, we were all living on the ragged edge of poverty, and we were all taking classes at the University of Michigan. There was a coal-stove in each unit, and a coal bin right outside the front door. My mother was appalled at our living conditions. These apartments made our house on Harpst Street look pretty good, and the next place we got would seem like a palace. But the one good thing about living there was the rent, twenty-five dollars a month.

We lived at Willow Run from August 1948 until February 1949 when a teacher in Saline told me that there might be a house available for us to rent at the Saline

Valley Farms. The farm was owned by Harold Gray. His grandfather had invested ten thousand dollars in the Ford Motor Company, and made millions when he sold his stock back to Henry Ford. Harold's parents were missionaries, and Harold was born in China. They returned to the U.S. before World War I, and Harold was drafted into the army, but he refused to serve, saying he was a conscientious objector. I'm convinced he truly was, but he was sentenced to Leavenworth Prison nevertheless. When he was released from prison after the war he bought a full section of land, six hundred and forty acres, south of Saline, and established a communal farm. His plan was to create a place where people could live and work and share in the profits of the farm.

Houses were built, orchards and gardens were planted, and a dairy was created. There was an area for chickens, and a canning factory, and a lake was created by damming a stream that ran through the farm. Harold also organized picnics, parties, and social activities for the people who lived on the farm. The eggs, milk, produce, and canned goods were then sold to customers in the surrounding area. It seemed like a good plan, and it worked for a period of time, but eventually failed financially. The people who were part of the commune had all invested money for a share in the operation, and lost whatever they had paid into it. Harold Gray was a warm and kind person whom we liked very much. While the farm wasn't successful financially, it still existed in the late forties. People rented houses on the farm, and enjoyed the social activities that were still held there. Most of the commune's activities had ceased to function, but the dairy was still in operation, and milk was delivered to customers in the Ann Arbor and Milan areas as long as we lived there. The canning factory also existed, and we canned fruits and vegetables for ourselves in the fall.

We borrowed the farm truck to move to the Valley Farms on a bitter cold February day in 1949. When I got in the truck I discovered that the driver's side window was stuck down, and I knew I was in for some cold rides that day. It was bearable during the day, but the last trip was made after dark, and it was bitterly cold. I drove alone in the truck while Marge followed in our car with Jack and Jim, but halfway to Saline I decided I was going to freeze solid. I stopped to get into the car, and told Marge I didn't think I could make it if I didn't get warmed up a little, so she turned the heater on high until I began to thaw out. I hated to crawl back into the truck, but I did, and survived the rest of the trip.

The house in Saline had two bedrooms, and rented for sixty-three dollars a month. That seems little enough now, but at the time I was making thirty-four hundred dollars a year, and the rent took seven hundred and fifty six dollars. It was the nicest place we had ever lived. We also thought the Valley Farms would be a wonderful place for our two boys, and it was. There were fields to roam, the lake for fishing and swimming in the summer and ice skating in the winter, and there were four other boys on the farm for company. Our kids remember the Valley Farms as an idyllic place to spend their childhood. It was a Tom Sawyer life that few children get to experience in the modern world.

We used some of the profit from our Harpst Street house to buy two pearl gray rugs for our living room, a forest green couch, a matching cranberry chair, and a bright yellow dinette table with two chairs and two stools for the boys. We had lived with junk for so long that new furniture in a nice house gave us a real lift. Marge found some inexpensive material that had the same colors as the couch and chair, and made drapes for the picture window. This used up the money from the sale of our house, but we both thought it was beautiful, and we loved it. After living in a trailer in Del Rio, Mother's house in Hillsdale, the disaster on Harpst Street, and the shanty at Willow Run, we were starting to feel respectable.

Jim was a funny little boy, in part because we would hear full sentences from this little kid who was only eighteen months old. Some small children came to visit us when Jim was not yet three years old, and they apparently annoyed him, because he told us, "Little kids irritate me." He was three when he told us, "It makes me nervous if I don't have some money in my pocket." I could understand that feeling, as I was nervous most of the time for the same reason. Jack and Jim got a small allowance each week, a penny for each year of their age. It wasn't much, but we lived out in the country and they didn't have any place to spend it anyway. But it was something, and I suppose it kept Jimmy from being too nervous, and if we needed two or three extra pennies when we were at the store we could always count on being able to borrow them from Jim.

We were expecting a third child in April of 1949, and hoped for a girl. We knew the baby's birth was imminent, so on the day she arrived I rode to school with a teacher, leaving the car for Marge. Around noon I had a call from Marge saying it was time to go to the hospital. She drove to school to pick me up, and I drove her to the University of Michigan Hospital in Ann Arbor. As usual, we didn't have to wait long for the arrival. A nurse came to the waiting room to tell me the baby had been born, and that it was a little girl. Marge could hear the conversation, and heard me say, "A little girl, well, what do you know, a little girl." We were delighted that after two boys we had a little girl in the family. Marge thought we might name her Ann Elizabeth, but for some reason I liked the name Debby, and Marge was willing to accept that name. It just seems to fit her.

She has been a joy to us, and I've told her, "If we could have just one little girl, I'm glad it was you." She was a sturdy little thing, always perky and outgoing, and we realized early on that she had music in her soul, with a natural talent to match. When she was still less than two years old she would walk up to the piano, reach over her head to reach the keyboard, and push the keys to hear the sound. In no time at all she began playing little tunes, first with one finger, and then with two fingers with each hand playing in thirds. She has an amazing ability to play a piece in any key, and can transpose to different keys at will in the middle of a song.

Debby's piano teacher once demonstrated a new piece before sending Debby home to practice. Debby took it home, practiced it, and returned for her next week's lesson to play it for her teacher. When Debby finished, the teacher said, "That was very nice, Debby, but you played it in the wrong key." Debby could hear a song, and then sit down and play it, so when her teacher played it for her Debby simply played it by ear in a key of her own choosing. Her playing has given me much pleasure, and I always enjoy listening to her. She once gave me a Father's Day present I treasure, a videotape of her playing some of my favorite songs.

Debby loved to have Marge tell her how thrilled I was when the nurse told me we had a little girl, and how I said, "A little girl, well what do you know, a little girl." Debby often came to sit on my lap for me to love her, and one time she looked up at me and said in her still imperfect speech, "You a vewy pwetty daddy." I have since told her, "You a vewy pwetty daughter." Debby never showed any of the moods or emotional behavior we heard about with the daughters of some of our friends. She was a good natured little girl, and nothing dampened her enthusiasm.

Two years later David was born on Saturday, May 26, 1951. He was late arriving, and I don't mean a day or two, or even a week. He was five weeks late. Poor Marge thought she was going to carry him around the rest of her life. That morning I got up and went to work in our garden. Jack and Jim were with Marge's parents, and Debby was with my mother in anticipation that David would probably be born sometime that year, so Marge was alone in the house. One of Jack's friends, Randy Karr, didn't know that Jack wasn't home, and came to the house to play with him. It was then that David decided he would enter the world, so Marge told Randy to run down to the garden and "Tell Mr. Ford to come up immediately!" I was an experienced husband by then, and I didn't have to guess why I was needed immediately. I ran to the house, and found Marge ready to leave.

I was dirty and sweaty, and since our other children hadn't threatened to be born at the first sign they were on their way, I felt I could take a quick shower. We then got in the car to drive to Ann Arbor, but when I got to Saline I realized the gas tank was nearly empty, so I stopped at a service station. I should have made sure the car had gas, but I hadn't. I then rushed to the hospital, as Marge kept saying the baby was coming. When I drove up to the emergency entrance Marge was put in a wheel chair, and wheeled into the hospital while I parked the car.

I brought a book to read, knowing from past experience that this could take a little time, and my job was simply to wait. I just got nicely settled with my book when a nurse came to announced that we had a new baby boy. We thought it would be nice for Debby to have a sister, but it was not to be, and there was no disappointment when David arrived. We had thought of names for a little boy, but didn't definitely settle on one until the night before his birth. That evening we attended a concert at the high school which included a song entitled, "*Little David, Play on Your Harp,*" and we both decided that if we had a boy that would be his name.

David was born full breech. He had his feet up around his head before birth, so after he was born he remained that way, with his feet right up by each ear, and it took several days before he got straightened out. In the process his feet slowly moved from his head, then up in the air, and finally straight out. During the time his feet were sticking straight up it was impossible to keep a blanket on him. When we tried it looked like he was under a tent. He was a handsome little fellow, with a cowlick over his right eye that Marge predicted he would learn to hate. David was a charmer with a ready smile, a happy and gentle little boy. He was our fourth child, and I have always felt that we were so busy with our other children that David didn't get his fair share of attention from me that the other three had.

Debby was his mentor, his warden, his mother, his boss, and his music teacher. Even though they were only two years apart, Debby took charge of David and taught school, taught him songs, and generally directed his life. David has since claimed, "I was twelve years old before I realized Debby wasn't my mother." Debby was a help to us, because she took over some of the things we would normally have to do.

When Marge was late in her pregnancy with David she was not as agile as she was normally. Debby sensed that Marge was at some disadvantage, so when she got in trouble Debby would crawl under a bed, and scoot as far away from the edge of the bed as possible, knowing Marge couldn't get under the bed after her. Marge decided that the first time Debby crawled under the bed after David was born that Marge was going to go right in after her. But after David arrived Marge was disappointed that Debby never again attempted that maneuver. Debby must have sensed that the times required new tactics.

There were four other boys living at the Valley Farms, Calvin and Randy Karr, and Robert and Alan Markert. They liked to ice skate on the lake during the winter, so we always inspected the lake to make sure the ice was safe. Even when we determined the ice was safe, everyone knew the middle of the lake was not safe because of the movement of the water, and the boys all knew they were supposed to stay near the edge. But during one hockey game Jack was chasing the puck too near the middle, and the ice gave way. Jack disappeared beneath the ice, and when he looked up the hole he had dropped through was black. He fought his way to the surface, and the other boys lay down on the ice, and held their hockey sticks out to him. Fortunately the ice held under his light weight, and he was able to crawl out. Then he came home, changed his clothes, and never said a word to us, knowing we'd never let him go ice skating there again. There were no adults present, so his rescue was up to the other boys. If they hadn't acted quickly his heavy clothing would have soon become water soaked and pulled him down. It still terrorizes me, knowing how close we came to losing that little boy that day.

I often marvel that any kid ever grows to maturity. The good Lord, or our guardian angel, must watch over us as we go through those years. The things that kids do blissfully are scary when we look back on them. Jack and Jim and their four friends once went exploring in the huge barn at the Valley Farms. The loft was filled with hay, and the boys had a great time making tunnels. Of course it was pitch black in those tunnels, the barn was huge, and they finally found themselves lost, with no idea which tunnel would lead them out. Then one of the boys struck a match to help them find their way. It's a wonder the dry hay didn't ignite, and burn the barn down with those six little fellows in it. I can just imagine that barn burning, and each family finally realizing their boys were gone. I wonder again, how do kids ever reach maturity?

As our family grew from two to three, and then to four, it became more and more difficult to make our income stretch to buy the things we needed. I was paid only for the months school was in session, which meant that my last pay of the school year was on June 20, and my next pay was on September 20. I received a small amount each month from the government G.I. Bill, but I had to find a job to help tide us over the summer. We didn't have a checking or savings account, because by the time I paid the bills there was nothing left to put in the bank.

I needed to find work during the summer months, and one year Harold Gray kindly gave me a job laying a floor in the attic of his garage. Another summer he hired me to paint one of the houses on the farm that was in terrible shape. I took classes towards my masters degree at the University of Michigan in the morning, and spent each afternoon that whole summer, and even into the fall, scraping and scrubbing the old paint with steel wool, and then giving it two coats of paint.

Just south of our house was a low flat area that we used for a garden. It was a fairly large garden, and I used it all to plant beans, corn, squash, tomatoes, beets, and broccoli. The soil had clay in it, so working the soil was hard work. We literally lived out of the garden during the summer months, and canned and froze vegetables for the winter. Marge always dealt with difficult times like a champion. She used to joke, "We're having corn, beans and tomatoes for lunch and we'll have tomatoes, beans and corn for supper." This was really more than a joke. We did exactly that during the week, with cracked eggs and cheese to provide protein. We had meat one day a week, on Sunday. It was invariably a pot roast, as that was about the cheapest cut of meat available, and by Sunday the anticipation of having a meal with meat made the pot roast taste like steak. One spring I bought a bushel of potatoes, cut them into pieces with two "eyes" each, and planted them with Jimmy's and Jack's help. Then I hilled them, weeded them, cultivated them, dusted them against insects, and finally dug them up in the fall. It was hard work. Shortly after digging them up I saw fifty pound bags of potatoes being sold in the grocery store for fifty cents. I never planted potatoes again.

In the summer of 1950 I completed my graduate work, and received my master's degree. About this time I was asked if I would be interested in being the swing man for two men at the Valley Farms who delivered milk. I took their routes on Saturday and Sunday, and they paid me ten dollars per day. That was enough to pay our rent, plus an extra seventeen dollars each month. I gladly accepted the offer, and got up at 3:15 a.m. every Saturday and Sunday morning to walk to the barn, get the milk truck out, load it with milk, and head out by 3:45 a.m. I delivered milk mostly in the Ann Arbor area, with a few stops in Saline. During the school year there were always evening school activities that could last as late as 11:00 p.m., and each Friday evening during football and basketball seasons there was a sock hop in the gym that ended at 11:00 p.m. I was expected to attend those dances, so by the time I locked up the school and drove home I got to bed about 11:45 p.m. Then I had to get up at 3:15 a.m. for the milk route. It was a good thing that I was young and had lots of energy. I actually enjoyed the job, seeing the sun come up, and the world beginning to stir. In the nice months of the year everything looked and smelled so fresh.

In spite of my extra jobs we continued to struggle to pay our bills. The last year I was at Saline, for the 1952-53 school year, I was paid five thousand dollars, and I asked to have my salary divided equally over a twelve-month period so we would have a steady and predictable income during the summer. It was a good idea, but we received a little less each payday, and as a result I found myself out of money a week before each payday. I don't mean we didn't have much. I mean we didn't have any. Two brothers ran a grocery store in Saline, and I had to ask them to let me charge my groceries until I got paid. Then my first stop after I got paid every month was to pay for the groceries I had charged. I would hate to face such financial problems again.

Trying to feed our family and pay our bills took a good deal of thought and time. I didn't have a wristwatch, and one Christmas Marge earned enough money to buy one for me by cleaning house for another woman at the Valley Farms. On another occasion Marge went into Saline with several other women who decided to stop for a coke. Marge had to say that she didn't want one, because she didn't have the nickel that it cost. One Christmas we were shopping in Ann Arbor, and the kids were with us. In a Woolworth store Jimmy saw a pretty blue parakeet, and was entranced with it. I could afford the parakeet, but I couldn't afford the cage, and it bothered me terribly that I couldn't buy it for that little boy who was so taken with that bird. I remember two Christmases when Marge and I agreed not to give each other a present, so we would have money for the kids' Christmas. Marge understood, but it hurt me to see her without a Christmas.

In spite of our struggles I remember standing outside at night on more than one occasion, looking up at the night sky, and thanking God for giving me a wonderful wife and five wonderful children. All parents love their children, but no father could love his wife and family more than I love mine. I can't understand men whose jobs come before their families. I loved my family completely, and they were always at the top of my list of priorities.

When I took the job in Saline I inherited the Girls Drum Corps, and a school band, of sorts. The Girls Drum Corps, a group of about thirty five girls, was well organized, wore white blouses and blue skirts, and had a drum beat of several measures, which they repeated over and over. The old adage that says, "If you can't play well play loud" fit these kids. They weren't very good, but they made so much noise that no one noticed.

The band, however, was even worse. It consisted of one trombone, one flute, one clarinet, a saxophone, and drums. Not one of them could read music, because the previous band director hadn't bothered to teach them. Within a short time I had a sixty piece band with a fair variety of instruments, but every one of the new members was a rank beginner who didn't even know how to hold the instrument, let alone play it. Some of those kids didn't know which end to blow through. The first day they came together was the darndest mess one could imagine. A cat and dog fight would have sounded more musical.

In the spring of my second year I took the band to the annual Michigan band contest. We played one number of our own choosing, and then were given a piece we had never seen before to see how well we could sight read. The ratings were from one to four, with one being the best. The first year we received a three, and I felt the judges had been merciful. The next year the band received a two. After that the Saline band became widely known as an outstanding organization that received a one rating routinely. Despite the improvement I was delighted when the school board hired a young student teacher, Art Katterjohn, to take over the band. Art had played in the University of Michigan marching band, and certainly knew more about bands than I did.

Kids have a penchant for giving teachers nicknames. The English teacher in Saline was Midge Haswell. She was a tall lanky woman, and the kids gave her the name Spider Legs, in private of course. When I later moved to Belleville we had a much married little English teacher who came to us as Phyllis Lawrence, then Gladding, then Dronefield-Watten. It was the last name the kids picked up on, calling her Mrs. Downright Rotten. The name didn't indicate the kids' dislike for her, it was just their sense of humor. Phyllis was well liked by her students, and I considered her an excellent teacher. She also had good classroom control, which shows that a teacher doesn't have to be big and tough to have good discipline.

I once hired a small man who had been a sergeant in the Polish army. He tried to run his class like an army unit, but teachers can only maintain good discipline by capturing their students' interest. You can't drive them. One teacher in a class of thirty kids can't use force to create either an orderly class or a good learning atmosphere. This teacher stood before his class at stiff attention, and tried to demand respect. The kids simply resisted him, and drove him crazy. I tried to help him, but he was so rigidly set in his approach that he wouldn't change. The final straw came when he heard a student say the word "sh-t" in his class. The teacher stood before the class and announced, "You say sh-t, I say sh-t!" He had to go. But the class had been in such poor control for a full semester that I felt sorry for any new teacher trying to bring them into line.

A young student teacher seemed to be doing well, so I hired him to finish out the year for the departing Polish sergeant. I talked to him at length about the troubles the sergeant had, and promised to help him any way I could. He started the first day of the second semester. After a couple of days I walked by his room and noticed that it was quiet and orderly. A student who had been trouble for the sergeant was standing at the front of the room giving a report. I couldn't even see the teacher. As I looked again I saw that the new teacher was sitting in the back of the room, and all the students were attentive and interested. That day after school I went to his room to tell him how pleased I was with the class, and found him helping a student to create a model solar system with the sun and the earth and all the planets. I looked at his bulletin boards, and they were filled with work his students had done. He was simply a natural teacher who made the subject interesting, and there was never one minute's trouble with that class for the rest of the year.

In the spring of 1953 I learned that Belleville High School was looking for a principal. Belleville was a small town with a big high school as the result of several school districts joining together. It was about twenty miles east of Saline, and had nine hundred students in grades seven through twelve. It continued to grow until we eventually had two thousand students in grades ten through twelve. I made an appointment with the Belleville superintendent for an interview, and after our interview he asked, "What salary would you have to have to come to Belleville?" I really didn't want to leave Saline, but we needed more money, so I told him I would need sixty five hundred to seven thousand dollars. I was making five thousand in Saline, and this would be a pretty nice increase. The superintendent called me the next day and offered me $6750, exactly halfway between $6500 and $7000. I hated to leave Saline and the great kids there, but $1750 attracted me like a moth to a flame. When I told Leo Jensen, the Saline superintendent, that I was leaving for more money he accepted my resignation with a warning, "I'll tell you something, Jack. You'll earn every penny of it." No truer statement was ever made. I earned every penny of it a hundred times over.

During my first year at Belleville we continued to live at the Saline Valley Farms. It took about thirty minutes to drive to Belleville, which in itself wasn't bad, but I had frequent evenings when I had to be at school, and there wasn't time to drive back and forth after school was out. As a result, I often left home in the morning and didn't get home again until eleven o'clock or later, and I was missing the evening meal and the social time with my family. There were always Friday night athletic events, and often Tuesday games, plus school concerts, dances, and board of education meetings that required my presence and took time from Marge and the kids. I was anxious to find a place for us in Belleville.

One evening the wife of a school board member told us of a house for sale on the southwest side of Belleville, so we drove over to look at it, and in the dark could see an old American two-story farmhouse about a mile and a half out of town. We drove back the next day, and could see it was a white frame house with a well house and work shop west of the house, and a large white barn thirty yards west of the workshop. North of the barn was a long chicken house, and behind that was an old fashioned outhouse. The outhouse was mostly a curiosity, but it was used on occasion.

There were five acres of property, a third of it used for the buildings, and a third planted in peach and pear trees. The remaining third was available for a nice garden and more fruit trees if we were so inclined. The property was triangular in shape. Elwell and Hull roads made two sides of the triangle, and a railroad track made the third side. When I enlisted in the Army Air Corps I rode the train down this track to St. Louis, and this was one of the houses that I had passed on that dark night twelve years earlier.

The owners asked twenty thousand for it, but accepted eighteen. That doesn't sound like much now, but I made just six thousand seven hundred and fifty dollars a year. For the next several weeks whenever I drove to Belleville I filled my trailer and car with household goods, and stored them in the empty chicken house. Finally around the middle of August I hired a man with a small truck to move our heavy items, and we were in our new home.

We lived there a year without curtains in the windows, because we didn't have the money to buy any. Jack and Jim slept on canvas cots because we couldn't afford beds. The second year I decided to give the boys the profits from the peach orchard so they could buy their own clothes and school lunches. Their mother overruled that idea to the extent that they had to buy two decent beds first. The boys put up a howl, but she was right, of course, and they got new beds.

The fruit trees seemed like a wonderful bonus. We all loved peaches, but there was more fruit than we could eat, so we sold the extra. By the time we moved into the house there were peaches and pears and plums hanging on the trees, just waiting to be picked. We sold enough fruit that first fall to pay the taxes on our property. It seemed like picking money off the trees, so I planted another hundred trees the next spring, giving us a total of two hundred trees. I was already mentally counting the money we were going to make. Life was beautiful.

What I didn't know was that fruit trees don't just grow quality fruit all by themselves. The first year all we had to do was pick the fruit. Then I discovered that fruit trees require a *lot* of work throughout the year. In March the trees had to be pruned, they had to be given a dormant spray against a fungus called curly leaf, and each week we had to spray for peach bore. Peach bore is a moth that plants its eggs in the bark of the tree. The eggs produce fat white worms that eat away at the tree, quickly killing it. Our battle against peach bore was never ending, and never very successful.

The trees had to be fertilized, and the ground cultivated and disked regularly to keep the weeds down. We sprayed each week throughout the spring and summer with an insecticide and a fungicide. After the fruit began to grow we had to thin the fruit by knocking about seventy five percent of the fruit off the trees so the remainder would grow to a nice size. Finally, we had to pick the fruit and sell it from a roadside stand. All this was in addition to my full time job and all the yard work, and the periodic painting and repairs. And rearing five children is not just a weekend recreational pastime. I remember seeing a cartoon entitled "The Winners" in which four little kids had taken down a big bully, with each kid holding an arm or a leg. But then the little kids were afraid to let go. I felt like one of those kids. I had this orchard and house and barn and all that went with it, and couldn't let go.

My biggest problem was lack of equipment. I had an old sprayer that came with the property, but no tractor to pull it. A neighbor had a tractor, and a few apple trees, but no sprayer, so we struck a bargain that I could use his tractor if I would spray his trees. He also had a disk that I used when my orchard needed disking. This arrangement worked until I borrowed five hundred dollars from the bank to buy a used Ford tractor and a broken disk that I was able to repair. I was suddenly independent.

About this time the sprayer rusted through, and was no longer usable. Something was always causing a crisis in my life, but I bought an old wooden sprayer, and thought I was in good shape, as a wooden sprayer wouldn't rust out. It didn't rust out, but that sprayer was the most temperamental piece of machinery ever built. It was difficult to start and never ran long enough to finish the entire orchard. It would stop running two thirds through the orchard, and refuse to start again. I never had anything that frustrated me more. I often told Marge, "I don't mind the work if I could just have a sprayer that would start and stay running until I finished." I struggled with that miserable sprayer until our youngest son went to college. Then I made a decision that I never regretted. I gave the sprayer to a neighbor, and said the worms could have the peaches and the trees and anything else out there that they wanted. I was free. I loved the outdoor work, the garden and the orchard, but I came to hate that sprayer.

A monumental burden was lifted from me when we gave up the orchard. Every morning I would walk out of the back door, look at what was left of the orchard, and say, "To hell with you." But this was after twenty years of suffering with that miserable sprayer. We did have all the fruit we wanted, and had truly tree ripened peaches, something I haven't had since, but we never made enough money to justify buying a new sprayer, so I struggled along with what I had.

Memories flow over me when I think of our farm in Belleville, the Christmases when the kids were little, and spring, when the fruit trees were in full bloom. But as often as not I see our boys out by the barn playing an improvised baseball game with a tennis ball. The rule was that the batter had to bat left handed. This worked pretty well for most of us, but Jim batted as well left handed as right handed, and we couldn't think of any way to further handicap him. We didn't have enough players to run bases, so boundaries were set for what would constitute a single, a double, and a triple. Over the house was a home run. Jack and Jim created most of the games that were played, and there was some game going on most of the time.

I loved our children, and teased and played with them as much as I could. I used to wrestle with Jack and Jim when they were young, and once told them that when they could beat me at wrestling I would buy them an ice cream cone. Long after I had forgotten about that promise Jim came into the kitchen one summer afternoon and said to me, "Dad, Jack and I would like to see if we can win that ice cream cone." I thought, "Those two boys are getting bigger and I'm getting older." I told Jim, "Go tell Jack I'll buy. I don't have to get beat up, too."

We moved to Belleville in August 1954, and in February 1956 Bruce was born. When David was born in 1951 I made up his birth announcement with the line: "We're mighty happy to have our four, but that's all there is, there ain't no more." But five years later there was. Bruce was born on his mother's birthday, February 28, and Marge has always called him her birthday boy.

Parents need to be imaginative sometimes. One time when Bruce was little I was convinced that he had done something that he denied. Finally I said to Bruce, "All right, I'm going to get the Magic Book." I went to our bookshelves and picked out an orange covered book (it was Cheaper by the Dozen) and began to thumb through the pages. I mumbled such things as "broke the window, hit your sister, ate the cake," etc. until I finally said, "Okay, here it is. It says you did it." When he heard that it was in the book Bruce confessed. I didn't want to punish him; I just wanted the truth. The threat of getting the Magic Book worked for weeks. I once was suspicious that Bruce had done something, and he asked me to go get the magic book and see. I knew then that he was innocent. But the Magic Book didn't work for long. Bruce either figured it out for himself, or someone put him wise, and I couldn't think of anything to replace it. When we moved to a condo in 1977 we had to get rid of many things we no longer had room for, and it seemed only fitting that Bruce should get the Magic Book.

When Bruce was three I drove him home one night under a full moon that lit up the sky. Looking for entertainment, I told him, "See that moon up there, Bruce? I'm going to make it move. Now watch." He looked at the moon through the back window of the car until I made a ninety-degree turn, which made the moon suddenly appear through a different window. He was impressed with the power of his dad, and I repeated the feat several times. Every time I came to a turn I said, "Moon, moon, with your big fat face, I want you to change your place." It's easy to be a hero to a three-year-old.

When Bruce was ten I took him with me one summer to pick strawberries at a local farm. I drove into the farmyard to tell the owner we were there, but when I got out of the car a large German Shepherd approached me. I hadn't been formally introduced to that dog, so I was very wary, and Bruce could see my obvious hesitancy as I shut the door behind me. After I took a half dozen timid steps towards the house Bruce rolled down his car window and yelled, "Sic em!" I froze for a moment until the dog began to wag his tail. Then I had to laugh, but my first inclination was to beat on Bruce, because he didn't know if that dog would bite. Perhaps this was his revenge for the Magic Book and the moveable moon.

One of my memories of the farm was tragic. The orchard was bordered by a railroad track, so it was easy for kids to help themselves to a few free peaches. One evening I stepped out on our back porch just as a train passed by. Suddenly I realized that the train had stopped, and was backing up. Soon the police arrived, and we learned that some boys from Detroit were gathering peaches in our orchard, and took off running when I came out on the porch. They all made it across the railroad track except for the last boy, who was struck by the train. The boy's father came to our house a couple of weeks later to see where his son had died, and I told him that I hadn't even been aware that the boys were there. It was a terrible experience that haunts me still.

I earned more in Belleville, but I didn't have the summer jobs I had in Saline, and our house payments were twice what the rent had been at the Valley Farms. It really was a struggle, and we kept falling further and further behind. Our children were growing older, and we couldn't see what we were going to do when Jack was ready for college. Our car was a seven year old Ford. The upholstery on the front seat was in tatters, so we put an Indian blanket over it to cover the springs. Some teeth on the gear of the starter had broken, and the starter wouldn't always catch. When that happened we had to put the car in gear, and then get out and rock the car back and forth until the flywheel turned to a spot with teeth. Murphy's Law says, "Anything that can happen, will happen, and at the worst possible moment." Murphy was a smart man.

Marge started substitute teaching to help us financially, and on the days she worked she took Bruce to the baby-sitter before she got herself ready to go to school. One morning she got in the car in her bathrobe, and took Bruce across town to the sitter. As she drove through Belleville her engine stopped, and when she tried to restart the engine the starter locked. It looked as if she would have to get out of the car on the main street of Belleville in her bathrobe and slippers to get help, but this time Murphy was foiled when a family friend came by and rescued her by rocking the car until it started. On top of everything else, we needed a new car.

Marge left Hillsdale College after her sophomore year to come to Texas. She was the first one in her family to attend college, and really wanted to earn her degree, but this meant night school in addition to substitute teaching and caring for the family. She did all of this so we could begin to pay off some of our mounting debts, and she took on more than anyone had a right to expect to keep us afloat financially. She had the responsibility for the house and five children, taught school all day, went to school in the evenings, and studied late into the night.

I tried to do as much as I could to help with the cooking, the laundry, and the ironing, but the responsibility was hers, and I know she was tired and worn out much of the time. I wished I had a career that paid enough that she wouldn't need to work, but by that time I had too many years towards retirement to change, and I couldn't have found anything that started at more than I was already making. I felt trapped, and so did Marge, but from that time on we began to gradually dig our way out. In our later years we were able to do things that we could only dream about during those hard years.

By the time Jack graduated from high school things were easier financially, thanks to Marge's teaching, but with college looming ahead our kids knew they had to work during the summer to help pay for their college education. When Jack was a junior in high school he dated a girl named Donna Wichello. Donna's father, Bill Wichello, owned a trailer hitch factory, and he was also a member of the local board of education, so I knew him well. He came from a poor family, and claimed that he and his brother took turns going to school because they shared a pair of shoes. Bill knew what poor was. During World War II he ran a small machine shop out of his garage to make parts for machine guns, but when the war ended he had to find something else to sell.

He invented a gadget to pull a clothesline taut, and called it "Draw-Tite." He was moderately successful with that product, but he wasn't getting rich. Then he took his family on a trip around Lake Michigan, and made himself a trailer hitch to pull the family trailer. Whenever he stopped people admired his trailer hitch, and asked where he got it, so he decided that making trailer hitches might sell, and he already had the perfect name for them, Draw-Tite! He arranged with the automakers to give him the specifications for the new cars coming out each year so he could have hitches ready for the new buyers. Bill eventually earned millions with his trailer hitches, but he continued to live in a modest house with his trailer hitch factory in the back. He had nationwide sales, but was always just the neighbor next door.

Bill asked Jack if he would like to work in the office on weekends, and of course Jack said he would. He worked at Bill's plant every weekend during Christmas and Easter vacations in high school, and during the summer while in college and law school. The others all followed in his footsteps, with Jim and David working at Draw-Tite, Debby at a Howard Johnson restaurant, and Bruce at a variety of tough jobs. One summer he got up at three o'clock every morning to drive to Detroit where he worked in extreme heat doing heavy manual work in a foundry. The work was so hot and demanding that he worked for fifteen minutes, and then got fifteen minutes off.

Jack graduated from high school in 1961, and chose to go to Hillsdale College, following in the footsteps of so many of his ancestors. It was a sad day when we took him to Hillsdale because we knew it was the beginning of the breakup of our family. Jim would leave in three more years, Debby in three after that, and David in just two years after Deb. Bruce was five years younger than David, so we knew he would be with us for a while yet.

Jack later attended Washington and Lee Law School, and became a Special Agent with the FBI in New York City before leaving to practice law in Sumter, South Carolina. While in New York Jack shot and killed one of the FBI's ten most wanted criminals during a stake out. The fight erupted late at night across a narrow alley in the heart of the city. Several shots missed Jack by inches. He enjoyed his years in the Bureau, but a few experiences like that made practicing law look attractive.

Jim graduated from high school in 1964, three years after Jack. He was always a conscientious student, often coming home from an evening athletic event, and sitting down to do his school work at eleven o'clock at night. I would try to get him to go to bed, but he stayed with it until it was done. One day he had a biology test the morning after a late track meet, and didn't have time to study as much as he wanted. I was the only one who could save him, so I waited until his biology class had just begun, and pulled a fire drill. The kids all filed out until I gave the signal to return to class, but knowing there was still time for the test I pulled a second fire drill immediately. A principal's kid ought to get some breaks.

Jim entered the University of Michigan in 1964. When he graduated in 1968 we were fighting the Vietnam War and he was subject to the draft. As I had before him, Jim elected to serve in the Air Force, entered pilot training, and found himself at Lackland Air Force Base, the same base I went to in 1942 when it was called "The Aviation Cadet

Reception Center." Jim spent three months at Lackland earning his commission, and then went to pilot training at Webb Air Force Base in Big Spring, Texas. This was the same field I flew to one Sunday morning twenty-five years earlier to retrieve a student who had gotten lost on a cross-country flight.

When Jim completed his training I flew down to be at the ceremony when he received his wings. Jim had given me many proud moments in high school, and here he gave me more. He won the award for being the best pilot in his class, and the Commander's Trophy as the best all around officer, a high honor. I brought my own favorite pair of sterling silver wings from my flying days in World War II, and I proudly pinned them on him. It was a proud moment for me.

For the next three years Jim flew the C-141, a four engine jet transport that took him all over the world. Then in 1972 he was sent to Vietnam for a combat tour of duty flying the C-47, a twin engine prop plane that was used for electronic surveillance. We always wondered where Jim was, where he was flying, if he was all right, and if he was in danger. We worried constantly about this son who had given us such pride and joy through the years, and seemed to have such promise. I couldn't bear the thought of losing him. I don't know how parents survive the loss of a child at any age. It was a happy day for us in June 1973 when Jim flew into Detroit Metro Airport, and we knew he was home from the war for good.

Debby graduated from Central Michigan University in 1971 with a teaching certificate. Jim was flying the C-141 out of Dover Air Force Base in Dover, Delaware at the time, and suggested to Deb that she go there to apply for a teaching job. That sounded exciting to Debby, and she drove to Dover where she did find a teaching job at the Air Force Base elementary school. While she was there she met Chas Erickson who was also a C-141 pilot. He and Debby were married in June 1974, and now live in Reisterstown, Maryland with their three children.

David graduated from high school two years after Debby, in 1969. He entered Michigan State University in the fall of 1969, and loved every minute he spent there. During David's freshman year I phoned him occasionally to see how he was getting along. One time I called him, and learned that David wasn't there. I asked where he was, and his roommate answered, "He's bar-hopping." We weren't sending David to college to go bar-hopping, so I told his roommate to have David call me when he returned. David never did call, but he obviously did have a conversation with his roommate. Whenever I called David after that his roommate always said, "He's at the library."

What David wanted most was to fly. After graduating from college he was accepted into the Navy flight program, and earned his Navy gold wings in 1974. I offered to fly down to Florida to see him get his wings, but David thought the ceremony wasn't going to be much, and told me not to come. I wish I had, as I had done so for Jim. It was a proud moment for me when I received my wings in 1942, I know it was for Jim, and I'm sure it must have been for David also. I wish I had been there to share his pride when his wings were pinned on him. David was a Navy pilot for six years, flying first out of the Philippine Islands delivering mail and other supplies to carriers at sea. After two years in the Philippines he was sent to Corpus Christi as a flight instructor. Marge cried when David left for the service, saying, "We'll never see him much anymore." She cried when Jim left, too, but as it turned out we see both of them more than the others. Parents love all of their children, but we love each child individually for the qualities that make them special to us. My mother once said that the child she loved most was the one who was having the most difficult time at that moment. I suspect every parent understands that statement.

Marge and I married in September 1942 and started life together with just the two of us. Ten months later Jack was born, and one by one our family increased until there were seven. Life was hectic, but always interesting, and we loved our family. I can't imagine better kids than we had, but one by one they left. Our family gradually became smaller and we knew we would soon be back where we started, with just the two of us. Finally Bruce was the only kid left at home. His life was almost like that of an only child.

In the fall of 1974, thirty-two years after we were married, we found ourselves alone again in an empty house. Bruce graduated from Michigan State in 1979, two years after we retired. He wasn't an eager student, but I know he now shares our belief that college is worthwhile, as it made it possible for him to fly in the Air Force, and become a pilot for Delta Airlines.

Bruce has been a loving son, with a wonderful sense of humor. We can always tell when Bruce is present by his hearty laugh. He came home from the service once on leave, and looked at the pictures on our bedroom wall of Jim and David and Bruce and me in our military pilot's uniforms. At the time Bruce was flying an A-7 jet fighter. Jim had flown cargo in the C-141, David had flown mail and supplies from the Philippines to carriers at sea, and I had been a flight instructor. Bruce stood looking at those pictures, pointed at Jim's picture and said, "truck driver." He pointed to David's picture and said, "mailman." Then he pointed to my picture and said, "Drivers Ed," adding, "I'm the only fighter pilot in the family."

My thirty-year career as a high school principal was filled with interesting experiences, and I could appreciate a harmless prank that didn't disrupt school or damage property. One morning some boys put a small greased pig in a girls' lavatory before the other students arrived. They hoped to see the girls scream, and watch the pig run down the hall with everyone trying to catch it. Unfortunately for the pranksters, a custodian checked that lavatory before the students arrived, found the pig, and captured it. The custodian was a part-time farmer, and was happy to take the pig home with him. I thought this was a great gag, and I never tried to find the kids who pulled it off. They deserved an award.

Many students drove to school, so we eventually hired a guard to stand at the entrance to the parking lot to provide security. Being in Michigan, we also built a shack for the guard to stand in during inclement weather. One morning the guard arrived for work, and discovered his guard shack was missing. I learned who masterminded the trick, and found him at our Vocational Building. I walked up to him in class, and watched him work on a project for a few minutes before I quietly and casually asked him, "How long do you think it would take you to get the guard shack back in our parking lot?" He grinned, and said, "Not long." I told him that I thought it was a good joke, but the guard needed his shack. This was in the morning, and before the lunch period was over the guard once again had his shack.

I had one new teacher who was not very popular with her students. She drove a Volkswagen Beetle, and one day after school she discovered that some students had lifted her car, and placed it on a pipe about eight inches off the ground. She couldn't move forward or backward, and failed to see anything funny about the situation. She stormed into my office demanding a pound of flesh from whomever was responsible. The car wasn't damaged in any way, and I didn't have much sympathy for her, but I did make arrangements to get her car lifted off the pipe so she could drive home. I later found out who was behind the joke, but I never told her.

Usually I waited until the school lunch periods were over before I ate my lunch. When the kids were all back in class I drove home to eat in peace and quiet. One day as I was driving home for lunch I saw two boys walking away from the school. I stopped beside them, rolled down my window, and asked where they were going. The larger of the two boys put his arms across his stomach, grimaced in pain, and said, "I'm sick to my stomach and I'm going home." He didn't have a pass from school, and obviously had just walked out of the building on a pretty fall day. I told him to hike right back so we would contact his parents and drive him home if he needed to go. I then turned to the smaller boy and asked him why he was there. I give him an "A" for coming up with the excuse that, "I forgot my glasses today, and I'm just following him."

One day I returned to my office and found Billy Thompson sitting in the outer office. I assumed he had been sent there by a teacher, but I couldn't imagine Billy having a large problem. He wasn't that kind of kid. It turned out he had come to the office to check out of school because his family was moving to Hawaii. I had no reason to doubt him until I asked what his father was going to do there, and he told me his father was going to be dealing in furs. I thought that was possible, but with my limited knowledge about the fur trade it seemed improbable, so I asked my secretary to call Billy's mother to verify his story. His mother replied that she would be right there. When I told her that Billy said his father was going to be dealing in the fur trade in Hawaii she looked stunned. Billy had his head down looking at the floor as he rubbed his forehead, shook his head from side to side, and said, "Now where did I ever get that idea?" Needless to say, Billy was at school the next day and every day thereafter.

Not all of the challenges at school came from the kids. In the early '60s one of Jack's friends gave us a baby crow. He was an ugly little bird when we first got him. We kept him in a one quart strawberry box, and fed him dog food until he was big enough to learn how to fly. For obvious reasons we named him Blackie. Blackie stayed around our property when he was young, but as he grew older he strayed farther from home. He first followed Marge to her school, where he was an amusing novelty until he started coming in through open classroom windows to beg for food. He later followed me to the high school, where he entertained students by riding on the tops of cars and busses as parents dropped their kids off for school. Eventually he discovered that the home economics room had food, and he could always be found there after the cars and busses had left. He finally became such a nuisance that I had to lock him in the chicken house when I left for school

A principal of a large high school is fair game for anyone with a grievance against the school, or the teachers, or the administration, and some students are just drawn to mischief. One night I heard a car stop in front of our house about two o'clock in the morning. I rolled out of bed, and saw three figures walking across the yard towards our house. I called out of the window, "What do you want boys?" They turned and ran to their car, as they made some unacceptable suggestions to me, and then roared off towards town. Jim and I ran down in our pajamas, jumped in our car, and followed them with our lights off. We followed them for a couple of miles until they turned into a driveway where one of the boys lived. I drove in right behind them, and as they got out of the car, I turned my headlights on. They pulled their coats over their heads and ran, but not before I recognized every one of them. I then called the police and learned that these boys had broken several windows that night. Monday morning I called all of them to my office, one at a time, and suspended them from school. One of the boys, Dennis Sohn, challenged my identification by saying, "How could you tell it was me? I had my coat over my head." You can see I wasn't dealing with a genius. I said, "Dennis, I'd know that big behind of yours anywhere." When his mother came to my office she wasn't nearly as concerned about what her son had done as she was that I had demeaned him.

Another boy, Steve Reed, came by our home one night with a carload of his friends who had formed a band. They threw a rock about the size of a baseball through our living room window, and I once again jumped in my car and finally found them. The next day I suspended Steve from school and notified his parents. The other boys were from another school, but I got their names and notified their parents also. Those parents said the boys would have to break up their band unless they made arrangements that were satisfactory to me to repair the damage. With that kind of parental cooperation dealing with kids was easy. The boys all came to see me, and said they would replace the window, but I wanted it done right so I did it myself. Then I kept the rock in my desk at school. Steve was subsequently sent to my office two or three times for minor problems, and each time I took the rock out and put it on my desk as we talked. I never mentioned it; I just let it sit there. When Steve saw it he became very cooperative.

I made every effort to have any evidence of a nighttime visit gone before the school buses came by the next morning. On more than one occasion I awoke in the morning to find that kids had strung toilet paper through the trees and bushes. It was usually done by kids who were honoring a friend, rather being malicious, and Bruce had friends who visited us occasionally. Still, wanting to beat the kids at their own game, I would get up as soon as it got light, get out my ladders, and clean the trees before the buses came by. I didn't want any kids who hadn't thought of it to get ideas of their own.

Our mailbox was taken several times. Each time the mailman found it, sometimes a mile or two away, and I put it right back on the post. One time someone put a firecracker in the box which exploded and blew the sides of the mailbox straight out. I was left with a flat piece of metal. The next morning I took the abused mailbox into my workshop, put it back together with stove bolts, and had it back on the post for the perpetrators to see when they drove by. There were other attempts to blow up the mailbox, but the stove bolts held firm, and all that ever happened was that it blew the door open.

One morning we awoke to find that the mailbox had been run over by a car. Jack was home from college, so he dug a hole, made a new post out of two by six lumber, put a big pipe in the middle, and then filled the whole thing with cement. Then we put the mailbox back on top, and waited for the next guy to try running over it. But as long as we lived there no one ever attacked the mailbox again. It was a disappointment. When we moved from the house after twenty-two years the original mailbox was still standing.

One year some kids repeatedly drove across our lawn during the night, leaving ruts and tire marks. We worked hard to have a nice looking home, and it was discouraging to have someone drive across the lawn not just once, but with regularity. They always followed the same path, so eventually I put a rake in the yard with the tines up, and waited. It wasn't long before I heard a car come by, and the sound of tires going flat. They didn't stop, but just kept going, and this time I didn't bother to follow them. It was the last time that happened.

Over the years student discipline became more and more difficult. About the time I thought I had seen behavior get as bad as it could get, racial problems between white and black students appeared. I was raised in Texas until I was thirteen, and had seen how black people were long subjected to discrimination in every aspect of their lives, from housing to jobs to demeaning ridicule. Blacks had to sit on the back seats of buses, and stand when those seats were filled even if seats in front were empty. Theaters, schools, restaurants, and hotels that served whites were not available to blacks. Public restrooms and drinking fountains were labeled: "Whites Only", and "Blacks Only." If whites were walking on the sidewalk black people would get off the sidewalk to get out of the way. A black person never went to the front door of a white home. He had to go to the back door and knock hat in hand. I was raised in that society as a young child, and lived in it until I was thirteen.

The Civil Rights Movement in the 1960s forced society to recognize that blacks were entitled to the same rights and privileges that white people enjoyed. With their new found equality many black people felt a sense of power, and the pendulum, as is often the case, swung in the other direction. In our school some black students became belligerent and aggressive to white students and the school staff. A common accusation was, "This is a racist school." If there was a confrontation between a black student and a white student it quickly escalated into one group against the other. It was difficult to deal with the black students because we spent most of our time trying to convince their parents that race was not an issue with us. We were only concerned with their child's behavior.

The situation finally came to a head one morning in March 1974. I had to make a trip to Ann Arbor, and when I returned there were police cars around the school, police with dogs, and a police helicopter overhead. As Marge always said, "Whenever there's trouble you are always gone." Some black students had confronted white students at the bottom of a stairwell during a change of classes, and things rapidly went from bad to worse. Soon students all over the school were gathering up rocks and boards and metal bars to "defend" themselves. Fortunately no actual fights broke out, but the potential was there for someone to get seriously injured. So we called the school buses to take the students home, and school was closed until further notice.

Any help is appreciated during times of trouble, and I remember a black principal from a neighboring school advising me to make reasonable and enforceable rules. I think we already had them, but it was sound advice. We first suspended the ring leaders, and then brought the students back one grade at a time, beginning with the sophomores. We met with them in the auditorium where I talked with them about the problem and what we expected from them. I repeated this with the juniors and then the seniors. In the meantime we hired adult supervisors to monitor the halls and grounds. The NAACP asked to attend the meetings with the students, and to have some of their members in the halls to see for themselves if there was any racism in the school, and I was delighted to have them, because they were good people. I knew they would see no racism, and we'd have no trouble from our black kids as long as the NAACP was there. The NAACP members were honest people, and everyone knew they would call the shots fairly. Things improved immediately, and were better for the last three years I was there, but of all the problems I encountered as a principal, these racial tensions were the most difficult.

Young teachers and principals have an advantage, because they relate better to the kids, and the kids accept them. I enjoyed that advantage in Saline and in my early years in Belleville, so maybe my view of how students changed towards the end of my career was partly due to my age. I spent twenty-four years in Belleville dealing with troublesome students, and in the later years it seemed as if that was all I dealt with. If it wasn't trouble, I didn't see it. When the assistant principals couldn't handle a problem, they brought it to me. I had all of the problems, but none of the fun of working with the good kids. Early in my career I remember thinking I was old enough to be these kids' father. It was a shock when I eventually recognized I was old enough to be their grandfather. It was time to go.

Marge and I decided to retire at the end of the school year in 1977. I had been a principal for thirty years, and was more than ready to retire. I had found the job tiring and unrewarding for a number of years, and I was just hanging on until I could let go. In 1975 we started looking for an area to build a retirement home in west Michigan, not far from the town where Marge lived as a schoolgirl. This seemed like a good area for us, as it would put us close to our parents, and it was near Lake Michigan, which we both enjoyed. Eventually we bought eight acres of heavily wooded property on the shore of Lake Michigan, and began to plan the home we would build.

We sold our farm in Belleville, and moved into an apartment for our last year there, but the people who bought our home still suffered occasional nocturnal visits from kids who didn't know we had moved. The new owners removed the flood lights I had mounted in the front yard, and when they complained about some vandalism, I told them, "I had those lights there for a reason."

My last day was at the end of July, 1977. In the interim I spent time with my replacement, trying to help him get acclimated. He stayed one year before deciding there must be better jobs elsewhere. The second man lasted five years, the third only six. They either weren't as tough as I was, or they were just a lot smarter, I'm not sure which. But despite the difficulties I still have happy memories of my years in education, including the dear friends I knew, many of whom are now gone. My life as a principal was interesting, rewarding, and at times exciting, but I was now retired. I hoped I might have thirty years of fun ahead of me, and I looked forward to getting at it. I was finally going to live the life I thought I would have when I quit school during my first recess in the first grade.

Retirement
1977-2002

I envied Henry Collins. Some people do what the rest of us only dream of doing. Henry was one of those. He was the principal of an inner city school in Detroit, where a school administrator's life can be a misery. One morning Henry didn't show up for school. When his secretary called him there was no answer. When they went to his house there was no one home. Henry didn't show up the next day, or the day after that, or any day thereafter. He and his wife had packed their house trailer and taken off for Mexico. They stayed until Henry figured out who he was and what he wanted to do. Then he drove back to Michigan many weeks later, walked into the superintendent's office, dropped his keys on the desk, and said, "I quit." He was my hero.

When my career was winding down I thought I would like to buy an Airstream house trailer, and start off like Henry Collins to just go where our desires took us, but as it turned out, retirement didn't begin that way. We bought the property on Lake Michigan, and began building a house three years before we retired. We moved in on December 23, 1977, and from that time until the following spring Marge and I worked every day, seven days a week, finishing the woodwork. Occasionally we would say to each other, "Lets take this Sunday off," and we'd feel like we really should be working as we sat and read or watched television.

When my mother was ninety-one she suffered several small strokes, and developed physical problems that required special care. We found a nursing home for her, as she required more care than Marge and I could give. A few years later we made the same decision for Marge's mother. My mother was not afraid of death. In fact she welcomed it in her last years, once saying seriously, "With any luck at all I'll be dead by spring." She was blessed with a keen mind, and faced life and death realistically. She believed, as I do, that the quality of life is what is important. She once told me, after becoming incapacitated, that, "Life just isn't much fun anymore." When we are young we fear dying too soon, and when we are old we fear living too long.

We took Mother directly from the hospital to a nursing home in Kalamazoo on October 24, 1979. Exactly one year later, on October 24, 1980, I was with her when she quietly took her last breath. I thought about both her life and mine during the two hours we watched as her breaths became more and more irregular and shallow, until finally she breathed her last, and the mother to whom I owed so much was gone. The night before she died her doctor told her she had an intestinal infarction. She was ninety two, and he said to her, "Mrs. Ford, you don't want an operation at your age do you?"

She replied, "Oh no."

The doctor then said to me in a most compassionate and tender voice, "It's time for the leaves to fall." I thought it was a beautiful way to express it. I had a wonderful mother, and I missed her after her death, but I know she lived a full life, and her death was expected and accepted. My dad, in contrast, died in the prime of his life. His death was a tragedy for us all. Mother outlived my dad by exactly forty nine and a half years to the day. Fifty years to the day after his funeral I stood by his grave as we buried my mother. Mother had asked to be cremated, and then we waited for the anniversary of my dad's funeral to hold that service for Mother.

I remained in the Air Force Reserves after the war, and the same year I retired from teaching I retired from the Air Force. I had a hazy idea that there were some benefits in addition to my pension, but I wasn't entirely sure what they might be. I had heard about being able to fly overseas on military aircraft, and soon discovered that the rumor was true. We could fly anywhere in the world on military aircraft if there were seats available.

We couldn't fly from just any air base. It had to be an air base where the large cargo planes were stationed, as they were the only ones that had seating for passengers. The most practical base for us was Dover Air Force Base in Dover, Delaware. This was the base where Jim was stationed for several years during the Vietnam War. On our first trip we drove into Dover before noon and found our way to the Passenger Terminal. As we drove in I saw a small Ford car with a medical symbol on the rear bumper that indicated the owner was a veterinarian. I said to Marge, "I wonder if that is someone coming here to try for a flight out." We followed that car to the terminal, and then followed the vet and his wife in to register.

The veterinarian was Merle Farris. He was known as Doc, and his wife was Myrna. They were from Morristown, Tennessee, near Knoxville, and had taken many space available flights. They were friendly, so I decided to stay near them. I didn't know what I was doing, and Doc was an expert. If they couldn't go where they had planned, they went wherever they could get a flight. Subconsciously I began to pick Doc's brain. I realized that we had to be flexible.

We planned to go to England, and then drive up to Scotland, while Doc and Myrna were hoping to get to Greece. After waiting two days at Dover for a flight we learned there was a flight from McGuire Air Force Base in New Jersey about two hours away. I decided to drive to McGuire, but first I wanted to let the Doc and Myrna know, so I went to their room in the visiting officer's quarters only to find them gone. I hated to leave without letting them know about the McGuire flight, but I had no idea where they were, so we left. When we arrived at McGuire we found there was a C-141 going to Frankfurt, Germany that evening. After checking in and getting listed for the flight I looked around, and there were Doc and Myrna. They were way ahead of us. I could see that Doc knew the ropes.

We got on that flight, but the plane landed at Ramstein instead of Frankfurt, so Doc, who was beginning to take care of us, said, "Follow me." He and Myrna took off with their luggage, and hurried to a building two or three blocks away. I followed without asking any questions. Doc knew where a bus would pick us up to go to Frankfurt, and once in Frankfurt Doc directed us to a hotel on the military side of the Frankfurt Airport that accepted military retirees. Only one room was available, so we agreed to share it.

Doc and Myrna got up early the next morning to catch a flight to Greece, but soon they were back, because the flight was filled, and there was no room for them. The following morning they again left early for their flight, but once again they were soon back, as they had not made that flight either. Time was getting short for Doc, who still had an active veterinary practice in Tennessee, so when we found a flight to Mildenhall, England the next day Doc and Myrna decided to go with us. When we arrived I rented a car, and offered to drop Doc and Myrna off in Cambridge where they could catch a train to London. After fifty years driving on the right side of the road, adjusting to left hand traffic made for an exciting ride, and if it was exciting for me it must have been doubly so for my passengers. When we left Doc and Myrna at the train station Marge said, "I'll bet they wonder if they'll ever see us again," implying that we wouldn't survive for long driving on the left side of the road.

Doc and Myrna always traveled by themselves so they could set their own pace and go their own way. But when we later called them to ask how their trip had gone in London, they said they were planning a trip to Spain that winter to a town called Neuva Andulucia on the Costa del Sol, and invited us to join them. We had never been to Spain, but we now had some experience with space available travel, so we accepted their offer. By the time we left Neuva Andulucia we had come to enjoy each other's company sufficiently that we decided to take future trips together.

For the next dozen years we traveled with Doc and Myrna, and always thoroughly enjoyed our time with them. We went to Spain three more winters, to England again, to Ireland, Germany, Austria, Portugal, Holland, Alaska, Mexico, Belgium, France, and Puerto Rico. They were the best traveling companions anyone could ask for, and we still stop to see them a couple of times each year to relive those trips we took together. Meeting them made all the trips we took after that a lot more fun than they would have been if we had traveled alone. We never knew what to expect when we walked into a terminal and checked the board for outgoing flights. There were times when we got on flights almost immediately, and other times when we wondered if we would live long enough to ever get on a flight.

The next winter we rented a casita in Spain, a small apartment with a living room, kitchen, two bedrooms, and a tiled bathroom, all for seventy five dollars a week. From the back patio we could see the Mediterranean Sea, and, on a clear day, the Rock of Gibraltar. I would love to spend another winter there. We were all younger then, and walked everywhere. With Doc and Myrna we drove to Gibraltar, took a tour of the Rock, walked the town, drove to the little mountain town of Ronda, and drove to Granada where we toured the Alhambra, a Moorish castle. We also took a boat trip across the Mediterranean Sea to Algiers, and were guided through the Kasbah, where a number of American soldiers disappeared during World War II at the hands of thieves. We were cautioned to keep with the group and not get separated. We led a fun and carefree life on our many trips with Doc and Myrna. I can't imagine a more wonderful life than we've had these past twenty years. Retirement has been the best life I've had since the day before I started first grade.

Our travels have been both enjoyable and enlightening. During one trip to Germany we decided to visit Berlin, which at that time required travel through the Russian sector at Helmstad. We reached the border after dark, and had to stop while the Russian authorities checked the papers for the train. Russian soldiers patrolled the area around the train, and we had been told not to communicate with the Russian soldiers in any way, either by voice or by motions. As I looked at those young Russian soldiers I could see that they were young kids who had a lousy assignment in a dark and lonely place. They were just doing their job. They weren't the cause of our problems with the Soviet Union. I looked out of the window of the train, and saw a young Russian soldier looking at me. I smiled and gave a slight nod of my head, and the young Russian soldier returned my smile and nod. I thought, "They are just like our own soldiers, young men trying to do what they are required to do."

In 1996 I told Marge that I would like to visit Spain one more time. Doc and Myrna were in their eighties, and didn't feel capable of the trip, so we went alone. I didn't make a reservation of any kind before leaving the United States, as we were familiar with the area, and anticipated no difficulty in finding an apartment. Three of our teenage granddaughters, Marjie, Megan, and Mary, were given trips to Spain as Christmas presents, and planned to join us after a few days, but when we arrived at Nueva Andulucia I discovered it wasn't the quiet little community we remembered. The rest of the world had discovered that area. It took us two days to find an apartment, and at a price of eight hundred dollars, a little more than the seventy-five dollars our first casita had cost! I was in a panic before we found that apartment, because if we were alone we could have just left, but not when we had three granddaughters coming.

We took the girls to all the places we had gone during our earlier visits with Doc and Myrna, but this time we had an advantage because Marjie and Megan both studied Spanish in high school, and we anticipated that they would be our interpreters. They did quite well with printed material, but in conversation they were as lost as we were. One day we took the bus to Marbella to go shopping. Some high school boys got on the bus, and immediately noticed Marjie and Megan, who are both blue eyed blondes who stood out among the dark haired, dark eyed Spaniards. One boy spoke to Megan in Spanish, but Megan, not comprehending a thing, just shrugged her shoulders. The boy tried a second time with the same result. He then spoke with his classmates and, for a third time, spoke to Megan, still getting the shrug and up turned palms. When the boys finally got off the bus Megan turned to her grandmother and said, "Three years of Spanish right down the drain."

It has been twenty-one years since I retired, and the yearning to travel that I felt so keenly when I was a high school principal has come to pass. Going to interesting places here and abroad is still my idea of fun. The only thing that makes it better is when our children and their families can go with us. For years my four sons and I took a trip out West every fall. We rode mules to the bottom of the Grand Canyon, visited Glacier National Park in Montana, and saw most of the scenic spots in between. From the day we arrived until the day we left we entertained each other with jokes and stories, and I cherish those memories. I can't imagine a retirement more fun and more interesting than the one we have enjoyed.

My daughter, Debby, once said to me, "Dad, isn't it wonderful that we have memory?" It truly is. Memories are a treasure. Recalling the events of my life is the next best thing to being able to relive them, and I do have many days in my life I would love to experience again. My story is the story of an ordinary man. Not famous. Not heroic. Not really much of anything. But every life is worth recording. How I wish my Grandfather Henry had written more of his life. I wish I had the memoirs of my great grandparents, and my great-great-grandparents. What would they find worth reporting? What did they find amusing? What were their feelings when they lost a child, and what was important in their lives? We are so involved with our own problems that we hardly have time to think of those who preceded us. For me, it was only after I retired that I began to reflect on my life. And then it became very important.

We need to look back on our lives to properly judge them. When I was young my day to day problems obscured the big picture, and I didn't always see my life as I do now. I saw the work, and the lack of time, and the lack of money, and the pressures, but for me that is all in the past, and I can now see the forest as well as the trees. As I look back I am grateful for all I was given. I was born into a loving and caring family that possessed good values, and they tried to pass those beliefs on to their children. Material things were desired, of course, but character was more important than possessions. My parents and grandparents gave me a name that was respected by all who knew them.

I found a beautiful wife whom I love and respect. She has been a wonderful wife to me, and a wonderful mother to our children. Her intelligence and good advice, her steadiness in stressful situations, and especially her ready and clever sense of humor endear her to me more than I can express. And we have been blessed with five successful loving children who lived by the same standards and values that I respected so much in my own parents and grandparents. They and Marge are my life and the center of my existence.

I have had a rich and interesting life from my childhood in Texas, school in Hillsdale, four years of flying during the war, and my career in education. It has been an exciting adventure, and I cherish every part of it. I also believe that some guardian angel has been riding on my shoulder to guide me, and to give me the wife and children that I have.

I wonder why I have been so favored.

Epilogue
By James Ford

Dad died at home on the afternoon of July 22, 2002. He died, as he lived, with humor, courage, grace, and love. One of his last requests was that I write an addendum to his memoir to record his struggle with prostate cancer. It is the final chapter that he was unable to write himself.

The first ominous sign appeared with an elevated PSA test in June 1996, and a year later a biopsy was positive for cancer. The next five years were a roller coaster of remissions, recurrences, doctor's visits, and medications. Lots of medications. When one stopped working he would try another. Through it all he and Mom attempted to get the most from every day that remained.

In July 2002, with time running out, we took one last trip over the Fourth of July to have a family reunion in the mountains of North Carolina, an area that he loved. It was a precious experience for him and for us, but it also left little doubt that the end was near. While we were there he developed double vision, but even that didn't dull his sense of humor, and he laughed when I suggested that his double vision meant he would enjoy the Fourth of July fireworks twice as much as anyone else.

From our return until his death we maintained a vigil at his bedside, recalling past memories, sharing stories, and enjoying the music that he loved. One of his favorites was Barcarol by Offenbach, which he first heard as a small boy listening to his parents' hand cranked Victrola. Playing it now helped close the circle. Debby and David, the musicians in the family, played for him every evening, Debby on the piano, and David on the violin. He especially enjoyed Ashoken Fairwell, which they played every night, and again at his funeral service.

Dad had a wonderful voice as a young man, and one of his few regrets was that the only recording of his singing, a record of the Lord's Prayer that he recorded in the 1940s, had become badly damaged from frequent use. He thought it was lost forever, but in those final days a recording studio was able to restore it through the miracle of modern technology. We played it for him several times, and again at his memorial service. The soloist at that service later complained that it was the first time his performance had been overshadowed by a dead man. In his prime Dad could sing.

The day before Dad died Mom was feeding him ice chips with a spoon, and when she dropped one on his cheek he said, "Nice shot." Mom asked him how he could make jokes at a time like that, and he replied, "I can't do anything else." At that point humor was the one gift he could give to us, and to himself. Throughout the final days it was Dad's strength and humor that kept us going. In times of crisis a man's true nature is exposed, and humor was part of Dad's soul. One night he fell while trying to walk to the bathroom, and lay on the floor until Bruce lifted him back into bed. After getting settled he told Bruce that he had fallen quite hard, and that Bruce should check to see if the floor was damaged. As Bruce started to instinctively do as he was told Dad stopped him, saying, "That's a joke, Son." One day he was too weak to talk, so we kept up the conversation, recalling memories, and telling him how much we loved him. Sensing that we were saying goodbye he mustered the strength to say, "I'm not going yet. This is just an act." And he was right. He lived another three days.

Mom and Dad talked at length about their life together, and how Mom would adjust to handling new responsibilities on her own. They had rarely spent a night apart in sixty years, and Mom said that Dad had taken care of her since she was seventeen. Mom asked him what he would like her to do with his wedding ring, and he told her that she could wear it around her neck. Then, after a pause added, "If it will fit over your head." It must have fit, because she wears it there today.

With the combination of diabetes and cancer Dad was on a regimen of tests and pills and insulin shots that controlled his life the last few years, and it only got worse as the cancer progressed. At one point he complained that he needed a "bwana boy" just to carry all of his pills and diabetic supplies. On several occasions he said that he would like to start a bon fire to burn all of those pills, so after the funeral we did just that on a small hillside behind their condo. I'm sure he appreciated it.

Much of the last week was spent reminiscing. He and Mom talked frequently about how they met, and he reminded us several times that she made him wait seven weeks for his first kiss. Finally Mom told him that she was sorry that she made him wait that long, and he responded, "I was sorry then." He was surrounded by love, and he knew it. Bruce told Dad that if love could heal he would have been cured long ago, and Dad replied, "I would live forever."

When Dad was confined to bed I set pictures of his parents on his bedside table, and hung a figure of Archangel Michael on his bedpost. Michael had earned this place of honor several months earlier when Dad was suffering from severe abdominal pain. Dad was doubled over in the kitchen waiting for Mom to drive him to the emergency room when he looked up and saw Michael hanging over their kitchen counter. In desperation he said, "Michael, I don't know if you can help me, but if you can now is the time." As soon as he said that the pain disappeared completely. Michael was treated with more respect after that, and I thought he belonged on Dad's bedpost to ease the journey.

Dad's love for his parents was as strong at the end as it had been when his father died seventy-one years earlier, and one night he dreamed that his parents were coming to visit him at his boyhood home in Wichita Falls. He said that he looked out the window to see his father and mother standing in the yard, but that he woke up before they came inside. I think the hope of a reunion made it less difficult for him to leave those of us who remain. Trying to make the impending separation less painful for him I reminded him that it wouldn't be long before the rest of us would come to join him. He responded, "I hope so," and then realizing the implications of that, added, "I mean I hope you join me, but not right away." The clarification made us both laugh.

Dad died peacefully on the afternoon of July 22nd with his family gathered around him. The funeral was as he wanted it. Debby and David played Ashoken Farewell, Jack gave the opening remarks, Bruce recited "High Flight", and I gave the eulogy. I was worried about getting through the eulogy, but it proved to be easier than the first time I gave it. A couple of days before Dad died I reminded him of the scene in *Tom Sawyer* in which Tom and Huck are falsely presumed to have drowned, and attend their own memorial service while hiding in the church rafters. Then I asked him if he would like to hear his eulogy, and he said he would, so I gave him a private reading. One thing he didn't hear was an addition I made on the day of the service. The newspaper that morning contained the last column ever written by Ann Landers. In it she gave her definition of success, and I included that at the end of the eulogy.

> *He has achieved success who has lived well, laughed often and loved much; who has enjoyed the trust of pure women, the respect of intelligent men and the love of little children; who has filled his niche and accomplished the task; who has left the world better than he found it, whether by an improved poppy, a perfect poem or a rescued soul; who has never lacked appreciation of Earth's beauty or failed to express it; who has always looked for the best in others and given the best he had; whose life was an inspiration; whose memory a benediction.*

By any of those criteria Dad's life was an unbounded success.

Book Five

James Ford
1946-
Chapter One

Nineteen sixty-eight was a tumultuous time for the country. The North Vietnamese launched the Tet offensive at the end of January, President Lyndon Johnson announced in March that he would not run for another term, Martin Luther King was assassinated in April, and Robert Kennedy was assassinated in June. Hundreds of soldiers were dying in Vietnam every week, and we watched much of it on the evening news. In the middle of this turmoil I got on a plane at Detroit Metropolitan Airport at the end of June to fly to San Antonio to start Officer Training School. I started on this adventure with mixed emotions. I was excited about the chance to fly, but I was deeply troubled by the war in Vietnam. Fortunately I was looking at three months of OTS, followed by a year of pilot training, and then additional months of training for my first operational assignment, and I thought that the war certainly had to be over by then. It never occurred to me that I would still be right in the middle of it five years later.

We flew out of Detroit late in the afternoon with a stop in Atlanta on the way to San Antonio. It was my first trip to Georgia, and as I looked out at the red clay that bordered the runway I little suspected that Georgia would later play such a large part in my life, attending law school at the University of Georgia, and marrying a girl from South Georgia. From Atlanta we flew on to San Antonio. New recruits were arriving from all over the country, and the Air Force had a bus waiting to transport us to the main training facility at Lackland Air Force Base. From there the officer candidates were transported to an auxiliary base at Medina a short distance away. We arrived in the early hours of the morning.

Even in the middle of the night the weather was oppressively hot and muggy. We received an orientation lecture in an auditorium where the speaker had to compete with the noise of the crickets, and then were taken to our rooms at 4:30 a.m. only to be awakened an hour later by the sound of someone screaming in the hallway, "Gentlemen, the time is Oh-Five Thirty. Get those overhead lights ON!" It was the wake up call I would hear every morning for the next three months. That evening our upperclassmen took us out into the hall for what they said was a competition to see who could yell the loudest. After choosing the lucky winner they informed him that he had just been selected to get up a little earlier every morning so he could give the wake up call for everyone else.

When we assembled in the hallway they announced that we had five minutes to get dressed and line up in formation to march to the chow hall for breakfast. Later we received haircuts and uniforms, and packed up all of our civilian clothes to ship home. We could keep one small box of personal items, and I used my space to keep a couple of poetry books that I had purchased at the airport in Detroit. Poetry books probably didn't bode well for my future as a warrior, but I kept them with me through both OTS and the year I spent in Vietnam. With little else to do for entertainment I memorized many of those poems, and can still recite them today. When John Quincy Adams was a young man his father recommended that he memorize poetry, telling him that once he memorized a poem he would never be alone. It's advice that has always worked for me.

The officer training that I went through was not the same experience Dad had in 1942. The haircuts were the same, but the programs were different. For starters my OTS training was only ninety days, instead of the full year that he had. He went through officer training and pilot training at the same time, and received both his wings and his lieutenant's bars at graduation. I went through three months of OTS to be commissioned as an officer, and then spent a year in pilot training as a second lieutenant. And my experience at OTS had little of the hazing that he had. There was some of it, but not much. Our days were filled with a few hours of academics, a few hours of marching, and a few hours of physical exercise, combined with room inspections, uniform inspections, military discipline, and military courtesy.

During my first full day at OTS an upperclassman mentioned to me that I could avoid morning work details and Saturday room inspections if I joined the OTS band. The band practiced in the morning while everyone else cleaned the bathrooms and polished the floors, and the band played on Saturday morning while everyone else stood inspection. The band seemed to be just the place I belonged. The only problem was that I didn't play an instrument, and I could barely read music. My musical education had ended after playing the cornet in the fifth and sixth grades, but I still remembered how to play the scale, so it was worth a try.

When the band held its auditions I was there. Fortunately the word had not gotten out that this was a good place to be, so few people showed up. It was such a small turnout that the director announced he would dispense with the auditions and take everyone. I was in. I was given a flugelhorn, which is basically a large cornet with a slightly mellower tone. It is easier to play than the cornet, but the disadvantage of the flugelhorn is that it doesn't play the melody. If I had played an instrument that played the melody I might have had a fighting chance, but there was no way I could follow the music playing harmony, and after one or two bars I was hopelessly lost. My salvation was silence. Once the band started playing no one knew if I was playing or not. I wasn't.

For six weeks I sat through daily rehearsals and Saturday parades without playing a note. I held the horn to my mouth and I kept in step, but I didn't play, except for once or twice when I got carried away by the spirit of the music and blew into the horn hoping for divine intervention. God might answer some prayers, but he didn't answer mine, at least not then, and the looks from the people around me soon returned me to silence. After six weeks we became upperclassmen, and were exempt from morning work details, so I resigned from the band and turned my flugelhorn over to a new underclassman who needed it more than I did, and probably had some idea how to play it.

I didn't find OTS all that unpleasant, and it certainly wasn't difficult. The academics weren't much of a challenge. The marching struck me as silly, but anyone could do it. I don't remember ever marching again after OTS, but the military is tradition if it is anything. Soldiers had to march in Napoleon's day, so it must be good training for jet pilots, and I assume that OTS and ROTC students still march today. I did have trouble with physical training, because we had to run a mile every morning. I injured a knee in college, and it would lock up on me if I ran very far, so I finessed this by jogging three laps while everyone else ran four. People became so spread out along the track that if I went slowly enough I could finish three laps about the same time everyone else finished four, and no one ever noticed.

We graduated at the end of September, and then headed off to pilot training bases throughout the south. During our last week at OTS the underclassmen handed out mock awards to various members of our class, and I received the "OTS is a joke award." I didn't fight the program; I just didn't take it seriously. For me it was a necessary step to flying jets, and nothing more. When my younger brothers went through officer training programs years later I advised them both to treat it as a game. If you get upset they win. If you remember that it's a game you win. And perhaps to some extent that is part of the purpose of the training. It is a natural selection process designed to weed out anyone who can't adjust and adapt. I'm sure that it's possible to take it seriously and still adapt, but it was easier to just treat it as a game. The only aspect that did start to wear on me was the confinement. We were isolated on the base for three months, but at least we knew that in three months it would be over. You can do anything for three months.

I adapted to OTS easily because I had lived with it for twenty-two years. Dad was a master at discipline and regimentation. The house was organized and scheduled, and he was the general. When he woke me up in the morning he wasn't nearly as gentle as OTS. They yelled in the hall; he flipped on the light and yelled in my ear. And nothing they did or said at OTS could upset me. Dad spent years building up our emotional calluses. Sometimes he called us by name, but usually it was "flange head" or "dimwit" or something similar. I had no idea what a flange head was, but he probably didn't either. If we did something wrong his typical response was to ask, "Are you dumb?" We would always say, "No," which set up his punch line, "Then don't act dumb." This worked until Bruce came along. When Bruce was still little Dad asked him one day, "Are you dumb?" and Bruce responded, "No, are you?" Dad had no answer for that, so he had to change his routine for Bruce. But it got him through his first four kids.

Our adult relatives were appalled at how he talked to us, warning that he would destroy our self image, but we knew better. All of his bluster was just a game. He was playing, and we knew it. It is proof that language means only what the speaker and the listener understand it to mean. When Dad called me names I heard terms of affection. I only grew concerned when he talked to me in quiet and respectful tones, because then I knew he was serious. OTS was just a quieter and gentler Dad, but the game was the same, and I felt right at home.

My best friend at OTS was Bill Harris*, a good old southern boy from Gastonia, North Carolina. Bill was a tall lanky fellow, about 6'3", who hadn't quite grown into his body yet. He was a gentle soul, but a bit uncoordinated, and I discovered somewhere along the way that Bill had trouble swinging his arms in coordination with his feet when he was marching, especially if he thought about it. So I occasionally entertained myself when I was marching behind him by whispering, "Arm swing, Harris." When he heard that he would start thinking about it, and soon his arms and legs would get completely out of sequence. He saw the humor in this the first couple of times, but then the novelty wore off, and he let me know that he didn't appreciate it. After that I kept quiet, and without my help Bill marched just like everyone else. We ended up going to the same pilot training base where he washed out during the T-37 phase. I greatly missed his company, but it may have been for the best. Flying isn't as difficult as many people think, but good coordination probably improves your chances for a long life.

*The names of several people mentioned in the remainder of this book have been changed to protect their privacy.

Chapter Two

After completing OTS I received orders to report for pilot training at Webb Air Force Base in Big Spring, Texas. The name comes from a natural spring south of town, but it is big only by West Texas standards. In any other part of the world it would be a small pond. But water is rare in West Texas, and Texans are loath to admit that anything in their state is small, so Big Spring it is.

Before reporting to pilot training I had a couple of weeks of leave, so I flew home and bought my first car, a brand new candy apple red Ford Mustang, for two thousand six hundred dollars. I then drove out to Big Spring, arriving late in the afternoon. Before entering the base I parked off the north end of the parallel runways, and watched the T-37s and T-38s takeoff and land. The T-37 was a small side by side twin engine jet with a top speed of three hundred and fifty knots. The T-38 was a sleek rocket that flew almost three hundred knots in the traffic pattern. I was mesmerized. To the uninitiated the traffic seemed to be chaotic. Planes were coming and going from every direction, and it was hard to imagine how they avoided collisions. I could hardly believe that in a few weeks I would be up there with them. The Air Force base is now gone, but in my mind's eye the sky over Big Spring will always be filled with jets. It was impressive during the day, and even more so after dark when the T-38 afterburners left long trails of fire across the night sky. It was a beautiful sight.

Before getting in jets we had to complete thirty hours in a Cessna-172 at the local civilian airport. The 172 was a cheap and safe way to eliminate those who had no aptitude for flying. It was basic training in the truest sense of the word, learning to takeoff and land, along with a few simple flight maneuvers such as lazy eights and stall recoveries. Many of my classmates were eliminated during this phase. I was scared to death of failure, but after the final check flight I was pleasantly surprised to find myself ranked first in the class. The check pilot might have been a poor judge of airmanship, but I began to have some confidence that I could get through this. I still had to handle jets, though, and I knew that I had a long way to go before earning the wings that my father had worn.

I had my first flight in the T-37 in December of 1968. Most of my preconceptions about flying jet fighters came from watching "Bridges at Toko-Ri" with William Holden, a movie about the air war in Korea. That movie ended badly for Holden, but I loved the flying scenes, and wondered if the real thing would be as exciting as the movie. My instructor was Captain Steve Piszczek, who had recently returned from a tour of duty in the back seat of an F-4 Phantom in Vietnam. The first flight was just a demonstration of basic flight maneuvers, and a tour of the area, and I remember thinking in the middle of it that it really was very much like the flying scenes from the movie, but with the added smell of JP4 exhaust, and G forces that pushed me down in the seat during aerobatics.

After demonstrating loops and rolls he asked if there was anything else I wanted to do, and I told him that I would like to see a spin. So he climbed up to twenty thousand feet, put the plane into a nose high stall, and kicked the rudder. The result was more violent than I had anticipated. The nose dropped abruptly, and as it did the plane flipped upside down. Then the nose dropped straight down before rising back up to the horizon where it began to spin. He demonstrated how to recover, and then we climbed back up and did a couple more before returning to the base. For the first time I began to think of myself as a real pilot.

My four months in the T-37 were the most stressful part of the year I spent in pilot training. Much of that was because everything was new, and I was constantly struggling to keep up. And part of it was because Capt. Piszczek was a frustrated fighter pilot who didn't appear to enjoy instructing, but in the Air Force, as in life, you don't always get what you want. He was stuck in the job for three years, and wasn't particularly patient with the mistakes that new pilots make time after time. He was pleasant on the ground, but an hour with him in the air seemed like a week. Of course an hour in the air with me probably seemed like a week to him, too.

My time in the T-37 was relatively successful, with the exception of two rides that I failed, the only failed rides that I had during the entire year. The first "pinked" flight was on my second solo. The procedure was for the instructor to take his student around the pattern a few times, and then do a full stop landing so the instructor could climb out at the end of the runway. He then stayed there to watch while the student flew a couple of touch and go landings by himself. On my first attempt I made a nice approach, but instead of settling down to the runway I let the plane slowly climb until I suddenly realized that I was twenty feet in the air at stall speed. It was bad enough that one of the other instructors standing beside the runway took off running to get away from the anticipated fireball. This plane had ancient jet engines that took seven or eight seconds to build up to speed, so as I headed for destruction the engines slowly began winding up to the high pitched whine they had at full power. Just before impact the engines caught, and I was able to accelerate and remain airborne.

The experience sent me to the base hospital. During my initial training flights with Captain Piszczek I had similar problems while landing, although not to the same degree. He wanted me to put the plane into a gentle descent over the runway, but I was just as likely to level off or climb as I was to descend. He asked a couple of times if I couldn't "feel" the plane leveling off, and I assured him I couldn't. So after my disastrous first solo I decided it was time for an eye exam. We needed 20/20 vision to get into pilot training, but once we were admitted we could wear glasses if necessary, and I knew my vision wasn't really 20/20. I passed the entrance exams by letting my eyes water until I had just enough tears to act as a lens so I could read the chart. This technique didn't improve my vision much, but it was all I needed to pass the test. The test I couldn't pass was landing the airplane. So I had my eyes tested, and as expected I did need glasses. As soon as I got them I could "feel" the plane climbing or descending as well as anyone else. Captain Piszczek thought he could feel these subtle changes, but he couldn't.

You can only see them, and with glasses I could see the same thing he was seeing. I also discovered that there were many more airplanes in the traffic pattern than I had realized. The sky was full of them.

My second failed ride came late in the program when I was flying with one of the other instructors instead of Captain Piszczek. I flew well, but he failed me for not maintaining a proper lookout for other aircraft. This was his first flight since being grounded several weeks earlier after he collided head on with a civilian aircraft during a cross country flight. It was a miracle anyone survived. His T-37 went under the civilian plane, severing the vertical tail of the T-37, and the landing gear of the civilian plane, but they were both able to land without injury. And now on his first day back he gave me a failed grade for not keeping a proper lookout. Maybe his standards had changed during the weeks he had off to think about it. Over the next year or two there probably wasn't a pilot in the Air Force who looked for other airplanes more diligently than he did.

The student in the plane with him during his midair collision was Gil Harder. Gil was an avid mountain climber from Colorado who later became my roommate when we were in T-38s. Gil was tough. He could hang by his fingertips from a ledge only a quarter inch wide. I couldn't tolerate the pain to even try that, but Gil practiced by hanging from the top of a door to toughen his fingertips. He shared some of his climbing books with me, and a couple of times took me out to a rock wall in the desert where he taught me to climb and rappel. His goal was to climb all the great peaks of the world. In 1978 he was caught in an avalanche during one of these expeditions while climbing in the Himalayas, but was able to dig his way out. The following year he went back to climb Annapurna, and this time the mountain kept him. He was a brave man who died doing what he loved, but much too young.

One new experience that we had to learn to adjust to in the T-37 was the G forces during a loop. A loop in the T-37 created only three or four Gs, compared to five or six Gs in the T-38, but even three or four Gs can be enough to cause blackouts in an inexperienced pilot. As the G forces drain the blood from your brain you first develop tunnel vision which blacks out everything except the center of your vision. It is like looking through a tube. Then if the G forces continue you become completely blind, and eventually unconscious. I never lost consciousness, but I did frequently develop tunnel vision, and occasionally complete blindness. When that happened the only cure was to release back pressure on the stick to reduce the G forces. It took only a few seconds to go from complete blindness to normal vision, and I was on my way again.

Experienced pilots avoid this is by tensing their abdominal and leg muscles as much as possible just before entering the maneuver. The contracted muscles counteract the forces of gravity, and push the blood back into your brain. If you squeeze hard enough you can withstand fairly high G forces, but it is a workout. A half hour of aerobatics in a jet is like a half hour of weight lifting.

The T-38 had higher G forces than the T-37, but I don't recall ever blacking out in the T-38. Part of that was due to experience, but part was also due to the G suits that we wore in the T-38. The G suit was a pneumatic suit around our legs and abdomen that plugged into an air pump in the airplane. As we started pulling Gs the plane would pump air into the G suit to squeeze our legs, helping to force blood from the extremities back into the brain. With the combination of the G suit and tensing our muscles as hard as possible we were able to withstand five or six Gs for twenty or thirty seconds, long enough to get over the top of a loop. G forces are related to speed, so the greatest force would be as we entered the loop at 500 knots. We then slowed to two hundred knots going over the top, which gave us a short respite until the speed picked up again on the way back down. Because of the speed of the T-38 we would gain at least two miles of altitude while going over the top of a loop, and then lose two miles of altitude on the way back down.

The other effect of G forces is that it prevents you from moving. At five Gs a one hundred fifty pound man weighs seven hundred and fifty pounds. An arm weighs maybe sixty or seventy pounds, and is too heavy to lift. I learned early on never to rest my hands on my knees while my instructor was demonstrating aerobatics, because if he told me to take the plane in the middle of a maneuver I would be unable to move my hand from my knee to the stick. The only way to withstand those forces was to brace my forearm on my thigh, with my hand resting on the stick, whether I was flying or not. You can move your hand enough under high G forces to fly the plane, but your arm won't be able to move until the maneuver is finished and the G forces return to normal.

Our T-37 training areas were north of Big Spring, and bordered the T-37 training areas for Reese Air Force Base in Lubbock, Texas. I didn't know it then, but at the same time I was flying out of Big Spring one of the students flying T-37s out of Reese was George W. Bush. In 1988 I sat next to him at a luncheon while he was in Kalamazoo to campaign for his father. I knew a little bit about his background, and tried to engage him in conversation about our common experiences. Our fathers were both military pilots during World War II, and we both went through pilot training at the same time in West Texas, so surely we could find something to talk about, but nothing clicked. He had no interest in talking to me. Most pilots enjoy recalling those years, and sharing stories, but he barely acknowledged that he had been in the Air Force. Given what we know now about his military career he may not have been very proud of it. I couldn't tell if he felt himself too superior to talk to me, or if he just had nothing to say. Whichever it was he clearly didn't have his father's intelligence or social skills. His father might become president, but it was obvious this guy was going nowhere.

Bush was a sharp contrast to John McCain. I also had dinner with McCain long before he became a senator, and he was as engaging and down to earth as Bush was haughty. We talked some about our experiences in Vietnam, and mine certainly paled compared to his, but he seemed to be genuinely interested. When we parted he thanked me for my service, and to this day he is the only person who has ever done so.

Late in the T-37 training I took a cross country flight with Captain Piszczek to the El Toro Marine base in southern California. There wasn't much range with the T-37, so along the way we had to land to refuel in Albuquerque, New Mexico, and Phoenix, Arizona. Everything went as expected on the way out, but on our return I realized something strange was afoot when he told me to flight plan our trip from Phoenix to Albuquerque for fifty feet above the ground. Regulations prohibited flying below four thousand feet, so my instructions were a clear sign that this would not be a typical flight. As soon as we got a short distance from Phoenix he took the plane down to fifty feet above the ground to show me what a real low level flight looked like. After we skimmed along for a while he offered me the controls, but I was more cautious than he was, and without realizing it I gradually let the altitude increase. Finally he said, "Take it back down - unless you're afraid." This was a direct challenge, so I descended until we were just barely above the ground, considerably lower than he had flown. I had to climb to clear telephone lines and trees, and then I would immediately drop back down to maybe twenty or thirty feet, all at three hundred knots. After a few minutes of this he said, "Okay Ford, take it back up. This is more than a body can bear." It was a satisfying moment.

Captain Piszczek did not go out of his way to boost my confidence. During that cross country we landed at El Toro after dark, and since it was a strange field, and I had little experience, he flew the approach himself. But during the descent he developed an ear block, and turned the plane over to me while he struggled to release the pressure. Eventually he was able to clear his ears, and once again took over for the landing, but the physical emergency obviously unnerved him. As he continued with the landing he thought about it out loud, "I wonder what I would do if I ever became incapacitated in an airplane with you. Would I eject, or would I let you try to land it by yourself?" After pondering the horror of that possibility for a moment he concluded, "I guess I'd let you try to land." I was flattered.

Throughout pilot training we spent only half the day flying. The other half was devoted to classroom instruction, physical exercise, parachute training, etc. It was a busy schedule. In the classroom we had courses on jet engines, electronics, weather, instrument procedures, and aerodynamics. We also went parasailing, experienced rapid decompression in an altitude chamber, and rode an ejection seat on a vertical rail. The ejection seat in the T-37 was an archaic explosive charge, as compared to the rocket seats that are used in modern aircraft. The shell exploded with enough force to throw the seat and the pilot fifty feet in the air. My father gave me a few kicks in the pants when I was young, but they were nothing compared to riding that ejection seat.

The altitude chamber demonstrated how insidious hypoxia can be. If we are choking the sense of suffocation occurs not because of lack of oxygen, but from the build up of carbon dioxide. That doesn't happen at altitude. There isn't enough oxygen at high altitude to support life, but the carbon dioxide is still exhaled freely, so a pilot can become unconscious without warning. In the altitude chamber we were taken up to thirty thousand feet and instructed to take off our oxygen masks. We were then told to write our names on a pad of paper, and count down by threes from one hundred. We wrote our name and serial number next to the number one hundred on the top line, then our name and serial number and the number ninety-seven below that, etc. After about a minute the instructor asked me how I was feeling, and I said, "Great." I obviously had the lung capacity of a Sherpa. Then he told me to replace my oxygen mask, and after a few breaths I looked at my pad of paper, and saw that I had counted down from one hundred to seventy. The first few lines were normal, but they deteriorated rapidly at the end. The last line was just scribbling. I was seconds from unconsciousness, but had no clue that anything was wrong. The message was clear; I'd better pay close attention to my oxygen supply.

Chapter Three

Flying the T-37 was a challenge. It wasn't a high performance jet, but it was a jet, and things happened quickly. Plus it was a twin engine jet with retractable landing gear, and we were constantly learning new skills, such as formation flying and instrument flying. After four months I began to get the hang of it just in time to transition into the T-38. The T-38 was much faster and more sophisticated than the T-37, and unlike the T-37, which had side by side seating, the T-38 had tandem cockpits, with the student in front, and the instructor behind. The engines had afterburners for extra power, and it was capable of flying faster than the speed of sound. The T-37 flew final approach at ninety knots; the T-38 flew final at up to one hundred seventy-five knots, depending on the fuel load. It truly lived up to its nickname as the "white rocket."

My instructor in T-38s was Neil Emmons, a first lieutenant who had just graduated from pilot training himself. I was his first student, so to some degree we learned together. He learned how to teach, and I learned how to fly. He was a study in contrast to Captain Piszczek. Lt. Emmons was friendly and patient, and always a pleasure to fly with. Part of that, no doubt, was because of his inexperience. He hadn't taught long enough to grow frustrated at seeing the same mistakes class after class. It would be interesting to know what his students thought of him after he had been there for a couple of years.

I took to the T-38 rapidly, and even with the increased speed I don't remember ever feeling that I was struggling to keep up. I enjoyed the aerobatics, and they came to me easily as well, possibly because my experience as a diver and a pole vaulter made me comfortable being upside down. I loved formation flying, and soon also felt comfortable flying instruments. I flew once with our flight commander, Major Mike Hagan, who told me that there were other students in the class who flew aerobatics and formation as well as I did, but that I had an advantage over them in flying instruments. I enjoyed the challenge of flying instruments while most of my classmates found it to be a chore.

We flew "fingertip" formation in the T-38 with three feet of wing tip clearance. The lead plane was in charge of navigation and maneuvering, and the planes flying on his wing just did whatever the lead did. The only job of the wingman was to stay in position. Major Hagan made this crystal clear when he talked to us before our first formation flight. He told us that he didn't want us watching where we were going, or looking at our instruments. Our only job was to remain three feet away from lead. When flying formation you have to put your complete faith in the lead, and do whatever he does. Then for emphasis Major Hagan added, "If the lead airplane flies into the ground I want to find a second hole three feet away from it." I took that as a joke, and usually stole occasional glances at my airspeed and altitude, but the joke lost much of its humor in 1982 when the Air Force Thunderbirds flew a four ship formation of T-38s into the ground while practicing a low altitude loop. At the accident site they found the hole created by the lead aircraft, and nearby the three holes of his wingmen. I don't know if any of them were former students of Major Hagan.

One of the closest calls I had while flying occurred during a four ship formation flight in the T-38. Only the lead plane had an instructor. The three planes flying wing were solo students. The student identified as number two flew three feet off lead's left wing. Number three was off his right wing, and number four was off the right wing of number three. I was flying number four, and Kirk Davis was flying number three. Kirk was a captain who had been in the Air Force for several years as a navigator, and was finally getting a chance to become a pilot. As the ranking officer in the class he was also our class commander. Kirk was a great guy personally, but not a smooth pilot, and I suspect that if he had not been a captain and a former navigator he probably would have washed out before ever getting to the T-38. This was the only time I ever flew formation with him, but I was aware of his reputation, so I was a little leery before we even took off.

Things went well until about halfway through the flight when Kirk abruptly banked to his right and headed straight at me. It was like a car in the left hand lane of a freeway suddenly veering into the right lane. Being only three feet away I had almost no time to react. In a reflex action I pushed the nose down, and at the same time did a 360 degree roll to the right. I have no idea how I missed him, but somehow I did. It could not have been by more than inches. I finished the roll underneath lead, and then found Kirk a hundred yards or so off to the right. Eventually we both rejoined the formation, but I gave him a wide berth for the rest of the flight. We landed four ship formations by flying in formation down the runway, and then peeling off one at a time for an overhead pattern, but when this formation returned to base there were three planes in fingertip formation, and a fourth plane a good twenty feet off to the right. The tower must have wondered who could fly formation that poorly, but appearances were the least of my concern. After the flight I asked Kirk what had happened, and his only explanation was that he had hit turbulence. If so, it was turbulence that didn't affect the plane three feet to his left, or me three feet to his right. At graduation Kirk was the only student who graduated with the restriction that he could not fly any plane that flew formation. It was a wise decision, but almost too late to save me.

We took several cross country flights in the T-38. In July Gil Harder and I took a formation cross country with our instructors to Denver so Gil could visit his mother. We ran into a line of thunderstorms in southern Colorado, and kept climbing to stay above them, eventually climbing to over fifty thousand feet, which was just about the ceiling for that plane. We avoided the storms, but it later occurred to me that we would have been in big trouble if we had lost an engine while over those thunderstorms, because the plane wouldn't have been able to maintain anything close to fifty thousand feet on one engine. As I accumulated more flying experience I tried to never put myself in a position where there was no escape if things turned sour.

Late in the summer Lt. Emmons and I took a cross country to Panama City, Florida to visit one of his friends who was stationed there. It was an uneventful flight until we lost one of our generators during the landing. The plane could fly on one generator, but we weren't allowed to take off with only one, so we had to stay in Florida for three days until a replacement could be shipped in. We spent one of those days deep sea fishing, and generally had a nice unexpected vacation. Finally they notified us that the generator had been replaced, and we took off to return to Texas. The take off roll was normal, but as soon as the wheels left the ground the plane started rolling uncontrollably, first to the left, and then back to the right. The plane had a computerized yaw damper to control the rudder, and as soon as I pulled the circuit breaker for the yaw damper the plane settled right down. One of the idiosyncrasies of that plane was that the instructor in the back did not have access to the circuit breaker panel, so he was at the mercy of the student in the front seat when a problem like this occurred. The yaw damper was designed to smooth out oscillations in the rudder, but when the maintenance crew in Florida replaced the generator they put it in 180 degrees out of phase, which caused the computer to alternately kick in full left rudder followed by full right rudder. It was a wild ride for a while.

We then climbed up to forty-three thousand feet for the trip back to Texas, but as soon as I leveled off the right engine flamed out from a malfunctioning fuel boost pump, and we had to divert into England AFB in Louisiana for another overnight stay. Little did I suspect that three years later I would be back at that base training to fly the C-47 for a tour in Vietnam. The next day we finally made it back to Big Spring after turning a two day cross country into a six day adventure.

My closest friend at Big Spring was Jack Kendall, and we could not have been more different. Jack was as laid back as I was intense. He was a used car salesman from Oklahoma, and he made more money during pilot training by buying and selling used cars than he earned from his Air Force salary. I never knew what car Jack would be driving. One day he would show up with a Corvette convertible, and as soon as he found a buyer for that he would sell it to buy something he liked better, always pocketing a profit in the transaction.

I worked as hard as I could in pilot training, afraid of failure and determined to finish as high as possible in the class so I could get the assignment of my choice when we graduated. I knew the Air Force would give our class a list of various airplanes, and the top graduate would get his pick. This continued down through the class until the last man in line got whatever was left. There were some very good airplanes, and some very bad airplanes on that list, and I wanted to have a choice. Jack, on the other hand, couldn't have cared less. When I was in my room studying in the evening Jack would often drop in and try to talk me into heading to a bar or to a party. His stock sales pitch was, "Why are you working so hard? It doesn't matter where you finish in the class. We'll all end up with the same wings when we graduate." If I heard that once, I heard it a hundred times.

As it turned out my hard work did pay off, and in October I was fortunate to win the Commander's Trophy as the top graduate in the class. There were actually three awards, one for best academics, one for best pilot, and the Commander's Trophy as best overall. I came in second in academics, but won the other two. It was a particularly proud and happy moment for me, because Dad flew down for the ceremony and we got to share it together. The next morning we had a parade on the flight line where we all received the wings that meant so much to us. The Air Force gave us standard issue wings, but Dad brought his favorite wings from World War II that he pinned on me himself. They were made of sterling silver, and were slightly larger and flatter than the standard issue. After the parade Jack Kendall walked up to me, studied my wings, and then his, and then mine again, and finally in his slow southern drawl said, "Well Ah guess Ah was wrong."

Jack, true to his plan, finished either last or next to last. I don't remember which it was, because the last two graduates both got EC-47s, the two planes on the list that no one else wanted. The EC-47 was a pre-World War II twin engine propeller driven airplane with a tail wheel, and canvas covered flight controls. The other one went to Nickey C. Lucas. Nick was an irreverent free spirit who had been raised by fundamentalist religious parents. Nick did not share their religious fervor, but he had sat through enough revival meetings to be able to entertain us at parties with hellfire and brimstone sermons. A few drinks improved his performance.

While Jack Kendall and Nick Lucas headed off to fight the war in their EC-47s I headed to Dover, Delaware to fly C-141s, the latest four engine jet transport in the Air Force inventory. Everything about the C-141 was as good as the EC-47 was bad. I would fly a modern jet airplane, I would get to fly all over the world, and I wouldn't get an assignment to Vietnam for at least two years. Sure to God the war had to be over by then. Plus the multi-engine jet experience would be an advantage if I decided to go into the airlines when I got out. I was grateful that I hadn't listened to Jack Kendall when he tried to get me to party instead of study.

As it turned out, I spent two and a half years in the C-141, but the war didn't end, and eventually my luck ran out. I finally received orders to go to Vietnam, and left for a one year tour of duty in June 1972. Along the way I stopped at Clark Air Force Base in the Philippines to go through jungle survival school. We spent a few days in the classroom, and then were taken out to the jungle to practice what we had learned. After a night in the jungle we were helicoptered back to Clark, and I walked to the bachelor officer's quarters where I was staying. I was hot and muddy and tired, looking forward to a shower and a nap. As I walked along the sidewalk a car passed me going in the other direction. I heard the driver slam on the brakes, and soon it was backing up as someone in the backseat rolled down his window. When the car got back to where I was standing Jack Kendall stuck his head out the window. It was the first time I had seen him in almost three years, and I had no idea where he was stationed, or what he was doing. He studied me for a moment, and then asked, "Ford, is that you? God, you look awful. I thought you were an escaped prisoner of war or something." Jack always knew just the right thing to say.

I asked him what he was doing in the Philippines, and he said that he was now flying C-141s out of the west coast, and had a stopover at Clark. So after his year in EC-47s he came back to the same plane I received out of pilot training. Then he asked me where I was going, and I told him that after my tour in C-141s I was headed to Vietnam to fly EC-47s. He broke out laughing, and reminded me that he had tried to warn me all through pilot training that class rank didn't make any difference. Then he rolled up the window, and I could see him still laughing as he drove off. I didn't see him again for twenty-five years. Then in the late '90s some of our classmates organized a class reunion at Wright Patterson Air Force Base in Dayton, Ohio. They scheduled a reception on the night we arrived, and when I walked in I saw Jack standing on the other side of the room. As soon as he saw me he came over laughing, reminding me of our last meeting, and of the fact that the top graduate and the bottom graduate in our class both ended up flying the very same airplanes during their Air Force careers. I wasn't sure if he had been laughing continuously since our meeting in the Philippines, or if the sight of me just brought it back to him.

Jack understood life, but I never learn. After the Air Force I went to law school, and then practiced law as a trial lawyer for thirty years. It is not an easy way to earn a living. Jack went back to selling used vehicles, but now he deals in airliners instead of cars. He buys used airliners from the U.S. or Europe, and sells them to third world countries. He has a large home on the Monterey Peninsula in California, works a couple of days a week, and has life by the tail. He is still smarter than I am.

I left the Philippines in early July 1972, spent about six weeks in Saigon, a few days in Danang, and then arrived at my final destination at Nakhon Phanom in northern Thailand in early September. After a brief orientation I went to my room to check it out. The room was a bit more Spartan than the Boy Scout cabins that I had camped in occasionally when I was young. And I was depressed. I was in a war that I didn't believe in, people were going to be shooting at me, I was stuck in the middle of nowhere for the next ten months, and I was flying a plane that I didn't like at all. And I knew that Jack Kendall was back in California somewhere having a good time. The room contained two bunks, a cheap dresser, and lots of cockroaches. I sat on one of the bunks feeling sorry for myself, and then took a look under the bed to see if anything was there. We all had duffle bags, called B4 bags, and I could see that a previous tenant had left his under this bunk. I pulled it out, and saw stenciled on the front the name Nickey C. Lucas. It must have been there for two years. So I worked as hard as I could in pilot training, and for my labors not only did I end up flying the same plane that the last two students in the class received, but I ended up at the same base, in the same squadron, in the same BOQ room, and in the same bed. Life isn't fair.

Of course I didn't know about all that when I graduated from pilot training. Then life was good, and I was looking forward to flying the C-141. But before leaving Big Spring Dad and I had a couple of days with nothing to do, so I drove him down to San Angelo to see the town where he and Mom were married, and where they spent their first two years of married life. He showed me the Cactus Hotel, and their first duplex, and then we visited his old friends Johnny Bonner and Fil Filburn. Johnny wasn't "rodeoing" any longer, but he was still ranching, and in yet another demonstration of what a small world we live in, Johnny's son went through pilot training with me at Webb, just as Dad and Johnny had gone through cadets together twenty-five years earlier. And Fil was the same boisterous personality that Dad describes in his memoir. He had probably calmed down some by 1969, so I can only imagine what he must have been like when he was in his twenties.

Chapter Four

My assignment out of Big Spring was the C-141 base in Dover, Delaware, but first I had to go through survival school at Fairchild AFB in Washington, and then two months of transition training in the C-141 at Altus AFB in Oklahoma. I arrived at Fairchild in mid November 1969 in the middle of an early winter storm. There were three phases to this survival school. First we had several days of classroom instruction, then we spent a few days in a mock prisoner of war camp, and we finished with five days in the mountains of Idaho for escape and evasion training. On the first day we were told heroic stories of men who had survived in the wilderness, and prisoners of war who had resisted despite torture and deprivation. The intended moral was that if we were captured we could resist, and if we went down in the wilderness we could survive. At the completion of the course I concluded that if I were captured I would tell them everything I knew, and if I went down in the wilderness I would shoot myself. It was not a pleasant two weeks.

The classroom work was interesting, and even the prisoner of war camp was tolerable, but the five days in the Idaho mountains were miserable. For five days we hiked through deep snow in sub zero temperatures with no food and little sleep. It didn't help that on the third day I got too close to the fire one night and burned a hole in one of my boots. Captain Piszczek had warned me that going through survival school was, "like practicing how to bleed," but he made it sound a lot nicer than it was.

The day I finished survival school I flew down to Altus, Oklahoma to start training in the C-141. I was so sick from the survival school experience that I don't remember much of the flight, and my first stop in Altus was the infirmary. Once I recovered the rest of my time there was uneventful. Altus is only sixty-five miles north of Wichita Falls where Dad had lived as a boy, so one weekend I drove down to visit his Aunt Lavern who still lived there. I had a short visit with her, and then she took me out to the cemetery where my Grandfather Robert was buried. It was a bright sunny day, and I envisioned Dad there on a similar day thirty-eight years earlier. I did not mourn for my grandfather, whom I had never known, but I did mourn for Dad, knowing how he suffered from the loss.

I finished training and drove to my new base in Dover, Delaware in early February 1970, and had my first trip to Saigon later that month. It was one of many trips that I would take to Vietnam over the next two and a half years, and with rare exception the route was always the same. We flew out of Dover to Anchorage by way of Buffalo, Thunder Bay, Grande Prairie, and then north to Alaska. In Anchorage the plane was picked up by another crew while we rested for fifteen hours. It is more accurate to say we rested for at least fifteen hours. Sometimes it was fifteen, and sometimes it was thirty. We never knew. If we went straight to bed we would wake in eight hours, and then might not get called for another fifteen hours, just about the time we were ready to sleep again. If we stayed awake for twelve hours before sleeping we would get the call at fifteen hours, after only three hours rest. We looked at the schedule to make our best guess as to when we were likely to get our next flight, but the guess was wrong more often than it was right.

From Anchorage we flew to Tokyo for another crew rest, and then from there into Vietnam. From Vietnam we flew to Okinawa for crew rest, and then back to Anchorage and home. The whole trip took about a week. We rested, but the planes didn't. It was at the height of the war, and there was a great need to ship weapons and material to the war zone as quickly as possible, so whenever we landed there would be another crew waiting to fly the next leg as soon as the plane was refueled. On one occasion I flew the same plane home from Anchorage that I had flown into Anchorage a few days earlier, but while I had made one trip into Vietnam, the plane had made three. I claimed at the time that I didn't really need a navigator because I could fly from

Dover to Saigon by just following the contrails of the planes ahead of me. It wasn't much of an exaggeration.

My first landing in Saigon was an emotional experience. For six years the war had dominated American news and politics like nothing we have known since. There were hundreds of American deaths every week, massive protests, and a national fixation on this small country that no one had even heard of ten years earlier. Saigon was the site of the worst fighting during the Tet Offensive in 1968, and we had all seen film of the fighting that raged throughout the city. My first arrival was at night, and as we came low over the city I could see the steamy canals and tin roofed huts that seemed so eerily foreign to anything I had seen in the U.S. or in Europe. I felt that I was entering the lion's den.

We were only on the ground in Saigon for a couple of hours, long enough to unload, refuel, and then load whatever it was they were shipping back home. We were always full in both directions. When I got back on the plane I was stunned to realize that one pallet contained a load of caskets. It was something that we picked up on almost every flight, but I never got used to it. The pallet of caskets was placed at the very front of the plane so it would be the last thing to go if we ever had to ditch our load to reduce weight. And it was always just one pallet per plane because of politics. Early in the war some photographer had taken a picture of a C-141 filled with caskets, and that image was not one that politicians in Washington wanted to see duplicated. One pallet of caskets per plane was much less of a public relations problem. On the trip home I stopped down in the cargo bay to look at the caskets and read the names of the young men I was taking home for the last time, and I realized that somewhere at the other end of the road were families suffering every parent's worst nightmare.

That first trip was exhausting. Every day we crossed five or six time zones, and then got up the next day to do it again. My biological clock was completely out of whack, and I had a terrible time trying to sleep. Part of that was from the disruption of my normal routine, and part was probably from the novelty of the adventure. It didn't improve much on the next trip, or the trip after that, and I wondered how anyone could survive that schedule, much less function safely as a pilot. But eventually I began to adjust. I grew accustomed to the constant time changes, and learned to sleep when I had the chance. Meals were also a problem. Most of our flights were at night; I'm not sure why. We were part of the Military Airlift Command, but referred to ourselves as the Midnight Air Command, because we usually flew at night, and landed in the early morning when nothing was being served except breakfast. I was never very fond of breakfast to begin with, and after a month or two of that I didn't care if I ever saw another egg.

Although I gradually adjusted to the routine, fatigue was always a problem. We flew most of the flights on autopilot, and would take turns sleeping during long trips over the ocean. This usually worked well, but not always. On one flight I woke up, looked around the cockpit, and realized that the entire crew had been asleep. One of the problems with sleeping was that we had a primitive computer in that plane that wasn't all that reliable. From time to time it would automatically put the plane into a 180 degree turn, and if we weren't paying attention we would start heading back whence we came. The turn was obvious when I was awake, but not when I was catching a nap. My salvation was that the computer would also turn the control yoke when it put the plane into a turn, so I learned to sleep with my leg draped over the yoke. I couldn't feel the plane turn, but if the yoke turned it would wake me up. Some things you have to learn from experience. They never taught this in pilot training, probably on the assumption that one of the pilots would always be awake.

I flew in and out of Southeast Asia many times over the next two and a half years, but not always into Saigon. Sometimes we flew into one of the bases in Thailand, or one of the other major bases in Vietnam, usually Cam Rahn Bay, or Danang. On occasion I would run into pilot training classmates on these bases, and once or twice I recognized someone's voice while they were talking with air traffic control. Then I would ask him to switch to an unused radio frequency so we could talk privately for a few minutes.

On one trip to U-Tapao Air Base in southern Thailand I ran into Steve Bennett at the officer's club. I was there overnight, and he was there on a ninety day rotation as a co-pilot in a B-52. We had a brief conversation and then went our separate ways. A year later Steve was shot down and killed while flying as a forward air controller in

Vietnam, and he was subsequently one of the few Air Force pilots to be awarded the Congressional Medal of Honor. He was hit while strafing enemy troops. Steve could have ejected, but chose instead to ditch in the ocean because a Marine spotter in the back seat erroneously thought his chute had been damaged. The Marine survived, but Steve died in the crash.

Steve was a nice man, and his death was a loss for him, his parents, his wife, and his infant daughter, Angela, who would never know him. Twenty-five years later I received a call one night from Angela. She was tracking down people who had known her father, trying to get to know him from their memories. In such ways do the tragedies of war continue to cause pain long after the people who started them have passed from the scene.

I didn't see much of the war while flying the C-141. We usually landed only at secure bases, and were in and out in a few hours, but I would occasionally see air attacks in progress. I was especially impressed with AC-130 gunships. The AC-130 had several large machine guns that fired out the left side of the plane. They claimed that this plane could make one pass over a football field, and put a bullet in every square inch. When the plane was working at night it looked as if a solid sheet of fire extended from the plane to the ground. It is amazing that the North Vietnamese persisted in the face of such firepower. Even more devastating were the B-52 bombers. I have seen many B-52 attacks from the air, and felt some of them on the ground. I felt the ground shake in Saigon one night from a B-52 strike twenty miles away. I can't imagine the horror of being in the target zone.

In late 1971 I landed at Phu Cat while a battle raged off the end of the runway. Air strikes were being directed by a forward air controller in a tiny single seat O-1 Birddog, a plane about the size of a Piper Cub. When we approached the base we were put in a holding pattern because the O-1 had been hit, and was making an emergency landing. The pilot got down safely, and I landed right behind him. We parked side by side, and when I walked over to his plane he was still pale and shaky. A quick glance inside his plane explained why. A North Vietnamese machine gun had raked his plane from nose to tail, leaving holes every couple of feet. One bullet came up between the seat and the control stick, passed between his feet, and missed his head by inches before exiting out the top. The next hole was a foot or so behind him. It made me shake just to see it.

I had a sense of foreboding whenever I flew into Vietnam, not for my own safety, but because of the thought of so much destruction occurring directly below me. I was comfortable and secure at twenty thousand feet, but I knew that people were dying just a few miles away. It seemed to be an evil with no end in sight. On the other hand I was also impressed with the beauty of the country, especially from the air. From a distance it is a tropical paradise with beautiful mountains and one of the world's most gorgeous coastlines. The waters off the Vietnamese coast are many shades of blue and green, and are dotted with coral reefs and islands. It is hard to imagine that such beauty and such brutality can exist side by side.

Only half of my flights were to Vietnam. The other half were to Europe, Africa, and the Mideast. Most months I would take one trip to Vietnam, have a week or so off, and then take a trip to Europe. We occasionally landed in England or Madrid, Spain, but our usual destination was Frankfurt, Germany. We would crew rest in Frankfurt, and then again at Incirlik AFB in Turkey before proceeding on to Lebanon, Iran, Saudi Arabia, or Ethiopia where the U.S. maintained a sophisticated satellite tracking station.

Ethiopia was particularly interesting to me. Haile Selassie was still the emperor, and it was like two countries in one. In the north Asmara was a European City that showed the influence of the long Italian occupation. To the south the capital city of Addis Ababa was very much an African city. The runway at Addis Ababa is nearly eight thousand feet in elevation, which makes landing there unusual, especially when combined with surrounding mountains, and primitive navigation aids. At eight thousand feet landing speeds are considerably higher than normal, and the plane's turn radius is much wider.

One of my flights to Addis Ababa was with Lt. Col. John Talley who had started his Air Force career during World War II. He was a check pilot who was considered to be a tough judge, but I enjoyed flying with him because he always had a useful suggestion or two. You can't fly for thirty years without learning something. There was no Air Force facility in Addis Ababa, so we stayed at the Hilton Hotel. The rest of the crew had dinner that night at the Hilton, but Col. Talley was an adventurous epicurean who persuaded me to have dinner with him at one of the local restaurants. He later almost killed himself eating toadstools that he mistook for mushrooms, but that's another story.

We caught a cab at the Hilton that took us through the dark winding dirt streets until we finally arrived at a simple single story restaurant where we sat on the floor, and ate a stew served on pita bread. We ate with our fingers, tearing off pieces of bread to scoop up the stew, and I have no idea what we were eating. It could have been eyeball stew for all I know, but I do know it was spicy. The next morning the crew assembled in the hotel lobby for the bus ride back to the airport, and we discovered that everyone in the crew was sick except for Col. Talley and me. My guess is that there were enough spices in that stew to kill any germs that tried to grow there.

Of course Ethiopia was our friend back then, as was Iran, while the Soviet Union was our enemy. We had to thread a needle to fly from Turkey to Iran without intruding on Soviet or Iraqi airspace. We accomplished this by following radio beacons from VOR stations on the ground, but we were aware that some years earlier the Soviet Union had shot down an Air Force plane after luring it into Soviet airspace by building a VOR station on Soviet territory with the same frequency as the one in Turkey.

The approach into Tehran was the steepest of any airport I ever flew into. Approaching from the north we cleared a mountain range, and then had to dive abruptly to get down to the runway. We stayed in a hotel in Tehran, but one evening we went to the American embassy for dinner and entertainment by a troupe of Iranian dancers. A few years later the Shah was overthrown, and the Americans in the embassy were held hostage for the better part of two years. As has been true of so many other countries, they were friends one year and enemies the next.

Libya had also been our friend until Gadhafi staged a successful coup, and ordered the Americans to leave. In the summer of 1970 I flew one of the last flights into Wheelus Air Force Base outside of Tripoli to evacuate the remaining American personnel. After landing we were surrounded by jeeps manned by Libyan soldiers with machine guns, and when I stepped out the door I was hit by temperatures that exceeded one hundred and twenty degrees in the shade. It was an oven. We were turning the base back to the Libyans, but they weren't getting much. The buildings still stood, but doors had been removed from their hinges, and electrical sockets had been removed from the walls. The U.S. administration apparently felt about as friendly towards Gadhafi as he felt towards them.

On most of these trips we would return, as we came, through Rhein-Main Air Base in Frankfurt. Just a few miles off the west end of the runway was the little town of Raunheim, the hometown of Christiane Moravetz who had been a German exchange student during my senior year in high school. I had visited her a couple of times in 1966 and 1967 during trips to Europe, so I knew where she lived, and I could easily pick out her house during final approach. If I had the time I would occasionally drive over to visit her family, or meet her at the officer's club for dinner. Her father had been a member of the Waffen S.S. during World War II while my father was a pilot in the Army Air Corps, and then their children became close friends. It is a strange world we live in.

During one of my flights to Europe I had two co-pilots, including Ed Kennedy, unrelated to the Massachusetts Kennedys. Ed was on his first flight to Europe. He was a bit macho, and refused to take my advice not to drink the water in Madrid. The next day we flew to Incirlik AFB in Turkey, and in the middle of the night I heard a knock at my door. It was the other co-pilot, telling me that Ed was sick and needed help. So we carted him off to the base hospital just barely coherent. They started to hook him up to an IV, but before they did they asked him if he was allergic to anything. In not much more than a whisper he said, "Cats." I'm pretty sure there weren't any cats in his IV.

Ed was in no condition to fly for a few days, so I proceeded on to Ethiopia without him. By the time we came back through Incirlik on our way home Ed was able to ride along as a passenger, and that night in Frankfurt he had recovered enough to take nourishment, so I took him to the officers club. He was also dehydrated and thirsty for something to drink. I waited until he drank about half his glass of water, and then told him, "Oh, by the way, you don't want to drink the water here either." There was a look of panic on his face until he realized I was joking. After Madrid I could have told him anything and he would have believed me.

I saw beautiful parts of the world in the C-141. The Vietnam coastline stands out, as do the mountains in eastern Turkey, the glaciers in Alaska, and the Greek islands. I had one flight into Beirut, Lebanon before it was destroyed during the Lebanese civil war, and I was struck by the beauty of the rolling green countryside. I'm not sure what I expected in Lebanon, but it wasn't that. One of the most beautiful sights was Tokyo Bay. I remember in particular one flight from Okinawa to Alaska that took me over Tokyo late at night. The sky was crystal clear, and the city surrounding the bay was aglow in lights. It was gorgeous. Twenty six years earlier other American pilots had seen Tokyo aglow, but then it was from the fire bomb attacks that burned much of the city to the ground. Fire bombing civilian populations has long been illegal under international law, but only if you lose. Miraculously the city had been resurrected from the ashes in only twenty six years. That was in large part due to the efficiency of capitalism. I visited East Berlin in the mid 1960s when many blocks of that city were still piles of rubble. Communism was a nice theory, but it had a few glitches in practice.

I also observed natural phenomena that I didn't see growing up in Michigan. I flew over Vietnam one night when a comet seemed to stretch over much of the night sky. I frequently saw the Northern Lights dancing over Alaska, and one afternoon when I was in U-Tapao, Thailand I spent the afternoon on the beach at the Gulf of Thailand. Late in the day clouds developed out in the bay, and then a funnel slowly descended down to the water. The funnel acted as a straw, and in a matter of minutes the clouds grew from fluffy cumulous to towering thunderheads that must have reached forty thousand feet. It was a water spout, which is essentially a tornado over water. And then as quickly as it appeared it was gone.

One night over the Atlantic I was startled to see the nose of the airplane start to glow with an eerie blue-green light. I watched it move inside, and soon the throttles and the instrument panel were also glowing. I thought perhaps we were in trouble until one of the older crewmembers told me that it was St. Elmo's Fire, an electrical luminescence named after the patron saint of sailors. Sometimes ships' masts would glow with St. Elmo's Fire during thunderstorms, and sailors regarded it as an auspicious omen that St. Elmo was looking out for them. I saw it on a few occasions after that, and it was always impressive.

Jet engines are far more reliable than internal combustion engines, and I never had a serious in-flight emergency in the C-141, although I had a few anxious moments usually related to weather. I landed in a couple of thunderstorms that made flight control a real challenge, and on one flight from Anchorage to Tokyo so much snow got packed into the wheel wells during takeoff that I was unable to retract the landing gear when I got airborne. The weather at Anchorage was just good enough to take-off, but not good enough to land, so I was preparing to divert to Fairbanks when the wheels finally came up and locked. I then proceeded on to Tokyo, but I worried that the wheels were so encased in a block of ice that they might fail to come down when I got ready to land. Fortunately everything worked as advertised on landing.

As is often the case, my closest call came from my own mistake. During a landing at McGuire AFB in New Jersey one evening I let a young co-pilot fly the approach in a two hundred foot overcast. That alone was questionable judgment, but I compounded it by not watching him as carefully as I should have. When we approached our minimum altitude the procedure was for the person flying the plane to monitor the instruments while the other pilot looked for the approach lights. So at three hundred feet I started looking for the runway while the co-pilot flew the plane. After searching for the runway for ten or fifteen seconds I glanced back at the airspeed indicator and realized that we were twenty-five knots below approach speed, and on the verge of a stall. I immediately pushed the throttles to full power and took control of the plane, and I'm sure the hundred or so passengers in the back were alarmed by the sudden roar of the engines. They should have been.

We got into that situation because the co-pilot started looking for the runway instead of concentrating on his instruments. While he looked for the runway he unintentionally leveled off, which caused the airspeed to decrease. His airspeed had been perfect up until then, so I had no clue that he was slowing down. If he had moved the throttles I would have heard the change in the engines, and would have known to check his speed, but this was so insidious that I never suspected he had leveled off. As with my disastrous first solo in the T-37 you can see it level off, but you can't feel it, and we were within a hair's breadth of putting that plane in the trees. It was the last time I ever stopped crosschecking the airspeed indicator, whether I was flying or not. Old pilots are safe pilots in part because of the mistakes they have made that didn't quite manage to kill them.

In the fall of 1971 I flew from Dover to Andrews AFB outside of Washington D.C. to pick up President Nixon's limousine and members of the Secret Service to accompany him on a trip to Maine and Chicago. Even though I was the aircraft commander the Secret Service would not let me get close to the limousine. In Chicago we parked next to Air Force One, and I had a close look at Nixon when he returned after his appearance in the city. I did not have friendly thoughts about Nixon, so maybe they were correct in not letting me get close to his car. On the way back to Washington the Secret Service broke out bottles of liquor to relax at the end of the day. I had my loadmaster advise them that liquor was not allowed on Air Force planes, and they sent a message back to me that was not polite at all. I had a pretty good idea where I stood in the pecking order, so they drank the rest of the way home.

Between trips I usually had a week or more off with nothing to do. I lived in Dover in an apartment complex on Silver Lake along with many other pilots and school teachers, and there was a party going on somewhere most of the time. In the summer we water-skied almost every day, and summer in Delaware is longer than the summers I had known in Michigan. One year we water-skied every month of the year except February when the lake was frozen solid the entire month. I did water-ski in January of that year when only half the lake was frozen. I was dumber then than I am now.

The two and a half years I spent in Dover were like the years many others experience in college, carefree and fun. There was always something going on in Dover, and we also took occasional trips down to the Delaware shore, or to Washington or Philadelphia. A couple of times we went snow skiing in the Pocono Mountains. I had never been skiing before, so I started on the kiddy slope, and after an hour or two I felt I was ready to take on the steepest slope they had. I had trouble getting on and off the ski-lift, but eventually I worked my way over to the slope and started down. And I was a natural. I couldn't turn or stop, but I could ski like the wind. I passed everybody on the mountain and got to the bottom in record time. I had found my sport.

Not smart enough to quit while I was ahead I decided to make one more run. This one started much like the first until I hit a mogul, and lost control. All I remember is seeing the trees and the snow and the sky, and the trees and the snow and the sky, and….. I finally came to rest half buried, and without skis, gloves, or hat. After taking stock of my injuries I limped back up the hill to collect my equipment, and then walked down to the bottom where I turned it in. After that I was a ski lounge skier.

I have fond memories of the friends I made in Dover. Some of them are gone now. The pilots and navigators included Juri Laurits, John White, Frank Petryszak, Jon Balk, Steve Hoffman, and Chas Erickson. There were also a number of young women, mostly schoolteachers, including Norma Benjamin, Margie McGinley, Bev Filer, Mimi Crowley, Peggy Reger, and Carolyn Morasco. In 1971 my sister Debby graduated from Central Michigan University with a teaching certificate, but no job, so I invited her down for a visit, and arranged for an interview at the base elementary school where she was offered a job. So for the next year I was able to share my friends with her. I also introduced her to Chas Erickson, one of the pilots in my squadron, and she has now been married to him for thirty two years.

For the first year and a half in the C-141 I was a co-pilot while I accumulated hours in the plane and became familiar with international flying. In a civilian airline it would have taken many years to become an aircraft commander, but one advantage of the military is that young men are given more responsibility than they can get anywhere else, and in July 1971 I was promoted to aircraft commander while still just a first lieutenant. Under Air Force rules that made me not only the aircraft commander, but also the crew commander in the air and on the ground. When we were on a trip I was responsible for all decisions involving the airplane, the mission, and the crew. It is a rather odd custom. It was not unusual to have a major or a lieutenant colonel as my navigator, but I was their commander even as a first lieutenant.

Mark Twain was a Mississippi riverboat captain as a young man, and later described it as the defining experience of his life. It was adventure, seeing parts of the country that few people had ever seen. It was prestige, riverboat captains being regarded with both awe and respect. And it was responsibility, having the safety of the boat and all of the passengers in his hands. For me the C-141 was my riverboat. It was all Mark Twain experienced and more. I remember flight planning a trip at the airport in Bangkok one time, and realizing that all of the airline captains in the room were in their forties and fifties, but there I was at age twenty-five doing the very same job they were doing, and with the same responsibility. I wouldn't trade it for anything.

I enjoyed flying the T-38 in pilot training with its speed and power and maneuverability, but I loved the C-141. I liked the responsibility, and I never tired of flying to distant parts of the world. It fit my personality as no fighter aircraft ever could. I liked the challenge of learning a very complicated machine, I felt a sense of accomplishment in learning all of the rules and procedures for international air travel, and I enjoyed working with a crew. But I also loved the airplane itself. It was just a joy to fly. Although primitive by present standards, it at the time had the most modern systems and instruments available, it was very responsive, and for a large cargo airplane it had power to spare. Even more than the T-38 I would pay big money for one more trip in a C-141.

But all good things come to an end, and I knew that I was due for an assignment to Vietnam. We could request the airplane that we wanted to fly in Vietnam, but there was no guarantee that the request would be granted. My only request was to fly a plane without guns. As the war dragged on I had grown more and more opposed to it, and my hope was to get an assignment to fly cargo or surveillance or rescue, or anything that didn't require me to kill for a war that seemed to me to be a terrible mistake.

Chapter Five

In December 1971 I received an assignment to fly AC-119s, a smaller version of the AC-130 gunships that I had seen at work on some of my trips to Vietnam. It placed me in the worst moral dilemma of my life. The AC-119 was a killing machine, with only limited knowledge of who would be on the receiving end. They might be enemy soldiers, or they might not. And even the enemy soldiers were just young men drafted to fight for their country. By December 1971 few people could think the U.S. was going to win that war. We stayed primarily because President Nixon did not want to be humiliated, and he was willing to sacrifice thousands of American soldiers, and tens of thousands of Vietnamese to postpone that fate. It might have been worth it to him, but it wasn't to me.

My temporary salvation came in the form of an Air Force flight surgeon, Bob Billings. He had flown with me on a couple of trips in the C-141, and when I got my assignment he offered to ground me for medical reasons until the AC-119 assignment was given to someone else, hopefully someone who wanted it. It wasn't the most honorable of solutions, but it was a solution, and I thought it was preferable to having blood on my hands for the rest of my life. I wasn't trying to avoid Vietnam. I was prepared to go there, and God forbid die there, but not to kill there.

Bob's plan worked, kind of. The assignment was withdrawn, but in a couple of months I was back on flying status, and I soon received another set of orders to fly the AC-119. This time I took the more direct, if not more honorable, approach of requesting help from my congressman and senators. I wrote letters stating my willingness to fly any plane in Vietnam that did not require me to kill, and asked them to intervene on my behalf. A few weeks later I received a response telling me that the Air Force had also refused that request. I didn't know what would happen next, but I did know that I would not fly the AC-119.

This time my salvation came in the form of orders changing my assignment from the AC-119 to the EC-47. The EC-47 was an unarmed plane that flew electronic surveillance missions. I can only assume that the Air Force decided to deny the request as a matter of policy, but to grant it in practice. Certainly someone along the line had done me a favor. It may have been for my benefit, or it may have been because the last thing the Air Force needed right then was a public relations problem. In any event I was relieved.

By the time all of this came to a head in the winter of 1972 I had spent years thinking about the war and searching for a solution that I could live with. But there was no easy answer. Some people thought that even paying taxes to support the war was immoral, while many others believed that our elected officials should decide what is moral. I was somewhere in-between. There may not be any significant difference between flying surveillance missions in support of the war, and dropping bombs, but it was enough to soothe my conscience. My uncles in the Civil War and my father in World War II would never have considered refusing an order on moral grounds, but in those wars I probably wouldn't have considered it either. This war, I thought, was different. I still do.

I did have a good role model. Back in 1916 Harold Gray became a conscientious objector while ministering to German prisoners of war on behalf of the YMCA. When he was later drafted he refused to serve, and was sent to prison at Leavenworth and Alcatraz. The prosecutor had requested the death penalty, but Harold escaped with a long prison term instead. After World War I ended he was released, with the notation on his discharge that his character was bad. In 1932 *Character Bad* became the title of a popular book describing his experiences and his pacifist beliefs. He then put his economic theories into practice by creating the Saline Valley cooperative farm south of Ann Arbor. His hope was to provide economic security to workers in an agrarian setting.

It was my good fortune to grow up on that farm. My first memories are of the small home that my parents rented a short distance from Harold Gray's home. They did not participate in the cooperative farm, but rented a home there while Dad served as the principal of Saline High School. No kid ever grew up in a more idyllic setting. We ran barefoot through the woods and fields, swam and fished in the lake in the summer, and went ice skating in the winter. In the fall we rode around in the farm truck while they harvested the wheat. A threshing machine drove beside the truck, cutting the wheat, and pouring it through a funnel into the bed of the truck where we were playing.

For me the Saline Valley Farms will always be sacred ground. It was a sad day when Harold's grand experiment failed in 1954, the same year we moved from Saline to Belleville. Over the years many of the farm's operations had slowly stopped functioning, and by the time we moved there in 1949 the orchard and many of the vegetable crops had been abandoned in favor of corn and wheat which were less labor intensive. The commercial cannery had also been closed, but the dairy herd and milk processing plant continued to operate. I have vivid memories of getting up at 3:15 in the morning on several occasions so I could accompany Dad when he drove the milk route on the weekend. The smell of that dairy will be with me until the day I die, but the dairy and the barns and the company store are all gone now, as is the house where I grew up. Only when I close my eyes can I see them as they were sixty years ago.

When I was only three or four I spent many days riding around with Harold Gray on his tractor while he pushed dirt. I have no idea where he was pushing that dirt, but it seemed to be one of his favorite activities, and I doubt he could have done it without my help. I would help him in the morning, and then wait on his doorstep after lunch until he had finished his nap so we could move more dirt in the afternoon. I don't know if he just tolerated me or if he enjoyed my company, but I enjoyed his. I knew he had gone to prison as a conscientious objector, but didn't know about his book until very recently. I wish I had known about that back in 1972 when I was struggling with my own conscience, because Harold was still alive then, and it would have been interesting to know if his views had changed since 1918. He refused to participate in any fashion during World War I, but I hope he would have understood my compromise. It's an honor to share a bad character with a man like Harold Gray.

I had my last flight in the C-141 in late April 1972, and left immediately for England AFB in Alexandria, Louisiana to transition into the EC-47. The "E" identified it as a C-47 that was equipped for electronic warfare. It was a bit of a shock the first time I got in a C-47. I had gone from flying a supersonic jet trainer in pilot training, to the large four engine jet transport in Dover, to this propeller driven relic that was designed in the 1920s. Throughout the 1930s and 1940s the civilian version of the C-47 (the DC-3) was the workhorse of civilian aviation. It is the plane that took my mother from Chicago to Texas to get married in 1942.

The C-47 had a tailwheel instead of a nosewheel, canvas covered flight controls, and could fly with the windows open. I had to learn how to fly with a variable pitch prop, and it took an engineering degree to operate the landing gear. Modern jets have a landing gear handle that is either up or down. In the C-47 there are several gear handles that have to be operated in exactly the right sequence. Get it screwed up and you can get stuck with one wheel up and the other wheel down. In retrospect I'm glad that I had the chance to fly a piece of history, but I can't say that I enjoyed it. My enthusiasm for the C-47 was exceeded only by my enthusiasm for the war.

In mid June I finished C-47 training and returned to Dover for a couple of days to say good-by to friends, and to see my parents who had driven down from Michigan to visit before I headed off to war. It was a sad farewell, knowing that I wouldn't be home for a year, if I came home at all. The EC-47 was not a dangerous assignment, but war is war, and we did lose two crews from my squadron during the year I was there, along with several close calls. In retrospect I'm sure the parting was more difficult for my parents than it was for me. I was going to a war zone where I had already spent some time, so it wasn't completely foreign to me, and I understand now what it means to be a parent. I would go to war any day before seeing one of my children go. I would even fly an AC-119 if it meant my kids could stay home. Some things are worth killing for.

The next morning I flew out of Dulles Airport for San Francisco, and took a military charter from there to the Philippines for jungle survival school. Jungle survival school was a pleasure compared to the survival school I had attended in Idaho. The only other survival school I attended was sea survival in April 1972 at Homestead AFB south of Miami. I had looked forward to that as a chance to go to southern Florida for a few days after a long winter. What more could I ask for? But as it turned out I was almost as cold at Homestead in April as I had been in Idaho in November. I arrived at Homestead in the middle of the worst cold spell of the year, and I don't think the temperature hit sixty degrees the whole time I was there. For three days I was soaking wet from morning 'til night, and nearly froze. Survival schools were just not kind to me. I figured that jungle survival should at least be warm.

Our teachers were Negritos, the Pygmy sized indigenous people who had made life miserable for their Japanese occupiers during World War II. They know the jungle like I know my own house. Much of the training was in how to hide in the jungle, and how to escape and evade capture if we were shot down. Before going into the jungle they took us out to a grassy hillside, and told us to close our eyes. Then one of the Negritos hid, and we had to find him. It shouldn't have been difficult, because there was no place to hide. The grass wasn't knee deep, and there wasn't a bush or a tree in sight.

When we couldn't find him the instructor told him to whistle. This narrowed the search somewhat, but still without success. When we finally gave up, the hidden Negrito reached out and grabbed one of my classmates by the ankle. He had somehow burrowed under the grass to the point where he was completely invisible.

Our job was much easier than his. We were taken into the jungle and given fifteen minutes to find a place to hide. It didn't look difficult, because there are millions of places to hide in a jungle, and you would think that we could have hidden there all day. We each had a rice chip that we had to turn over to any Negrito who found us, and the Negrito could turn it in for rice. It was his pay for assisting in the training, and we soon discovered that the Negritos were as good at finding us as they were at hiding. We might as well have had Neon lights on our heads. I was hoping that the North Vietnamese weren't half as good as these guys.

Compared to the mountains of Idaho the jungle was like a supermarket. With a little knowledge you can find any number of edible plants, and potable water is inside every stick of bamboo. We spent one night out camping, and the Negritos cooked up a feast from plants that they found easily. My most surprising discovery was the noise. The jungle is almost silent during the day, but it makes a racket at night. Every animal and insect starts hollering as soon as the sun goes down, and every rat that runs by sounds like a horse crashing through the underbrush. It wasn't a very restful night, which may have been part of the reason that I looked a little disheveled when I ran into Jack Kendall the next morning back at Clark.

I realized somewhere along the way that my orders still had me going to the AC-119 squadron at Nakhon Phanom, Thailand. The Air Force had changed my training orders, but forgot to change my final destination. So I went to base operations at Clark for instructions, and they told me to proceed on to Saigon, and wait there for further orders. I had been to Tan Son Nhut AFB in Saigon many times, but this time it was different. When I stepped off the plane I was hit by the heat and the smell, and the depression of knowing that this would be my home for the next twelve months. It was an altogether different feeling than I ever had during my frequent three hour turn-arounds in the C-141. It didn't even seem like the same place.

There were several EC-47 squadrons scattered around Vietnam, so I got a room on base, and waited for someone to tell me where to go next. Every couple of days I would check in with the personnel office, and they would tell me that they were working on it. There was an EC-47 squadron at Tan Son Nhut, so eventually I decided to be proactive and just report to them, but when I did the officer in charge told me that they had all the pilots they needed, and that I should catch a ride up to Danang and wait there for orders. This I knew was a really bad idea. Danang was a hellhole compared to Tan Son Nhut, so if I had to wait somewhere for orders I would wait right there in Saigon thank you very much.

So I waited. And I waited. And I waited. Altogether I sat there with nothing to do for almost six weeks. No one ever said the military is efficient. I read, worked out, went to the officers' club for dinner, and slept. Without much to do I also tried to improve my room. It had a couple of small windows, and a previous resident had put masking tape all over them, making it look like a prison cell. So I got a razor blade and meticulously removed all the tape, giving me a nice view of the barbed wire fence outside. When I casually mentioned to someone what I had done he told me that the tape was there to keep the windows from shattering in the event of a rocket attack. So the next day I was back in my prison cell.

In those days the Air Force had an odd mix of officers. At least half of the young officers were only there because of the threat of the draft. It was either the Air Force or the jungle, and nobody in his right mind wanted to be in the jungle, but there were also many career officers. They enjoyed the military life, and planned to stay for at least twenty years to qualify for retirement. There was also a real psychological difference between pilots who flew fighters, and pilots like myself who gravitated towards transports. Transport pilots were civilians at heart. In many ways we were just airline pilots. We got our airplane safely from one place to another and then went home. The fighter pilots were adrenaline junkies who tended to be more militaristic and aggressive. I suppose you need that attitude to be effective in the job, just as you would probably find a very different psychological profile between professional golfers and professional football players. The fighter pilots were football players.

Today the Air Force recognizes those differences, and has different training programs for pilots who are destined to go into fighters, and pilots who are headed for multi-engines. In the 1960s and 70s everyone trained in the T-38, and the theory was that every pilot was a warrior. The official slogan back then was "Every man a tiger." But I wasn't a tiger, and I knew it. I think I was a very good transport pilot, but I wasn't a warrior.

Those differences became clear to me at the officers club at Tan Son Nhut. It was a good place to eat, but it also had cheap alcohol, continuous poker games for small or large pots, and a piano bar that tended to become more raucous as the evening wore on. As in previous wars, the Vietnam War also had its own songs. Some of those songs I enjoyed, but I drew the line at "Napalm Sticks to Kids." Late in the evening the warriors would sing that one with gusto, but even in the numbed atmosphere of a prolonged war I couldn't understand how anyone could find the song amusing. It had multiple verses, some of which went like this:

> Little kids sucking on their mother's tit
> Gooks down in a fifty foot pit
> Dow Chemical doesn't give a shit
> Napalm sticks to kids.

> Little school children in a free fire zone
> Books under their arms as they're walking home
> Last one in line goes home alone
> Napalm sticks to kids

> Killing gooks is lots of fun
> When you get one who's pregnant
> It's two for one
> Napalm sticks to kids.

> Chorus:

> Napalm, napalm
> Napalm, napalm
> Dow Chemical doesn't give a shit
> Napalm sticks to kids.

After six weeks in limbo I finally received orders assigning me to the squadron at Saigon, so I took my orders and returned to the same man who six weeks earlier had told me to wait in Danang. He wasn't happy that I had stayed in Saigon, but it didn't matter, I was going to Danang anyway. He told me that the squadron in Saigon was being shut down, and that the entire squadron would be leaving on a C-130 for

Danang the next morning. I had been to Danang often enough to know that it was not a nice place, and that it received rocket attacks on a regular basis. I haven't been drunk many times in my life, but that night I made an exception.

I arrived in Danang the next morning, and was immediately issued a helmet and a flak vest. The regulations required everyone to wear those whenever we were outside. They also assigned me to a room on the second floor of a barracks made out of plywood. Each airplane at Danang was placed in a concrete bunker, but the people lived in plywood buildings. As a new arrival I was on the second floor, because everyone with seniority was on the ground floor. There was a reason for this. They stacked sandbags around the base of the building to protect the ground floor from rocket attacks, but there was no way to protect the second floor. If you lived through the first six months on the second floor you got to move downstairs for the remainder of your tour.

There was some grass at Tan Son Nhut, but Danang was just dirt and dust, and the prospect of spending ten months there was daunting. I went to my room, upstairs, got settled in, and decided to take a shower to revive myself from the night before, but this didn't improve my mood any. The shower was made out of plastic, and when I stepped into it I saw multiple rays of sunshine filtering through shrapnel holes from previous rocket attacks. To make me feel even worse the veterans told me that not long before a pilot had been severely wounded by shrapnel while asleep in his bed, upstairs.

When rockets explode the shrapnel is thrown upwards. On the second level it would enter through the floor, so I scrounged a second flak vest, and that night I laid the helmet and the two flak vests next to my bed. With the sound of the first rocket I planned to roll out of bed, and ride out the rest of the attack on top of the flak vests and the helmet. It wasn't a great plan, but it was the best I could think of.

That night I had the opportunity to put my plan into action. Around three a.m. I was awakened by the sound of an explosion, and bailed out of bed onto the flak vests, with my head in the helmet. But there were no other explosions, and as I fully woke up I realized that the sound I heard came from the afterburners of an F-4 taking off on a mission. There were no rockets. Then lifting my head from the helmet I came face to face with my roommate who was returning from a trip to the bathroom, and who had witnessed my act of heroism. In some situations there just isn't any good explanation.

The next morning we all reported to the EC-47 squadron at Danang, and learned that half of us would stay there, and the other half would go to Nakhon Phanom (NKP) in northern Thailand. Every other man alphabetically was selected for NKP, and I was, thank you God, one of those chosen to leave. I had never been to NKP, but it had to be better than Danang. And it was. Compared to Danang NKP was a paradise, green and lush with vegetation. There were no rocket attacks, no sandbags, and no flak vests. I still didn't look forward to ten months at NKP, but it was a big improvement over either Danang or Saigon. So I grabbed my B4 bag and headed off to find my room, which just happened to be Nickey C. Lucas's old room.

NKP was carved out of the jungle in the mid sixties as the war began to heat up, and most of the buildings were simple structures put up quickly. They are all gone now, and the jungle has returned, but in 1972 it was a thriving enterprise, the home of forward air controllers and special operation squadrons that supported the air war in Laos and North Vietnam. The EC-47 was used for electronic surveillance to listen to North Vietnamese radio transmissions, plot their positions, and call in air strikes. My job was just to fly the airplane. All of the spying was performed by highly trained enlisted men who operated the sophisticated top secret equipment in the back, and I have no doubt that the equipment we carried was worth far more than the airplane. In fact, we were warned that if we ever had to crash land that we should get away from the plane, because the Air Force would immediately send in fighter bombers to destroy it to prevent the equipment from falling into enemy hands.

I was a member of the 361st Tactical Electronics Warfare Squadron, called the 361st TEWS for short. Our call sign was Baron, and we all lived in a long row of cabins built a few feet above the ground to avoid flooding during the monsoon season. There was also a squadron of Nails, the call sign for the OV-10 forward air controllers, and a squadron of Jolly Green rescue helicopters. My squadron shared a common courtyard with the Jolly Greens. In the middle of the courtyard was a large cage for Buffy, a Malaysian Sun Bear that one of the Jolly Green pilots had picked up out of the jungle when he was just a cub. He was full grown in 1972, about the size of a small black bear, and with a taste for beer. Most afternoons the Jolly Green pilot who cared for him would let him out to exercise and walk around. He also liked to wrestle, and he could keep it up indefinitely without getting tired. He would go through two or three opponents, and still be ready for all takers. At the end of the war he was shipped to a zoo in St. Louis where I'm sure they took good care of him, but I suspect he had to give up his daily beer habit.

NKP Air Base was a few miles from the town of Nakhon Phanom, a small town on the Mekong River that served as the border between northern Thailand and Laos. Across the river we could see the Laotian town of Thaket, but we weren't allowed to go there. Laos was Indian country. Most of it was controlled by the North Vietnamese and the Communist Pathet Lao guerillas. The Ho Chi Minh Trail ran through Laos, and it was the North's lifeline to the South. The air war in Laos was a spectacularly unsuccessful attempt to cut that lifeline. Rumor had it that Nakhon Phanom was a rest and recreation center for both sides, with Communist forces slipping across the river to escape the battles in Laos. There, amongst the bars and brothels, both sides coexisted in perfect harmony until it came time to return to the war.

Chapter Six

I flew my first combat mission in September as co-pilot for George Spitz. Everyone had to fly a few missions as co-pilot to become familiar with the procedures and the territory, and my first mission was to the Barrel Roll in northern Laos. The southern panhandle of Laos was called the Steel Tiger. Most of my flying that year was in the Barrel Roll, a mountainous land in the foothills of the Himalayas. In the middle of all this was a flat plain called the Plain of Jars. It received its name because of the ancient clay jars that were found there. The Plain of Jars had changed hands several times during the war, but by the time I arrived it was firmly controlled by the North Vietnamese.

The EC-47 carried no oxygen, so we were not allowed to fly above ten thousand feet. This made things a little dicey in the north, because many of the mountains in the Barrel Roll were over nine thousand feet. Flying that slow and that low to the ground meant that we had to be very careful where we flew if we wanted to stay alive. We were sitting ducks for anti-aircraft artillery, especially if radar controlled, and the only way to survive was to know where the guns were, and to stay a safe distance away. Every time an aircraft was shot at the pilot noted the gun position, and reported it when he landed. Then before each flight we would be briefed on all the known gun emplacements in the area where we were flying.

This worked well most of the time, but every once in awhile the sneaky little bastards would move one of the guns, so I never knew for sure where the guns were located on any given day. The one thing I did know was that the guns would be next to a road. An anti-aircraft gun is a big piece of equipment that has to be hauled around by a truck. You wouldn't find one out in the middle of the jungle. In our missions we loitered over an area for eight hours, so there were a couple of common sense precautions that we took to minimize the risk. First, I never flew down a road. Guns could be anywhere on a road, and if I flew down a road I was bound to find one sooner or later. The solution was to cross roads only at right angles. Another precaution was to never cross a road at the same place twice. If we set up a pattern of crossing a road routinely at the same place there was a good chance that a gun would be there waiting for us before our eight hour mission was completed.

Staying away from the roads usually kept us away from the guns, but not always. In order to accurately plot the position of enemy radios the navigator first had to know where he was. This was in the days before global positioning or modern computers, so the navigator had to constantly update his position by flying over a known point on the ground. One of our favorite spots to do this was a pretty waterfall deep in the jungle in southern Laos. It was a safe spot miles from any town or any road, and we grew complacent. But someone on the ground was watching, and apparently grew frustrated from seeing us fly over the same spot unmolested day after day. Eventually Major Ray Martinez discovered just how frustrated they had become when he took a direct hit from an anti-aircraft shell while flying over that waterfall. How they had lugged an anti-aircraft gun through the jungle I will never know. The explosion blew a three foot hole in his wingtip, and sent shrapnel through several seats, but no one was hit, and the plane returned to Nakhon Phanom without difficulty. It was the last visit any of us paid to that waterfall. I assume the North Vietnamese eventually dragged the gun out of the jungle the same way they had dragged it in, but no one was willing to bet his life on it.

George Spitz was in his second tour of duty in Thailand. He certainly knew what was safe, and what wasn't, and nothing was more dangerous than flying directly over the Plain of Jars in northern Laos. There was no military reason to do it, but on my first mission with him that's exactly what he did, and in short order the anti-aircraft fire opened up, fortunately without success. If anyone had taken me over the Plain after

I became familiar with the territory there would have been a fight in the cockpit, but on this first mission I was too naïve to realize where he was taking me. There are some people who crave adrenaline, and I can only assume that George was one of them.

Another area that we avoided was the Ho Chi Minh Trail itself. We flew close to it, but you needed a death wish to fly over it. And then in early 1973 some bureaucrat in a basement office in Washington decided that sending EC-47s over the Trail was a good idea. Here we were in the last days of the war, and they were asking us to go on a suicide mission. Plus there was no reason to do it, because we could easily monitor enemy radios and plot positions from miles away. There was a rebellion among the pilots, so they asked for a volunteer, and George Spitz stepped forward. He reported anti-aircraft fire as he entered the area, but still didn't turn back. Fifteen minutes later everyone on the plane was dead, and the next day the bureaucrats decided that maybe it wasn't really such a good idea to fly over the Trail after all.

At the time of George Spitz's fatal flight I was working as a scheduler in addition to flying missions. Every day I made out a schedule that was posted in strategic locations around the base so the pilots could see when and where they were flying the next day. We were all greatly relieved of course when the missions over the Trail were abandoned. I waited for about a week, and then one day posted schedules in all the usual places except for one copy that went up next to the room of a friend of mine. For him I made up a bogus schedule showing him on a mission over the Trail the next day. Then I sat and waited. In a matter of minutes he was pounding on my door, wanting to know who made the decision to go back over the Trail. I gave him time to ponder how he wanted to spend his last evening before finally admitting that it was just a hoax.

One of my best friends at NKP was Bob Kohn, an Air Force Academy graduate. Bob was a good man, but I thought he was a little shaky as a pilot. His first assignment out of pilot training was flying tankers for the Strategic Air Command, which was an indication that he didn't finish very high in his class. No one would choose to fly tankers if he had a choice. I flew with him once as his co-pilot right after getting to NKP, and I had some misgivings about his control of the plane, and a few of the decisions he made. I liked Bob, but I wasn't comfortable flying with him.

In early November Bob and I took a trip into town one evening just to check the place out. We caught a bus from the base, and then hired two pedicabs (a bicycle pulling a passenger cab) as transportation in town. We rode around for two or three hours, and then headed back to the bus stop to catch the last bus to the base. Along the way we decided to have a race, so we put the two pedicab drivers in the back, and pedaled the bicycles ourselves. When we reached top speed Bob lost control of his pedicab and ended up in the ditch with a bent front wheel. It was an omen.

Bob's roommate was Milt Ward, and in mid November Milt's girlfriend flew over from the states for a visit. During that week Bob moved in with me, and slept on a mattress on the floor. He had an early flight on November 21, and went to sleep early the night before, so when I came in later I had to step over him to get to my bunk. It was the last time I would see him alive. His mission was uneventful, but he let his co-pilot land, and the co-pilot lost control on touchdown, veering off to the left. The C-47 was stable in the air, but difficult to control on the ground. Bob overcorrected, veered off the runway to the right, and jumped a ditch before becoming airborne. While clearing a tree line beside the runway he clipped a tree with his right propeller. If he had just done nothing except come around to land he would have been okay, but he immediately called for the co-pilot to shut down the right engine. Instead of shutting down the right engine the co-pilot shut down the left engine, and they nose dived into the trees. Bob died in the crash, although surprisingly the co-pilot and several others survived.

As is true of most aircraft crashes this one was caused by a combination of mistakes; you can usually survive one or two. But I am reminded of a comment made by one of my instructors in pilot training who said, "There are only two kinds of pilots, those who have, and those who will." Sooner or later we will all make mistakes. You just hope that you don't do it often, and that luck is with you when you do. Luck wasn't with Bob that day.

I took Bob's death pretty hard. The squadron commander put me in charge of completing all of the necessary paperwork, and shipping his belongings home to his parents, but when I went through his possessions I found many letters from his girlfriend, and decided that those letters should be returned to her. So I bundled them up and sent them back to her with a brief cover letter, assuming that she had certainly been notified of his death. She hadn't. The first she knew about it was when she received my letter in the mail. I received a nice letter back from her, but I'm sorry that she had to hear about Bob's death in that manner.

Bob is buried at the Air Force Academy, and I have visited his grave a couple of times when I was out in Colorado. He was only twenty-five when he died, and he has missed so much. I can only wonder what he would have done with his life if he had lived. His death was such a waste, as most war deaths are.

Before transferring to NKP, Bob picked up a mongrel puppy from Quality Control at Tan Son Nhut in Saigon. In honor of where he came from, Bob named him QC. After Bob's death a couple of us shared duties as QC's adoptive parents, and he became the squadron mascot. I thought that the squadron mascot should have at least one combat mission under his belt, so one morning I snuck him onto the plane with me. QC sat in the back while I went through my pre-flight routine, but as soon as I started the take-off roll he came running up the aisle and jumped in my lap. As I left the ground he took one look out the window, and then stuck his head under my arm, and that's where he stayed until we landed. When the word got out that our mascot was a combat veteran I received a message from the squadron commander suggesting that this should be QC's last mission. As near as I could tell that was just fine with QC.

Most of my flights out of NKP were routine. There was a war going on, but from a plane it was almost like watching it on TV. I could sit and watch fighter planes dropping bombs and napalm down below me, but I had a sense that none of it was real. Occasionally I had to remind myself that it was real. One day up in northern Laos I watched an artillery duel between two mountain tops. First the shells would land on the mountain off to my left, and then a few moments later I would see the return fire exploding on the mountain to my right. I watched this for a couple of minutes before realizing that all these artillery shells going back and forth were sailing right through the airspace where I was flying. The rest of the battle I watched from a safe distance.

Flights in the EC-47 were tiring. Many of the flights started with briefings at four or five in the morning, and we often didn't get home until late in the afternoon. This was especially true for missions over South Vietnam because it would take us a couple of hours each way just to get to and from the target area, and we often had to stop in Ubon to refuel on the way home, adding another hour to the day. Then we would have dinner, try to catch a few hours sleep, and get up at two or three the next morning to do it all over again. And this was all hand flying. The EC-47 didn't have an autopilot, so we were working the whole time.

Airline pilots today usually fly about sixty hours a month, but in the Air Force we could fly up to one hundred thirty hours in a month, and that didn't count time on the ground for briefings, pre-flight procedures, etc. In December 1972 I flew eighty hours in thirteen days, and the result was exhaustion. At the end of that marathon I had a mission with a relatively young co-pilot over Pleiku in the Central Highlands of South Vietnam. We had a three a.m. wake up, and by mid morning I was dragging. I tried to stay awake, but it was a losing battle. Suddenly I woke up and realized that the plane was in a nose down left bank. I quickly corrected, but just as quickly started dozing again. The next time I woke up the co-pilot was flying. I don't know what position the plane was in when he decided that someone should be flying it.

The need to periodically update the navigator's position almost got Ray Martinez killed over that jungle waterfall, but it saved my life in January 1973 while I was flying a mission in northern Laos close to the Plain of Jars. My job was just to orbit over the area while the spies in the back did their work, and this mission started out like any other. All I had to do was keep the airplane in the air, and stay in my assigned area. In the middle of the mission I found myself crossing a road that ran northwest from the Plain of Jars to the little town of Muong Soui. I had been flying straight and level for five or ten minutes when the navigator asked me to turn back to the south so he could update his position. As I banked the plane to the right I immediately started hearing explosions, and when I looked back to my left I saw tracers from the anti-aircraft shells shooting by my left wingtip. If I had not started my turn exactly when I did those shells would have hit me dead center. They were probably on their way before I even started my turn. Pilots in World War II said that they knew anti-aircraft artillery was close if they could hear the explosions over the roar of their own engines, and I could clearly hear these shells exploding.

It is a strange sensation to know that someone is trying to kill you. After his first battle at the age of twenty-two George Washington wrote that there was "something charming" in the sound of bullets. Winston Churchill said, "There is nothing in life so exhilarating as to be shot at without result." My first thought was, "My God, be careful down there. You almost hit me with that one." They obviously didn't understand that I was just doing my job, and that I bore them no ill will. But after being bombed for years I'm sure they didn't see my role as benignly as I did.

A couple of weeks later I was scheduled for another early morning mission north of the Plain of Jars. Our takeoff was scheduled at four a.m. so we could be in the area by dawn, but before we took off we needed a weather briefing, a security briefing for all the known gun positions, and a crew briefing to plan our flight. These were usually routine, and I would go through them half asleep. But when the navigator, Lt. Col. Nicklas, gave his briefing I was instantly wide awake, because he had flight planned our route to take us directly over the Muong Soui road where I had nearly been shot down two weeks earlier. I had no desire to give them a second chance.

I advised Col. Nicklas about my close call, and told him that I wanted to avoid that road by flying over the mountains west of Muong Soui, a diversion that would add maybe ten minutes to the flight. But this didn't satisfy Col. Nicklas, because it would result in us arriving in our area a few minutes late. There was no military significance to that, but there was bureaucratic significance. The career officers in the squadron had to be evaluated somehow, and one of the methods was to grade them according to on-time arrivals in the target area. If we diverted around Muong Soui it would be a black mark against the squadron. We debated whether the lives of everyone on the plane were more important than a late arrival, but I made no headway with Col. Nicklas. He was adamant.

The problem for Col. Nicklas was that he might be a lieutenant colonel, and he might be the navigator, but he wasn't the mission commander. I was. And unless he could figure out some way to fly that plane from the navigator's seat we weren't going to fly over the Muong Soui road. Finally I told Col. Nicklas that I was sorry, but we were going to fly my route, not his. He responded that he was the navigator, and if I didn't accept his flight plan he wasn't going. I considered that option for a couple of seconds, told him, "Then I guess you're not going," and went to call the back up navigator.

There was always a navigator on stand-by in case someone got sick or was unable to fly for any reason. The stand-by navigator that night was Pete Schwartz. Schwartz and I went through OTS together, and he was nearing the end of his tour at NKP. He had already left mentally, and when I called his room I discovered that even though he was on stand-by he had left the base to spend the night in town with his Thai girlfriend. So I had to call the duty officer to tell him that I was without a navigator. The duty officer then came down and ordered Col. Nicklas to get back on the plane. He could complain about it later if he wanted to.

When we landed Col. Nicklas requested an immediate meeting with the squadron commander and other base officials. They asked me why I wouldn't fly his route, and I told them that I thought we had already lost enough men that month, and that flying over the Muong Soui road was a foolish risk. Then the squadron commander asked if I thought that anything over there was worth dying for, and I told him that I didn't think so, other than rescuing a downed pilot. The war was a lost cause. This was only two or three weeks before the Paris Peace Accords were signed, so I wasn't saying anything that should have come as a shock.

The meeting broke up without any resolution, and I never heard another word about it. I didn't really expect to. I was convinced that my decision was the proper one, and, in any event, all the commanders on the base were pilots, not navigators. One principle they would all defend was that the pilot is the boss on the airplane, and I knew they would be reluctant to undermine that authority even if they thought I was wrong. The squadron commander later wrote a nice letter of recommendation for me when I applied to law school, so I guess he didn't hold the incident against me.

Chapter Seven

I don't know what happened to Schwartz for abandoning his post to spend the night with his girlfriend. Probably nothing. If Laos was Indian country, the bases in the war zone were like the Old West. There was no law, or at least no law as we know it. The officers club had cheap alcohol, topless dancers, slot machines, and a general atmosphere of moral indifference. Prostitutes were in all the bars that lined the main gate to every base, and you couldn't sit in a bar for thirty seconds without finding one in your lap. But they knew their trade, and they would be gone as quickly as they arrived if they sensed they were wasting their time.

Some of the officers, like Schwartz, wanted a more stable relationship, and found a tilac. Tilacs were wives for the year, and when the officer returned home at the end of the year his tilac would move on to someone else. Schwartz's tilac was Niwat. Niwat was drop dead gorgeous. I don't know where Schwartz found her, but she was a prize. Rumor had it that she was previously the tilac of the former base commander. September 17, 1972 was the 25th anniversary of the establishment of the Air Force, and to honor the day the base had a celebration. There were Thai kick boxing and other forms of entertainment, but the highlight of the day was a beauty contest among the tilacs. Every squadron entered one contestant, but it was really no contest at all. Niwat won in a walk. When Schwartz went home he told Niwat that he would send for her, but a month went by, and then two, and Niwat was still waiting. Eventually she moved on to someone else. A girl can only wait so long.

Niwat reminded me of Nately's Whore, a character in the novel *Catch 22* by Joseph Heller. I read that book right after pilot training, and thought it was the funniest satire I had ever read. Then I read it again when I was in Thailand, and was disappointed that it was no longer funny. In order to be humorous satire has to be an exaggeration, and after five years in the Air Force I had either done everything in Heller's novel myself, or knew someone who had.

Schwartz flew as my navigator on his last flight, and had a special request. Before he went home he wanted to buzz the Mekong River. Our mission that day was once again in the Barrel Roll in northern Laos, and we got there by following the Mekong a hundred miles north to where the river makes a sweeping turn to the west. We then left the river to head north across the mountains to our target area. On the way north I maintained normal cruising altitude of ten thousand feet, but on the return home I gave him the ride that he requested. When we got back to the river I dropped down almost to the water, well below the height of the trees that lined both banks. The river is quite wide, and I had no trouble following its course as we headed south. We would have been an easy target for any soldier with a rifle, but the chances of that happening were pretty slim. There would be no reason for soldiers to sit along the river waiting for a plane to make itself an easy target.

As we headed down the river we passed over many fishermen out in their boats. The radial engines on the EC-47 make a racket, and it had to be impressive to be in the middle of a sleepy river when something like that passes a few feet over your head, but despite the noise, and the novelty of a plane at that altitude, most of the fishermen didn't even look up. I would barely clear the masts of their boats, but so far as I could tell they didn't know I was there. They were probably just scared. They didn't know what my intentions were, and they didn't want to look like targets. So they kept their heads down, and continued fishing as if they had no interest in me at all, but their wives probably heard about it that evening.

There were many ways to abort a mission if we didn't feel like flying, but I never did, except once. On Christmas Day 1972 I had an afternoon mission in southern Laos. We took off about two in the afternoon, and were scheduled to land at ten that night.

It wasn't much of a Christmas, but at least the officers club planned a fancy turkey dinner, and I was looking forward to it. But they only served dinner until nine, and I wasn't due to land until ten. Perhaps the North Vietnamese took the day off, because we intercepted almost no radio transmissions all afternoon, and by eight p.m. I had had enough. I called the base to tell them that I was returning because of an overheated engine, but when I landed I told the maintenance officer not to spend a lot of time trying to reproduce the problem, and I think he understood. Then my crew and I all had a Christmas dinner.

After Christmas I took R&R in Hawaii. We had several places to choose from, but Hawaii seemed to me to be the closest to civilization. I didn't have any plans other than to just get away from the war. I only spent a few days in Hawaii, but what struck me was the ability to walk down the street and see people leading normal lives. It was the routine aspects of life that we all take for granted that I missed the most. I saw people going about their daily activities, and thought that this wasn't real. What was real was the war. My body was in Honolulu, but my mind was back in Southeast Asia. I had the same feelings when I returned home for good in June, and it took me months to get over it. I was happy to be home, but I didn't feel as if that was where I belonged.

On New Year's Day I called Bob Kohn's parents from Honolulu. We didn't have access to long distance phones in Thailand, so this was the first opportunity I had to talk to Bob's parents since his death in November. His father was a retired Air Force pilot, and I thought that he would appreciate hearing from one of Bob's friends, and that he would want to know how Bob died. The squadron commander would not allow me to give any details when I wrote to Bob's parents after the accident, and I hoped to ease their minds at least a little. But it turned out that the squadron commander knew what he was doing. Bob's father didn't really want to talk to me, and he had no interest in the details of the accident. I don't think I would react like that if I were in his shoes, but we all deal with loss in our own way.

Shortly after I returned from R&R I had a night mission in southern Laos, just a short distance across the river from NKP. We took off at dusk, and things started out well, but two hours into the flight the cockpit suddenly filled with acrid smoke, making it difficult to breathe or see. I could smell that it was an electrical fire, so I shut down the generators and the battery, killing all electrical power to the plane. In a few minutes the smoke cleared, but I was left with a blacked out airplane at night. The standard procedure for an electrical fire was to turn equipment back on one at a time until the fire started again, and then you would know where the short was located. But the plane could fly without electrical power, and the fire had been bad enough that I didn't want to press my luck by giving it a second chance. So I decided to just return and land.

I didn't need any navigational aids. I had flown in Laos long enough to know that country better than I knew any other part of the world, and I could find my way home easily from the lights of the towns and the shadow of the Mekong. We all carried hand held emergency radios in case we got shot down, and I had the navigator use his to call the base to let them know we were on our way. I also carried a small pocket flashlight that I held in my mouth to illuminate the airspeed indicator, which was the only instrument I really needed to get down safely. I expected the landing to be a little dicey without landing lights, but I did have help from the lights that lined the runway.

I had things well under control until final approach when the left engine quit. I had enough power in the right engine to make it to the runway, but I couldn't feather the left engine without electrical power, and without that engine I had only one chance to land, because the C-47 could not take off or even maintain altitude with one engine windmilling. So I came to a stop, left the plane sitting on the runway, and got out to kiss the ground. It reminded me of a sign over the equipment shack at pilot training, which was manned by enlisted men who were not on flying status. It said, "I'd rather be down here wishing I was up there, than up there wishing I was down here." That night I was happy to be back on the ground. For our efforts we were selected as the Air Force aircrew of the month in Southeast Asia, and I received a nice certificate signed by the commanding general of the Pacific Air Force. But of course there weren't many aircrews still flying in Southeast Asia by then, so they probably didn't have many to choose from. My real reward was being able to walk away from the landing.

When the Paris Peace Accords were signed in late February 1973 the B-52s and the fighter jets stopped their attacks, but the EC-47s continued to fly. It was a violation of the Peace Accords, but it continued unabated until I left at the end of May. We flew surveillance missions over both Laos and Vietnam, so we were concerned that if we were shot down over Vietnam we might be executed as spies instead of being protected as prisoners of war. Plus we were still being shot at while everyone else was standing down. There was enough mumbling in the ranks to result in a visit from one of the commanding generals of the Pacific Air Force Command who assured us that our mission was still important. Then someone asked him what our status would be if we were shot down in Vietnam, and he replied that it was a moot question because we were no longer flying there. He said that to pilots who were flying there every day. I don't think he was lying; he probably just didn't know. The question was never answered to anyone's satisfaction, but we kept on flying, and fortunately no one ever had to find out if we were spies or not.

In April 1973 I ferried a plane from NKP to Taiwan for routine maintenance, refueling at Tan Son Nhut AFB in Saigon, and at Clark AFB in the Philippines along the way. By this time all the Americans had left South Vietnam, and Tan Son Nhut had been returned to the South Vietnamese. It was eerie to see Tan Son Nhut like that. It was one of the busiest airports in the world when I flew in and out in the C-141, but now the air traffic was at a trickle, and the American air traffic controllers had all been replaced by Vietnamese who struggled with the English language. It felt like a ghost town.

I have always liked Chinese food, so I was looking forward to the trip to Taiwan. On the flight over I talked about the opportunity to eat Chinese food from a real Chinese restaurant, and promised to take the crew out to eat when we got to Taipei. It was the real reason I was going to Taiwan. Repairing the plane was secondary. I built it up to the point that my crew began to have some of the same anticipation I did.

We got into Taipei early in the evening, checked into a hotel, and then met to go to this feast that I had promised. Someone at the hotel recommended a restaurant within walking distance, and off we went, but when I looked at the menu it was written in Chinese, and no one in the restaurant spoke English. I hadn't planned on this. I had been to many Chinese restaurants in the U.S., and every single one had a menu in

English. I finally just pointed to something on the menu, but whatever they brought us was inedible, maybe boiled squid, maybe boiled rubber, I couldn't tell which. I was disappointed, and my credibility was shot. I don't remember where we ate after that, but I do know that I wasn't leading.

We had extensive training in what to do if we found ourselves on the ground in hostile territory. We carried a survival vest with maps, signal mirrors, a hand held radio, a survival knife, and a thirty-eight revolver. We also had private information known only to us so rescue helicopters could verify that they weren't being lured into a trap. But in times of stress your mind can short out, and one pilot could not remember any of his personal information when he was down in hostile territory. Without the correct answers the helicopter pilot wouldn't come to get him, and this set the pilot off on a tirade as he realized that the helicopter was leaving him there for either capture or death. But his profanity was so fluent and so colorful that the helicopter crew decided that no North Vietnamese would be able to duplicate that, so they came back and picked him up. It just goes to prove that sometimes a lack of religious training can be an advantage.

All of the survival training would only come in handy if we made it to the ground alive, and in the EC-47 the chances of that happening were slim to none, especially for the pilots. We carried parachutes, but the cockpits were too small to wear them, so they were stored in the rear next to the door. We were supposed to wear a parachute harness so that in an emergency we could quickly go to the back and snap on the parachute before bailing out, but we would never be able to get there if the plane wasn't under control. In a spinning plane your chances would be zero. If the plane was under control my plan was to crash land if at all possible. I could think of scenarios where I might bail out, but they weren't very realistic, so I never wore the parachute harness, and in the entire year I spent in the war zone I never loaded my handgun. I thought there was more danger of shooting myself loading and unloading it every day than there was of ending up on the ground with an unloaded weapon. And if I did get down safely I didn't think a revolver would be of much use against automatic weapons anyway. It was mostly just a security blanket.

I always tried to plan for any possible contingency, and in the EC-47 I could foresee several scenarios that would call for drastic action. One grim possibility of course was that we would find ourselves going down deep in enemy territory. Laos was Indian country, and we knew that they didn't take prisoners. The enemy took prisoners in North Vietnam, and occasionally in South Vietnam, but never in Laos. If you went down in Laos surrender wasn't an option, so one thing we all thought about was whether we should save the last bullet for ourselves. I knew it was the smart thing to do, but knowing it and doing it are two different things. I have no idea what I would have done if faced with that choice.

Much of my flying was deep in enemy territory in northern Laos near the North Vietnamese border. I only flew into North Vietnam once, and that was just so I could say that I had been there. It wasn't a smart thing to do, but sometimes young men do foolish things. Being that far from friendly territory, I did give thought to what I would do if I lost power or got shot down close to the North Vietnamese border. The instinct would be to head west for home, but my plan was just the opposite. If I had the plane under control I planned to glide as far into North Vietnam as possible before bailing out or crash landing. The chances of rescue were just as good there as in Laos, plus it held out the hope that if we weren't rescued we would be captured instead of executed.

One day some of the pilots were discussing what they would do if they ordered a bailout, and a crewmember refused to jump. A couple of pilots said they would return to the cockpit and do their best to crash land. That didn't make a lot of sense to me, because the only way I would order a bailout in the first place was if I didn't think that a crash landing was survivable. I told my friends that I would follow the John Talley protocol. Lt. Col. Talley was the old World War II pilot who took me on my restaurant adventure in Addis Ababa. He was a font of sound advice. After World War II he flew C-47s in Germany, and during one night flight his plane was struck by lightening, knocking out both engines. He ordered a bailout, and remained at the controls long enough to give everyone a chance to get out. Then he got up and headed for the door himself. He told me that when he got to the tail he found the entire crew standing next to the door with their parachutes on. Without saying a word he ran around them and jumped out the door. He thought that once the crew saw the pilot bail out it would help them decide what they wanted to do.

This was a variation of what Capt. Piszczek told me early in pilot training. In that plane, with ejection seats, the order was to "Eject." He emphasized that if he gave the order I was to eject immediately, and that if he said, "Eject," and I said, "What?" I would be talking to myself. That actually happened to an instructor in a T-38 in Texas in the late sixties. He ordered an ejection, and then punched out immediately. The student stayed with the plane, got it back under control, and brought it home for a safe landing. Then they had to send a helicopter out to pick up the instructor. There are some situations in life so embarrassing that you can never live them down.

As the year wore on I started thinking about what I would do with the rest of my life. Lacking a better alternative I decided to attend law school. I had no idea what practicing law entailed, but I assumed I would sit behind a desk, enjoy intellectual stimulation, pass out sage advice, and make lots of money. By the time I discovered that practicing law is really just a knife fight it was too late to reverse course.

Chapter Eight

I took the Law School Aptitude Test (LSAT) as a senior at the University of Michigan and had a 693, which was a pretty good score, placing me in the top two percent, but the score was only good for five years, so I had to take the test again to apply for the fall semester of 1973. Having been out of school for five years I had some misgivings about retaking the test, but I had no choice. So I took the LSAT all by myself one Saturday at the base at NKP, and when the scores came back a few weeks later I was thrilled to see that I had improved to a 764. The average at Yale that year was 718, so I thought a 764 should get me in anywhere, but I thought wrong. I applied to four schools, but the University of Michigan and the University of North Carolina both turned me down. I was accepted at William and Mary, and the University of Georgia, and opted for Georgia.

I chose Georgia for two important reasons. It was warm, and my roommate at NKP told me it had a pretty campus. I didn't know any more about choosing a law school than I did about practicing law, but I haven't regretted my choice. It was a pretty campus, it was warm, and it was a good law school. I could have done much worse.

With my law school acceptance in hand I flew my last combat mission at the end of May, and caught a charter back to San Francisco to be discharged from the Air Force. That trip is a blur. I know I took a C-130 out of NKP, but I don't remember where it took me, or where I caught the charter to return home. It was an emotional time. I had taken my last flight as an Air Force pilot, survived the war, deserted my friends who were still there, and returned home. The discharge from the Air Force was in itself disorienting. The Air Force had been my identity and my home for five years. The organization and regimentation in the military provides a strange sense of security. You always know where you will be, what you will do, and how you fit in. And then all of a sudden I was a civilian again. I felt naked.

The Air Force had not been what I expected. As a student at the University of Michigan in the late sixties I was in the middle of the anti-war fervor that was sweeping the country. We had demonstrations on campus, visits from anti-war activists, and daily exposure to news reports from Vietnam. The country was divided, and leaders in the military were not highly regarded, at least not on most college campuses. I did not participate in the anti-war activities, but I was affected by them, and when I joined the Air Force I expected to find senior officers who were mindlessly militaristic. What I found was quite different. Most of the officers supported the war, but they were all thoughtful decent men. I seldom encountered anyone in the Air Force whom I didn't respect, whether senior officers, junior officers, or enlisted men. We were in many ways a real band of brothers, and I have never been part of any organization either before or since that had better people.

We often don't appreciate what we have until it is gone. Experiences that didn't seem so great at the time may look quite different in retrospect. I know my dad didn't fully appreciate his Air Force career until years later, but I was grateful for it even at the time, and I was always aware that I was having a unique experience. Pilot training was stressful, and I recall other students lamenting that they would hate to go through all of that work and then not be able to fly after they graduated, but even in pilot training I felt fortunate to fly those planes. If my career had ended right there I would have been grateful for the opportunity. I could have done without Vietnam, but the years I spent in the C-141 at Dover were three of the best years of my life, and I knew it. I also knew it would end, and I tried to burn the experience into my memory so I would be able to carry it with me. I can close my eyes now and see my last landing in the C-141. I remember the day, I know which runway I landed on, and where I touched down. I was a lucky man. But then it was over.

I flew home to Detroit in June 1973, ending the adventure that had started at that same airport five years earlier. Mom and Dad met me, and took me home to the farmhouse where we had lived since 1954. They were having an early summer heat wave, with temperatures around eighty degrees, and after a long winter the Michiganders were basking in the sun. But I was freezing. I had just returned from a country where afternoon temperatures often reached one hundred and ten degrees, and inside the airplane it was frequently over one hundred and thirty degrees on the ground. I wore leather flying boots that were usually soaked through before we even got airborne, and on days off I could play tennis for hours in that heat, my body having made the adjustment. During one cold spell in Thailand I tried to play tennis, but the chill made me miserable, and I soon gave up. When I got back to my room I checked the thermometer, and it was eighty-two degrees. So adapting to Michigan weather was just one more of the adjustments that I had to make. In the meantime I wore a jacket while everyone else was in short sleeves.

Aside from my years in the Air Force, Michigan was the only home I knew. I was the last Ford to be born in Hillsdale, but I didn't live there for long. We moved from Hillsdale soon after I was born, first to Ann Arbor, and then to Willow Village, but my first memory is of our house at the Saline Valley Farms. Life was different then, and mostly for the better. We had the run of the farm, nearly six hundred acres, and led the life of Tom Sawyer. We would have preferred Huck Finn, but parents have something to say about that. When we moved to the farm in 1949 I only had to share my parents' attention with Jack, who was three years older, but soon Debby and then David joined us.

One advantage of a rural childhood is that siblings often grow closer out of necessity, because there usually isn't anyone else to play with. Jack was a good older brother, but I still resent the fact that he was always Gene Autry when we played cowboys. I was Roy Rodgers, which wasn't bad, but I knew Gene Autry was the plum role, and I never got to play it. Other games turned out even worse. One day we snuck into the garage to pretend that we were driving the car. When it was my turn to drive Jack had time on his hands to explore other things, and discovered the cigarette lighter. When he pulled it out it glowed red, and for lack of a better idea he placed it against my right cheek. I carried a half moon scar reminder of that incident for many years. I can still see it now, but only because I know where to look.

We didn't have money, but we were never poor. No kids ever had better parents, and we were rich with love and attention. Besides, kids never know if they are poor or not. I assumed that everyone ate meat only on Sunday. In the summer we ate out of our garden, but we never went hungry. I wore hand-me-down clothes and darned socks, but I was warm and safe, and life was good.

We were blessed that television was not yet popular. No one on the farm had a television until I was five, and we got our first set when I was six. Until then we had radio, and adventures were usually more exciting on the radio than they are on television. We regularly listened to "The Lone Ranger" and "Let's Pretend", along with popular classics such as "Amos and Andy." It never occurred to us that "Amos and Andy" could be objectionable. We had one radio in the kitchen, and I often curled up on the counter with my head next to the radio listening to Art Linkletter's "House Party" while my mother cooked supper. I spent many afternoons on that counter top. Kids today should be so lucky.

I have vivid memories of sitting in my mother's lap while she rocked me and sang "When the Red Red Robin Comes Bob Bob Bobbin Along." She probably sang other songs also, but that's the one I remember. And in the evenings Dad would read to us, sometimes children's stories, but not always. Our favorite was *Hunter*, the true life memoir of a big game hunter in Africa during the early years of the twentieth century. Hearing that story at my father's side transported me to another land and another time in a way that no television ever could.

Years later I tried to bribe my own children into exercising their imaginations, promising them two hundred and fifty dollars each if they could go an entire year without watching television. They all accepted the challenge and completed the year successfully. When it came time to collect their reward Dad asked my son, John, what he planned to do with his new found wealth, and John told his grandfather that he was going to buy a television. You can't fight progress.

We did things on the farm that we probably had no business doing at that age. We made bows out of willow branches, and bought real arrows from a hardware store in town. We hunted with them regularly, but never hit anything so far as I can remember. I also got a BB gun when I was seven, and had about as much luck hunting with that as I did with the bow and arrow. Our arsenal was completed with sling-shots made from inner tube tires. Kids lost out when tubeless tires were invented. We also had some old truck tire inner tubes that were great for floating around in the lake. On dry land we could curl up in the middle of them, while a buddy rolled the tire across the yard, or we could stack them up and make a fort. I have more good memories of playing with those tires than I do of any present that anyone ever bought me.

I forget how much life has changed in sixty years. I spent years without television, and then had only a couple of channels in black and white. I bought my first color television when I was twenty-five. We heated our house in Saline with coal. There was a coal bin in the basement, and the coal truck ran a funnel through the basement window to fill it. In those days getting a lump of coal in your stocking for Christmas was a real threat. Santa knew where he could find a lump of coal if he needed one. Cars had running boards, and if your parents were brave they would let you ride on them, but only slowly. I often sat in my father's lap while he drove down the highway. Today he would get arrested for that. When not in his lap I liked to lie on the ledge behind the back seat so I could look out the rear window. Today he'd get arrested for that, too.

I clearly remember standing out in our front yard with Dad one evening in the early fifties as we gazed up at the heavens and speculated about what was up there. Even at that young age I was stunned when he told me that he expected men to fly to the moon in my lifetime. He said it wouldn't happen in his lifetime, but it might in mine, and he got my imagination churning. Little did he suspect that it would not only happen in his lifetime, but in his mother's lifetime as well. She was a member of the amazing generation that grew up with horses, and died with space travel.

In the summer Jack and I often got up early to collect worms for the day's fishing. After a rain we could collect them on the surface, but if that didn't work a couple shovels full of dirt would usually produce all the bait we needed. The lake was full of catfish, sunfish, blue gills, and large mouth bass. We knew that bass were predators, so we often bought fancy spinners that looked like small fish when we reeled them in. This was good entertainment for an hour or so, and then when we grew bored we would switch to worms to actually catch fish. I don't know of anyone who ever caught a bass using a spinner.

I wouldn't have dreamed of letting one of my kids go fishing unsupervised in deep water when they were six or seven years old, but Jack and I fished off the dock all the time. Of course we had grown up on the lake, and were competent swimmers, so there wouldn't have been much danger if we did fall in. After fishing we went home and waited for Dad to take us swimming in the afternoon. I don't know if we actually went swimming every day, or if it just seems that way in my memory, but I'm sure that we didn't miss many days.

Up the hill from our house was a large duplex shared by the Karrs and the Markerts. Calvin Karr and Alan Markert were four years older than I was, and their younger brothers, Randy Karr and Robert Markert, were Jack's age. Despite the age difference I usually accompanied them on whatever adventure they had planned for the day. I owe Jack for that, because he seldom went anywhere without me. One crescent scar is a small price to pay for a brother like that.

In the early fifties we saw a movie about the magician, Harry Houdini, and in short order we all became magicians and escape artists. We escaped from cardboard boxes, burlap sacks, and anything else we could think of. After an afternoon of perfecting our latest tricks we often put on a magic show for our parents in the evening. I recall one show in the Markert's basement when Alan was going to make water disappear by pouring it down a funnel. He did that behind a card table covered by a blanket, and it was my job to sit under the table to catch the water in a jar. Then he turned the lights off so I could make my escape. Once I was gone Alan turned the lights back on and removed the blanket with a flourish to prove that the water had indeed disappeared.

The only flaw in the program was that we never practiced it. Alan told me to sit under the table, to catch the water in the jar, and to escape upstairs while the lights were off, but he didn't tell me to take the jar with me. So when he removed the blanket there in full sight sat the jar full of water. In desperation he kicked it, which sent the water flying, but that didn't do a thing to make his humiliation less conspicuous, and to the sound of laughter he came charging upstairs with murder on his mind. He was four years older than I was, so he might have accomplished his mission if Jack had not intervened to save me. One crescent scar is a small price to pay for a brother like that, too.

The Markert boys' father was Clement Markert, a biology professor at the University of Michigan, and we occasionally received free biology lessons from him when we were fishing or out walking in the woods. In the 1930s he fought in the Spanish Civil War along with other American volunteers who opposed the fascist revolution of Francisco Franco. Franco was an ally of Hitler, so one might think that Markert's service in Spain would be respected, but not during the anticommunist hysteria of the early fifties when those who fought against Franco were suspected of having leftist sympathies. In 1954 he refused to discuss his political beliefs when questioned by one of Joe McCarthy's subcommittees, and was stripped of his position at the University. He later had a distinguished career at Yale, but it is sad that he had to suffer from one of our periodic witch hunts.

Johnny and Mae Rule lived just a short distance from our house. They were about sixty years old at the time. Johnny was an immigrant from England who came over as a young man to work in the iron mines in Michigan's Upper Peninsula. On the farm he served as the caretaker. Both Johnny and Mae were like grandparents to me. Most afternoons I would knock on their door, and Mae always offered me cookies and milk. Johnny spoke longingly of England, and the siblings that he had left there, but he never returned. When I was in college I took a trip to Europe in 1966, and before I left I visited Johnny and Mae, and got the address of his only surviving sister in Cornwall. I then stopped in to see her, but it's sad that Johnny couldn't make the trip himself.

Johnny had a raspberry patch that I loved to raid. It was surrounded by a wire fence, but I often snuck in when the sight of those berries was too enticing to resist. And I think he caught me every time. Maybe he had some Negrito in him. I thought I was invisible, but nothing occurred on that farm that Johnny didn't see. Fortunately he never held it against me. He chased me out of his raspberry patch many times, but I was just as quickly forgiven. One day my mother learned that I had been caught again, and that evening at supper I received a lecture about my transgressions. Johnny often brought us a gift of raspberries, and she warned me that if I kept stealing them that he would stop sharing his berries with us. She just got the words out of her mouth when we saw Johnny walk past our dining room window delivering yet another bowl of raspberries. Grandchildren get cut a lot of slack even if they are adopted grandchildren.

Someone on the farm owned a large German Shepherd named Diablo, and never was a dog more appropriately named. I was scared to death of Diablo. He wasn't a modern German Shepherd. He was like one of those prehistoric tigers that were twice the size of present day tigers. I had to look up to see Diablo's eyes. When I grew tired of getting caught in Johnny's raspberry patch I resorted to stealing just those berries that I could reach through the fence. I wasn't actually in his berry patch; I was just policing the perimeter. One afternoon as I crouched down next to the fence silently eating what I could reach I felt a warm breath on my neck, and when I turned around I stared up into the face of the devil himself. I instinctively screamed, since concealing my crime was at that moment the least of my worries. I have no idea what happened to Diablo. I went blank after that. I do remember that adults came running from all directions, and of course there was no way to hide what I had been doing. I can't say that the experience cured me of crime, but it did cure me of that crime. I don't remember ever raiding Johnny's raspberries again after that.

One of the advantages of having a brother almost three years older was that I got to do everything three years younger than he did. When he got a BB gun I got a BB gun. When he got a bicycle I got a bicycle. And when he got us in trouble it was his fault. You can't blame me; I was just following him. We got the bicycles when Jack was nine and I was six. He got a twenty-six inch bike, and I got a twenty-four inch bike, but even the twenty-four inch was much too big for me. I couldn't touch the pedals even with the seat all the way down, so Dad bolted large wooden blocks to the pedals. Then I could pedal, but I still couldn't come close to touching the ground. Getting started was easy, but stopping was a controlled crash. I either had to stop close enough to something I could grab onto, or in open ground just stop and jump. It's a wonder the bike survived. I had a basket on the front of the bike for a while, but that ended when I got caught in a rut while going full speed down a steep dirt road, and the bike flipped. I survived unhurt, but the basket was totaled. When I told Dad my basket was bent he grabbed some tools to go out and straighten it, but when he saw the damage he just removed it. The accident happened because I was racing down the hill trying to keep up with my brother who was three years older, and riding a bigger bike. He didn't always protect me.

We were about the same age when Jack decided to visit Max Haswell's chicken house. Max operated a large egg business for the cooperative farm, and had a long two story chicken house full of layers. We wandered in one afternoon and decided that it would be fun to take a couple of the eggs and throw them against the side of the chicken house. It was fun, so we went back in and got a couple more. That was fun too, so we kept at it, and we visited most of Max's chickens before we quit. Then we stayed to greet Max when he came out to collect eggs. Crime is a serious problem in this country, but one thing society has going for it is that most criminals aren't very smart. Jack even asked Max if he thought he would collect many eggs that day.

Max didn't collect many eggs that day, and when he took a look at the back wall of his chicken house it didn't take him long to figure out why. A couple of days later Mom received a letter from Max describing his discovery, and identifying the primary suspects. Things turned really ugly after that. For starters we both got spankings, and were sent to bed in the middle of the afternoon. Sometimes putting the blame on my older brother took the heat off of me, but I don't recall that it did a thing for me that day. We also spent weeks paying off the damage out of our meager allowances. This experience didn't end my criminal career either, but it did cure me of throwing eggs.

Many years later I came home from work one day to find my five year old son, Jimmy, and two of his friends painting our brick walk and the side of our house with black paint that they found in the garage. I reacted to this much the same way Max probably reacted when he looked at the back of his chicken house. One of Jimmy's friends went home and told his mother that Jimmy's father had lost his mind, but I only remember suggesting that painting the house black wasn't a good idea. Perhaps I lost my mind and my memory.

That evening after I found my mind I told Jimmy a bedtime story before he went to sleep. I talked about the need to be respectful of property and to behave responsibly, but I didn't want to put too much guilt on him, so I also told him about my transgressions at Max Haswell's chicken house, and I finished by confessing that, "What I did was as bad as painting the house black, wasn't it?" Jimmy thought about this for a moment, and then responded, "I don't think so. I think what you did was worse." Children can be aggravating like that. He had me, and we both knew it. Confronted by this tough judge I admitted that what I had done was indeed worse than what he had done. Then we both went to bed appropriately chastised.

In addition to Max Haswell's chickens, the farm also had a large dairy herd that supplied the farm's milk routes. Every morning the cows walked from the barn to the pasture just south of our house, and in the evening they retraced their steps. I don't remember anyone driving them. They seemed to know where they were going, and when to return. There was a large field in front of our house to the west, and the cow path was at the far end of that field at the top of a gentle rise. From our house the cows looked as if they were walking across the horizon, heading south in the morning and north at the end of the day.

At the entrance to the farm there was the company store, and behind that the dairy and the cannery. Behind the dairy was a large barn that housed the cows and enough hay to sustain them through the winter. The hay was stored in bales, and if we stacked the bales just right we could create a maze of tunnels high enough to crawl through. A kid can play for hours in a good hay mow.

One day Jack and I were up in the barn with the Karr and Markert brothers, playing in the tunnels, when we came to an intersection, and didn't know which way to turn. Randy Karr solved the problem by lighting a match so we could see. With all the dry hay and the hay dust it's a wonder that it didn't catch fire. Fortunately Jack saw the danger, and yelled at Randy to put the match out. It's events like this that make you wonder how any kid lives long enough to grow up.

Chapter Nine

In 1951 I made the trip into town to start kindergarten, and Dad took me down to the kindergarten room to introduce me to Mrs. Coates. I had recently learned how to do cartwheels, and decided to make an entrance by doing one through the classroom door. I knew that a good cartwheel would leave folks impressed, but what it got me was a warning by Mrs. Coates that we didn't do such things in school. So I had my first reprimand before we were even formally introduced.

Dad didn't need an introduction, because he was the school principal. Saline was a small town then, and there was one school for K through twelve. In fact, through thirteen years of school I only spent one year when Dad didn't have his office in my school, and that was the year we stayed in Saline after he took a job at Belleville. So doing the cartwheel was one of my few transgressions while I was in school. I was one kid who really didn't want to get sent to the principal's office.

I don't remember ever not liking school. The worst part of kindergarten was nap time. I stopped taking naps when I was two, and I had no desire to start again when I was five, but other than that kindergarten suited me just fine. I attended Saline through the second grade, made friends, and enjoyed learning how to read. "Fun with Dick and Jane" was big back then, and I'm not sure anyone has come up with a better reading primer during the intervening years. We had three recesses a day, but no cafeteria. The kids who walked to school had lunch at home. The rest of us carried lunch boxes, and ate in the classroom. My favorite sandwich was beef heart. Dad got me started eating beef heart, but then he would eat anything. He probably would have liked Colonel

Talley. When I was in second grade the school started selling hot dogs on Thursdays, and I considered that a great treat. It was real progress when we could get hot food right there in school.

In first grade I suffered a trauma that emotionally scarred me for life. I was too casual zipping up my pants in the bathroom one day, and got caught in the zipper. Sometimes when you get something caught in a zipper it comes right out, and other times it takes pliers. This was one of those pliers' situations. I couldn't get loose myself, and Miss Bales wasn't any more successful, so she walked me down the hall to the office to let Dad work on it. I remember the walk clearly, but I don't know if I remember it because of embarrassment or pain. I think I had moved past the embarrassment stage by then, so it must have been the pain.

Dad freed me, but he wasn't gentle about it. There probably wasn't any gentle way to do it. The only good result of the experience was that it never happened again. This is something that no man ever does twice. When my son, John, was four he wore pajamas that zipped from his neck down to his knee. They were probably designed by a woman. One night I heard him get up to use the bathroom, followed moments later by a piercing scream, and he assures me that it never happened to him again either.

In August 1954 we moved from Saline to a five acre farm in Belleville. I was sad to leave the Valley Farms, but also excited about the adventure. It was a new house, a new town, and a new school. The new house was twice the size of our house in Saline, with a big tree house in the side yard and a hundred peach trees ripe for picking. We moved from a very large farm to a very small farm, but this farm was ours, and it needed attention. That fall we just picked the peaches, and sold them on a stand in the front yard, not having any concept of the work that went into getting them to that stage. We got a lot smarter the next year.

There were also a couple acres of field corn that we harvested by hand that fall. Then we went around with knives to chop down the stalks. The next year we expanded the peach orchard, and that was the end of the field corn, but as long as we lived there we had a large garden with sweet corn, squash, beans, peas, and tomatoes. A garden like that tends to spoil you for anything you buy in a grocery store. There is nothing better than sweet corn that goes straight from the garden to the table in the time it takes you to husk it and cook it.

That was also the fall that Jack and I took up smoking. With all that field corn there were plenty of corn cobs to make pipes, and lots of corn silk for tobacco. So we harvested a nice crop of corn silk and stored it in the barn to dry. Then after a few days we stuffed it in our pipes, and we were ready to go. It was exciting, but not exactly what we had hoped for. If smoking corn silk doesn't cure you of the habit I don't know what will. Maybe we should try marketing it next to nicotine patches. We pretended to like it, but before long we found other ways to entertain ourselves.

Through the spring and summer the peaches had to be sprayed once a week, and that was a two man job. Jack and I alternated driving the tractor, and Dad walked behind spraying the trees. From what we now know about pesticides it's a wonder any of us survived. We had no protective clothing or masks, and by the time we finished with the orchard we were all soaking wet. We couldn't hear Dad's instructions over the noise of the sprayer's engine, so when he wanted to get our attention he turned the spray on us. When we complained he just assured us that it would kill any germs we had growing on us.

Dad was the organizer and the disciplinarian. He was never harsh or mean, but the thought of defying him never even occurred to us. We didn't know what he would do, but he would do something, and we weren't interested in finding out what it would be. Some people can rule just with the force of their personality, and Dad was one of those. It probably wasn't the punishment that we feared so much as his displeasure. There is a story about a young private in the Confederate Army who was taken in front of General Lee for discipline, and as the soldier stood there shaking Lee told him, "Son, you don't have to be afraid. You will get justice here." The soldier replied, "General, that's what I'm afraid of." Like that young soldier, none of us wanted justice from Dad.

Dad was a morning person, and every morning we would hear him whistling or singing in the shower before it was time for us to get up. When he was through he would flip on our light and yell, "Come on girls. Wake up." Then he took breakfast orders, anything we wanted. All through school he was a short order cook. One kid might ask for oatmeal, another fried eggs, another pancakes, and whatever we asked for was waiting for us by the time we got downstairs.

Mom was an anchor of stability, but Dad was the engine that kept things moving. He had a great sense of humor, and loved to play. If we had a game going he was usually ready to join in. He also gave us some wonderful trips to Washington D.C., Quebec, and out to California in 1959. I should probably give Mom equal credit, but I know these were his idea. He loved to travel, and he knew that memories were more valuable than material things.

During the trip to Quebec in 1956 Mom and Dad rented only one motel room, so Jack and I slept in the back of the station wagon. But by three or four in the morning we were freezing in that station wagon, and knocked on the door of the motel so we could warm up. After a couple of days of this Mom and Dad finally got tired of being awakened in the middle of the night, so they said they would sleep in the car, and we could have the room. About three the next morning they were pounding on our door, and after that we got two motel rooms.

The trip out west in 1959 was a three week marathon, driving across the northern states to Oregon, then down through California to Ensenada, Mexico, and home via New Mexico and Colorado. The trip was planned as only Dad could plan it. He knew where we would stop every night, what time we would get up, and what we would see. As part of his flight plan he even scheduled the cities where he would stop for gas. When Dad traveled nothing was left to chance. With a long way to go, and a short time to get there, we drove non-stop for the first thirty-six hours, finally stopping in Spearfish, South Dakota. Then Dad went out to wash the car, and came back to the motel with a quart of ice cream. Finding us all sound asleep he woke us up to eat the ice cream before we collapsed again.

We participated in few organized activities while we lived on the farm. Jack and I were in Boy Scouts for a couple of years, but our hearts weren't in it. Anything that required regimentation went against our grain. We much preferred to make our own entertainment, and we had football or baseball games going most of the time. All you had to do was take a ball out into the yard, and pretty soon neighborhood boys would start to show up. We chose our sport, we chose when we wanted to play, we made up the rules, and we refereed. Adults were seldom involved unless they wanted to play, and right field was usually out. It didn't take many kids to make a game, but we never had enough players to cover the entire field.

When we weren't playing sports I spent much of my time reading. I could ride my bike to the library in town, and it became a well worn path. I read all the Little House books, and then moved on to bigger adventures. There was a series of Indian stories that I loved, plus the Halliburton travel adventures, and any book I could find about flying. I watched some television, but reading was my primary escape.

As we grew older we started making up games. If no one else was around we invented games we could play by ourselves. One basketball and a hoop can keep a kid busy for hours. I also played complete baseball games by myself, hitting green apples with a plastic bat. Norm Cash and Charlie Maxwell were Detroit Tiger heroes then, and in my backyard they came up in the ninth inning with the bases loaded time after time. They were both left handed, so I batted left handed. This came in handy years later when we devised a baseball game using a tennis ball. The rules required everyone to bat left handed, and I already had years of practice hitting green apples with a plastic bat. By then I could hit better left handed than I could right.

Keeping the lawn mowed was a never ending job. The previous owners claimed that it was a seven mile walk to mow the lawn, but it seemed longer. With a push mower it took four or five hours, and the lawn was large enough that we seldom mowed it all at one time. We did a section at a time, and by the time we finished the last section the first needed mowing again. In addition to the yard and the orchard we also had a garden to weed, leaves to rake, and when we got older the house and the barn to paint. We didn't work nearly as hard as we thought we did, but there was always enough to do to keep us out of trouble.

When we moved to the farm there were a few bantam chickens there that I adopted as pets. They ran free during the summer, and I fed them by tossing chicken feed in the yard. They knew the routine, and when I called them they would come running. We had a chicken house that they could enter and leave at will, but usually they would roost outside during the night. They couldn't fly much, but they could fly well enough to get onto low branches. In the winter I kept them in the chicken house, and they required a lot more attention. Every morning before school I had to knock the ice out of their water pans, and replace it with warm drinking water. If I was late with their feeding they would be in a stir next to the door when I tried to get in, and sometimes it was impossible for me to get in without letting a few of them escape. So occasionally I had to climb up on the roof and pour chicken feed down the air vent. Then while the chickens were attacking the food in the middle of the floor it gave me a chance to get in the door to feed them properly.

We got most of our eggs from these chickens, but over time the flock increased to the point that they were no longer pets, and we had to do something to thin them out. Naturally Dad saw this before I did. He explained that chickens could also be eaten, and either we had to eat some of these or they were going to take the place over. So I had to learn that not all food comes cleaned and dressed from the grocery store. Dad dispatched the unlucky fryers with an axe and a chopping block, and it gave me a new understanding of the phrase, "like a chicken with its head cut off." It is about as grotesque as it sounds. They would run around and flap their wings, and I shiver a little to think of it. Then we dropped them in a bucket of boiling water so we could pluck the feathers. It has been fifty years, but I could still identify the smell of a scalded chicken when it comes out of the water.

The term "pecking order" is not just an expression. It's a fact, and chickens know exactly where they fit into their society. The king of my flock was an old rooster, and there was no doubt about who was in charge. He ran his flock pretty much the way Dad ran his, so I started calling Dad "the old rooster." The original old rooster was supreme for a few years, but then he grew old, and one morning I found him dead. He had some competition, so I suspect the death was not natural. I kept the flock for another year or two, but it wasn't the same without the old rooster, and my school activities started interfering with my farming, so we gave the remaining chickens to a neighbor. I was glad to be rid of the responsibility, but I still think there is no finer looking bird than a bantam rooster.

When I was sixteen I painted the house. It was a two story farm house, so it took me a good part of the summer to finish the job. When I was finally done Dad announced that he was going to pay me by giving me the sprayer. Jack and I kept the profits from the orchard for our spending money, so I guess Dad considered the sprayer to be a capital contribution to the business. On the other hand the orchard always got sprayed before I owned the sprayer, so I didn't see a lot of benefit from ownership. Besides, I was going to go off to college in a couple of years, and I wouldn't be able to take the sprayer with me, so we finally compromised on a new suit instead of the sprayer. The truth is that Dad hated that sprayer. I think he was looking for an excuse to give it away.

The money that Jack and I received from the orchard was good financial training. Dad financed the spray and fertilizer, but Jack and I kept the profits. We put the money in a savings account at the bank, and that money paid for our clothes, school lunches, and spending money for the year. The first year we were sleeping on old army cots, and Mom insisted that we use our profits to buy beds, but after that the money was pretty much ours to spend as we wanted. On a good year we could have three or four hundred dollars in the bank by the middle of September, and in years when the crop wasn't as good we might have only two hundred. It was an education in business, and in budgeting. We knew that was all the money we would get for the year, so if it ran out we would be broke until the next fall. It proved to be good training for my life as a lawyer. As a trial lawyer I made money when I settled a case. I might feel affluent at the moment, but I knew it could be six or twelve months before I saw another payday, and I never knew from year to year what my income would be. So my early training in frugality continues to be useful. In the back of my mind I still have to get through the year with three hundred dollars from the fruit stand. My kids thought I was just cheap, but they never raised peaches.

At an early age Jack and I started hunting on our farm, and on forty acres of woods and fields on the other side of the railroad tracks that formed the northern border of our property. There wasn't anything there except a few rabbits and pheasants and crows, so we didn't kill much, but we spent hours trying. As was true with the BB gun in Saline I also got a shotgun three years younger than Jack did. I had no business with a shotgun, but I had one. I started when I was twelve with an old 410 that my father had as a boy. It had a hammer that I was too small to cock with my thumb, so I put the stock on the ground and cocked it with the palm of my hand. Then I would go hunting with the gun cocked. In retrospect it makes riding on Dad's lap in the car seem pretty safe.

I loved the hours that I spent in the woods, and the thrill of the hunt, and the smell of gunpowder. I was trying to sneak up on crows, but in my mind I was hunting lions in Africa. The crows were never in much danger by the way. They are a smart bird, and no one is going to sneak up on a crow. They also know when they are being hunted, and when they're not. When I was unarmed I could walk right up to the tree they were in, and they would sit there and scold me, but if I had a shotgun in my hands I couldn't get within a hundred yards of them.

I did shoot a couple of crows, and it was one of those that put an end to my hunting career. I knocked one out of a tree one day, but didn't kill him. I finished him off by hitting him over the head with the barrel of my gun, and I can still remember the look in his eyes as he lay there waiting for me. He wanted to live as much as I did, and the experience took away any stomach that I had for the hunt. It wasn't long after that when I put my guns away, and I haven't hunted since. I loved the time in the woods, and the challenge of the hunt, but I couldn't take any pleasure from success.

The railroad tracks were a source of both sport and carnage. For several years we used the trains for target practice with our peaches. They were just box cars, so we weren't trying to do any damage. The real test was to put a peach through the open door of an empty box car. Wide open wasn't tough, but if the door was just cracked it was a real test to lead it properly on a train that was traveling at forty or fifty miles per hour. Visually it looked as if the peach was curving towards the door instead of the door catching up with the peach. But our fun came to an end when we were visited by a railroad detective who told us they were getting tired of cleaning peaches off their cars. We should have thought about that without being told, but I don't remember that we did.

Over the years there were some terrible car/train collisions on those tracks. There were no lights or gates, and the rails were raised just high enough that a car's lights at night would not pick up the train until the last second. Seeing how little was left of some of those cars gave me a respect for trains that persists until today. If you live for long next to a railroad crossing you will always feel nervous when you drive over a railroad track. Occasionally I stood next to the tracks as a test of courage, but my feet invariably shuffled backwards a little when the train approached.

In February 1956 my youngest brother, Bruce, was born just a few days before my tenth birthday. He was a robust little kid, never lacking in self confidence, and always eager to play any sport. David was gentle, or even timid, but Bruce loved a physical challenge. When he was seven he asked to join in a football game that some of my high school friends were playing in the front yard. We let him run with the ball, but when he was tagged he kept right on running until we called him back. Only then did he realize the rules, dropping the ball in disgust, and saying, "Aw, do you mean it's not tackle." I was old enough to have almost a parent child relationship with Bruce, and I thoroughly enjoyed that little boy.

Chapter Ten

When I was in fifth grade Mom started teaching. Dad was the high school principal, and Mom had her classroom next to mine, so I never had a chance. Across the courtyard from my room was the metal shop where my Uncle Max taught. I was surrounded. One day I looked out the window and saw Uncle Max's students lining up in the courtyard. He had bet the kids that he could beat them in a twenty yard race, with them running forward and him running backward, and he beat most of them. He was still in his thirties then, as was Dad. They both died of cancer, frail and in their eighties, but I remember them in their prime. They will always be in their prime so long as I remember them that way.

I had my first girlfriend in fifth grade. Her name was Cheryl Meece, and she was in my mother's class. I walked her to class in the morning and to the bus in the afternoon. What more could you ask of a girlfriend. I still have a soft spot in my heart for Cheryl. No one can claim I'm not loyal.

In sixth grade my teacher was Clyde Batzer. I don't remember much about his classroom, but recess was big that year. Clyde played football in college, and we had a football game going most days, even in the winter. He punted and played quarterback for both teams, so we had to learn how to catch, and he's the one who talked me into playing football in junior high. Once I got started I was stuck with it for six years despite the fact that I had no desire to get hit or to hit anyone else. I discovered to my dismay that there's a big difference between touch football and tackle.

I have a few good memories of football, but the injuries are more vivid. In seventh grade I sprained an ankle, and had to wear a cast for a couple of weeks. In ninth grade I had my appendix removed. That wasn't a football injury, but it happened during football season so it counts as far as I'm concerned. Tenth grade started well. I was the only member of my class to play on the varsity team that year, even though I weighed one hundred thirty pounds, but I was quick when I was scared. I scored our only touchdown at homecoming that year, and got promoted to first string halfback, but immediately sprained another ankle and sat out the rest of the year. I had a problem with ankles.

My junior year I moved to defense. I did reasonably well until half way through the season when we played Plymouth High School. Their fullback was a kid named Hugh Sarah, who weighed two hundred twenty-five pounds and was the defending state shot-put champion. Late in the first half I had a head on collision with Sarah. He did a somersault in the air, and then got up and ran back to the huddle. I nosed into the turf with a bruise that went from my ear to my elbow, and didn't play for the next two weeks. When I came back I was a different man, and there were no more head on collisions after that if I could possibly avoid them. I was in survival mode. I liked pass defense, but I prayed that the line wouldn't let anyone through who weighed more than one hundred fifty pounds. For the most part they didn't. Frank Nunley played linebacker in front of me, and he didn't miss many tackles. Later he was the starting middle linebacker for the San Francisco 49ers, so I picked a good man to play behind. It was a happy day when we finished our last game my senior year. We lost, and I couldn't have cared less.

I was also a diver for a couple of years, but the sport that I enjoyed was track. I desperately wanted to break the twenty year old school pole vault record of eleven feet eight inches, but never quite made it. Eleven feet eight inches is nothing these days, but we jumped with steel poles back then, and anything over eleven feet was pretty good. I jumped eleven nine in practice as a senior, but practice didn't count, so the record stood until fiberglass poles became popular a few years later. I did win the conference championship my sophomore year, but that wasn't the same as the school record. My junior year I was out with another sprained ankle, and in my senior year the championship went to a kid from Redford Union who had the first fiberglass pole I had ever seen. With my steel pole I was like a man carrying a knife in a gun fight. I pole vaulted for a couple of years with modest success at the University of Michigan until a knee injury ended my career my sophomore year. Then I put the sport on hold until I came out of retirement to coach my children when they took up the sport.

All through high school we spent every Thanksgiving in Hillsdale with my Grandmother Ford. It was a time for all of the aunts and uncles and cousins to gather once again in the town where they grew up and went to college. Until her death in 1969 Cousin Edna also joined us. One year we took her out to the farm that Darwin and Edwin and Alton had cleared in the 1850s. The old farmhouse was still standing then. It was deserted, and in very poor condition, but Edna gave us a tour of the home that she had shared with Darwin and Julia in the 1880s and 1890s. Regrettably most of that history meant nothing to me then. I'm grateful for what she wrote, but I would love to have a day to spend with Edna now.

Jack attended college at Hillsdale, and every year the college hosted a Model United Nations Assembly for high schools from Michigan, Indiana, and Ohio. It was a big production with several hundred students representing the various countries of the United Nations. The president of the foreign relations club at Hillsdale served as the secretary general of the assembly, but on the first day the high school students elected a president to preside over the rest of the sessions. During my senior year in high school I ran for president and won. Jack was the president of the college's foreign relations club that year, so we had a lock on things. He was the secretary general, and I was the president, and for a couple of days we ran the show. Dad was there as a chaperone, and Mom came to watch, so it was an exciting weekend.

The assembly met in the old College Baptist Church where Great Grandfather Henry served as pastor from 1919 to 1923, and where Dad and Grandfather Robert once sang in the choir. It seems that Hillsdale was a magnet that just kept pulling this family back for the better part of two centuries. My son, Jim, was the last to graduate from the college in 2001, and I doubt that there will be any more, but I expect that for several generations Hillsdale will still be remembered as the old country. Dad is buried there now in the family plot next to Henry, and someday I hope to join him. Edna wrote that all roads led to the farm, but the road actually ran right through the farm on its way to Oak Grove Cemetery.

I found math easy, and I liked physics. So naturally I was a history major in college. There weren't many history majors at Michigan who took physics classes to raise their grade point average, but I did. I struggled with the humanities, which just goes to demonstrate what dumb choices I have made from time to time. There's no reason to do something I'm good at when I can do something difficult instead. Roger Rosenblatt wrote a great little book a few years ago titled *Rules for Aging*. One of his recommendations was "Do not go left." The analogy comes from basketball players who spend years learning to go to their left so they can double their options. That might be a good strategy for basketball players, but for the rest of us Rosenblatt says we should play to our strengths. But his advice came too late for me. I have spent my life trying to go to my left.

My physics teacher in high school was a man named Ed Sprague who went into teaching after leaving one of the auto companies, and he didn't know any more about physics than I did. If we asked a question he usually couldn't answer it until he went home to get an explanation from his wife. That's not my supposition; it's what he told us. I finally told Dad that he should sit in on some of these classes, because he had a teacher who was incompetent. After a couple of visits from the principal, Mr. Sprague was gone, replaced by Mac McCoy, a retired teacher in his seventies who just came back to finish the year. Mr. McCoy knew physics, but he was more interesting when we got him to talk about his life. He was born around 1890, and before the turn of the century had traveled out to Oklahoma with his family in a covered wagon. It is another example of just how far the world had come in sixty-five years. Like my grandmother he grew up with horses, and lived to see men walk on the moon.

I had a couple of girlfriends in high school. When I was a sophomore I dated Diane Hidenfelter, the daughter of the football and track coach. She was over at our house one day, and I sat down at the piano and asked her if there was anything that she wanted to hear. I wasn't serious, because the only song I knew how to play was Moon

River. My sister Debby was the piano player, and she had laboriously taught me how to play that one song. So I could hardly believe it when Diane said she would like me to play Moon River, which I did flawlessly. Life would have been so much easier if I could have saved just a little of that luck for the stock market or the horse track. I can still play Moon River by the way. Moon River and only Moon River.

My senior year I dated Judy Harrison, but it wasn't a placid relationship. Judy worked at the local root beer stand, and during one of our out periods I stopped to buy a hamburger, which I ordered with everything except sweet relish. I can't stand sweet relish. When Judy brought the hamburger it had nothing on it except sweet relish, and I ate it without comment. Her birthday was in September, but for some reason I was late getting her a birthday card, so I bought her a card that said on the front, "I'll bet you think I forgot your birthday." On the inside it said, "Well, I did." The following March I received a card from Judy a couple of days after my birthday. On the front it said, "I didn't forget your birthday." And on the inside it said, "I couldn't remember your name." I still have it. Like most high school romances ours didn't survive college, but my affection for her did.

In May 1964 we took a school field trip to the University of Michigan football stadium to see President Lyndon Johnson give the commencement address at Michigan's graduation ceremony. It was during that speech that he announced his "Great Society" program to eliminate poverty in America. Much of his legislation over the next four years was based on that program, but the moment was totally lost on me. I had no idea that he had said anything of consequence. I felt better a few years later when one of my history professors at Michigan, Bradford Perkins, discussed his own graduation from Harvard in 1947. At that graduation Secretary of State George Marshall announced the Marshall Plan to rebuild Europe after World War II, but Dr. Perkins confessed that at the time he was totally unaware that Marshall had said anything of importance. Maybe we just weren't paying attention.

I finished high school as the salutatorian of my class, just a few thousandths of a point behind the valedictorian, Nancy Kotlarczyk. Nancy deserved to win. I had help. I only got help one time, but I got it when I needed it. During my senior year I had a biology test the morning after an evening track meet, and I knew I wasn't ready for the test. There was no way I could get ready, so just as the class started that day Dad pulled a fire drill. When we got back into class there was still time for the test, so Dad pulled another fire drill. He was a great dad, and a great principal, and this was his only crime. I am indebted. As the salutatorian I gave the opening remarks at graduation, and I used the opportunity to thank the parents. I thanked all of the parents, but I'm sure my parents knew it was intended for them.

That summer I worked at the Draw -Tite trailer hitch company assembling hitches, and loading trucks. It was a great opportunity to earn money for college, but I did earn it. I worked six days a week from six in the morning to six thirty at night, with two fifteen minute breaks, and a half hour for lunch. On Saturday I quit at four thirty, for a seventy hour work week. The money was fantastic, but the schedule was grueling. I assembled hitches in the morning, but most of the afternoon was spent loading trucks by hand. The hitches were heavy, and the trucks were like furnaces on hot days. I earned around two thousand dollars for the summer, which was big money in 1964, but I learned that there was no way I wanted to do manual labor for a living.

I was also a little envious of Jack, who had a job there working in the office, a white collar job. He came over to help in shipping after the office closed at four thirty, so he did get some taste of how the rest of us lived. George Renton was our supervisor, and part owner of the company, and naturally he tried to keep things moving. One afternoon he wanted us to unload an open bed truck full of hitches just as a thunderstorm passed through. We balked because of the threat of lightening, but George would have none of it. As we cowered under shelter he told us that there was no danger of lightening, and to get out there and unload that truck. He no more than got the words out of his mouth when a bolt of lighting hit a tree next to the truck, and the whole load of hitches started sparking. Without saying another word George turned and walked away.

I found the hours as tough as the work. I am not a morning person, and getting up at five every morning just about killed me. I grew more lethargic as the week wore on. Jack was better at it than I was, and he would usually have something started for breakfast by the time I got downstairs. One day we had company, so Jack and I slept in our parents' travel trailer. When the alarm went off Jack was up and out the door to start breakfast while I tried to drag myself out of bed. Finally I looked over at the clock and realized that he had set the alarm for four a.m. instead of five. Some people might have gotten up at that point to tell their brother, who was cooking them breakfast, that he had another hour to sleep, but if I did that I would have to get out of bed and walk to the house. On the other hand, if I just stayed in bed I knew he would come looking for me sooner or later, which he did. He claims that when he got there I still didn't tell him the time, but just pointed at the clock. I am reminded of that incident several times a year.

Chapter Eleven

I started at the University of Michigan in August 1964. I was offered a full scholarship at Albion College, but chose Michigan instead. If I had it to do over I would go to a small school. Universities are fine for postgraduate work, but I'm sure I would have been happier at a small college. I realized that I was in trouble right out of the box. Michigan required four semesters of a foreign language, and on the first day in Mademoiselle Quick's French class I discovered that everyone else had studied a language in high school, most had taken French, and one had gone to school in France. I had never taken a language, and probably didn't have much aptitude for it to begin with. I survived with four semesters of Cs, but I spent half my time studying French and three fourths of my time worrying about it.

That spring I pledged the Lambda Chi fraternity, but it didn't take long for me to conclude that I wasn't fraternity material. A few weeks into it I got a call one evening telling me that the pledge class had to go immediately to the fraternity house for some spur of the moment activity. I was studying for a test the next day, and told them I couldn't go. They didn't accept that excuse, and when push came to shove I told them that I wasn't all that excited about being a member anyway, so they could remove me from their pledge class. It all worked out for the best. The next fall I received a call just before school started from my freshman dorm director offering me a job as a dorm counselor. It paid most of my room and board, so I was more than happy to accept. I already had a tuition scholarship, and worked another summer at Draw-Tite, so with the counseling job I was paying my way through school and saving money while I was at it. I eventually paid my entire way through college, took two trips to Europe, and graduated with fifteen hundred dollars in the bank.

The first trip was in 1966 after my sophomore year. I went with Dick Wells, and we spent almost two months making the grand tour of Europe. We rented a car in Paris, and started by driving down to the Running of the Bulls in Pamplona, Spain. The actual running of the bulls takes place early every morning. The rest of the day is a drunken revelry, especially at night. The first night we bought two bottles of champagne and a bucket of ice for two dollars. There were two of us, and two bottles of champagne, so we each drank one. It was my first experience with alcohol, and I had not yet learned that I am a cheap drunk. A whole bottle of champagne made me comatose.

I'm also a happy drunk. I remember a young Spanish girl walking by in front of me, and I gave her a friendly pat as she walked by, to which she took serious exception. She turned and slapped me, and then slapped Dick just in case she had missed the real culprit with her first assault. I learned several things from that. First, Spanish girls have no sense of humor. Second, I probably shouldn't drink. And third, a bottle of champagne can make your face numb. She hit me hard enough to almost knock me down, and I didn't feel a thing.

I woke up the next morning in the public square. I had lots of company because all the hotels had sold out long ago. Dick and I planned to run with the bulls that morning, but we were late arriving, and there was no way to get close to the street, much less in it, so we climbed up the side of a building near the bull ring, and watched from a distance. What I saw left me quite satisfied to be a spectator instead of a participant. Then we attended the bullfights in the afternoon, and left for Barcelona.

We traveled up the French Riviera, across Switzerland, down the coast of Italy to Rome, and then north to Venice, Berlin, Amsterdam, and Sweden. From there I took a ferry across the North Sea to London before flying home on a Pan Am jet out of Heathrow. When I got on the plane I walked through the first class section and saw four young men who looked vaguely familiar, but I couldn't place them. One of them said, "Hello sport," but I walked on without responding, and only later did I realize that the four young men were the Beatles, and the one who spoke was Paul McCartney.

They were on one of their first tours in the U.S., and when we landed in Boston the plane was met by a throng of frenzied Beatles' fans.

The following year I worked half the summer at Draw-Tite, and then took an abbreviated tour of northern Europe with Jack. I met him in Munich, and from there we went to Frankfurt to spend a couple of days with Christiane Moravetz, the former high school exchange student who lived just off the end of the runway at Rhein Main Air Force Base. Her father was a popular television sports journalist in Germany who was away on assignment when we arrived. That night Jack and I slept in Christiane's room, while she slept with one of her sisters. In the middle of the night Chris' father came home, and as luck would have it both he and Jack got up at the same time the next morning to use the bathroom. They met in the hallway, Bruno Moravetz coming out of his bedroom, and Jack coming out of his daughter's bedroom. Jack spoke no German, and Herr Moravetz spoke no English, so an explanation was impossible.

From Frankfurt we went to Helmstadt to pick up one of the three highways that crossed East Germany to Berlin. We were driving a Renault that Jack had leased in Paris, and before entering East Germany we stopped at a gas station to have the oil changed. We then headed for Berlin, but about halfway there the transmission ground to a halt. We later discovered that our "mechanic" in Helmstadt had drained the transmission oil instead of the engine oil, so the engine had twice the oil it should, and the transmission was dry.

I stayed with the car while Jack hitchhiked into Berlin to call a wrecker, but in a couple of hours he returned unsuccessful. He had neglected to take his passport with him, apparently not anticipating any difficulty in getting out of East Germany without identification. So I suggested that this time Jack should stay with the car while I hitchhiked into Berlin – **with my passport.**

When I arrived at the border the East German police invited me into their "office" so I could explain why I was trying to hitchhike across the border without the car I had when I entered East Germany. The building was next to a wooden guard tower, and the room looked like something out of a cold war movie. There wasn't a stick of furniture in it except a single chair in the middle of the room, with a bare light bulb hanging over it. The chair was for me while I tried to explain that my car had broken down on the autobahn, and I needed to have it towed into West Berlin so we could get it fixed. The guards were skeptical, but not hostile, and eventually I was allowed into West Berlin, but with the provision that the tow truck would have to pick up the car without me. So I made the call, and then waited there at the border until after midnight when the wrecker, with Jack and the car, finally returned.

Eventually we had a new transmission installed, at a cost we couldn't afford, and were back on our way. But before returning to West Germany we spent a day driving through East Berlin, and the contrast with the West was striking. West Berlin could just as easily have been New York or Chicago. The streets were jammed with traffic, the buildings alive with lights, and the sidewalks full of shoppers. East Berlin, on the other hand, was a ghost town. The main street didn't have half a dozen cars on it at rush hour, the buildings were dark and drab, and whole blocks of the city were still just rubble from the bombing during World War II. It was a bleak life indeed.

Back in the west we headed north to Copenhagen and then Oslo. We planned to go from Oslo to England, but after looking at the map decided to keep heading north around the tip of Scandinavia, and down to Helsinki instead. It was a trip of roughly two thousand miles over primitive roads that we completed in five days, in large part because we had twenty-four hours of daylight. It was a trip of stark beauty with fjords and mountains that gave the impression that we were on top of the world. In fact we were, or at least about as close to the top of the world as one could get in an automobile.

Along the way we picked up a British hitchhiker who was traveling with a backpack and a guitar. Guitars were required luggage for college tourists in 1967. His goal was to get to Nordkapp, the northernmost point in Norway, but the highway to Finland crossed about fifty miles south of there, and with our time constraints Jack and I decided to head for Helsinki instead of Nordkapp, leaving our passenger to complete the journey on his own. At the junction of the road to Nordkapp he got out, hoping to catch a ride with someone else heading to that remote outpost, and we drove off leaving him sitting on his backpack out there on the tundra in the middle of nowhere. I don't recall that we had seen another car in the last couple of hours. Over the years I have often wondered what happened to that courageous traveler. I suspect that I could return today and find his remains still sitting there at that intersection, but maybe someone came along eventually and took pity on him.

The road traveled through the heart of Lapland, and we frequently saw the camps of these nomads, and the reindeer that were the heart of their existence. They lived in teepees very much like those of the Plains Indians, and occasionally set up camp next to the road to sell their wares to the rare tourist who ventured that far north. At one of these camps Jack and I invested in a reindeer hide. I don't know what we planned to do with it, but the price was too good to pass up, so we tossed it in the back of the car, and headed for Helsinki. All went well for a day or two, but then we began to notice a faint odor. The day after that it was a strong odor. The day after that we had to drive with the windows open. Then we began to understand the difference between a tanned hide and an untanned hide. This was not a tanned hide.

After another day or two the investment that had become a problem turned into a crisis. We couldn't stand another day in the car with that hide, and if we ever did get it back to Paris we couldn't imagine being allowed to put it on an airplane, so we stopped at a post office, carefully sealed the hide in a cardboard box, and mailed it to our Uncle Bill in Ohio. We then entertained visions of his rapt anticipation as he opened this gift shipped to him all the way from Europe. If we had thought more about it we would have sent it C.O.D.

From Helsinki we took the ferry across the Baltic Sea to Stockholm. It's a beautiful trip, winding through hundreds of small islands that dot that part of the Baltic. It was a warm summer afternoon, the sun was shining, they served a nice lunch, and then the motion of the boat started to take its effect. People stretched out on the deck chairs at the rear of the boat, and soon many of them were drifting off to sleep. As we traveled between the islands sea gulls began to follow the boat, waiting for garbage to be thrown overboard. At first there were just a few birds, then a few more, and before long we had an armada.

The birds had no trouble keeping up with the boat. With a few flaps of their wings they could glide long distances before having to flap again. They followed along at the stern, with the front edge of the flock over the back third of the boat, and there they stayed for the entire crossing. They had obviously done this before. And like birds everywhere they occasionally had to relieve themselves. At first just a few of these missiles landed on the deck, but the pace picked up as more birds joined us. After awhile the occasional missile turned into more of a bombardment.

Jack and I watched all of this from a covered lobby that overlooked the rear deck, and as the bird activity increased the passengers on the deck started heading for cover. Eventually there was only one man left, obviously a sound sleeper. He was stretched out on his back, soaking up the sun, mouth agape, and out cold. Jack and I watched him for an hour, waiting for the first direct hit, but it never came. This man led a charmed life. By the time he finally awoke the rear deck was covered, but he hadn't been touched. When he got up you could almost see his silhouette as the only dark spot on a deck painted white. I would have bet big money that no one could spend an hour on that deck without getting plastered, but he did.

When I returned to school that fall I discovered that my financial status had improved. Because of an unexpected resignation I was promoted from resident advisor to dorm director. In addition to free room and board I now had a two room apartment with kitchen and private bath, and a salary of one hundred dollars per month. With my tuition scholarship I was going to school and putting money in the bank.

I also had to hire a replacement for myself as one of the four resident advisors, and I chose Norm Wilhelmsen, a dental school student who had lived across the hall from me when we were freshmen. The dormitory staff in those days was responsible for both counseling and discipline, or at least for preventing chaos. For the most part the job wasn't difficult, but there were a few challenges, and pranks were common. One of my favorites was a kid who inserted plastic tubing into the urinals so the water sprayed straight out when they were flushed. Residents would wake up in the middle of the night, stumble into the bathroom, use the urinal, and then get shot in the stomach with a stream of cold water when they pulled the handle. I didn't have to worry about discipline in that case; his friends and roommates took care of it for me.

Some pranks I heard about, but didn't see. One student returned to his room one evening to find it completely packed from floor to ceiling with crumpled up newspapers. Another student had his room at the end of the hallway. One Saturday night while he was out drinking, his friends cut off access to his room by building a false brick wall across the hallway. That story may be apocryphal, but I'd like to think it happened.

Occasionally their judgment was more questionable. One night a student squirted lighter fluid under the door of a friend, ignited it, and then pounded on the door, so he could enjoy the panic when his friend awoke from a sound sleep to find his room on fire. I think he pretty much got the reaction he was hoping for. One year in the middle of the night during final exams a couple of students plugged up all the drains on the fourth floor, turned on all the bathroom faucets, and then removed the faucet handles. I discovered their work when the water reached the basement.

My apartment was on the ground floor across the hall from Norm Wilhelmsen's room, and most afternoons I would wait for him to return from class so we could go to dinner together. Somewhere along the way I heard that you can make a shaving cream bomb using rubber tubing from a chemistry lab by tying a knot in one end, filling the tube with shaving cream, and then closing a door on the open end. When the door is opened the tube takes off like a rocket spraying shaving cream everywhere. It works like a charm.

One afternoon I obtained some of the tubing, made my bomb, and put it in Norm's door. Then I cut off any exposed tubing, wiped away the excess shaving cream, and waited. I also passed the word that the residents might want to stick around on the ground floor that afternoon to watch. Right at five o'clock Norm returned and walked by my open door to put his books away before going to dinner. Moments later he was covered in shaving cream, as was most of his room. I helped him clean up before we went to dinner, and by that time his sense of humor was beginning to return.

The next day I assembled the residents again at the anointed hour. At five o'clock Norm walked by my apartment, and I heard his footsteps stop as he inspected his door before opening. This time he could see the tubing pinched in the door, and a faint touch of shaving cream surrounding it. There was a prolonged pause, and then I heard his footsteps returning. He walked into my room, dropped his coat and books on my sofa, and said, "Want to go to dinner?"

"Sure," I said, and we headed off together. The route to the cafeteria took us by Norm's room, and as I walked past it Norm threw open the door as he ducked for cover. And then in front of my assembled audience a half inch piece of tubing with a dab of shaving cream on it fell harmlessly to the floor. Revenge, they say, is best served cold, and by the time Norm got even I had forgotten all about the bomb. He hadn't. Most evenings I studied at the graduate library until it closed, because I liked the quiet, and the smell, and the atmosphere of that old building. Then when the library closed I would walk back to the dorm, usually arriving around midnight.

All of the resident advisors had master keys, and on occasion when Norm or I received a care package from home we would leave a sample in the other's room. Late one winter evening when I opened my door I could see from the light that filtered in from the hall that there was a small plate on my desk. My mouth began to water as I anticipated a plate of cookies from Norm's mother. "What a friend," I thought as I walked over to sample one, not stopping to turn on the light. Then just before picking one up I realized that they were not cookies at all. It was a plate full of rat's heads from a biology study that Norm was working on. We were even, but I would have preferred a shaving cream bomb any day.

Chapter Twelve

───

There isn't a big market for history majors, so as my senior year progressed I had to think about what I would do to support myself after I graduated. In the winter of 1968 I took the Law School Aptitude Test, but before I started law school there was the Air Force and the Vietnam War. Then I went to law school. I started at the University of Georgia Law School in September 1973, went straight through two summers, and graduated in December 1975. I had saved fifteen thousand dollars while in the Air Force, not a small sum back then, and also received a monthly check from the G.I. Bill, so I was able to complete law school debt free. I also got married and took a honeymoon to Europe, so it is obvious that a dollar in 1973 was not the same as a dollar today. I think about that from time to time as I contemplate what my retirement needs might be in twenty years.

Law school was surprisingly easier and less stressful than my undergraduate classes at Michigan. Law school is more logical than the humanities, so I was pretty much in my element. I also had the advantage of being fresh. Those who went directly from college to law school were tired before they started, but I relished the opportunity to go back to school. If fatigue did start to set in I could rejuvenate myself by remembering where I had been a year earlier. Law school really was a pretty good life. I spent twenty-eight months there and didn't get shot at once. My final advantage was simply maturity. Law school professors can be intimidating, but as a twenty-eight year old veteran I think I found them much less intimidating than did my younger classmates. That may not have improved my grades, but it did reduce my stress level.

All of those factors helped me to finish the critical first year first in my class. I maintained that through the second year, and through two thirds of my third year. Then I got married and slid a few places before I graduated. It was all Hattie's fault. One of her favorite bits of doggerel is:

> He lost his job, his house burned down, he led a terrible life.
>
> But he took it like a man, and blamed it on his wife.

My most memorable law school professor was Perry Sentell who taught torts. Professor Sentell was a showman. His classes were based on intimidation and theatrics, but always with a sense of humor. His crowning glory was the annual presentation of the *Palsgraf* case. *Palsgraf v. Long Island Railway Co.* was a 1928 case from New York, written by future U. S. Supreme Court Justice Benjamin Cardozo. The case established that defendants are not responsible for injuries caused by negligence unless the specific injury is foreseeable. In *Palsgraf* a railway employee negligently knocked a package of fireworks from a passenger's hands, setting off an explosion that knocked over a scale that injured Mrs. Palsgraf. Mrs. Palsgraf won her case at trial, only to see Justice Cardozo take it away from her on appeal.

Most law students read the *Palsgraf* case, but Professor Sentell's students will never forget it. The lecture occurred in the spring, and by early winter we began to get hints from the upperclassmen that this would not be an ordinary class. As the date approached the anticipation increased. We were warned to be on time, to be prepared, and to dress for the occasion. The mood was like opening night on Broadway.

When the day finally arrived there was no difficulty in finding the lecture hall. Railroad tracks drawn in chalk led from the arch in the quadrangle to the law school, through the common areas, and down the hall to Professor Sentell's room. Students from the previous year had festooned the entrance with balloons and banners, and decorated the stage to replicate a railroad station, complete with the offending scale, and an electric train that circled the lectern. We were in our seats early, and the aisles were packed with second and third year students who returned to see the show. It was the hottest ticket in town.

The class began with a reenactment of the accident itself. Professor Sentell played all of the parts, including Mrs. Palsgraf's young children who danced with excitement as they waited for the train to take them to Rockaway Beach. Then the injured Mrs. Palsgraf walked into her lawyer's office with the plea, "Counselor, can you help me?" The student selected to answer that question was in for a long hour. As the rest of us sighed in relief the unlucky nominee rose to his feet to answer a barrage of questions that took the case from the first office visit through breaking the sad news to Mrs. Palsgraf years later that her victory had been snatched from her by a four to three vote in the state's highest court.

Most law school classes are dry and academic, but this lecture was the first indication for many of us that the law affects real people in dramatic ways. I thought about that years later when I had my own *Palsgraf* case, representing the family of Rick Husted, a young father killed in a motorcycle accident. In the trial court the family was awarded a judgment of four million dollars against the truck driver who killed him. Then we tried to collect from the truck driver's insurance company, and the appeal dragged on for ten years. The Michigan insurance statute says that an insurance company must pay whenever their insured causes an accident while driving "a motor vehicle," but Auto Owners refused to pay because their insured wasn't driving his own vehicle. He was driving his employer's vehicle, and Auto Owners didn't think it should have to pay for that regardless of what the statute said.

When the case was argued to the Michigan Supreme Court five of the seven justices agreed that "a motor vehicle" means any motor vehicle. The language of the statute couldn't be much clearer. But the written opinion was slow in coming, and in the meantime two of the Democratic justices retired, replaced by two Republicans. By the time the written opinion came out the initial five to two majority in favor of the family had turned into a four to three majority for the insurance company. The majority acknowledged that "a" does mean "any" in standard English, but nevertheless concluded that the Legislature couldn't possibly have meant what it said when it passed that law. Like Mrs. Palsgraf's lawyer I was left with the task of informing my client that her victory had been snatched away from her, and that she would be left to raise her young grandson on her own. It was one of many cases over the years that showed the pervasive influence of partisan politics in Michigan's judicial system and probably many other states as well. And I found little solace in the dissenting Republican justice's statement that his Republican colleagues' decision was "unconscionable." It was unconscionable, but my client still lost.

The case brought to mind Mrs. Palsgraf's plea, "Counselor, can you help me?" Her lawyer, foolishly relying on existing law, answered, "Of course." And then the law changed. Over the years I have many times warned clients that the law isn't what the Supreme Court said it was yesterday. The law is what the Supreme Court will say it is tomorrow. Like the rest of us, judges see facts and law through the prism of their own prejudices and biases, and often their own financial interest. A judge who receives large campaign contributions from business groups will usually see things business's way. It's human nature.

Professor Sentell was trying to warn us of this with his *Palsgraf* lecture, and it did sink in, even if the full significance only became apparent later. The annual production also achieved some well deserved notoriety for Professor Sentell. At most home football games it was customary for the public address announcer to fill slow moments by announcing, "Professor Sentell, please call Mrs. Palsgraf." She also received occasional invitations to White House events, care of Professor Sentell's home address.

At the end of my first year I continued with summer school, hoping to graduate as quickly as possible. I was then twenty-eight, living on my savings, and eager to get a paying job. During that summer session one of my classmates, Kathy Horne, thought I should meet a young army widow who was taking summer classes to get a master's degree in education. Hattie Taylor's husband had been a helicopter pilot who was shot down and killed only a few weeks after his arrival in Vietnam. Hattie then returned to her South Georgia roots to teach school, but spent her summers living in Athens with Katrina Douglas while they both attended summer school. Katrina was the widow of a Navy pilot, so they had something in common. Kathy knew I had been a pilot also, and arranged a blind date.

I drove over to meet Hattie at her apartment, took her to dinner, and then to a movie, "Chinatown" with Jack Nicholson. In the movie Nicholson tells his co-star, Faye Dunaway, that she has something in her eye. Leaning forward to ostensibly examine her eye, he kisses her instead. When I took Hattie back to her apartment that evening I told her that she had something in her eye. Caught off guard she held still while I maneuvered for a better look. That's when I knew this was going to be easy.

Things moved rapidly after that. I knew a good deal when I saw one. In August Hattie vacationed in Gatlinburg, Tennessee with her brother and sister, and I drove up with her on my way back to Michigan for a visit home between semesters. The following month I drove down to South Georgia one Friday after school to take her to Hilton Head, S.C. to spend the weekend on Jack's sailboat. She lived in Graham, and I could find that on the map, but I didn't know how to get to her parents' farm. "No problem," she said. "Just drive into Graham, stop at the convenience store on the left, and tell them that you want to call Hattie Lou." That was my first clue that the small town I came from in Michigan bore little resemblance to the small town she came from in South Georgia. Her hometown was a flashing light and a convenience store. There wasn't anything else. But her instructions worked as advertised, and when I stopped at the store Cousin Lonnie got on the phone immediately, and Hattie drove over to lead me home.

That Christmas I invited her to spend the holiday in Michigan, and when we got back to Georgia I proposed. I ordered a ring from the company that sold class rings at Belleville High School, but it took awhile for it to arrive. In the meantime I promised her one. Then we waited, and we waited. In April Hattie came to Athens for the weekend, and Saturday night we sat on the floor of my apartment watching a movie on TV. Actually, she watched the movie. I was busy making a substitute engagement ring that would have to suffice until the real one arrived. With a couple pairs of pliers and some wire I laboriously twisted the wire to make a ring with swirls on the top to resemble a diamond. Hattie checked on my progress periodically, and occasionally I put the "ring" on her finger to adjust it for size. Then when I was finished I asked to size it one last time, and she held out her hand while paying little attention to what I was doing. It fit perfectly, so I just left it there. We continued to watch the movie, and at a slow point in the action Hattie looked down to see my finished work, and discovered the real diamond on her finger. It had arrived in the mail that afternoon.

We were married August 23, 1975 in the small Methodist Church that Hattie had attended all her life. It sat out in the country, about a quarter mile behind the convenience store where I made my first stop in Graham a year earlier. August 23rd was a steaming hot day, but Hattie chose to wear the same wool wedding dress that my Great-Grandmother Sarah wore when she married my Great-Grandfather Henry in 1880. That dress has been worn by many Ford brides over the years, most recently by our daughter, Mary, in 2004. With luck it may have a few more weddings in it.

After a brief honeymoon in Europe we returned for my last semester of law school a week after classes had started. Hattie also attended class that fall to complete her master's degree in math education. Then I had to look for a job. I was interested in climate, but Hattie was smart enough to realize that family was more important, and encouraged me to live either in Georgia near her family, or in Michigan near mine. As much as I dislike cold weather I opted for Michigan, and Hattie was kind enough to go with me. In South Georgia slang she had "married bad," but tried to make the best of it.

In early December I was invited to interview with The Upjohn Company, a pharmaceutical company headquartered in Kalamazoo. They had a small in-house legal department, and had never before hired directly out of law school, but the General Counsel, Gerry Thomas, was willing to give me a chance. I took Hattie with me, and we arrived in Kalamazoo after an early winter snowstorm. I dropped her off at the downtown mall to shop and look around while I interviewed, but she was totally unprepared for Michigan weather, and was wearing open toed shoes in six inches of snow. Her first stop was a shoe store to buy boots.

The interview went well, and I was offered the job, starting in January 1976. Upjohn paid to have our few pieces of furniture moved from Athens to Kalamazoo, and the van arrived a day or two after New Years in the middle of another snowstorm. Every time the front door of the apartment was opened it let in a cloud of snow that covered the entryway. Hattie now owned boots, but she had never seen snow like this, and had no idea how to get rid of it. She caught on quickly, however, when she saw me pick up a broom and start sweeping. With constant sweeping we were able to hold our own until all of the furniture was safely inside.

I made our first marital purchase that winter. It was the year of the winter Olympics, and I wanted a color television to watch them. I didn't have the money to buy a television, but I did have a job, so I bought a small color set for two hundred and forty dollars on the installment plan. I expected to pay it off quickly, but soon discovered that marriage was more expensive than I had anticipated. I was still paying on it a year later.

I was hired by Upjohn to help defend their product liability lawsuits. Most of these were for Cleocin, an antibiotic that occasionally caused severe colitis. They didn't know why it caused colitis, or what to do about it, but there was no question that Cleocin was the cause, and the consequences could be catastrophic, and by the time I arrived in 1976 there had been over one hundred reported deaths. I worked with Ken Cyrus on these cases, but we didn't actually try them ourselves. Our job was just to coordinate the many attorneys around the country who represented Upjohn in their own communities. They tried the cases, while Ken and I supplied the documents, and the company witnesses, and made sure that everyone followed the same script.

After three years of law school I was well prepared to be an appellate judge, but I knew nothing about practicing law. In the days of Abraham Lincoln a lawyer studied law by working as an apprentice. He would meet with clients, do research, draft documents, and study law books when things were slow. By the time he became a lawyer he was ready to open his own office. It doesn't work that way today. Modern law students spend three years studying the theory of law. I had no idea how to draft a document, and had never seen a complaint or an answer. I was like a surgeon who had read lots of books, but never touched a scalpel.

My inexperience surfaced almost immediately. My first assignment was to help one of our local defense lawyers respond to a motion. Gerry Thomas stopped in my office that morning, and asked me to draft an affidavit for one of our employees to sign. I took some notes, and told Gerry that I would be happy to. Only after he left did I ask myself, "What the hell is an affidavit?" An hour in the library fortunately answered that question, and gave me some examples to copy. I was a corporate lawyer with one of America's largest pharmaceutical firms, a magna cum laude graduate of my law school class, and had no clue what an affidavit was.

Chapter Thirteen

I discovered rather quickly that trials in the real world bear little resemblance to the cases I studied in law school. I was no longer dealing with theoretical questions. The cases at Upjohn involved tragic injuries and real money. I also discovered that judges are unpredictable and inconsistent. One judge could rule one way, another just the opposite. Nor was the litigation a search for the truth. Both sides just wanted to win. Company representatives were carefully prepared to repeat the company line, and not to stray from the planned defense. When opposing lawyers requested records they were fought at every turn. If unable to get the judge to limit the request, we studied the questions word by word to look for any excuse to withhold records that we knew would be damaging. If a lawyer came to Kalamazoo to review the records we would overwhelm him with boxes of innocuous documents, hoping that he would tire before finding the needle in the haystack. To help him tire quickly we put him in a closed room with no windows, and no access to food or drink. It was all ethical, but it wasn't a search for the truth. And the opposing lawyers used similar tactics. Litigation with a major corporation is war, not sport.

Most product liability cases follow a familiar pattern. The initial cases are fought ruthlessly, and the first injured plaintiffs to go to trial seldom have enough information to win. They are just the advance guard, sacrificing themselves for those who follow. But with every case the plaintiffs' lawyers discover more documents, and accumulate more testimony. Over time the balance of power begins to shift until eventually enough smoking guns are discovered to make a convincing case. The company might win the first five or ten cases, but sooner or later a plaintiff will win, and then the flood gates will open. After the first loss manufacturers have little choice but to start settling cases to try to contain the damage. The truth usually comes out in the end, but it takes a battle and several years to get there.

I saw this pattern not only at Upjohn, but also years later after I switched sides, and went into private practice. In the early 1980's I represented Sylvia Jolicoeur who was seriously burned when the gas tank of her International Harvester tractor exploded. I soon discovered that this had been a common occurrence since the early 1960's. On warm days enough pressure could build up in the gas tank to eventually blow the gas cap, soaking the driver in a geyser of gasoline. Then the gas would ignite. But over the years International Harvester had won every case. They claimed there was nothing wrong with their tractors, that the drivers must have opened the gas caps themselves, that it would be impossible for the gas to ignite spontaneously, etc. Juries bought it every time.

Then while I was still investigating Mrs. Jolicoeur's injury I learned of a case in East St. Louis, Illinois that changed the rules of the game. In that case, as in all the others, International Harvester told the lawyers and the court that it had no records dating back to the 1960's. But during this trial one of the Harvester employees let it slip that he knew where the records were. They had all been boxed up and shipped to the company's law firm in Chicago. International Harvester didn't have the records, but it sure knew where they were. The judge then stopped the trial, and sent a truck to Chicago to retrieve the documents.

The records were damning. For almost twenty years International Harvester had known about this problem with their gas tanks, they knew what caused it, and they knew how to fix it. But they did nothing. The explosions occurred for two reasons. First, the gas tank was placed over the engine, where engine heat could turn liquid gasoline to gas vapor. Second, the vent holes on the gas caps were too small to allow the vapor to escape. When enough pressure built up the caps would blow.

In the records from the 1960's some of the Harvester engineers discussed the problem, and how to fix it. Larger vent holes would have been sufficient, but this fix was vetoed by management because it would result in lower gas mileage, making the tractors less competitive. The company refused to make changes even after one vice president described the tractor as the most dangerous on the market, and wrote a memo stating that he refused to be part of it any longer. Despite all of this the tractors stayed on the market, farmers continued to be torched, and International Harvester continued to win every trial. So long as they kept winning they had no motivation to fix anything.

All of that changed with the discovery of the documents that had been hidden in Chicago. When the trial resumed the jury awarded the farmer a judgment of fifteen million dollars, and suddenly Harvester started settling cases. They also designed a replacement cap with a larger vent hole, and extra tongs to prevent it from being blown off. The fix cost only a few dollars per tractor.

One of Upjohn's first Cleocin cases to go to trial was a death case in Oklahoma City. We knew Cleocin caused the death, so the issue came down to the adequacy of the warning in the package insert. Upjohn warned that Cleocin could cause pseudomembranous colitis, but the plaintiff claimed that the warning wasn't specific enough to really put doctors on notice that this was a different and more deadly form of colitis than what they were used to. As is often the case, the trial came down to a battle of the experts, and no expense was spared. For weeks the jury heard experts from both sides go into great detail about various forms of colitis, and what the language in the package insert would mean to the average doctor. In the end Upjohn won, as defendants usually do in the early cases, and the jury concluded that Upjohn's warnings had been sufficient.

With a growing number of trials waiting in the wings we were eager to talk to the jury to find out what we had done right. We wanted to determine which of our experts had been the most convincing, and how the jury had resolved the highly technical discussions of the causes and consequences of various forms of colitis. What we learned was stunning. Some of the jurors just wanted to go home, but one of the men was willing to talk. We caught up with him on the sidewalk on his way to his car, and asked him what we had done to convince him that a doctor reading our package insert should have been able to anticipate the possibility of this terrible side effect. He looked at us almost dismissively for even asking such a silly question. "The witnesses were all a waste of time," he said. "We didn't pay attention to any of that."

"Then why did you decide that the warnings in our package insert were adequate?" we wanted to know, still hoping for some revelation that would be helpful in future cases.

"It was simple," he replied. "Anyone should know that if you swallow a pill it will get down into your intestines."

The jury had sat through weeks of trial with absolutely no clue what the debate was all about. We could have been speaking Greek, and they would have understood just as much. It was an experience that I saw repeated time after time over the years. Lawyers focus on a few facts that determine the outcome logically, but we often have no idea what the jury will find important.

One of my early trials in private practice was a paternity case. Cindy Knowles met my client, Tim Schmidt, at a party. It was their only date, but the magic worked, and nine months later she was the mother of a little boy. Tim admitted the relationship, but denied he was the father. At trial Cindy testified that he had to be the father, because there was no one else. This was in the days before DNA testing made paternity cases obsolete, so the jury had to listen to the testimony, and come to a decision based on little more than their best guess.

Actually, they had more than just a guess to go on in this case. I had a hair problem to contend with. Tim's hair was bright red. He looked like Ronald McDonald, and the child was a clone. At just a few months of age he was already sporting a fine head of orange hair, and I had no answer for that. The case looked hopeless, but Tim wanted his day in court, so we went to trial.

The prosecution lasted most of the morning, with several witnesses describing the night in question. At ten minutes to twelve the prosecution rested, and the judge suggested that we break for lunch, as it made no sense to start the defense case that close to the break. We could come back after lunch and still have a chance of finishing before five. But I told the judge I would like to get started, and he agreed. So I called my first witness at ten to twelve, and two witnesses later I rested my case before noon.

Witnesses don't take very long when they don't have anything to say that can help you.

The jury deliberations lasted about an hour, and when the jury filed back into the courtroom I was prepared for the justice that I expected Tim was about to receive. Then to my surprise they announced that they had concluded that he was not the father, and by the miracle of American justice he was spared eighteen years of child support. Poor Cindy and her baby were on their own.

After stopping to express my condolences to Cindy, who was not all that inclined to accept them, I ran to catch up with the jury foreman to ask what he possibly could have been thinking. His explanation was not unlike the juror I had talked to in Oklahoma: since Cindy admitted that this was a one night affair the jury assumed that she was a loose woman who might have consorted with others also. It was a moral decision that placed all the responsibility on her, and had little to do with who was the probable father.

Sometimes trials are decided by events that don't even occur in the courtroom. It might be pure fantasy, or something that one of the jurors read, or unspoken clues that only the jurors see. One year my father was called as a juror to sit on a criminal trial for a young black man accused of selling drugs. The trial lasted several days, and in the end he was found guilty. Always eager to understand how juries think, I asked Dad what convinced him that the defendant was a drug dealer.

"It had nothing to do with the trial itself," he told me. "We decided it the second day of trial while we were all having lunch across the street." The defendant was free on bail, and also went out for lunch. "While we were waiting for our order we saw the defendant drive up and park in front of the restaurant. He was driving a new Cadillac, and we figured that there was no way he could buy a car like that if he wasn't selling drugs."

I don't know what evidence the lawyers were thinking about when they gave their closing arguments that day, but they were wasting their time. The defendant went to prison for driving a Cadillac. On the other hand, how did he pay for that car? Perhaps he belonged in prison. Even if juries flip a coin they are still right fifty percent of the time.

Sometimes I have wished that juries would flip a coin. They can be dangerous when they try to think. Adam Mallon was a motorcycle rider who broke a leg when a car turned in front of him. Motorcycles have provided a consistent supply of clients for me over the years, often with just this type of accident. It wasn't a major case, but it was a bad break, and the other driver had no excuse. She turned in front of the motorcycle because she wasn't paying attention, and just never saw him. There wasn't anything that Adam could have done to avoid her. The police officer on the scene gave the defendant a ticket, but at trial we were not allowed to tell the jury about the ticket because of Michigan's rules of evidence. The officer couldn't testify about the ticket because he wasn't there when the accident happened. Only actual eye witnesses are allowed to testify about who was at fault.

Adam did win his case, but the award was meager, and to add insult to injury the jury found Adam fifty percent at fault. A few days later I called the jury foreman to ask her why the jury thought this accident was half Adam's fault. "You didn't tell us who got the ticket," she explained, "and since you didn't tell us who got the ticket we assumed that your client must have gotten it. We didn't know what he did wrong, but if he got a ticket he must have done something, so we found him fifty percent at fault." It is from such experience that lawyers learn how to try cases. After that I always asked the police officer who got the ticket. The defense lawyer would object, and the judge would explain why the witness could not answer, but at least the jury knew I wasn't trying to conceal something from them.

Most of 1976 was a learning experience for me. I was learning how to be a lawyer, and how to be a husband, sometimes with spotty results at both. One of the nice benefits of moving to Kalamazoo was the chance to spend time with my grandparents who lived only twenty minutes away. By then Grandma was slipping into Alzheimer's, but Grandpa was as sharp as ever, and at the age of seventy-seven was still serving as the Register of Deeds for Van Buren County. He always wanted to be a lawyer, and would no doubt have been a good one, but his education was cut short when he lost both hands in a railroad accident at the age of fifteen.

We visited them often, and also frequently had them over to our apartment. Late that summer they stopped in on a Saturday afternoon while our neighbors, Trav and Armida Pearse, were in the process of moving out. We watched them make frequent trips in and out of their apartment, and I casually mentioned to Grandpa that Armida's father was in his sixties when she was born. Even more surprisingly, she had a younger brother who was born when her father was in his seventies. That news clearly impressed Grandpa, but all he said was, "Oh geez, don't tell your grandmother."

I took the Michigan Bar Exam in July, and received the news in November that I had passed. Grandpa then arranged to have the formal admission ceremony at the courthouse in Paw Paw where he had his office. It was a proud event for both of us. Grandpa was much of the reason that I chose a legal career, and to some degree I'm sure he was living his dream vicariously through me. But, sadly, a few days before the ceremony Grandpa died of a heart attack while driving home from a meeting in Lansing. Three days after his funeral we went through with the admission ceremony, as he had planned it, but it was a bittersweet moment. The man who would have enjoyed it the most wasn't there.

In the spring of 1977 I spent several weeks attending a trial in Houston. The flood gates hadn't opened yet, so we were still winning all of these cases, but the numbers were increasing, and a company lawyer always had to be in attendance. This case was more stressful for me than most, because Hattie was expecting our first child at any minute. Late one Friday afternoon she called to tell me that she thought the day had arrived. I didn't know how long it would take to get back to Kalamazoo, but I wanted to be there if I could, so excusing myself from the courtroom I caught a cab to the airport, bought a teddy bear from one of the airport shops, and took the first flight to Chicago. I called home again from Chicago, and learned that we weren't parents yet, but probably would be before the night was over.

There were only a limited number of daily flights from Chicago to Kalamazoo, and I arrived in Chicago close to midnight after the last flight of the day had departed, so

I rented a car and drove home as fast as I dared. I arrived at three in the morning, and was relieved to see that Hattie was still there. And she stayed there until Jimmy was born five days later.

On the day of his arrival Hattie's contractions started coming five minutes apart shortly after midnight, so we packed up and headed for the hospital. Not having been through this before, I assumed that by breakfast I would be a father. But breakfast came and went (I missed it), and lunch came and went (I missed that too), and still there was no baby. After nineteen hours of hard labor Jimmy finally appeared, but even then he had to be dragged kicking and screaming with the aid of forceps. The forceps left a couple of significant bruises, but other than that he was in good shape.

Throughout the process Hattie announced repeatedly that we would be a one child family, and I don't think her concern was over the fact that I had gone almost twenty-four hours without eating. It wasn't until after the delivery that she began to look more favorably on the whole experience. Jimmy was a placid newborn. He didn't cry at all, and seemed to be amazed at the dramatic new world he had entered. His eyes were wide open, taking everything in. I expected the same reaction when John was born two years later, but John arrived with his eyes shut, and howling at the top of his lungs. That should have been a clue that all kids are different. They can have the same parents, and be raised in the same house, and be as different as night and day.

Parenthood was a shock. My brother, Jack, had warned me, but I still wasn't ready for it. He said, "Remember how much your life changed when you got married? Well, that's nothing compared to how much it will change when you have a baby." Sleep was the first thing to go. I expected a month or two of middle of the night feedings, but I didn't expect it to last for four years. It wouldn't have lasted that long if I had known what I was doing, but I didn't, and it did. Hattie knew enough to just let him cry on occasion, but I couldn't stand it. As a result he never learned to go to sleep by himself. I would walk him, or rock him, or bounce him in his bed until he fell asleep. Then when he awoke during the night I would go through the process again, over and over and over. When I got tired of walking with him I would put him in a little wagon. The wagon had a ten foot rope, so I could sit and read the paper, give the wagon a push with my foot, and then reel it back in with the rope. After awhile the constant motion would put him to sleep, and then I could put him in bed.

When John was born twenty-one months later I had two of them keeping me awake at night. Then Mary was born two years after John, and I had three. After years of sleepless nights I finally reached the end of my rope. When Mary was four months old I couldn't take it any longer, and let her cry herself to sleep one night. It almost killed me. The next night she cried a little, but not as much. After that the crying stopped, and we all slept through the night without interruption. I finally learned how to get infants to sleep through the night, and of course never again had any use for this new found knowledge. It was like Dad's experience with cars. He owned cars for sixty years, and claimed that he never had the same problem twice. As soon as he learned how to fix something it would never break again. It was always something new. And now that I understood how to get children to sleep, there were no more children. This time when Hattie announced she wasn't having any more babies she meant it.

Chapter Fourteen

I rapidly grew weary of my job at Upjohn. It was a wonderful company to work for, and the people couldn't have been nicer, but it was a company, and I was not a company man. I was young and ambitious, and wanted to try cases myself instead of watching other lawyers try them. I was also confident that I could try cases as well as the lawyers we hired to try them for us, which meant that I didn't really understand what they were doing. I was about to learn that trial work is a whole lot harder than it looks.

I had also grown weary of committee meetings. Corporations run on committee meetings. Every department had endless meetings, and a company lawyer was expected to attend most of them. Experience has probably proven this to be a smart management technique, but there is nothing more boring than a committee. If I go to hell I don't expect to burn; I expect to spend eternity on a committee.

The more I learned about Cleocin the less tenable our position seemed to be. It was indeed a powerful antibiotic that saved many lives, but it was also often promoted by sales representatives for minor conditions that could have been better treated by safer drugs. The final straw was a lengthy trial in St. Petersburg, Florida over the death of Anna Martinez, a sixteen year old girl who had taken Cleocin for acne. She was an only child, otherwise in perfect health, and the trial testimony of her devastated parents was gripping. Anna spent days in the hospital, and despite excellent medical care her condition continued to deteriorate. On the day she died her mother was with her when she suddenly took a turn for the worse. As the hospital staff rushed her back to surgery she turned to her mother and said, "Take care of Daddy." It was the last time they saw her alive.

To my amazement Upjohn won that case, as we had won all the others, but I didn't feel good about it. Try as I might I couldn't get that little girl's last words out of my memory. They linger there today. Lawyers don't have to believe in their client's case. We try cases every day for clients we don't like or don't believe. It comes with the territory, especially for lawyers who defend criminal cases. Most lawyers don't get to pick their cases. They just have to take what comes, and do the best job they can.

But this was different. No one was forcing me to work for Upjohn or any other corporation. I was still young enough to change, although I could see that the option wouldn't be there for long. Corporate attorneys have limited market value. They don't have any trial experience, and they don't have any clients. If they leave one company their only option usually is to work for some other company in a similar job. If I wanted to break out of that cycle I had to do it soon.

In September 1977 I resigned from Upjohn to take a job as a trial attorney with a small firm in Kalamazoo that was trying to develop a personal injury practice. It's what I thought I wanted to do, although by temperament it probably wasn't a good fit for me. I would have been happier and more successful as an appellate attorney, or as a law school professor, but I was drawn to the drama of the courtroom. Once again I was trying to go to my left.

I stopped working at Upjohn in early September, and took a few days off before starting my new job on the seventeenth. While I was between jobs I had lunch one day at a Chinese restaurant, and decided that the fortune cookie would tell me if my new job was a wise move. Fortune cookies are more interesting if you ask them the question in advance. What it said was unlike any other fortune cookie I have ever seen. It read, "On the seventeenth of the month you will make a business move that will result in financial success." Fortune cookies lie.

Nineteen seventy-seven was a busy year for me. In addition to changing jobs we also bought our first house, and were learning to care for a new baby. I was somewhat prepared for the job and the house, but I was not prepared for how a child could change my life. Over the years I had read about parents who lost children as infants or toddlers. It was sad, of course, but subconsciously I didn't consider it to be as tragic as losing a teenager or someone you had known all your life. After all, how attached could you be to a child you had known for only a few months, especially one who couldn't talk? Even after Jimmy was born I didn't realize how much he meant to me.

Those naïve assumptions changed in September. When Jimmy was four months old he caught a cold, and developed a cough. Then the cough got worse, and became a bark. We took him to the pediatrician who told us that he had croup, but that it was nothing serious. Just put him in a steamy bathroom, and he should be fine. That evening the cough got worse, he struggled to breathe, and the steamy bathroom didn't do much to help. At a loss, I called my mother. Mom arrived in about an hour, and immediately recognized the seriousness of the situation, "If he were my child, I would take him to the emergency room."

That was all the encouragement we needed, but when we got to the hospital we were startled by their response. We knew he was struggling, but the hospital staff treated it like a crisis, setting off alarms, and calling for help. Jimmy was moving air, but just barely. Fortunately the treatment worked, and after a few days he was released to go home. Aside from the scare, what impressed me the most was Jimmy's reaction to the crisis. He was only four months old, and I didn't expect him to know his parents from anyone else, but in a room full of doctors and nurses he paid no attention to them. They held a mask over his face, and poked him with needles, but through it all his eyes were on me. If I walked to the other side of the room his eyes followed. He knew nothing about hospitals, but he knew me, and he was looking to me to save him.

That was the first time I understood what it meant to be a parent. This little boy was my responsibility, and I would have to protect him for the next eighteen years. The fact that I thought it would be for only eighteen years showed that I still didn't get it, but I was learning. I was also surprised by my own emotion. This little four month old boy who couldn't talk was the most important person in my life. I didn't care what happened to me so long as he survived.

I loved Jimmy as an infant, but I really started to enjoy him when he learned to talk. I discovered then that there was a lot more going on in that little head than I had suspected. One of our first joint projects was a comedy routine that allowed me to be his straight man. When we were with friends I would start by asking him a question, "Hey Jimmy, how old are you?"

"Two."

"When's your birthday?"

"May 12th."

"What are you good for?"

"Nothing." It always drew laughs, and he got to be the star.

I also discovered that negotiating skills are innate. One night I was getting him dressed for bed, when he asked to use my toothbrush to brush his teeth. I loved him, but not that much, and told him that he would have to use his own. A brief argument ensued before he gave up and changed the subject. "Are we buddies?" he asked.

Touched by this show of affection I said, "Sure, Jimmy, we're buddies."

"Well then," he responded, "let me use your toothbrush." It was a magnificent effort, albeit unsuccessful.

We relied heavily on Mom and Dad. They lent us money to buy the house, helped care for Jimmy, and were a primary source of information. What I didn't know about children and houses, which was plenty, I sought from them. Dad helped me paint, he wallpapered, and he helped sand the floors. And when things broke down he usually had some idea about how to fix them, although sometimes his diagnostic procedures left something to be desired.

They came over one weekend while I was trying to figure out why I had a puddle of water on my basement floor. I looked everywhere, and couldn't determine the source. No pipes were leaking, the water heater was dry, and I just couldn't figure it out. Dad was as stumped as I was, and then had a sudden insight. Water softeners use salt, so if it was coming from the water softener it would be salty. He reached down and stuck his finger in the water, and then tasted it with the tip of his tongue. "It's not salty," he announced, "so it can't be the water softener." We still didn't know.

They stopped in again the next weekend, and by then I had discovered the source of the puddle. I brought it up while we were talking in the front yard. "Remember that puddle in my basement that wasn't salty?" I asked.

"Sure. Did you ever find out where it came from?"

"As a matter of fact, I did. The sewer was backing up."

Dad remained nonchalant. Tasting sewer water didn't bother him. "Well, it didn't hurt me any," he said with stoic bravado. Then he turned and spit several times before he realized what he was doing.

Chapter Fifteen

I had seen many trials on television, and sat through several with The Upjohn Company, but none of that prepared me for my life as a trial lawyer. Television lawyers don't live in a panic over where their next case is coming from, or how they're going to pay the rent. They always know just what question to ask to break their case open, and they hardly ever lose. Their clients are always innocent, they never spend hours in the library searching for cases that don't exist, and they always have the perfect response on the tip of their tongue when some totally unexpected testimony or legal argument blindsides them at the worst possible moment. In the real world no defendant ever confesses on the witness stand, and I have yet to see a case won with outstanding oratory. Usually my biggest job was just trying to figure out what really happened. Someone would come into my office with a significant injury, and I had to figure out why. Things often turned out not to be as they first seemed.

One of my first clients was Betty Johnson. Betty and her husband were retired, and liked to travel in a recreational vehicle that they rented from a local dealer. All went well until Betty received a severe electrical shock when they stopped at a campground out in Arizona. She survived, but dislocated both shoulders, and had a difficult time. My job was to figure out why she got shocked.

After talking with them for a while I discovered some additional facts that might help me. They carried an extension cord to plug into the power outlet when they stopped, but this hadn't caused a short at any other campsite. They also told me that they had a three pronged plug, but used a cheater plug in Arizona because the outlet there only accepted two pronged plugs. But they had also done that before without any problem. I needed an electrical expert.

Arthur Konkle was an electrical engineer who occasionally testified in legal cases, and he agreed to inspect the R.V. to see if he could figure out what had happened. After filing suit, and going through some legal wrangling, the court ordered the dealer to let us have the R.V. for an afternoon. So I found myself with Art on the dealer's lot in that unheated R.V. on a freezing cold February afternoon. This wasn't looking much like the warm office full of books that I had envisioned when I applied to law school.

Fortunately Art was good at what he did, and before long he had closed in on the problem. He was able to determine that there was a short in the R.V. between the neutral electrical wire and the skin of the R.V. This would cause no problem with a three pronged plug, but with a cheater plug the neutral line would be powered if the plug was plugged in upside down. And if the neutral line was powered the skin of the R.V. would be hot. This is obviously what happened out in Arizona, and as Betty climbed into the R.V. she touched the skin of the R.V. while her foot was grounded, thereby causing the shock.

But we weren't done. That told us what happened, but it didn't tell us where the short came from. We had no way to prove if the short was caused by the manufacturer, or the dealer, or even the Johnsons themselves. To build a solid case I needed to find the short, and that was like looking for a needle in a haystack. Art hooked up a nine volt circuit through the skin of the trailer, and attached a flashlight. So long as the light stayed on we knew the short still existed. The light would go out if the short was removed. Then we started with the most likely sources, taking apart all of the electrical outlets, but found nothing. Then we moved on to appliances and lights and anything else of an electrical nature, but still nothing. After three hours we were both freezing, and the chance of finding the short seemed pretty slim.

Finally Art was ready to give up. There were all kinds of electrical wires under the skin of the R.V. and he guessed that one of the rivets had probably hit one of the wires, but it was only a guess. Without removing all of the rivets there was no way to prove his theory, and that would of course destroy the vehicle. The only other thing he had not taken apart was the ceiling air conditioner. "I can do that if you want," he said, "but the problem is most likely from one of the rivets."

"We've come this far," I answered. "Let's give it a try." I didn't want to get that close without exhausting all possibilities.

The air conditioning unit was held on with half a dozen large screws, and when Art removed the first one the light went out. Once we got inside we could see that this was not a factory installed air conditioner. It was installed by the dealer, who used a three wire cord to connect it to the R.V.'s electrical system. Then when the air conditioner was screwed into place one of the screws went through the cord, shorting out the ground wire to the neutral wire. So we removed the wire, and replaced it with one that was undamaged so the R.V. would be safe in the future. The wire that we removed, with the screw still in it, became my primary trial exhibit.

Since it was not a manufacturing defect the manufacturer was dismissed, and soon thereafter the dealer's insurance company settled. The settlement had nothing to do with my ability as a trial lawyer. It was just a puzzle, and once we solved the puzzle the case was over. In large law firms these puzzles are solved by experts and investigators, but in a small firm in a small town I was more often than not my own expert and my own investigator. One of the interesting aspects of trial law is that it is a never ending education, and every case is different. In electrical cases I had to become an electrical engineer. If a ladder collapsed I was a ladder expert. In medical malpractice cases I had to know more about the drug or the disease than the defendant doctor knew. Usually it wasn't as hard as it may sound. Doctors know a tremendous amount about a great many things, but their knowledge is usually broader than it is deep, and after a few hours in the library I could know more than they did about a specific drug or a specific disease. And to be fair, they could do the same with many aspects of the law. They might never know as much about the law as I do, but with a little study they could easily know more than I do about a specific area of the law.

Early in my career I became an expert on punch presses. I have had several clients who lost fingers in presses, although fortunately those injuries are less common now than they were years ago when most presses were operated by foot pedals. The operator would place a part in the press, remove his hands, step on the foot pedal to activate the press, and then reach back in to remove the part after it had been stamped. Over an eight hour shift this routine could get very old and very mechanical. If the operator lost concentration and stepped on the foot pedal while his hands were in the machine he could lose his fingers or even his hands.

As courts became less tolerant of these injuries the manufacturers started adding safety devices to reduce the number of accidents. One solution was an electric beam to stop the press when the operator's hands were in the danger zone. More commonly the foot pedal was replaced by two hand buttons so the press would not come down unless the operator pushed both buttons simultaneously. When these safety devices work they make injury almost impossible, but when the safety devices fail tragedy is almost guaranteed.

Cindy Young was a twenty-two year old girl who operated a press for a small tool and die company near Lake Michigan. This press had two hand buttons, but she was still maimed when the press double cycled. She pushed both buttons to operate the press, and then reached in to remove the part after the press had cycled, but when her hand was in the press it automatically recycled a second time on its own, severing three fingers and about half of her right palm. All she had left was the thumb and index finger. My job was to figure out why it double cycled. If the press had a design flaw she could sue the manufacturer. If the malfunction was caused by the way her employer serviced the machine she would be limited to partial payment of her lost wages under workers compensation. The press was fifteen years old, so proving a design defect would not be easy.

At the time I knew absolutely nothing about punch presses, so to prepare for Cindy's case I had to learn how presses are designed, and how to read electrical blueprints. I started by hiring an electrical engineer to analyze the design, and then had him teach me what he found.

There was no question that this press had in fact double cycled. After Cindy was injured her employer called the manufacturer, who sent out a company engineer, Tom Sparks, to examine the press. Sparks was able to duplicate the double cycle, but that still didn't tell us why. He did give us some clues, however. Most presses have three limit switches that control the press. The top and bottom limit switches stop the press at the top and bottom of the cycle, and both switches are adjustable to accommodate the many different operations that the press can be used for. The middle limit switch changes the speed of the press in mid cycle, and also allows the press to complete the cycle after that point even if the hand buttons are released.

When Sparks was finished with his examination he removed the hands free function of the middle limit switch, although he claimed there was nothing wrong with the press as originally designed. All of this took him three days, and was completed long before I ever met Cindy, so one of our problems was to reconstruct the press as it was at the time of the accident, and before Sparks modified it. Fortunately the original blueprints for the press were still available, and provided all the information we needed. Although this was a tragedy for Cindy it is an ill wind that doesn't blow some good for someone, and Sparks turned out to be the beneficiary of this tragedy. After three days at the company he left his wife, and ran off with the company's bookkeeper. He apparently hadn't spent all of his time examining the press.

I hired Bob Ewell, an engineer from Chicago, to review the blueprints. After a couple of weeks he called me back, and said that he had found a design defect that allowed the press to double cycle under one unique set of circumstances. First the top limit switch and the middle limit switch had to be set very close to each other. Then the operator had to hold both hand buttons through the entire downward and upward travel. If all of this occurred the press would double cycle without the buttons being pushed again, and that is obviously what happened to Cindy. But now we had to prove it.

I got permission from the court to examine the press with my expert, and arranged to meet him at the company. Convinced that we would be able to make the press double cycle, I brought a video camera. Then I sat back and waited for Ewell to wire the press exactly as it was when it left the factory, and to place the limit switches exactly where they were when Cindy was injured. By that time I had learned how to read the electrical blueprints, and I knew the press had to double cycle. It had to. When all these circuits tripped at the same time the press would come down twice.

It didn't. We pulled out the blueprints to check every wire in that press, and they were all as they had been when the press left the factory. We put the limit switches exactly where Sparks had found them when he examined the press after the injury. It double cycled for him, so it had to double cycle for us, but it didn't. Nothing we tried made it double cycle. Finally Ewell gave up. He packed up his briefcase and sat down next to the door waiting for me to leave. I wanted to keep trying, but he knew the game was over. He had been an engineer for a long time, and he explained to me that sometimes the theory just doesn't work in practice. That's the danger when you try a reenactment. If it doesn't work your whole case goes up in smoke. Sometimes you're better off just arguing the theory.

There was a case in Kalamazoo many years ago that showed just how dangerous reenactments can be. The theory in that case was that a gun misfired without the hammer being pulled all the way back. The defense argued that it couldn't happen, and had a gun expert to prove it. At trial the expert dismissed the plaintiff's claim as nonsense. The gun couldn't fire when the hammer was in an intermediate position, "and if you don't believe me then just give me the gun and I'll show you." With considerable flair the expert put the hammer in the intermediate position, and pulled the trigger to prove that nothing would happen. And nothing did happen, except for a very loud click as the hammer came down on the firing pin. It was a click that could be heard all over the courtroom, and brought both the expert and the defense to a complete standstill. For a lawyer a reenactment gone bad can ruin your entire day.

I knew Ewell was right. We were wasting our time, but knowing when to quit has never been my strong suit, and I continued to play with the press while he waited impatiently for me to give up. I tried several wiring changes to no avail, and then in frustration more than anything else turned my attention to the limit switches. These were mechanical switches that were tripped as the press moved up and down, and I could trip them with my hand if I pushed hard enough. I hit the upper and lower switches, and could hear them click as they were tripped. Then I hit the middle switch with a downward motion, and heard it click, but when I hit it with an upward motion there was nothing but silence.

As soon as that happened I knew that we had found our answer. The switch that was designed in the blueprints tripped in both directions, and the press would only double cycle if it tripped going up. If the switch was replaced by a switch that only tripped going down it would be impossible to double cycle. I then talked to the plant manager, who confirmed that when Sparks examined the press he also replaced the two way limit switch with a one way switch. He didn't mention this in his report, but he had obviously recognized that the two way switch was the defect, and he did correct it. All of this got Ewell up off his chair, and when the one way switch was replaced with a two way switch the press double cycled just as we knew it should. And I got the videotape that I came for.

The manufacturer never made a settlement offer on that case until after we picked a jury and gave our opening statements. By that time I had constructed a couple of models of the press with limit switches connected to flashing lights, and I explained to the jury how the press worked, and why it double cycled. Sparks sat at the defense table on behalf of the manufacturer, and I later learned from the defense lawyer that in the middle of my opening statement he leaned over to his lawyer and said, "They understand it." At that point he knew the game was over, and after I finished the opening statement we had a brief recess, and the case was settled. But they didn't pay a dime so long as they thought there was a chance that the defect could be concealed.

A few years later another press case played out very differently. Ron Adkins lost most of his hand at a tool and die shop in Kalamazoo when his press also double cycled. Once again I turned to Bob Ewell to determine the cause, and once again he found a design defect by examining the blueprints. According to his analysis the press would have double cycled in certain configurations on the day it left the manufacturer. The manufacturer of course denied it, but unlike the manufacturer in Cindy's case, this manufacturer honestly believed that there was nothing wrong with the press, and that Ron's employer must have altered it in some way.

After filing suit I scheduled the depositions of the manufacturer's engineers and executives. The company had several locations around the country, and for reasons I no longer remember we settled on Springfield, Illinois as a central location for the depositions. I flew in from Kalamazoo, the defense lawyer flew in from Grand Rapids, and at least some of the company's employees flew in from Buffalo. I was prepared for a long day.

The first witness was the company's chief engineer, and after a few preliminaries I got straight to the point. I asked him if he understood how we claimed the injury happened, and he said he did. Then I asked if he understood that we claimed the press would double cycle on the day it left the assembly line, and he said he did understand, but had been convinced that we were wrong. Finally I asked him, if he was so sure we were wrong, had he taken a new press off the line, and configured it the way Ron's press was set up at the time of his injury to see if it would double cycle? He said they had. "Well, what did it do?"

"It double cycled."

"Were you shocked by that?"

"I certainly was."

"Well, what are you going to do about it?"

He said that the company had already redesigned the press, and that they were sending out warnings to all of the current owners, telling them how to correct the defect. It's the way companies should react, but so often don't. The case was pretty much over at that point. I finished quickly with him, and took cursory depositions of the other employees, but once the chief engineer admitted that he had confirmed the defect there wasn't much left for me to do. I would like to think that there are people out there today who have all of their fingers because of this case, but not one of them has any idea that I exist, or that the press they're working on was ever modified. The "tort reform" movement that is so strong today, especially in Michigan, thinks only of company profits, and ignores the tremendous good that private lawsuits have accomplished. Lawsuits are an inefficient method of compensating victims, but they are an extraordinarily effective way to correct corporate misconduct and improve public safety. The irony is that many of the people who are alive and healthy today because of product liability lawsuits would probably be the first to condemn them if they ever sat on a jury.

Having finished the depositions in half the time expected we all had the rest of the day off to spend in Springfield before our flights left that evening. I was the only one with a rental car, so I loaded up the defense attorney and the company witnesses in my car, and set off sightseeing. We toured Abraham Lincoln's office, and his home, and then drove out to see his memorial at the cemetery where he is buried. That still gave us time for a quick dinner before the trip to the airport, and we all left as friends. In a perfect world all cases would end as this one did.

Chapter Sixteen

I learned early on that many defendants and many defense experts will lie to defeat legitimate claims. Defendant doctors and corporations lie to avoid financial responsibility, and defendant experts lie for money. There is a cottage industry for experts in all fields who are willing to say whatever a lawyer wants them to say, at least if the lawyer is willing to pay. The same can no doubt be said of plaintiffs' experts, but I didn't defend cases, so I didn't see that first hand. Lying defendants and lying defense experts were an everyday experience, although occasionally a defendant would throw me a curve by telling the truth when he could easily have gotten away with a lie. There is hope for human nature.

My first experience with the ugly underbelly of litigation was a product liability case against General Motors. Bobby Hawkins bought a new General Motors pickup truck in the late seventies. It was a big truck with two gas tanks, one on either side of the truck bed. From the first day he had trouble with the gas supply operating intermittently. He took it back to the dealer, and thought they had it fixed, but on the third day that he owned it he was driving home late at night when the engine suddenly quit once again. So Bobby pulled over to the side of the road, took out his flashlight, and crawled under the truck to see if he could determine the problem. Just as he stuck his head under the truck it caught fire, resulting in significant burns to his face and hands.

I filed suit against both General Motors and the local dealer, claiming that they sold Bobby a defective truck. General Motors then sent out one of their engineers to inspect the truck to see if he could figure out what had happened. Once that was completed we started taking depositions. Bobby went first, and described what happened that night. He knew there was a problem with the fuel system, and was hoping he might be able to see something when he looked under the truck. But he said the fire started as soon as he got under the truck, and before he could see anything amiss.

The next deposition was the General Motors' engineer. I scheduled the deposition at the office of G.M.'s attorney, Grant Gruel, in Grand Rapids. Grant was a very experienced attorney who represented G.M. throughout western Michigan. I was inexperienced and clearly overmatched compared to someone with Grant's reputation. I had not yet tried a case, and had never faced a defense lawyer like Grant, or a defendant with the financial resources of General Motors. I was prepared for a brawl, but I also knew that trucks aren't designed to catch fire. I didn't know if I would win, but I was pretty sure that I should win.

Before we got started with the engineer's deposition Grant asked to speak to me privately in his office. He closed the door, and said, "Jim, before you take this deposition I think you should see some photographs that our engineer took when he inspected the truck." They clearly showed that the gas line to the tank had been disconnected. Grant told me that the photographs proved that Bobby had tried to fix the problem himself. He had obviously climbed under the truck and disconnected the gas line, thereby causing the leak that burned him. The accident was his fault, and once that information came out the case would be over.

But all was not lost. Grant also had an offer for me. If I would just dismiss General Motors without taking their engineer's deposition Grant promised that he would not tell the dealer's attorney what the engineer had found. Then I could still proceed with the case against the dealer, but I had to make my decision on the spot. Once the deposition began the offer would be revoked, and Bobby would not be able to recover against either defendant.

The photographs and the offer set me back on my heels. There was no question that the gas line had been disconnected, and it didn't happen by accident. Bobby was under the truck, and there was no one else who could have disconnected it. I could see my case going down the drain, but the offer wasn't very attractive either. If Bobby caused his own injury he didn't deserve compensation from anyone, and in any event I didn't trust Grant to keep his promise. Once G.M. was dismissed they would find some way to alert their dealer. I was inexperienced, but I was reasonably sure that information like this would come out sooner or later. So I told Grant thanks but no thanks. We would take the deposition as scheduled and live with the consequences.

The deposition proceeded as advertised. The engineer told us how he went to the junkyard to examine the truck. He had to get a tow truck to turn it over, but as soon as he looked at the underside of the truck he could see that the gas line had been disconnected. So he took his photographs of the smoking gun, and drove back to Detroit, convinced that he had an air tight defense for his employer. There was no way to shake his story, and I didn't even try. It was a long drive back to Kalamazoo as I thought about how to confront my client with this damning evidence.

I expected a confession when I showed Bobby the photographs, but he didn't blink. He assured me that the truth was as he had told me on the first day. He hadn't touched a thing before the fire started. He was so convincing that I was tempted to believe him despite the photographs. On the other hand, someone had deliberately disconnected the gas line, and there were no other suspects. It had to be Bobby.

My next call was to Adolph Wolf. Adolph was a fire expert who made his living by investigating and testifying in fire cases. If you wanted to know what caused a fire, or where it started, Adolph was your man. Fortunately I had contacted Adolph after my first meeting with Bobby, and asked him to go take a look at the truck. G.M. didn't know it, but Adolph had been out to the junkyard before the G.M. engineer got there. Adolph also had the truck turned over, and took his own pictures. Those photographs, Adolph assured me, told a very different story. When Adolph inspected the truck all of the gas lines were still firmly attached. When I got copies of his photographs there was no doubt about it.

Now it was my turn to invite Grant into my office. "Grant, before this case goes to trial I think you should see some photographs of the underside of that truck that my expert took before your engineer got to it." With one glance Grant knew the game was over. The only person who could have disconnected the gas line was the G.M. engineer himself, and if Adolph had not beaten him out to the junkyard the fraud would have worked. Grant studied the photographs for a few minutes, and then asked, "How much do you want?" We settled the case several days later for about twice what I thought it was worth. And then I began to understand how cases were defended in the real world. Personal injury suits are for real money, and they will try to beat you any way they can.

Chapter Seventeen

Our family grew rapidly. John was born in 1979 and Mary followed in 1981. Hattie was teaching, I was struggling to build a law practice, and we had our hands full with three children under the age of four. My office was on the eighth floor of what was then the Industrial State Bank Building, overlooking Bronson Park. Bronson Park is the geographical and cultural center of Kalamazoo. It is surrounded by churches and governmental buildings, and is the site for frequent concerts, art fairs, and political gatherings. Abraham Lincoln stood there to give a speech during his only visit to Kalamazoo in 1856. The park was filled with flowers and majestic shade trees surrounding a fountain in the center, an oasis of calm in the heart of a busy city.

May 13, 1980, was a beautiful spring day as I stood in my window looking down on the park, thinking how lucky I was to have that view. While most offices in town looked out on concrete I viewed a remnant of nature in full bloom, and I wondered how many of the old trees had been there when Lincoln gave his speech, and the stories some of them could tell. It really was a civic and historical treasure.

By mid afternoon the skies darkened, and a typical Midwestern spring storm seemed to be brewing. I occasionally glanced out my window, but saw nothing out of the ordinary, and I had cases to work on. Then we heard warning sirens, but that also wasn't unusual. I had heard them before when storms were approaching, and didn't take them seriously. Besides, wind and rain and lightening are no threat when you are inside a modern building.

A little after four o'clock I briefly stopped what I was doing to look at the approaching storm, and when I looked over the park to the hills off to the west I saw the unmistakable silhouette of a tornado headed directly at us. I had no idea how quickly a tornado moved, but I knew I did not want to be up on the eighth floor if it hit our building, so I yelled to the other people in the office that a tornado was coming, and then led the way to the basement. Someone had to lead. In other words, I took off running down nine flights of stairs.

The tornado took longer to arrive than I had expected, but when it did get there it was obvious that we had been hit. I could hear the rumble, and as it passed directly overhead my ears popped from the drop in air pressure. A few minutes later we headed back upstairs to inspect the damage, and found little left of our offices. All of the windows had blown in, along with branches and other debris. Most of the ceiling tiles were down, and I had a large potted plant hanging in my window that had blown through the opposite wall, leaving a hole the size of a basketball.

Looking out at Bronson Park I could see that many of those century old trees that I had admired just a couple of hours earlier were now destroyed. One of the largest, a big oak on the corner, lay on top of a motorcyclist who was dead. People were beginning to venture out, but most were in a daze. To make it all seem even more unreal, there was no sign of the storm that had caused all of this destruction. The sky was blue and sunny, and there wasn't so much as a breeze. There was no calm before this storm, but there was an eerie calm after.

It was months before we were able to move back into our office, but we were luckier than some. On the west side of the building all of our windows blew in. It was a shambles, but all of our papers and files were still there. They were mixed in a pile of debris, but little by little we could retrieve them and put them back where they belonged. Offices on the east side of the building were less fortunate. On that side of the building the windows were sucked out, taking all of the office contents along with them. Some of those papers were later found miles away. Most were never seen again. Lawyers who may have spent years putting a case together had nothing to show for it.

My car was parked on the north side of the building. I found it with the windows blown out, and a large slice through the hood, but there was no way to drive it home. With trees and wires down I knew it would be there for a few days, so I simply abandoned it and walked the two miles to get home. It was actually a very pleasant walk in the nicest weather we had seen all year.

The next day I returned to examine my car more closely. I pulled leaves and branches out of the front seat, and under the dash I discovered papers that had been sucked out of a law office on the east side of our building. One of them was a letter to the lawyer from a client trying to collect on a promissory note. He had clearly grown frustrated with his debtor's refusal to pay, and was ready to do something about it. After describing his increasing aggravation he wrote to the lawyer, "I have finally had enough, and I want you to file suit immediately. Enclosed is the promissory note." The letter was under my dash, but I suspect the promissory note was somewhere between Kalamazoo and Detroit. I hope he kept a copy.

Hattie and I had worked constantly to fix up our modest house. It took me two years to finish painting the outside, so we could live in a yellow house instead of the pink house that we bought. There is no accounting for taste. The inside was a constant renovation project of painting, papering, sanding floors, new carpets, new kitchen appliances, etc. Gradually it was turning into our house, but it was small, and with a one car garage. In Michigan it is more than a luxury to have your car covered in the winter. We liked our house, but it wasn't our dream house either. That house was just down the street.

In 1981 the Osborn house went on the market. It was an old colonial with a three car garage and two landscaped acres in the middle of the city. It sat on the highest hill in Kalamazoo, looking over the lights of the city, but in the summer when the leaves were out you couldn't even tell that you were in a city. That was our dream house, and now it was available.

We made an offer, and after some negotiating the house was ours. Then we had to sell the one we were living in. As is often the case our renovations picked up speed when we thought about selling, hoping that a little paint here and some paper there could result in a higher selling price. The old decorating was good enough for us, but it might not be good enough to entice a buyer.

Our first project was Mary's bedroom. This room must have had half a dozen layers of wallpaper on it, and it was cracked and ugly. So I rented a steamer, and went to work. Like most of my other jobs it took me three times as long as I anticipated. Removing that wallpaper was like removing cement. I would steam and scrape, and then steam and scrape, and then steam and scrape some more. It took me almost a week of working constantly during every spare minute to finally get down to bare plaster.

Then I called my paper hanger. Dad had been papering houses for years. He hated the job, but he was good at it, and I had no idea what I was doing. So like usual Dad came over to help. We started early Saturday morning, and worked through the afternoon, putting up a light yellow paper with small flowers. It brightened the room, and had to help with potential buyers. After we finished we put away the ladders and the buckets and all of the equipment, and went downstairs for dinner before Dad and Mom returned to their home on Lake Michigan. We at least owed them a meal for their labor.

After dinner we saw them off, and I was feeling good about my day. Practicing law often doesn't show results for years, and you never know if it will all come to naught, but when you paint or paper a house the progress is instantaneous and obvious. You can see what you've accomplished, and I knew this was a day well spent. Feeling content, I went back upstairs to admire my work, and discovered that two small boys, ages four and two, had also been busy while I was saying goodbye to Mom and Dad. My brand new light yellow wallpaper was now decorated with crayon drawings and scribbling in several bright colors. I apparently wasn't the only one who was proud of my work that day. The artists were allowed to live when I discovered that the artwork could be removed.

When we had our house ready to sell we contacted a realtor, and waited for the offers to start pouring in. There was some activity, but not as much as we had hoped, so we took the next step of scheduling an open house on a Sunday afternoon in October. With three little kids creating messes quicker than we could clean them up, we were a blur of activity that morning trying to get everything as spotless as possible. Mary wasn't walking yet, so we put her in a walker while we were busy cleaning. The walker had wheels, and allowed her to motor around the house before she was strong enough to stand on her own.

An hour before the open house was set to start we were finishing up the last details when I suddenly heard a frightening crash, and knew immediately what had happened. In our haste and confusion we had left the basement door open, and Mary had gone down the wooden stairs strapped in her walker. When I got to her she was unconscious. Probably the worst thing to do in that situation would be to move her, but I wasn't thinking rationally. I picked her up and ran to the car to take her to the hospital, leaving Hattie to watch the boys. Of course Hattie was as distraught as I was, and as I climbed into the car in the driveway Hattie stood in the front doorway shouting, "Don't leave me." At the time there were a couple of people walking by on the sidewalk, and I can only imagine what they thought they were witnessing.

By the time I got to the hospital Mary was starting to come around, but not completely, and it was with a sense of both panic and relief that I turned her over to the emergency room. After making sure she was stabilized they took her in for x-rays, and then brought her back to her room to await the results. A few minutes later the x-ray technician came into the room and knelt at the head of her bed so he could hold her head perfectly still. You didn't have to be a doctor to know that this was a bad sign, and after some prodding I got him to admit that his first look at the x-rays showed a probable broken neck. It was as low a feeling as I have ever had. I was devastated at the possible consequences for Mary, and overcome with guilt for leaving the basement door open. When one of the nurses asked me how she was injured I told her, "Her father was an idiot." I thought that pretty well summed it up.

Fortunately the initial impression of the x-ray technician proved to be incorrect. When a radiologist looked at the films he concluded that her neck was not broken, although she did have a skull fracture that required a couple of days in the hospital. I have no memory of what happened with the open house. I have no memory of when or how Hattie got to the hospital. I have no memory of what we did with the boys. But I will never forget the image of that emergency room tech holding Mary's neck.

Chapter Eighteen

My first big case was a tragic house explosion. Mr. and Mrs. Gleason were home canning tomatoes one summer afternoon while employees of the City of Portage were installing a new water line from the street to their basement. The procedure was fairly simple. First they dug a hole in the front yard where they would connect to the water main. Then they went into the basement to knock out a cement block where the new line would come into the house. All that was left was to run a line from the basement to the water main.

At one time the only way to run a waterline from a house to the road was to dig a trench. But modern technology has made the job easier and quicker, and now a tunnel can be dug rapidly with a pneumatic tunneling device called a Pneumagopher. All they had to do was aim it through the removed cement block in the basement, and in a few minutes it would show up at the hole they had dug out by the street, saving both time and the yard.

As with other forms of technology, sometimes the gopher worked better in theory than it did in practice. One problem was that there was no way to control it after they turned it loose. They just had to aim it as best they could, and then hope that it hit its target, but sometimes it could hit a root or a rock that would cause it to veer off course. Usually it worked well, but not always. If it veered off track it could be pulled back and fired again, but the danger was that it could strike electrical wires or gas lines. That's why state law required the city employees to hand dig to expose any of those underground pipes. This could eliminate the danger, but it also required someone to hand dig, and it was easier and quicker just to aim it and hope.

As luck would have it there was a gas line that crossed the Gleason's front yard above the intended path of the Pneumagopher, so to make sure that the Pneumagopher went under the gas main the employees lined up the gopher with a level. If they started it below the gas main, and lined it up to travel a level path, it should miss the gas main by a foot or two. Having faith in their ability to line up the Pneumagopher, the City of Portage employees decided not to hand dig around the gas main as the law required, but as he used his level to aim from the Gleason's basement the employee dropped the level down through the cement blocks. Without a level he could only aim the Pneumagopher by sight, but this was enough for the onsite supervisor who instructed the operator to, "Let it go."

Moments later the two employees in the basement were met with a blast of natural gas blowing through the tunnel that the Pneumagopher had created. Realizing that they had hit the gas main they raced to their truck to call the fire department. As the Gleasons worked in their kitchen they saw the two employees bolt up the basement stairs, through the kitchen, and out the back door without saying a word. When they looked out their front window they saw the employees climb into the City truck parked out by the street. Clearly something was wrong.

Alarmed by the behavior of the City employees Mr. and Mrs. Gleason walked out to the truck to ask what had happened. When they approached the truck one of the employees rolled down his window and said to Mr. Gleason, "We hit a gas main. You need to go back in and turn off all the pilot lights." Doing as he was told, Mr. Gleason walked back into the kitchen just as the house exploded. He lived for several days before the severe burns finally took his life.

The case dragged on for a couple of years before the city finally agreed to a settlement. The details of the accident weren't at all obvious when the case started. They had to be dragged out of witnesses a piece at a time. Only after months of depositions did the picture begin to come into focus. The case also demonstrated what every lawyer is taught in law school: "stop while you're ahead."

In addition to proving liability I also had to prove the pain that Mr. Gleason went through before he died. My main witness was the burn physician who cared for him, but physician witnesses are often a challenge. They tend to hate lawsuits and lawyers, and drawing testimony out of them can be tedious. Dr. Newman was no exception. He went through the history of the injury in dry detail, but getting him to humanize it was like pulling teeth. The more I worked at it the more clinical he became. I established that Mr. Gleason died of his burns, but not much more. There was nothing in his testimony to trigger the emotions of the jury, and any lawyer knows that juries decide most issues with their emotions, and not their heads.

Finally I gave up. If the jury was ever going to understand what Mr. Gleason had gone through, it would have to come from his own family. But before we went home the defense lawyers also had a chance to ask questions. First up was John LaParl, a sly old defense lawyer who represented the city. Mr. LaParl had no questions. He knew when he was winning.

Next up was Bill Kramer who represented the Pneumagopher manufacturer. Mr. Kramer, God bless him, did have some questions. I had established that burn patients go through daily debridement in a Hubbard tank to remove dead skin, but when Dr. Newman described it to me it was a dry clinical description, the kind of thing you might hear in a medical school lecture. Mr. Kramer, not satisfied with that, wanted to get the doctor to say that it wasn't really all that painful. After all, the patients are given pain medication before the treatment begins. So he challenged the doctor head on, "Dr. Newman, isn't it true that patients are given medication to minimize the pain before they go in the Hubbard tank?"

At that question my laconic doctor came alive. He might not be fond of trial lawyers, but he didn't much care for defense lawyers either, especially one who was trying to put words in his mouth. "Well, I'll tell you what I'll do," said Dr. Newman. "You come up to the burn unit some afternoon while we're debriding a patient, and stand outside the door and listen to him scream, and then you tell me if you think it hurts."

With that John LaParl stood up, slammed his briefcase closed, and walked out of the room. He clearly wanted to punch his co-counsel before he left, but managed to restrain himself. With one extra question Mr. Kramer created the vivid visual image that I hadn't come close to establishing in an hour of questioning. "Stop while you're ahead." Maybe the people who write law books do know what they're talking about.

There are times, however, when it pays to go against the conventional wisdom. The first case I ever tried was against Bill Dark, a crafty defense lawyer twenty years my senior. I represented a young boy who suffered a broken leg when a dumpster fell on him, and Bill beat me mercilessly. A few years later he beat me again in a case involving a fatal automobile accident. I was beginning to think I'd never win.

I never did break even with Bill, but I did win one case against him. It involved an athletic young black man, six foot two inches tall and one hundred eighty pounds, who claimed he was assaulted by the vice president of an international corporation headquartered in Kalamazoo. The vice president was fifty years old, and stood only about five foot eight, but my client said that the defendant had kicked him in the back and knocked him down a flight of stairs. He injured his elbow in the fall, and required surgery.

By the time I got the case the defendant had already won the criminal case that was brought against him. It isn't an easy task to convince an all white jury that a small middle aged corporate executive assaulted a young black man twice his size. The criminal jury didn't believe it, but I liked my client, and I did believe him. The trick was getting the jury to believe him, and the job didn't get any easier when the defendant's insurance company hired Bill Dark to defend him.

I thought that my only chance would be if I could convince the jury that the vice president had a temper. The incident had occurred on a Sunday afternoon at an apartment building that the vice president owned. One of the apartments in that complex was rented to a young black woman who was a friend of my client, and the problems started when she had a fight with her boyfriend, and he responded by damaging the apartment. She then called my client to come over and help her move out. As luck would have it, my client arrived just before the vice president, who had been called about the disturbance. Up until then he had been sitting home drinking beer, and watching a football game. When he arrived he put two and two together, and came up with six. Thinking that my client was the one who had damaged the apartment he couldn't resist the temptation to kick him in the back when he had the chance. But I still had to get the jury to believe that the vice president's temper was that volatile.

The conventional wisdom says that a plaintiff's lawyer should always have his own witnesses testify first. The theory is based on the belief that the plaintiff should get in as much good testimony as he can before the defendant has a chance to say anything. But I have never liked that strategy. I prefer to let the defendant take his best shot right out of the gate, and then I hope that my witnesses can chip away at that testimony. Juries are always justifiably skeptical of what they hear from the witness stand, so I would rather have them wondering what the defendant is lying about before they start wondering what my client is lying about. It's sort of a first liar loses theory. Like most theories, sometimes it works and sometimes it doesn't.

This time it worked. The first witness I called to the stand was the vice president himself. He had just returned from a long international trip, and he was tired. Bill Dark also hadn't had time to prepare him, expecting that he would have a day or two to do that before I rested my case. Calling him as my first witness caught them both by surprise. After a few preliminaries I started to focus on the incident. I first established that he owned the apartment, and that he had been called that afternoon by someone who warned him that his apartment was being damaged. He then jumped in his car, and arrived just in time to see my client and the tenant packing up to leave. The apartment, according to the vice president, was pretty well destroyed.

"Did it make you angry when you saw the damage to your apartment?" I asked.

There was a long pause as he clenched his teeth, and looked from side to side. "What kind of a question is that?"

"It's a straight forward question," I responded. "Were you angry when you saw the damage to your apartment?"

Again there was a long pause. Then he looked at Bill and said, "Do I have to answer that?" The decision wasn't up to Bill of course. It was up to the judge, but Bill knew what the decision would be, so he told his client that he did have to answer the question. This time the pause was even longer. His face started to turn red, and he glared at me before finally blurting out, "F--K YEA." After that demonstration the jury didn't have much trouble concluding that this was a man who was capable of losing his temper.

After the trial Bill stopped me in the hallway to ask what had inspired me to call his client as my first witness. I had no idea that the defendant had just returned from an international trip, or that Bill hadn't had a chance to go over his testimony, so I told him that it just seemed to me to be a good way to start. Bill nodded silently, and then turned and slowly walked away. Over his shoulder he said, "Good move."

Chapter Nineteen

*W*hen Mr. Edwards called me he was adamant that he had to talk to me immediately. It was too sensitive to discuss on the phone, but he assured me that he had a case of substantial value, and he wanted to get it started as soon as possible, so I agreed to meet with him the next afternoon. When he walked into my office I saw a middle aged man of obviously limited means. He was neatly but modestly dressed, and had the air of someone who had suffered a few hard knocks in his life. "What can I do for you, Mr. Edwards?" I asked. He said that he wanted to sue the Battle Creek Enquirer, a local newspaper. Usually a comment like that would mean he wanted to sue for libel, but not this time. Slowly he started telling me his story. Some months ago, he explained, he had grown lonely, and was looking for companionship. So he turned to the personal ads in the paper, and one in particular caught his eye. It was a forty-two year old single lady of high moral standing who sought male companionship for dancing and long walks on lazy summer evenings.

This was exactly what he was looking for also, so he called her, and they hit it off immediately. One thing led to another, and soon they were living together. Life was good. Then one day their tranquility was shattered by the sudden appearance of a former boyfriend, hers not his. Mr. Edwards and the boyfriend didn't get along nearly as well with each other as they did with their common girlfriend, and soon a fight ensued. It was a fight that Mr. Edwards was losing badly until he grabbed a butcher knife. After that things went downhill rapidly for the former boyfriend. He survived, but just barely, and Mr. Edwards was charged with attempted murder. His trial was scheduled to start in two weeks.

"I don't handle criminal cases," I told him. "You need to hire a criminal defense lawyer. Besides, what does this have to do with the Battle Creek Enquirer?"

"It's their fault that I'm in this mess," he responded. "I called this woman because her ad said she was forty-two. Now I find out that she's really forty-seven. I would never date anyone that old. If the paper hadn't printed her false ad I would never have met her, and if I hadn't met her I would never have stabbed her boyfriend with a butcher knife. Plus," he added, "I don't have time to be in court in two weeks. I have an important meeting with the President at that time, and have to leave immediately." With that he pulled out a bus ticket from Kalamazoo to Washington D.C. to prove his story. As gently as possible I told Mr. Edwardse that I regrettably wasn't taking any newspaper cases that week. Then I escorted him to the door. But before he left I gave him the names of a couple of lawyers I wasn't all that fond of, and suggested that he give them a call. If anyone could help him I was sure they could.

Over a thirty year career I talked to many Mr. Edwards. The world is full of them, and most of them have my phone number. Usually I remain composed when I talk to them, but many times I've had to put the phone down until my laughter subsided. I have heard stories that no one could make up. I have also discovered that the mentally ill have a speech pattern that is almost instantly identifiable. It is like Justice Potter Stewart's description of pornography; I can't define it or describe it, but I know it when I hear it. With rare exception I can tell within seconds if I am talking to someone who is under psychiatric care. There is something in their cadence or in the inflection in their voice that is a dead giveaway. I don't know what criteria psychiatrists use now to diagnose mental illness, but when it is perfected the voice alone will be all they need.

My father used to say that being a high school principal would have been a good job if he just didn't have to deal with teachers and students. And sometimes being a lawyer could be a good job if we just didn't have to deal with judges and clients. No matter how careful I tried to be in accepting clients, there were a few that slipped through the net, and more than once I have wished that I had never met either my client or his case. Sometimes it was my fault, but on occasion I have had clients tell me one thing, only to learn later that the truth was quite different. Over the years I think I have become better at picking up on stories that don't quite ring true, but not always. All lawyers have had clients tell us they can't get out of bed, only to see them later on secret surveillance videos raking their yard or painting their house.

On at least one occasion my own client did the surveillance work for the defense. They didn't have to hire an investigator to follow him. He had suffered a broken leg in an automobile accident, and he was still crippled when we got to trial two years later. He used crutches every time he came into my office, and complained about how the injury had changed his life. Most of the activities he once enjoyed were now impossible. It was a good case.

Then two days before trial I sat down with the Sunday paper, and on the front page of the local section there was a story about a folk dancing club that had just held its annual celebration. Along with the article was a picture of several local cloggers in full stride out on the dance floor being led by none other than my crippled client. My two years of work went right down the drain, but justice was probably served.

On other occasions I have won cases without ever being sure who was telling the truth. One of my more tragic clients was Keith Butler, a young quadriplegic who had been shot in the throat by a close friend while they were playing with a gun. They were both drunk at the time, and they were both teenagers. By the time I got involved the shooter had already been sentenced to a couple of years in state prison for negligent discharge of a firearm. He wasn't worth suing, because he had no money, but Keith told me that his teenage friend had purchased the alcohol that evening at a local grocery store, which was obviously illegal. The store of course had both money and an insurance policy. If the story was true the case had substantial value.

The shooter testified twice from prison that he purchased the liquor that evening from the store, just as Keith said. There were no other witnesses, so the store was pretty much stuck with his testimony. He was in prison, which usually doesn't do much for a witness's credibility, but it's hard to attack someone's credibility when you have no other story, and in this case the store didn't have another story. I felt fairly confident as the trial date approached.

Then just a couple of weeks before trial the roof caved in. Keith called me one day to tell me that the shooter was threatening to recant his story at trial unless he got a share of whatever money Keith received. I still didn't know what actually happened that night, but I did know that my case was in serious trouble, and it was time for another trip to the prison for a face to face talk with my star witness.

It is always a little eerie to visit someone in prison. Hearing the doors slam shut behind you is unsettling even when you know that it's only temporary. I haven't been there often, but when I have visited a client or a witness we usually end up in a small conference room. But this witness wasn't my client, so we didn't rate that same degree of privacy. Instead, we were taken to a small classroom where we could talk while being watched by one of the guards. I took the witness to one of the desks in the back, and asked him to tell me what was going on.

He claimed that he and Keith had concocted the grocery store story just to start a lawsuit. The scheme, he said, was for them to share the proceeds, and now Keith was backing out. Unless he got his share of the money he planned to tell the court that he had lied in his deposition testimony, and that it was really his uncle who bought the liquor. Whether the new story was true or not was anybody's guess, but it didn't matter. Once a jury heard his new testimony the case would be over.

A few days later the insurance company offered over five hundred thousand dollars to settle the claim. It wasn't a lot of money for a quadriplegic, but it looked very good compared to the disaster that I foresaw if we went to trial. My only question was whether I had any ethical obligation to reveal that the key witness was planning to change his testimony, and after looking at it carefully I decided that I didn't. After all, I still didn't know who was telling the truth, but I did know that the witness had testified twice under oath, and I had as much reason to believe him then as I had to believe him now. So the case was settled, but I still don't know if justice was done.

In addition to a cash settlement Keith agreed to accept the majority of his settlement as a "structured settlement" that would pay him roughly forty thousand dollars a year tax free for the rest of his life. It wasn't a huge amount, but it was enough to provide him with a lifetime of protection. He would always have a place to live and enough to eat. I have seen so many clients lose their settlements that I always try to steer them into a structured settlement if I can. And I knew that if Keith received half a million dollars in cash that it would disappear overnight. With a structured settlement he could never go hungry for long, because a new check would arrive every month. He was the perfect candidate for a structure, and I felt pretty good about the security that I was able to give him.

It worked well for a few years, and then one day out of the blue he called me to ask me to help him sell a year of his structure for cash. He told me that he wanted to buy a house, and that he needed a down payment. I knew there were unscrupulous companies out there that would be delighted to give him seventy percent in cash for the right to receive the full structure themselves. They couldn't find a more lucrative investment. They pay him twenty-eight thousand now, and then collect the full forty thousand over the following year for almost a fifty percent profit.

The problem was how he was going to live for the next year if he sold a year of payments. He had no other income, and I could see only disaster in this plan, so I refused. A couple of weeks later I received another call from him saying that he had found a lawyer who was willing to help, but he needed a copy of his file because he had lost his settlement documents. The ethical rules were clear that I had to turn over his file when he requested it, but again I refused. He could have filed a grievance against me, but he didn't. His new lawyer was able to get copies from the original insurance company, and in short order his year's worth of settlement payments had been sold.

Two months later I heard from him again. His family and his friends had run off with his money, and he was destitute. Now he wanted me to help him sell off a second year of payments so he would have something to live on, but again I refused. He was just digging the hole deeper, and in another two months he would be two years behind, so I told him that somehow he had to figure out how to hold on for ten months until his monthly payments started up again. A short time later he committed suicide. I hope it wasn't my fault, but it's a burden I have to live with.

Most of my clients over the years have been a joy to work with. Almost all of them were coping with some tragedy in their life, but most were honest and appreciative of anything I could do to help them. Still, people are people, and if a lawyer isn't careful the attorney-client relationship can turn sour in a hurry, and once that happens it is nearly impossible to resurrect. But after thirty years I have discovered a few tricks of the trade to remain on good terms with the people I represent, and the first rule is brutal honesty. As a young lawyer I was insecure enough to think that I had to know everything, or at least that my clients had to believe that I knew everything, and that is a recipe for disaster. People are pretty good at recognizing when you're bluffing, and in the long run it just doesn't work. But they will be very understanding if you tell them that you don't know all the answers, but will do your best to find out. Based on my experience with medical malpractice suits the same rule applies to doctors. The doctor who says he doesn't know will never hurt you. The doctor who wants you to believe that he knows everything is an accident looking for a place to happen.

Rule number two is to never tell a new client what his case is worth. That of course is the first question most clients have, and if a lawyer is foolish enough to attempt an answer he will regret it ten times over. There is simply no way to know what a case is worth, especially in the early stages before all the facts have come out, but once the lawyer mentions a number it will be written in stone in the client's mind. So I always tell them that the value isn't for us to decide. Ultimately a case is worth what a jury of six strangers will give you for it, or what an insurance company is willing to pay so they won't find out what the jury will give.

And the problem with predicting what a jury will do is that we don't know who will sit on that jury. We might draw jurors friendly to injured people, or we might draw jurors who love insurance companies, and the lawyers have very little control over who ends up on that jury. We also don't know how any of the witnesses will perform once they get in the courtroom, or what rulings the judge may give during the trial. But even at the end of the trial, when we know who is on the jury, and after hearing all of the witnesses, it is still impossible to predict the outcome with any degree of reliability. Some years ago a local federal judge ordered a mock trial in an attempt to figure out what a case was worth without going through lengthy litigation. So he called in twelve jurors, and gave both lawyers a few hours to present their cases before sending the jury out to deliberate. Then to make it more interesting he split the jury into two six man panels. When they came back one panel awarded three and a half million dollars to the plaintiff. The other panel awarded zero. So I guess if the plaintiff's lawyer had been smart enough to see into the future during his first office visit with that client, he could have told him that his case was worth something between zero and three and a half million.

Of course lawyers do start to get a feel for the value of cases after handling enough of them, and sooner or later the plaintiff will look to us for guidance in making a demand. Most clients will go along with our recommendation, but there are always a few who have inflated expectations, and the worst thing a lawyer can do is to tell them that their demands are unrealistic. As soon as the lawyer says that he becomes the enemy, and the client will never listen to him again. So the first thing I do is agree with my client that if I were in his shoes I would want a million dollars for my broken leg too. And then I slowly start telling him about all the things that can go wrong, and the many juries in this area that have brought back shockingly low verdicts for injuries far worse than his. But of course if he wants to take that gamble I'll be right there with him. So now it's his decision, instead of me telling him to lower his demand, and given enough information clients almost inevitably make the right decision. As a last resort I offer my unrealistic client an option. Instead of going to trial to get that hundred thousand you think your case is worth, why not just accept the fifty thousand the insurance company has offered, and then go bet it on one spin of the roulette wheel in Las Vegas, because at least there you have almost a fifty-fifty chance of doubling your money, and that's probably much better odds than you'll get with a Kalamazoo jury. When they start to look at it like that they usually decide to take the fifty, and I haven't had one yet who tried to double it in Vegas.

Chapter Twenty

I spent five years with my first law firm, although by the end of five years only one of the original partners was left. Law firms can be a caldron of egos and personalities and financial jealousy, and over the years new people came in as some of the original partners left or were forced out. With each change the character of the firm changed, and the more it changed the less comfortable I felt. Then in 1983 it merged with another local firm, and was no longer recognizable.

When I first joined the firm, salaries were based on a somewhat crude expression that forms the basis for many law firms, "you eat what you kill." Each lawyer was paid according to the number of clients he brought in, and the fees that he collected. If you produced money for the firm you were paid accordingly. After the merger that changed. The senior partner of the new firm wanted a disproportionate amount of the income to go to him regardless of what he produced. To make the arrangement permanent he also wanted everyone to sign a partnership agreement with severe financial penalties if any lawyer left the firm. Everyone signed except me.

The issue came to a head at a Saturday morning firm meeting. I was willing to live with the compensation agreement, but not the penalty for leaving. The only protection I had was the freedom to walk away, and I wasn't willing to give that up. After a short discussion they told me that I either signed the new agreement, or I was out, and it wasn't a tough decision. If I left then I could at least do so with no penalties. I told them I was out.

I was out, but I didn't know where. I had enough clients and enough cases to keep going for a while, but I didn't know for how long. And I had no office. In a few days I had to either find an office or another law firm that would have me. My refuge was Mark Zarbock. Mark was a brilliant Harvard Law School graduate, twenty years older than I was, who had fallen on hard times. Years earlier he was one of the leading corporate attorneys in Kalamazoo until alcohol and a divorce wiped out everything he had accomplished. After extensive surgery to repair the damage that alcohol had done to his liver, and a year off to recuperate, he was making a comeback as a trial lawyer. He had an office, I needed a place to go, and the deal was made.

The day I moved out of my old office I received a letter demanding that I repay the firm twenty thousand dollars. They claimed that under our compensation agreement I had been overpaid for the work I had done that year, and the firm wanted to be reimbursed. When I challenged the calculations they sent a letter to all of my clients telling them that I owed the old firm money, and asking my clients to pressure me to pay what I owed. It demonstrated what every lawyer knows; the breakup of a law firm is like a divorce, and sometimes it can turn ugly in a hurry.

The argument continued for several months. During that time the firm sent me periodic letters claiming that my fair share of the company profits was twenty thousand less than I had received. I waited until the firm's fiscal year ended in July, and then requested a copy of their year end accounting. They could say anything in a letter, but they couldn't fudge the year end accounting, because they used that to determine their own compensation. I never did see the year end accounting, but a few days later I did receive another letter from the firm offering to just call everything even. And that's how we left it.

It was a scary time for me. I had three kids, a new house, and a very uncertain future. At such times we all look for comfort, and I found mine in an unlikely place, the letters of my Grandfather Robert. I never knew him of course. He died fifteen years before I was born. I did know about him from the stories my father and grandmother told, but it was superficial at best. Then in 1983, just shortly before the change in law firms, I received copies of the letters he had sent home over the last twenty years of his life. Those letters described in great detail his struggle to support his family during the Great Depression, and in a strange way they gave me hope. If my grandparents could survive the Depression certainly I could survive starting my own office. It's a blessing to have grandparents. Sometimes they can give you strength long after they are gone.

I had spent my first two years at Upjohn immersed in medical issues related to the drug cases, and read enough medical records and medical depositions to begin to feel comfortable with doctors and with the science of medicine. Like many other things, it isn't all that difficult once you understand the language. It isn't brain surgery, usually.

When I joined Mark I knew that I would have to establish a niche if I wanted to survive, and medical malpractice seemed like a logical choice. I found medicine interesting, I thought I had accumulated more medical knowledge than most lawyers, and I was willing to do it. Most lawyers aren't. It is simply too difficult and too expensive. No lawyer in his right mind would take on a malpractice case if he had enough automobile cases to keep himself busy, but I didn't have enough auto cases. If I could establish a reputation for handling malpractice cases competently I thought I might corner that market, and if I did it well enough I would have a steady source of income. I was confident that there was enough malpractice in Kalamazoo to keep several lawyers busy.

Shortly after joining Mark I received a call from a young woman telling me that her twenty-one year old sister, Carla, was near death at Borgess Hospital. The next day she came to see me, and related the events as she knew them. It all started a couple of years earlier when Carla went to see Dr. White, her family physician in South Haven. She was concerned about a mole on her thigh, and wanted it removed. Dr. White told her that the mole was benign, and nothing to worry about, but he did remove it as she requested. A few months later it was back, and the doctor removed it again. Six months later it was removed a third time. Now Carla was dying of metastatic melanoma that had spread to her brain. When I visited her in the hospital it was obvious that she was experiencing a horrific death.

After Carla died I filed suit alleging that Dr. White failed to send the mole to pathology, and that if the cancer had been diagnosed promptly Carla's chances of survival would have been almost ninety percent. Then we started down the long road that all malpractice cases take, conducting discovery, finding expert witnesses, and flying around the country to take expert depositions. I had to prove the standard of care for a family practitioner, and I had to have cancer experts describe how Carla could have been saved if the mole had been sent to pathology at the outset. It took two years to get the case to trial.

Most malpractice cases settled in those days, but this one didn't because any settlement would have come directly out of Dr. White's pocket. He had attended some seminars instructing doctors how to avoid malpractice suits by hiding all of their assets in joint accounts with their wives, and then canceling their malpractice coverage. Once the patient's attorney found out that the doctor was uncollectible, so the theory went, the case would be dropped. I was tempted to drop it, but I had seen Carla in the hospital, and I wasn't walking away from this one.

As the case progressed I learned about melanoma by talking to the expert witnesses, and by reading everything I could find in the medical literature. I became a frequent guest in the hospital's public library. One thing I discovered was that the diameter of the mole was critical for diagnosis. Any mole greater than six millimeters had to be regarded as suspicious for melanoma.

Dr. White also knew the warning signs for melanoma, and he testified in his deposition that Carla's mole was smaller than six millimeters. I didn't know if he was telling the truth, but it didn't make much difference, because, true or false, that was his testimony and I had no way to disprove it. Once the mole was removed it ended up in the good doctor's trash basket. There were other reasons for the doctor to be suspicious, but the small size of the mole would be difficult for me to overcome in front of a jury. I knew it was an uphill struggle.

One problem in any death case is that you don't have a client sitting beside you. For the jury, the decedent isn't a real person; she is just a name. The real person is the forlorn doctor at the defense table who is another victim of greedy trial lawyers filing frivolous law suits. If we were to have any chance I had to somehow humanize Carla for the jury. They had to get to know her to counteract their natural sympathy for the doctor.

One way to accomplish that was to show the jury photographs. If they could put a face with the name, and see how Carla interacted with her family, my hope was that they would care enough to at least pay attention to how she died. So a couple of weeks before trial I drove over to her parents' house to look through their photo albums. I didn't need many pictures, but I hoped for three or four to demonstrate who Carla was, and what she meant to her family. And then I hit the jackpot. In law, as in many other endeavors, it is better to be lucky than good.

Carla lived near Lake Michigan. She liked to fish, and one photograph in the album was taken just a couple of months before she had the mole removed for the first time. It showed her holding a large fish that she had caught that afternoon. She was wearing shorts, and the mole on her thigh was clearly visible. Better yet, she was standing next to an eight inch cinderblock wall. When I enlarged the photograph I could measure the size of the mole by using the cinderblocks for comparison. It was unquestionably much larger than Dr. White had testified, and substantially larger than the six millimeter warning sign for melanoma.

When Dr. White was on the witness stand he again told the jury how small the mole was. This was the heart of his defense, and he was confident that his testimony would be the last word. Physicians have great credibility with juries, and if he said it was a small mole the jury would undoubtedly believe him. The defense also relied on two physician experts who said that the standard of care did not require every mole to be sent to pathology; it was a matter of professional judgment. Malpractice defense lawyers routinely argue that everything a doctor does is a matter of judgment, and that it is unfair to second guess him.

The first expert was Dr. Jensen, a family physician from Dr. White's home town. Dr. Jensen said this case was typical of what was wrong with trial lawyers and medical malpractice cases in general. In his mind it was a waste of money to send all moles to pathology. Doing so was an example of defensive medicine, spending money just to avoid being sued. The risk of melanoma was small, he said, and not worth the cost of pathology.

Then I asked Dr. Jensen if he sent every mole to pathology, and he said, "I didn't before, but I do now." He only made the change, he told me, because of this case. It was a waste of money, but he didn't want to end up in the defendant's chair like his colleague, Dr. White. But he did admit that the only way to catch all melanomas was to send them to pathology. You can't tell just by looking. If you don't send them to pathology a few patients will die because of delayed treatment, but so long as the death of his patient was the only consequence of guessing wrong Dr. Jensen was willing to take that chance. Sending the mole to pathology just wasn't worth the cost. But if the risk of guessing wrong meant that he might also get sued, then the cost of pathology became unimportant. He would send every mole to pathology to avoid that. For him, what constituted "defensive medicine" depended on who was at risk. Like some of his colleagues Dr. Jensen cared more about his own pocketbook than he cared about his patients' lives. When his money was at stake the cost of defensive medicine was no longer a waste of money.

The second defense witness was Dr. Grekin, a local dermatologist. Dr. Grekin also told the jury that it wasn't necessary to send all moles to pathology. Doctors have to use their judgment, he said, even though it is subject to human error. Doctors, like the rest of us, aren't perfect. It was a persuasive argument, one that I expected the jury would accept. Truth be told, I accepted it myself. But my argument wasn't that every mole had to go to pathology. My argument was that this mole had to go to pathology. Dr. White's lawyer had very carefully not asked him that question.

One cardinal rule of trial practice is to quit while you are ahead. Another is to never ask a question if you don't know what the answer will be. I thought about that when I stood up to cross examine Dr. Grekin. He hurt me with his testimony, but he would hurt me even worse if he told the jury that this mole didn't have to go to pathology. It was possible that his lawyer had set a trap, hoping I would ask that question myself, making the answer all the more damaging. On the other hand, if Dr. Grekin thought Dr. White complied with the standard of care for this mole he would probably have said so. It would take real courage for the defense lawyer to leave that question unasked, hoping that I would ask it for him. So I decided to take the chance.

I started slowly, reviewing Dr. Grekin's testimony that it wasn't ALWAYS necessary to send moles to pathology, not that it was NEVER necessary. Then we moved into the facts of this case. I asked the doctor to assume some facts hypothetically, all facts that I knew would come out as the case progressed. I told him to assume the mole had changed, that it was a large mole, and that it had grown back twice. "If all of these facts are true, then wouldn't you agree with me that Dr. White violated the standard of care by not sending the mole to pathology for a definitive diagnosis?" I held my breath waiting for the answer.

There was a long pause as Dr. Grekin thought about my question, and obviously the impact his answer would have on the colleague he was trying to defend. Most defense experts in malpractice cases will say whatever is necessary to defend the case. That is, after all, why they were chosen to be experts in the first place. Defense lawyers know who will cover for them and who won't. But Dr. Grekin was different. Dr. White didn't have malpractice insurance, so he didn't have the insurance company's usual stable of expert witnesses to go to. Dr. Grekin was just a practicing doctor, and he was honest. He wanted to help Dr. White, but there was a limit to how far he would go, and saying that Dr. White complied with the standard of care in this case was beyond that limit. His shoulders slumped as he responded almost in a whisper, "Yes, he violated the standard of care."

I introduced the photographs when Carla's parents were on the stand, but still didn't mention the mole on her thigh. I had the smoking gun in evidence, but I wanted to delay discussing it until final argument when I thought it would have maximum impact. I also expected that it would blindside the defense attorney when it was too late for him to respond. I have been in that position myself, and it is no fun to find yourself at the end of a trial with your pants down around your ankles.

When Dr. White was on the witness stand I gave him a chance to explain why he decided to gamble with Carla's life. He had to admit that he knew it might be melanoma, he knew he couldn't determine what it was without sending it to pathology, and he knew if he guessed wrong it would be a death sentence. "Then why, knowing all of that, did you tell her it was benign even though you knew it might be cancer?"

"Because I thought it was probably benign, it would cost thirty dollars to have it tested, and she didn't have any medical insurance to pay for it."

The jury didn't accept that as a good explanation, especially when they realized he had not told the truth about the size of the mole, and awarded the family five hundred thousand dollars, at that time the largest jury award ever returned in that rural community. But getting a judgment and collecting a judgment are two different things. Dr. White had been to the seminars, he had all of his investments in his wife's name, and he was still confident that he could exempt all of that from collection. To avoid garnishment of his income he filed for bankruptcy, and it appeared that the seminar advice might work after all.

One asset that was vulnerable was his IRA retirement account, containing a little over two hundred thousand dollars. The rules on such accounts are complex, but after a year of litigation in bankruptcy court he finally agreed to pay most of his IRA to settle the case. After trying the case twice, once in state court, and once in bankruptcy court, I thought we were finally done, but before I could distribute the settlement I received a lien from the IRS claiming a large portion of the settlement as punishment for invading Dr. White's IRA before he turned fifty-nine and a half. Another year of litigation ensued with the IRS before a federal judge finally split the baby, and gave the IRS about half of what it was seeking. After four years and three trials the family eventually received less than a third of what the jury awarded.

The response of the medical community was almost immediate. Within a couple of months the State Medical Society persuaded friendly state legislators to introduce a bill to make doctors' pension plans immune from collection. A physician could have millions of dollars in joint assets with his wife, and millions of dollars in a pension plan, and it all would be exempt from collection regardless of how negligent he was, or how much injury his negligence caused.

When the bill came up for a vote in the legislature I appeared on behalf of the Michigan Trial Lawyers' Association. We did not oppose the request for immunity for doctors' pension plans, but argued that a doctor should only get immunity if he carried at least two hundred thousand dollars in malpractice insurance. If I needed insurance to drive my car, it only seemed reasonable to require a surgeon to carry insurance to perform brain surgery. It might be reasonable, but it wasn't political.

When it was my turn to testify a staffer came to escort me to the hearing room, but before we entered he advised me to keep my remarks brief. "You will have a chance to testify," he said, "but you should know before we go in that the decision has already been made to make doctors' pension plans immune from collection, and they will not be required to carry insurance."

I was startled both by the decision, and by the fact that it had been made before the legislators even heard any testimony. I started arguing my case to the staffer, but he cut me short. "Look," he said, "I'll give it to you straight. This year the Michigan State Medical Society has donated five hundred and fifty thousand dollars to house members. The Trial Lawyers Association has donated only two hundred and fifty thousand. If you want to block bills like this you are going to have to donate as much money as they do. So you can come in and testify, but the decision has already been made." It was my first experience with how democracy works in the real world, but it was not my last.

Some years later the state's automobile insurers sponsored a ballot initiative to effectively eliminate recovery for injuries suffered in automobile accidents. The legislature wouldn't pass that bill, so the insurers hoped to do better with the public, holding out the promise that eliminating liability would reduce their insurance premiums. It is an attractive argument, because most people assume they will never be the person who gets hurt. But after a bruising campaign it was soundly defeated at the polls. The insurers then turned once again to the legislature. The same election that defeated the ballot proposal gave control of both houses to the Republicans, so the insurance companies correctly assumed that they could now get from the legislature what the people had defeated.

As the bill worked its way through the legislative process the Kalamazoo Trial Lawyers Association invited our Republican state senator to talk to us about the bill. He supported it, of course, so after his talk the lawyers began to ask pointed questions about how this bill would deprive the most vulnerable citizens of their right to seek justice in court. Finally the senator had had enough. "Look," he said, "I know this bill isn't reasonable. But you're talking about people's rights. I'm talking about money. The insurance companies give money to both Democrats and Republicans. The Trial Lawyers only donate to Democrats. If you want us to be reasonable you're going to have to start paying both sides just like the insurance companies do." I wasn't surprised to know he thought like that, but I was surprised to hear him say it publicly.

Chapter Twenty-One

Our new home was a hundred yards off the street, and surrounded by woods. You couldn't find a more tranquil setting in the middle of the city. To the west was a city park, and on the north and east the hillside fell off too steeply to build. We had the privacy of the country and the convenience of the city, but we were isolated.

A year after we moved in I received a call one morning from the Kalamazoo Police Department. The dispatcher asked me my name, and then told me that she regretted to inform me that my wife had been attacked. She didn't know the extent of Hattie's injuries, but she did say that the police were with her. I was home in five minutes, and found a driveway full of police cars. Hattie was physically uninjured, but badly shaken. She told me that around ten a.m. a young black man knocked on our front door asking for directions. She helped him as best she could, but as he started to leave he suddenly burst through the door and knocked her to the floor. When she asked him what he was doing, he responded, "I'm going to kill you."

Mary, who was three, was the only child at home, and Hattie yelled to her to call 911. Mary ran to the phone to do what she was told, but before she could make the call the intruder realized that Hattie wasn't alone, and left her to get the phone away from Mary. This energized Hattie, who then turned on her attacker to protect Mary. The assailant didn't realize that he had invaded the home of a girl who grew up tossing tobacco bales in South Georgia, and when the fight started in earnest he had his hands full. While they wrestled, Mary escaped out the back door, and ran to a neighbor's home to ask for help. Realizing that things weren't going according to plan the attacker then picked up a screw driver to wield as a weapon, and demanded money. For his efforts he got one dollar, all the money Hattie had in her purse. He then fled out the back door and across the city park.

By the time I got home tracking dogs were already on his scent, while officers took statements and dusted for prints, all of which turned up nothing. The dogs also lost his trail at a nearby grocery store. A couple of hours later the police left, and Hattie and I were alone. Then my initial shock started to turn to anger. I wanted to find that man, and I wanted to find him today.

When I first got home I stood amid a phalanx of police cars parked in my driveway, and between conversations with the officers I could hear the chatter over their police radios. After they left and the dust settled I recalled hearing the dispatcher mention a suspicious person who had been reported earlier that morning about half a mile south of our house. With nothing else to go on I set out to find the person who made that call.

I had heard the dispatcher say that the suspicious person was seen near the intersection of Cork and Rose, so I drove down to that intersection and started knocking on doors. While I was doing that a police car drove by, and then stopped. The office recognized me and wanted to know what I was doing. When I told him of the suspicious person report he insisted that I was mistaken. He said he was the officer in charge of the investigation, and if any such report had been made he would know about it. "That may be," I told him, "but there was a report because I heard it myself." To satisfy me he called in to dispatch to ask about it, and in a few minutes the dispatcher called back to say that there had been such a report, and that it came from the next house down the street.

The officer and I went to the home together, and in a few minutes we had a name. The young resident said he had gone to high school with a young black man named David Jones. He must have known Jones well, because when he saw Jones in his front yard that morning he called the police. What's more, the description fit. The only problem was that he hadn't actually seen Jones' face. He only saw Jones from the back as he was walking away, but he was confident that the identification was accurate.

The next day the police brought a bunch of mug shots for Hattie to identify. She couldn't. She knew what her assailant looked like, but she couldn't be sure from any of the mug shots. With that the police officers gave up. If she couldn't identify him from the mug shots there wasn't anything more they could do. The police are quite restricted in what they can do to investigate a crime, and any official act that taints an identification can result in the dismissal of the charges. But I wasn't the police, and I didn't have those restrictions. I was still convinced that David Jones was our man, and I wasn't about to give up.

I found out when he graduated from high school, and located a copy of that year's high school yearbook from one of his classmates. When I showed this to Hattie she recognized him immediately. Even more convincing was when I showed a group picture to our daughter, Mary, and she was able to pick him out of the crowd. Now I was convinced, but I still had to persuade the police to arrest him, and that wasn't easy. They understandably were worried about how the identification would hold up in court, but after a few hours with the lead detective and the assistant prosecutor they finally agreed to pick him up on a probation violation. He still denied the crime, but it didn't appear that our case was going to get any stronger, so after a few days the prosecutor agreed to charge him.

His arraignment was in front of District Court Judge Jim Coyle. When Judge Coyle heard the details of the crime he ordered Jones held on a fifty thousand dollar bond, which Jones couldn't pay, so for at least the next few weeks we knew where Jones would be. What Judge Coyle didn't remember was that he had seen Jones before. He didn't remember the meeting, but Jones did, and on his way back to the jail Jones ranted against his excessive bond, claiming that Judge Coyle was just out to get him.

On rare occasion justice is poetic, and this was one of those times. It wasn't Jones' first exposure to the criminal justice system. At the tender age of twenty-one he was already a three time offender, and as luck would have it one of those previous offenses was for burglarizing Judge Coyle's house. When Jones walked into the courtroom for his arraignment Judge Coyle didn't recognize Jones, but Jones recognized Judge Coyle, and understandably assumed that he might not fare well in front of that judge. It just wasn't his day.

Eventually Jones pled guilty, and was sentenced to twenty to thirty years in prison. He belonged there, but twenty years is a long time, and in Michigan inmates have to serve their minimum sentence before becoming eligible for parole. By the time he got out he had spent half his life behind bars. When he did finally become eligible for parole Hattie wrote a letter to the parole board asking that he be released. He committed the crime while seeking money for drugs, but he also hadn't hurt her when he certainly had the chance. He could have killed both Hattie and Mary when the robbery went bad, but he simply fled instead. After twenty years it was time to give him a chance.

A year after his release I was crossing the street to the courthouse one afternoon when I found a cell phone lying on the pavement. After court I brought it back to my office, and went through the phone numbers in it to try to locate the owner. One number, identified as "Mom," seemed a good place to start, so I called her. She answered the call, and told me that the phone belonged to her son, David. Her name was Mrs. Jones. She was taking a bus trip that afternoon, so I arranged to meet her at the bus station to return the phone. I never told her who I was.

Chapter Twenty-Two

Medical malpractice cases are the most difficult cases I have handled. By comparison, automobile cases are a walk in the park. There are a variety of reasons for this. Today in Michigan the Legislature and the Supreme Court have created an endless series of procedural hurdles to make it nearly impossible for injured patients to even get a case to trial. These technicalities are designed to make it appear in theory that justice still exists, while in practice shielding bad doctors from ever being held responsible. Money talks, and nowhere does it talk louder than in the court system. Wealthy special interests get favors at every step of the way, not just in their ability to afford multiple lawyers and expert witnesses, but also from the Legislature and the courts.

Justice in medical malpractice cases was an uphill struggle for any injured patient even before the law became corrupted. An automobile driver who causes an accident might convince himself that it wasn't his fault, but he won't be upset if his insurance company settles the claim. Usually he is just happy to have it all behind him. That is not the case with doctors. Doctors are among the brightest and most ambitious people we have. They are proud of their status, and accustomed to almost servile deference. A malpractice suit threatens their ego and their self respect even if it doesn't cost them a penny. It is usually no threat to their professional status, but they are still unwilling to admit to themselves, much less anyone else, that they could have made a mistake. As a result most of these cases are a fight to the death.

In this fight the doctor and his insurance company have most of the weapons, not the least of which is money. Litigation is expensive, and malpractice litigation is extremely expensive. There are experts to hire, travel and research costs, and court reporters' fees. The experts are all physicians, accustomed to physicians' fees, and usually charge three hundred to a thousand dollars per hour for their testimony, sometimes more. When multiple defendants are involved there are multiple experts, each one often costing five to ten thousand dollars for preparation even before you get to trial, and it is not unusual to have fifty thousand to one hundred thousand dollars in expenses before a case is over. If the patient's lawyer wins he gets his money back, but if he loses it is gone forever. For a small town lawyer the risk is enormous. And statistically the doctor will win these cases at least ninety percent of the time. To survive, a trial lawyer has to be both extraordinarily cautious about the cases he accepts, and extremely frugal in how he spends his money. One loss can wipe out several wins.

Defendants of course have no such concerns. The doctor is supported by an insurance company with assets in the hundreds of millions, sometimes billions. If the patient's lawyer can afford one expert the insurance company will hire three. They also provide a stable of experts for the defense, while the patient's lawyer must struggle to find someone willing to testify. If I have a medical question I usually go to the medical library to find the answer for myself. A defense lawyer can simply call his client. It is a David versus Goliath struggle that the public doesn't begin to understand.

The public doesn't understand because they learn most of what they know about the legal system from advertising. Insurance companies and the Chamber of Commerce spend millions of dollars convincing the public that they are the victims. They claim, without any foundation, that good doctors are being driven out of business, and they want potential jurors to believe that it is up to them to put a stop to it. And there is no comparable counterweight to that public relations juggernaut. When the lie is repeated often enough and loud enough people do believe. If I did not see the process from the inside I would probably believe it myself.

A huge problem for any plaintiff's lawyer is simply finding a doctor who is willing to testify against another doctor. Few doctors want anything to do with the legal system, and would never testify against a colleague under any circumstances. The list of available experts is small, and rarely will the most qualified doctors agree to testify. Almost never will a Michigan doctor agree to testify against another Michigan doctor. The consequences are simply too grave. Many physicians have told me that they would like to help, but they know their colleagues will ostracize them and refuse to refer patients if they do, and they can't afford to jeopardize their practice just to help one patient.

At one time medical schools were a good source of experts. These professors are among the most skilled in their fields, they tend to be more interested in the science of medicine than in the financial profit from medicine, and they aren't worried about where their next patient is coming from. For years the University of Michigan Medical School was a rich source of expert witness in all specialties, and if they believed a case had merit they had great credibility with jurors.

In short order the physicians of the state, many of them University of Michigan graduates, grew weary of having world class experts testify against them. So they banded together and let the university know that if it didn't do something to put an end to this testimony the alumni would cut off funding for their alma mater. The university then responded with the 1988 "Goldman Memo" warning its physicians not to cooperate with plaintiffs in malpractice cases. Included was a list of plaintiffs' attorneys that they could not to talk to, and the threat that any physician who testified against another physician would be stripped of his malpractice coverage. Once again we were back looking for out of state witnesses.

Defendants face no such problem. There is hardly a physician in the state who would not come to the aid of a colleague. In a matter of minutes they can get a parade of "experts" willing to defend whatever the defendant did. If the defendant cuts off the wrong leg it is most likely the patient's fault. He probably flipped over on the table while the surgeon wasn't looking. The jury usually has no way of knowing who is lying, and who is telling the truth. Faced with a battle of opposing experts they will give the benefit of the doubt to the defendant doctor every time. His defense may be utter nonsense, but if he can get a couple of his colleagues to repeat it under oath he has the case practically won.

On occasion I was able to anticipate how a defendant doctor would try to defend a case, and then set a trap so his own testimony would destroy his case. It required a degree of deception, because if the doctor knew where I was going he would be able to alter his testimony accordingly. But if he didn't know where I was going I could sometimes get an honest answer without the doctor having any idea that he was saying something damaging.

Dr. Burns was one of those doctors. He ran a fertility clinic in Grand Rapids for women who had trouble conceiving. One of his patients was Gloria Tanis. Gloria went to Dr. Burns for treatment of endometriosis, a condition that causes the uterine lining to grow in places where it shouldn't. Dr. Burns performed laparoscopic surgery to remove those cells, but in the process punctured Gloria's colon. She then developed severe peritonitis that scarred her tubes, and left her permanently sterile. The surgery that was designed to improve her fertility had sadly caused exactly the opposite result.

I knew that it was not malpractice to puncture the colon during a laparoscopy. The initial entry is done blindly, and a punctured colon is one of the risks that can't be avoided. Our real claim was that the doctor's office did not recognize and treat the injury before Gloria's tubes became permanently scarred. She called his office two days after surgery complaining of severe abdominal pain, but was put off for three days by a nurse who said that those symptoms were normal. My experts told me that the standard of care required an immediate exam under those circumstances.

The problem was that this would be an easy case to defend. All the doctor had to do was parade in two or three experts to testify that the damage was already done by the time of the first phone call. If the damage was already done then the doctor's delay didn't matter. It is what has become popularly known as the "so what" defense. It is one of the routine fall back positions when negligence is obvious. And I knew, as do all defense lawyers, that it wouldn't matter if I brought in two or three experts to say that Gloria's injury was treatable when she first called the office. With juries the tie always goes to the doctor.

My only hope was to set a trap to get the doctor to testify against himself. So I filed a complaint alleging that the doctor committed malpractice by puncturing the colon, even though I knew that wasn't malpractice. I said nothing about the delay in treatment. Then I scheduled his deposition. Both the doctor and his lawyer were supremely confident. They knew puncturing the colon wasn't malpractice, and that it would be easy for them to defend that claim. Usually I challenge doctors during depositions, but I let Dr. Burns get on a roll. He knew the statistics and the literature regarding colon punctures, and easily handled every question. Then I baited the trap.

I had a copy of Dr. Burns' office chart, and I knew that it said nothing about the phone call two days after surgery. So I finished up by telling Dr. Burns that I wanted to make sure I understood all of his defenses. I told him that I understood that my client started having significant pain two days post surgery. "You don't claim that this injury is in any way her fault for not calling your office that day, do you?" Oh he certainly did. What doctor could resist that softball? "Well even if she had called on the second day it wouldn't have made any difference in the outcome would it?" This softball probably looked like the size of a basketball. Not only could he deny that he was negligent, but he could put all the blame on her. So he told me that her failure to call certainly did make a difference, because if she had called immediately he would have gone back in and repaired the wound before the tubes were damaged. With that answer the trap snapped shut.

I then went back to my office, dropped the claim of negligence for puncturing the colon, and replaced it with the claim that his nurse was negligent for not responding to the phone call on day two. Although the phone call was not recorded in the doctor's chart, it was a long distance call from Kalamazoo, and I had my client's phone records to prove that she spent half an hour on the phone with the nurse that day.

Now the defense was back to where I knew they would be before the case ever started. They brought in experts to swear under oath that my client's fallopian tubes were already destroyed by the day of the phone call, but their problem was that I had the defendant doctor's sworn testimony that he could have prevented the injury if she had called him on that day. The defense experts said they thought Dr. Burns was wrong about that, but the defense lawyer knew he couldn't go to trial when Dr. Burns agreed with my experts instead of his own. Dr. Burns could change his opinion when he got to trial, but that wouldn't sell either. They decided to pay instead.

I'm not sure what the truth was in that case. It's possible I suppose that the damage was already done on day two. There's no way to know. What I am certain about is that Dr. Burns would have testified under oath to whatever opinion helped his defense the most. If he thought saying it was treatable on day two would help him, that's what he would testify. If he thought saying it was not treatable would help him, that's what he would testify. I just gave him enough rope to hang himself.

In most malpractice cases the plaintiff's only chance is the medical literature. Experts can and will say almost anything, but medical literature rarely lies. When they are writing for peer review journals or writing textbooks they tell the truth. The only effective way to break down a defense expert, in my experience, is to show that his testimony conflicts with every medical book that has ever been written. When you do that you have a chance to win.

Unfortunately not every error can be pointed out in a textbook. There is no textbook that can tell a jury how to read a CT scan or an EKG. It may be markedly abnormal, but if the defense experts all say it is normal the jury doesn't know whom to believe. Plaintiffs seldom win those cases, and I will rarely take one even if I know there was malpractice. Any case that a jury can't figure out by itself from the medical literature is a good way for a plaintiff's lawyer to go broke.

If you are really lucky you can find a medical article that the defense expert wrote himself. A number of years ago I had a case for a woman who suffered from advanced breast cancer, caused because her family doctor ignored a breast lump. The doctor's excuse was that she didn't do a biopsy because she thought it probably wasn't cancer, even though she couldn't be sure. I argued that all unknown lumps had to be biopsied. The defense claimed it was a professional judgment call to biopsy or not, and argued that the doctor's judgment should not be second guessed just because we now know she was wrong. After all, nobody's perfect.

The defense had an outstanding expert, Dr. Ken Denton from the Michigan State Medical School. I took Dr. Denton's deposition, and he testified at great length, and with real conviction, that it was not the standard of care to biopsy every unknown lump. It is a matter of judgment, he said, based on years of training, experience, and intuition. Doctors know when a lump is suspicious, and it was not this defendant doctor's fault that this cancer didn't look suspicious. To biopsy every unknown breast lump would be a waste of time and money.

That would normally sell to any West Michigan jury, and the defense knew it. What the defense didn't know was that Dr. Denton was a prolific writer, published in many medical journals and textbooks. And while he might be willing to testify one way in a malpractice case to help a colleague, he had something very different to say when he was telling doctors how to practice medicine. His message to them was clear: every unexplained breast lump must be biopsied. You can't tell what it is by feeling it or taking x-rays. When I shared those articles with the defense counsel the case settled quickly.

Chapter Twenty-Three

*A*nother advantage that doctors have is that the records are in their control, and most cases depend on what is or is not in those records. When a doctor knows he is in trouble the temptation is often irresistible to go back and get rid of the evidence. A former document examiner for the Michigan State Police told me once that when he reviews medical records in malpractice cases he finds alterations well over fifty percent of the time. By the time a patient's lawyer gets to the records the medical care can look outstanding.

One of my early cases was against a local nursing home. My client's mother died there from bed sores that eventually became large and infected. Of course the nursing home can't guarantee success. Some people die regardless of how carefully they are treated. I didn't know if this was a legitimate case, but I agreed to get copies of the mother's nursing home records to see what kind of treatment she received. If those records did not show that she was being turned and checked regularly there might be a case. But if the records showed that she was receiving good care then we would just have to accept it as God's will.

The woman died in November 1993, so I was primarily concerned with her medical records for the previous two months, and when I reviewed them I was impressed with how thorough the nursing staff had been. They checked her and turned her several times a day. They washed her and treated the bed sores and did everything exactly according to the book. With that kind of documented medical care the case had no chance.

There was only one small problem. According to the nursing home records they provided all of this outstanding care in October and November 1994, a year after the woman died. It wasn't difficult to figure out what had happened. I didn't request the records until the summer of 1994, and by then the staff had been dating all of their records "1994" for at least six months. So when they went back to forge the records for their deceased former resident it was a simple oversight that led them to date the records with the wrong year, much the same way many of us tend to put the wrong year on checks that we write in January. I didn't need a document examiner to prove the forgery in that case. Once I pointed out the dates to the defense attorney his enthusiasm waned noticeably, and the case settled.

Other forgeries were more difficult to prove. Linda Martin was a young mother who lost a son shortly after birth from the effects of a placental abruption, a condition where the placenta separates from the uterus. A small abruption is survivable, but over two or three days this abruption progressed to the point that her fetus was not getting sufficient oxygen. He was born alive with severe brain damage, and died a few days later.

Linda was upset with her obstetrician, Dr. Chandra Singe, for not recognizing the condition before it caused such severe damage. She had seen Dr. Singe two days before the boy's birth, complaining of significant abdominal pain, but the doctor ignored her complaints and did nothing. If a caesarian section had been performed then the baby would have been fine. Pain in the uterus is a classic warning sign for a placental abruption, so I was interested in looking at the doctor's office records to see why she had not acted sooner. I have learned through long experience not to trust what my clients tell me. Cases are almost inevitably won or lost on the basis of what is in the medical chart. Even if the patient is telling the truth no jury will believe her unless it is confirmed by the medical records.

Dr. Singe's office records confirmed that Linda had an emergency visit complaining of pain, but the pain obviously had nothing to do with an abrupted placenta. The pain she complained about was in her thighs, and she specifically denied pain in the uterus. Normally I would have stopped there, but there was something about the case that made me suspicious, and I filed suit anyway so I could delve beyond the records to try to find out what really happened. The records showed nothing close to malpractice, but it also didn't make sense for a pregnant woman to have a placental abruption without uterine pain, and there was something that caused Linda to request an emergency appointment that day. I hoped that a deposition of Dr. Singe might provide some answers. It didn't. She stuck to the information in the office chart. The pain was reported to be in the inguinal area and the thighs, and not in the uterus as Linda now claimed. If Linda said that she came in with pain in her uterus she was lying. In a credibility contest between a patient and a doctor the doctor will win every time. I didn't like our chances.

The case meandered through the legal process for over a year while we waited for trial, and from time to time I would review it to try to find some way to convince a jury that it was Linda who was telling the truth. If I only had to contend with the doctor's testimony we might have a slim chance, but here it was even worse. The doctor had written in her records at the time of the office visit that there was no uterine pain. It really did look hopeless.

Shortly before trial I was reviewing the records again when I noticed something that had escaped me before. The office record was written on lined paper, and every entry was on one of the lines except for the entries relating to the location of the pain. That was written at the bottom of the page between the lines. It could be that she compressed the entries to get them all on the page, but it didn't look right. I asked to see the original, and the defense attorney refused.

I then filed a motion that was granted by the judge to require the doctor to produce the original record so I could have a document examiner review it. Document examiners are amazing in their ability to prove forgeries, and I was optimistic that he could prove this entry was altered after the office visit to cover the doctor's mistake. Unfortunately he was unable to do that with this record. He could not tell me when the suspicious entries were written, but he did give me something. He confirmed that they were written with a different ink than the rest of the page.

I produced the document examiner's report to the defense attorney, and waited for an explanation. It wasn't long in coming. "The doctor carries two pens in her pocket," he told me. "Sometimes she will make several entries with one pen, examine the patient, and then pull out a pen to make another entry. If she pulls out the other pen it will be written in a different ink." He assured me that she had not touched the record since the date of the office visit two days before the child was born. It was a little shaky, but still good enough to sell to most West Michigan juries, and the defense lawyer knew it. I knew this case was still a long shot, but we had to give it a try. Besides, the insurance company was offering practically nothing to settle, so we didn't have much choice. I had invested thousands of dollars for experts, and court reporters, and the document examiner, but there was no escape except to go through the trial and take my beating.

A few days before trial, I took the deposition of the pediatrician who cared for the boy after he was born. I was throwing good money after bad, but I couldn't go to trial at all without testimony that the boy died from lack of oxygen caused by the abrupted placenta. I expected it to be a very short deposition, just to make sure that I had the damage testimony that I needed.

The doctor testified as I anticipated. He could not comment on what Dr. Singe did or did not do. He could only tell us what was wrong with the boy, and what caused his death. He had almost finished his testimony when I wanted to ask him a specific question from the records, and to do that I walked around behind him so I could point to the entry that I wanted him to talk about. As I did so I noticed that he had a copy of Dr. Singe's office record in front of him, and none of the suspicious entries about the location of the pain were on his copy.

I asked the pediatrician how he obtained his copy, and he told me that the day after the child was born he requested a copy of the pre-natal records so he could make his chart complete. Dr. Singe's office then sent him the copy that I saw before me. It was one of the more dramatic moments I have witnessed while practicing law. It wasn't an in court confession so popular in movies, but it was close. Dr. Singe had testified under oath that she made this entry two days before the boy was born. And now we could prove that it hadn't been made until at least the day after he was born. By then she knew Linda had suffered an abrupted placenta, and in a panic she pulled the chart and altered the notes of the last office visit to cover her mistake. She could come up with an excuse for the second pen, but she could not think of an excuse for the pediatrician's copy, and the case settled.

It is a small world. A few years after I finished that case my niece, Meg, attended physician's assistants school in Georgia. The program required her to do rotations in various specialties, and she chose to do her obstetrics rotation in Kalamazoo while she stayed with us. As luck would have it she was assigned to work with Dr. Singe. I warned Meg about my case against Dr. Singe, and she wisely decided that it probably wouldn't be a good idea to let the doctor know that she was my niece. So when Meg started work there she gave the doctor a fictitious name of the relatives she was staying with. This worked until one day when Hattie left a message for her to call Hattie Ford. The doctor picked up on that, and said to Meg, "I thought you said you were living with the Wards."

Sensing disaster, Meg responded, "Oh, I am. You know how the receptionist gets everything wrong." And with that justifiable bit of deception she got a passing grade for her rotation.

Deceit is often a matter of official hospital policy. Nurses who want to keep their jobs know better than to write anything in a hospital chart that could later come back to haunt the hospital in a malpractice suit, but deceit isn't always just a matter of omission. Sometimes nurses receive a direct order to lie. Mazie Ferguson's case was one of those. Mazie was a neighbor, well into her eighties, who often babysat our children. She was a gentle soul, and the kids loved her. She lived in a modest house with her husband, Bob, a cat, a dog, and a pet rooster that woke us up every morning. The rooster violated a city ordinance, but neighbors would overlook things with Mazie that they probably wouldn't have tolerated from anyone else.

In 1986 Bob died suddenly, leaving Mazie all alone after a long marriage. Hattie and I were worried about how she would handle the loss, and how she would manage on her own, but Mazie was philosophical. At the graveside she told me that she mourned for her husband, but added, "We all have to face death sooner or later, don't we?" Little did she realize just how soon she would have to face it herself.

A few days later Mazie called to tell me that she was having back pains, and asked me to drive her to the hospital. After a long wait in the lobby she was finally examined, and found to be having a heart attack. After emergency treatment she was eventually admitted to the cardiac unit on the sixth floor. Her condition was stable, but the combination of age and various medications and the strange surroundings left her confused. She wanted to get out of bed, and she wanted to go home. To keep her quiet and in bed they put her in a Posey vest, and secured the vest to the bed.

She seemed to be on her way to recovery when tragedy struck a few days later. At two o'clock in the morning her daughter received a call from the hospital that Mazie had suddenly died in bed from a second heart attack, and within two weeks of her husband's death I was back at the cemetery for Mazie. But death is a part of life, and soon things returned to normal. The pets were all given away, and the house was listed for sale. Then one afternoon I received a call from Mazie's daughter telling me that the hospital wanted to meet with her to discuss her mother's death, implying that perhaps not everything was as it seemed. The daughter was understandably suspicious, and asked me to go with her. We met at the hospital the next morning, and as soon as I walked in I could tell that this was not a typical meeting. They didn't have a doctor there to explain what happened. This was a room full of hospital executives and lawyers. It was confession time.

The hospital's lawyer spoke first. "Your mother didn't die the way we told you she died," he said. There was no way to sugar coat this, and he just wanted to get it over with. It was painful enough for him to admit these things to her, and my presence surely didn't help his mood any. "She did die from a heart attack, but she didn't die in bed. We actually found her body in the basement stairwell. It appears that she untied the Posey vest, walked down seven flights of stairs, and suffered another heart attack before anyone realized she was gone."

The obvious question was why they were admitting it now, and that answer came next. "We received a telephone call from the Kalamazoo Gazette," he said. "They know what happened, and are going to print the story this week. We thought it would be better if you heard it from us before you read about it in the paper."

If I had known this story from the outset I might not have even taken the case. After all, nobody directly caused Mazie's death. She untied herself, and walked down the stairs on her own, most likely trying to walk home. And she was eighty-seven years old. No jury would award much, if anything, under those circumstances. But a lying hospital was an entirely different matter, so I filed suit alleging that the hospital was negligent in her supervision. They knew she was confused, they knew she wanted to walk home, and they improperly secured the Posey vest so that she could easily untie it.

An even tawdrier story emerged when we took the depositions of the hospital nurses. One of them, I knew, was the angel who blew the whistle on the hospital by slipping the story to the newspaper. I never found out who she was, but she has my admiration. The beauty of the whole episode was that the hospital panicked prematurely. When the story did come out in the paper it contained no names, and only a few details about a woman who was found dead in the hospital stairwell. If the hospital hadn't blinked it could have ridden out the storm. Neither Mazie's daughter nor I would have ever associated that story with Mazie. After all, Mazie died in bed.

What the nurses told us was all more or less consistent. Sometime after midnight they discovered that Mazie was not in her room. They first searched the floor, and when they couldn't find her there they called in security to search the entire hospital. It took them almost an hour to find her body, and when they finally realized what had happened, the head nurse called the hospital vice president who was on call to handle emergencies. She told him of their discovery, and that she was going to call Mazie's daughter to tell her what had happened.

"Not if you want to keep your job," was the vice president's reply. He told her to take Mazie's body back up to the sixth floor, tuck her back into bed, and then call the daughter to report that they had found her there during their rounds. The nurse did what she was told, and it would have worked perfectly except for the nurse with a conscience. Even then the hospital's defense attorney put up a spirited fight. The case dragged on, and there were no settlement offers until the eve of trial. As a last ditch effort the defense lawyer asked the judge to exclude the evidence of the cover-up, arguing that it was all irrelevant because it occurred after Mazie died, not before. When the judge denied that motion the case settled for several times what it would have cost them if they had allowed the nurse to tell the truth at the outset. Truth be told, it probably wouldn't have cost them anything if they had done that.

Chapter Twenty-Four

While all of this was going on my brother Jack's marriage was slowly disintegrating. I felt bad about it, because I liked Anne, and I had been the best man at their wedding in 1970. I remember the wedding clearly because I took leave from the Air Force to attend, and when I flew back to the Philadelphia Airport after the wedding I discovered that my red Ford Mustang had been stolen out of the parking lot while I was gone. I still look twice whenever I see an antique red Ford Mustang. It has to be out there somewhere.

But true love is rare, people change, and after seventeen years this marriage had reached the end of the road. The divorce was Jack's doing. As is often the case, he met someone else, and he was willing to go through the torment of a divorce for the sake of a new life. Not only the torment, but also the expense, and this one looked like it was going to be costly. According to South Carolina law Jack was the party at fault, and would therefore be stuck with very substantial alimony unless he could prove that Anne had also found someone new. In a sane world why would it matter? They were separated, so why shouldn't she find someone else? But the law is the law, and if Jack could prove that she had a new boyfriend it was going to save him a lot of money. You almost wonder why separated husbands in South Carolina don't hire suitors to woo their ex-wives. It could become a cottage industry.

Jack was convinced that Anne had a boyfriend, but he couldn't prove it. He searched the house, he checked the mail, and he even hired a private investigator to tail her. All of these efforts came up with nothing. One of the unfortunate side effects of divorce litigation is that it makes adversaries out of people who are already going through an emotional wringer, and it almost forces them to throw gasoline on a fire that desperately needs water. In any event all this sleuthing was getting Jack nowhere. The date of the divorce was rapidly approaching, and alimony was going to be part of it.

Jack and I have always been close, and he called me regularly to talk about the devastating effect that the divorce was having on his emotions, his children, and his finances. And he talked about his frustration at not being able to prove that Anne had a new boyfriend. He didn't care if she had a boyfriend, but he didn't look forward to years of alimony either.

A couple of weeks before his divorce went to court I called Jack one afternoon at his office. I asked him if his private investigator had been able to come up with anything, and he told me that they had nothing. He had finally resigned himself to the fact that alimony was going to be part of his life. "Would it help any," I asked, "if I were to send you an explicit letter from Anne to her new boyfriend?"

There was a stunned pause, followed by, "You've got to be kidding me."

"No," I said, "I'm not. You know you can always count on me to take care of you, and since you couldn't do it yourself I had to do it for you. It was a little more difficult to solve this from up here in Kalamazoo, but I'm holding the letter in my hand as we speak."

No novelist could make this stuff up, and if he did no one would believe it. I had actually discovered the evidence that Jack so desperately needed by walking out to my mailbox to retrieve a package that Anne had sent to her boyfriend in Maine. The letter was inside. It took me a while to figure out how it ended up in my mailbox in Michigan, but once I did the explanation was quite simple. You really couldn't make this up.

The previous Christmas Hattie and I had sent a Christmas present to Jack and Anne while they were still together. Then came the separation, the lawyers, and finally the new boyfriend. A few days before my phone call to Jack, Anne sent a book to her boyfriend, and enclosed the letter. She grabbed the first available box to mail it in, which just happened to be the same box Hattie and I had sent to them a year earlier. Then she put her boyfriend's address on the front, but forgot to change the return address, which was ours. And finally, she wrote down the wrong address for her boyfriend. When it was undeliverable as addressed it was returned – to me. And two weeks later they were divorced. Without alimony.

As loyal as I was to Jack, I felt bad for Anne. She was going through at least as much trauma as Jack was, and this had to be a bitter blow. Her lawyer made some threat about reporting me to the FBI for tampering with the U.S. Mail, but I wasn't too concerned, since I had simply opened a package that I found addressed to me in my own mailbox, and I was pretty sure that was legal. Over time Anne forgave me, and a few years later she sadly developed pancreatic cancer. At the time she was living near Boston with a new husband. I had a deposition scheduled in Boston shortly before she died, and I called to ask if I could come to see her. It was the first time I had seen her since they separated, and it was the last time I saw her. We sat in her kitchen for an hour talking about the odd way I found her letter, but also about the many memories we shared of family gatherings, and about her illness which she faced with amazing courage. I miss her.

Chapter Twenty-Five

A lawyer who works full time for an insurance company is under enormous pressure to do whatever it takes to win his case. If he resists on ethical grounds there are plenty of others with fewer scruples who will be happy to take his place. What the insurance company wants is victory. How the lawyer gets it is his problem. A few years ago I won a medical malpractice verdict against a very good defense lawyer who had won over twenty trials in a row. My case was the first case he had lost for his insurance company in several years, but this one he did lose, and within two weeks the company was at his office with a truck to pick up all of his files. He was fired. They weren't about to tolerate incompetence.

The news of that firing was probably known by every defense lawyer in the state before the sun went down that day, and the message was clear; if you want to keep your job you'd better keep your insurance company happy. Early in my career I had a number of medical malpractice cases against a defense law firm with an excellent reputation, and a very good record. Then one day one of the lawyers in that firm agreed to represent a patient in Ohio who had a good case against her doctor. The lawyer probably thought that it was a safe thing to do, considering that it was in a different state, and against a different insurance company, but he thought wrong. When his own insurance company client found out about it they fired him and his entire firm on the spot. They wanted ideological purity in their lawyers, and didn't want anything to do with a lawyer who would ever sue a doctor, regardless of how justified it was, or what state it was in.

Suddenly faced with unemployment the lawyer did the only thing he knew how to do, he changed sides. If he could no longer earn a living by defending doctors, surely he could make a living by suing them. He understood medicine, he understood the law, and he had been trying malpractice cases for years. Maybe getting fired was just a blessing in disguise. And there was a side benefit. Finally he could start earning some of those enormous contingent fees he had always dreamed about, instead of working by the hour.

Once he stopped defending cases I never saw him again, because now all my cases were being assigned to his replacement. But a couple of years later he happened to call me for some reason, and before he hung up I asked him how he liked being a plaintiff's lawyer, and how it compared to defending these cases. He didn't have to think about his answer. He didn't like it, he found it to be "infinitely more difficult" than doing defense work, and he was desperate to get back to representing insurance companies where the work was easier, and where he got paid every week. And it was a safe bet that if he ever did get rehired he would do whatever it took to keep the company happy. With that kind of pressure it is no wonder that some defense lawyers are willing to cut ethical corners.

A number of years ago I represented a young mother who lost her son in a cave-in of loose dirt near her home. An excavation company had dropped a large pile of dirt there, and when the boy climbed on it, it collapsed and buried him. My first job was to find out which company put it there. There were three construction projects going on in the neighborhood, and I knew one of them must have done it, but I didn't know which one. They all denied it, so I sued them all. Many people may not understand that shotgun approach to litigation, but it is often the only way to get to the truth. Without a lawsuit you can't force anyone to tell you anything.

All three companies filed answers denying responsibility. That was no surprise. In thirty years I have never had a defendant file an answer admitting the injury was his fault. If a plaintiff files suit without solid proof, both the lawyer and the plaintiff can be sanctioned with substantial fines. It happens regularly. The rules are the same for defendants, but are never enforced. Defendants can deny anything with impunity.

Plaintiffs are often sanctioned for filing frivolous complaints, but I have never heard of a defendant being sanctioned for filing a frivolous answer. It just doesn't happen.

After receiving the answers to the complaint I followed up by sending interrogatories, asking specifically if any of the companies ever dug in that area, if they had digging equipment in the area, or if their lawyers had taken any statements from any potential witnesses. Everything was denied. One of the defense lawyers signed the denial himself under oath. They knew nothing, had conducted no discovery, and had no witness statements. If I was going to prove this case it would be without their help.

At a loss as to what to do next, I scheduled depositions of the companies' insurance claims adjusters, and subpoenaed their claims files. It was a long shot, but I was hoping to find something that could at least start me on the right trail. At 5:15 p.m. on the evening before the depositions were scheduled to begin there was a knock on my door, and I opened it to find two of the defense attorneys holding boxes full of documents. Those documents proved that the lawyers' clients had dumped the dirt that caused the death. There were several witness statements that the lawyers had taken, and company records that confirmed their involvement. The claims adjusters apparently weren't willing to perjure themselves under oath, and the lawyers were hoping that by giving me the records all would be forgiven. "All right," one of them said, "now you've got what you have been asking for. Let's just forget about it and get on with the case."

I was relieved to finally have the proof that I needed, but I was irate that the lawyers had been lying to me and to the court. For the only time in my career I filed a motion asking the judge to find both defense lawyers in contempt of court for lying under oath, and for signing court documents that they knew to be untrue. Because they were long time members of the Kalamazoo Bar Association no local judge would hear the motion, and called in a visiting judge from Grand Rapids instead. At the hearing the lawyers pretty much just threw themselves on the mercy of the court, which was a smart move. They were fined just twelve hundred dollars apiece, a trivial amount. They both probably billed more than that for preparing the false answers.

But as with doctors, some lawyers surprise me with their honesty. I think most of the defense lawyers I have opposed over the years can be trusted. There are very specific ethical rules for lawyers to follow, and most do follow them. The witnesses often lie, but I can't blame the lawyers for that. I'm sure that some of my clients have lied also. One notable example of an honest defense lawyer involved a suit against a psychologist for having a homosexual relationship with her patient. The psychologist admitted the affair, but denied that the plaintiff was her patient. The psychologist claimed that she only treated my client's son, and since my client wasn't her patient there was nothing professionally unethical about the affair.

One easy way to determine if my client was a patient was to get the psychologist's appointment calendar. If my client was scheduled for therapy sessions it would be convincing evidence that she was a patient. The problem was that there were other patients listed on that calendar also, and I had no right to see those names. So we compromised, and the psychologist agreed to give me a copy of the calendar with all the times blacked out except for the dates and times when my client claimed to have appointments. When the copies were produced all of those dates were for my client's son. There were no appointments for my client. Someone was lying, but I wasn't sure who.

Then I had one of those experiences that make me proud to be a lawyer. There were two defense lawyers in the case, one representing the psychologist, and another representing the psychologist's professional corporation. A couple of days after the psychologist's deposition the lawyer for her professional corporation called me. He was calling, he said, to tell me that the records produced at the deposition had been forged. On my copy of the calendar I could only see the name of my client's son, but the two defense lawyers had seen the original, and on the original it was obvious that the defendant had erased my client's name, and written in the son's name instead. This made the professional corporation as liable as the psychologist, but the lawyer told me that his conscience and his commitment to ethical standards would not allow him to let the fraud stand. That kind of honesty occurs regularly, but it doesn't make good fiction. You will never see it in novels or on television. On the other hand, the lawyer told me that his co-counsel was furious with him for revealing the truth, arguing instead that they should try to settle the case quickly for a modest amount while they still had the advantage. Not all lawyers are honest.

One of the most egregious cases of lawyer misconduct involved Carroll Jones, an elderly lawyer from Jones, Michigan. He and his sister also owned the Jones Bank. It wasn't a big town, and they owned most of it. My client was Dennis Brown. Most clients can give me the salient facts about their case in just a few minutes. The details may take longer, but in a few minutes I have a pretty good understanding of what the case is about. But Mr. Brown had a long story, and it got more and more bizarre as he droned on.

Mr. Brown grew up in Jones. He went to school there, his sister worked in the Jones Bank, and, as is the case in most small towns, everybody knew everybody else. They knew each other's parents, their children, their hobbies, and most of the good and the bad things that they had done during their lives. Anonymity does not exist in towns like Jones.

Mr. Brown owned a small farm just outside of town. He married his childhood sweetheart, Sandy, they had a couple of children, and for a number of years life was good. They didn't have much money, but they really didn't need much. They were getting by. Then about five years before he came to see me Mr. Brown discovered that he had a problem. His wife, it seems, had grown bored sitting home alone all day while he was out working in the fields. To assuage her boredom she started going shopping, and discovered that she enjoyed it. She enjoyed it a lot. She enjoyed it more than she could afford it, and had to borrow money from the bank to feed her habit. Eventually she ran up several thousand dollars in debt.

When Mr. Brown found out what his wife had been up to he went to the bank and spoke to the bank president. The president, as it turned out, was Attorney Jones' sister. Mr. Brown told her that he would pay off his wife's debts if the bank promised to never again lend her any money. He would pay the debt this time, but he didn't want to find himself in the same bind in the future. The president agreed.

Life then returned to normal in the Brown household until just shortly before he came to see me. Their children were getting bigger, and Mr. Brown decided to make some home repairs, but when he went to a local savings and loan to borrow money for the repairs he was refused. The savings and loan would not accept a mortgage on the house because the bank already had one. This was news to Mr. Brown because the bank couldn't get a mortgage without his signature, and he hadn't signed anything. His wife had some explaining to do, and when he went home to confront her everything came pouring out.

The first thing he had to know was that she had a boyfriend, another farmer who lived a few miles away. That was the good news. The bad news was that she had sunk back into her borrow and spend habit. At first the bank accepted her promissory notes, but when the debt reached forty thousand dollars the bank wanted to be repaid. Sandy had no money, so the bank helped her out with a plan. If she didn't have the money to pay the notes the bank would be happy to accept a mortgage on her house instead. It was a win-win deal for everyone. Sandy didn't have to pay the notes, and the bank got security for its loans.

The only catch was that she couldn't give a mortgage without her husband's signature, and that would defeat the whole purpose. Her immediate concern was to keep him from discovering anything. Her husband was unable to come into the bank, she told the president, but he would be happy to sign the mortgage if the president would drive it out to his house. The address she gave was the address of her boyfriend.

The president accepted the offer, and headed out to protect the bank's loan by getting Mr. Brown's signature on the mortgage. The president had known Mr. Brown all of his life, but took the mortgage to the address Sandy gave her. When she pulled into the driveway the boyfriend was waiting, according to the plan, and he did sign the mortgage, but not before the president greeted him by saying, "Mr. Brown, you sure have changed." Mr. Brown may have changed, but the president had the signature that she needed, and she promptly had it recorded with the Register of Deeds where it was later discovered when Mr. Brown attempted to take out his new loan.

When Sandy finished her confession Mr. Brown knew he had a major problem that he couldn't solve by himself. He needed legal help, and he went where everyone in that small town went, to Carroll Jones. It didn't occur to Mr. Brown that Mr. Jones also owned the bank. Mr. Jones listened patiently to the story, and when it was over he told Mr. Brown that he was in even more trouble than he realized. "This is bank fraud," Mr. Jones explained to his new client. "If we don't get this taken care of your wife is going to prison. What's more, everyone will believe that you were in on it with her, so you are probably going to prison, too. The only way I might save you is if I can talk the bank into letting you sign a legitimate mortgage." He left immediately to walk across the street to talk to his sister, the bank president, and returned a few minutes later with a mortgage for Mr. Brown to sign. Then he presented his client with a bill for his services.

There are few ethical rules that Attorney Jones didn't violate in that transaction, conflict of interest being the most obvious. He knew his bank was going to be out forty thousand dollars unless he could con his client into signing a new mortgage. He also threatened criminal prosecution to persuade Mr. Brown to cover the debt, itself a felony in Michigan. I sued the bank and Attorney Jones, and eventually the bank cancelled the mortgage, but they all got off easy. I don't know what happened to Mr. Brown, or his wife, or the boyfriend.

Chapter Twenty-Six

It's fascinating how kids who grow up in the same house with the same parents can be so different. Jimmy was fearless, and would try anything. On his third birthday he decided that it was time to ride a two wheel bicycle. He started in the morning, and by the time I got home that evening he was riding it up and down the sidewalk. He looked as if he had been in a fifteen round fight, but he was riding the bike. It should have been no surprise to me when he later became interested in diving, pole vaulting, and skydiving.

John was always a happy kid. Maybe it was due to birth order, although he could get upset on occasion. When he was four Hattie scolded him for some transgression, and he didn't like it. When the lecture was over he came downstairs and told me that, "Mama's not my best friend anymore." Still not quite satisfied, he added, "And you're not either." Then he paused to reflect, presumably on the fact that I hadn't done anything to him, and that he was now quite alone so far as friends were concerned. Deciding to hedge his bet without completely losing face he added, "But I do like you a little bit." I was flattered.

John loved music, and still does. Both of my parents were music majors, and my sister, Debby, and brother, David, are musical, but the gene skipped over me and landed on John. Once we started him on piano lessons we couldn't keep him away from it. When he got older I occasionally fell asleep listening to him playing at night, and awoke to the sound of the piano in the morning.

School, on the other hand, was just for making friends. He had some of his grandfather in him. When John was in the first grade he got a part in "A Mid Summer Night's Dream" at a local theater. A couple of weeks later I received a note from his teacher telling me that John had stopped working. When I confronted him with the accusation he made no effort to deny it. "Dad, I don't need to learn how to read," he said. "I'm going to be an actor." He had found his calling at the age of six, and wasn't about to waste any more effort on school work.

Mary, the youngest, was always responsible and reliable. Well, most of the time anyway. The poor little girl was born with a cleft palate that went undiagnosed far too long, and she didn't get corrective surgery until she was four. Before the surgery no one could understand a word she said, but she has been making up for it ever since.

I have lots of guilt with my children, as most parents probably do. I wonder if I gave them every opportunity, and I know I didn't give them enough time. I always worked long hours, but not because the job was more important than they were. Usually I didn't have much choice. The law is a jealous mistress, and demands more than most lawyers really want to give. One of my regrets is that Mary never got the tree house she wanted. I was always going to build one for her later, but later never came. She deserved a tree house.

When I did cater to their desires I often botched the job. Jimmy was desperate for a dog, and when he was five I finally gave in. After some research I decided on a Cockapoo, half Cocker spaniel, and half Toy Poodle. They usually weigh about twenty pounds, and make good house pets. Then when I saw some Cockapoo puppies advertised in the paper Jimmy had his dog. But it didn't take long for me to realize that I had been swindled. Frisky didn't have any more Cocker spaniel or Poodle in him than I did. By the time he was six months old he weighed eighty pounds, and looked like a Black Lab/German Sheppard mix.

We had a large pen in the backyard, but I could not keep that dog contained. No matter what I tried I could not prevent him from going under or over the fence, and when he got out he usually headed for the local elementary school. After all, that's where the action was. The school administration, however, was not nearly as happy to see Frisky as he was to see them. One of the milder complaints was from a bus driver who had to slam on his brakes to avoid a squirrel that Frisky chased into the street. The final straw came when our baby sitter reported seeing Frisky in front of the school engaged in a game of tug of war with a blind man's cane. I can only assume that the tap tap tap must have seemed like a direct challenge.

The dog had to go. But how do you give away a little boy's dog? There isn't any good way, but the best I could think of was to send the dog to Hattie's parents' farm down in Georgia. That way Frisky would have all the room he needed to run free, and Jimmy could still see him when we went down to visit. It wasn't a good solution, but it was a solution. All I had to do was get the dog to Georgia.

We were heading south for Christmas that year, so I hooked up the trailer, put the dog house in the trailer, put the dog in the dog house, and started out. This worked well until we got to Indianapolis, and I let the dog out to take a break. By then he had been in the dog house for several hours, and there was no way on God's green earth he was going back in it. I pushed and shoved, and tried to bribe him with food, but there was just no way it was going to happen. So I tied him to both sides of the trailer, giving him enough rope to move around, and started out once again. I hadn't gone far before other drivers started blowing their horns, and making gestures towards the trailer, and when I stopped to check I found Frisky completely entangled in the rope.

We stopped for the night at a motel near Nashville, and when we left the next morning I assumed that Frisky was now sufficiently familiar with the routine that I could give him a little more freedom. Instead of ropes tied to both sides of the trailer, I used just one rope tied to the front. This gave him enough room to move around, but not enough rope to go over the rear gate. And he had enough rope to go into the dog house if he wanted to get out of the wind. I was looking forward to an uneventful trip.

I didn't go fifty yards before horns started blaring once again, and when I looked back Frisky was gone. He didn't have enough rope to go over the rear gate, but he did have enough rope to jump over the side. He was apparently as eager to get out of the trailer as he was to get out of the pen in our back yard. The problem was that the rope was long enough for him to go over the side, but not quite long enough to reach all the way to the ground. Only his hind legs could touch the ground, and that's where I found him running for all he was worth on two legs trying to keep up with the rapidly accelerating car. He was doing a pretty good job of it, too. It's surprising what you can do sometimes with the proper motivation.

Eventually Frisky arrived at his new home none the worse for wear. It was a large farm, he had the run of the place, and all would be good. But the next morning when I woke up I discovered that he had spread trash all over the front yard, so I immediately threw on my shoes, and cleaned up the mess before Hattie's parents woke up. I wanted to be on my way back to Michigan before they got wise to what I had done to them. When we returned home I bought Jimmy a hamster to make up for the dog, but even I knew that was a sorry trade, and a couple of years later Jimmy finally got the dog he wanted, a small Shih Tzu puppy. This time I checked his papers.

I don't hunt, I don't fish, I don't ski, and I don't go camping, all things that many fathers do with their children. After two weeks at Air Force survival school in November 1969 I promised myself that I would never spend another night in the woods if I could avoid it, and so far I've lived up to that promise. As a result my kids missed out on some of the bonding that comes from these experiences, but I hope I made up for some of that with pole vaulting. I coached all three of them in high school, and for us that common experience provided what many other kids get from fishing or camping.

I started with Jimmy when he was in ninth grade. He thought vaulting sounded like fun, but he wasn't at all eager for me to coach him. He probably didn't think I knew much about it, and he didn't want me to offend the school's coach by interfering. Ted Duckett was the coach, and he invited me to get involved, but it was a hard sell with my son. It took me awhile to gain his confidence so that he welcomed my help, and wasn't embarrassed by it. He had a couple of practice sessions before I stopped by for the first time. He was just learning how to leave the ground, and the first thing that was obvious to me was that he was jumping off the wrong foot. I told him to jump off his left foot, but he assured me that he had been taught to jump off his right. I hadn't jumped in twenty-five years, but I knew that wasn't going to work. When Ted stopped by I told him that Jim needed to jump off his left foot, and Ted responded that the vaulter they had the previous year jumped off his right. I digested that for a moment, and then asked, "Was he left handed?"

"Now that you mention it he was left handed."

So Jim started jumping off his left foot, and I established a little credibility. I still had a long way to go, but it was a start. I knew enough to teach him the basics, and by the time of the first meet he was able to compete effectively. He won that first meet against two other schools, and earned a varsity letter as a freshman in his first competition. We were on our way, but he still had some misgivings about having me coach him. The turning point occurred a few weeks later when I was late getting to practice. He started jumping with a new pole that day, and kept getting thrown far to the right with every jump. In fact he was going so far to the right that he kept missing the pit, and his confidence was shaken. The school's coaches had given him all kinds of suggestions, none of which helped a bit, and by the time I got there he was pretty rattled. I watched a couple of jumps, and realized that he was bending the pole in the wrong direction, and that the cure was simply to rotate the pole in his hands about forty-five degrees. As soon as he did that he started landing in the center of the pit again, and we worked as a team after that.

Jimmy was a much better athlete than I had been. He was fast and athletic and fearless. Anything I asked him to try he did without hesitation, and that is unusual in a sport where one bad landing can cause serious injury. Most kids have to be brought along slowly to build up their confidence, but Jimmy would try anything. It didn't take long for him to progress beyond my knowledge of the sport, and I had to struggle to keep ahead of him. My salvation was a video camera. I frequently videotaped Jim's jumps, and then compared his technique with films of world class vaulters, and little by little I learned what worked and what didn't.

Jim had quite a bit of success in the sport, setting the school record, and placing twice in the state meet, but I probably had more fun than he did. I like the sport, I loved spending time with him in a common project, and it was a welcome break from practicing law. Many days I found myself in my office thinking about what I wanted him to work on at practice that afternoon instead of paying attention to my cases. Practicing law was work. Coaching Jim was play.

John was also a good vaulter, but he didn't enjoy it the way Jimmy did. Music and theater were more important to John, and he gave up pole vaulting after his junior year. I regretted that I couldn't maintain that common interest with John the way I had with Jimmy, but all kids are different. We all have to march to our own drummer, and I didn't try to pressure him to change his mind. I would have been miserable if someone forced me to sing in the high school choir instead of playing sports, and I understood that music was where John found his pleasure.

I thought I was out of the sport permanently, but then in Mary's junior year Michigan introduced pole vaulting for girls, and I was back in business. Kind of. That year the school hired a pole vaulting coach, so I didn't have the same involvement with her as I had with the boys. My biggest frustration with her was that she just wasn't running. Vaulting is a speed event, and she was jogging down the runway. She thought she was sprinting, but she wasn't. Finally one day at practice I told her I was going to race her when she jumped. I was wearing a suit and dress shoes, but I picked up a pole and told her that I would run beside her when she jumped, and that I planned to outrun her.

Mary has a competitive streak, and the thought of an old man in a business suit outrunning her was more than she wanted to endure. When a few of her teammates stopped to watch there was no way she was going to let me beat her. It was close, but she did beat me as I remember, and for the first time she learned what it felt like to really sprint with the pole. She was almost unbeatable after that, and ended up finishing second in the state finals that year. During her senior year the school's pole vaulting coach got involved with other things, and I gradually became as involved with her training as I had been with the boys. She still holds the school record.

Ultimately I think Mary got more out of the sport than either of her brothers. Until she started vaulting her only sport was soccer, and she was an indifferent soccer player at best. She was more interested in socializing with her teammates than she was in soccer, and she didn't think she was good at it. But when she became successful with pole vaulting I saw a whole new girl start to blossom. When she first tried out she told me that she didn't expect to be good enough to make the team. But she did make the team, and at her first meet she won first place against two other schools. I don't think I have seen her more excited either before or since. It was as if a whole new world had opened up for her. She found something that she was very good at, and she knew she was good at it. She rarely lost during the next two years, and it left her with a confidence and a sense of accomplishment that has stuck with her to this day. The only person who enjoyed it more than she did was her father.

Chapter Twenty-Seven

ost of the doctors that I sued over the years were good doctors. Making a mistake doesn't mean you are a bad doctor. Everyone makes mistakes. They should take responsibility for their mistakes, which is why I file suit, but it doesn't make them bad doctors. On two occasions I have even gone to doctors for treatment after suing them. That may be surprising, but even more surprising is that they agreed to treat me. It just goes to prove that, while many doctors take this process very personally, the best ones don't. Good doctors understand that they are not infallible, and when they make a mistake they usually figure it out for themselves long before I get involved.

A few years ago I sued a very good general surgeon who accidentally clamped off an artery to the liver while performing gall bladder surgery. The case was aggressively defended, as they all are, claiming that the patient suffered another unrelated emergency, and that the destroyed liver had nothing to do with her death. But deep down the doctor knew better, and when the case finally settled on the eve of trial he asked to speak to me privately. Surprisingly, his attorney let him do it.

We met in a conference room at the courthouse, and it was immediately obvious that this death was haunting him. He didn't want to think that he had killed my client's mother, but deep down he knew he had, and he wanted the family to know how sorry he was. I don't routinely console the doctors I sue, but I did this time. He would save many lives during his career, but part of the price he would pay was the knowledge that he had also taken some lives along the way, because you probably can't perform surgery day after day without a few catastrophic mistakes. Most he would get away with, but a few would be deadly.

I analogized surgery to the years I spent in the Air Force. I told him, and I suspect it is not far from the truth, that I never flew a mission without making a potentially fatal mistake. But the stars were never aligned against me, and I always got away with it. You just try to be as careful as you can, and make as few mistakes as possible, and then you have to be able to forgive yourself when you fail. Afterwards he apologized directly to my client, and she forgave him. I think they both found the tragedy easier to live with after that.

Although most doctors are very good, I have seen some notable exceptions. A few were truly incompetent, including a neurosurgeon who had never been able to hold a job, repeatedly failed the test to become board certified, lost his operating privileges at several hospitals, and left a long trail of malpractice suits before he injured my client while performing a neck fusion. Before he even got to the vertebrae he accidentally tore the esophagus, leaving my client unable to eat solid food without gagging. His life really was a misery.

For once I was almost looking forward to the liability aspect of a case. This doctor's record was so bad that I couldn't wait to cross examine him regarding all the exams he had failed, all the hospitals that had fired him, and all the patients he had injured. But I still needed an expert to testify that he violated the standard of care in this case, and for one of the few times in my career another local neurosurgeon agreed to provide that testimony. Everything looked good until a couple of days before trial when my expert suddenly decided that he was too busy to testify, and without his testimony my case would be thrown out before it ever got to a jury.

I was desperate when I showed up for a pretrial hearing the next day, and then the heavens smiled on me. The defense lawyer knew that his client's history was going to be a disaster, and the only way for him to keep that out of evidence was to admit negligence. So he told the judge that he would admit malpractice, but deny that my client was injured. With the admission of negligence I no longer needed an expert. It was like having an enemy soldier surrender while you're holding an empty gun. I never told the defense lawyer that all he had to do was hang in there for one more day and the case would have gone away. In thirty years of trying medical malpractice cases that was the only time a defendant admitted liability, and it couldn't have come at a better time.

But I still had to prove that my client had a serious injury that prevented him from swallowing normally. The trial was interesting because the surgeon's malpractice insurance company hired a private investigator to follow my client around for weeks, hoping to get pictures of him eating without difficulty. Eventually they trailed him to Burger King, and videotaped him eating in his car. The defense lawyer dropped the tape on me just a week before trial, and the first couple of times I looked at it I thought we were in big trouble. My client claimed that he always choked when he ate, but there was no choking on this tape.

But after looking at it for the fourth or fifth time I suddenly realized that there was a clock on the tape, and it didn't run continuously. There were some gaps that weren't noticeable unless you looked at the clock, and obviously the tape had been spliced to eliminate the gagging episodes. It would stop with my client's head in one position, and start up again when he was back in that position, but with significant time missing. It was done skillfully, but why they didn't do something about the clock I'll never know. I ran the tape in slow motion for the jury, and had them watch the clock, and I think the case was pretty much over when they saw that.

My children claim that my job makes me see danger everywhere, and keeps me from trusting anyone. It's not quite that bad, but they have a point. I have handled so many motorcycle accidents that I wouldn't ride one on a bet. If you ride a motorcycle it is just a matter of time. And while I respect doctors I don't really trust them. I always review my own lab results, and I never take a drug without reading the package insert. Actually I do trust doctors. It just never hurts to double check. Over the years I have had three cases in which doctors diagnosed cancer, but then forgot to notify their patients. In each case the patient only learned of the diagnosis months later after the cancer had grown beyond the point of being treatable.

Some of the doctors that I've sued had problems that went far beyond their medical ability. Dr. Kleeman was one of those. He had been a binge drinker since he was in college, and it only got worse over time. By the time Cathy Amerson met him the hospital had already sent him to rehab once or twice, but now he was back working in the obstetrical clinic. On the night Cathy went into labor Dr. Kleeman was the obstetrician on call.

As soon as Cathy and her husband saw Dr. Kleeman they knew something was seriously wrong. He wasn't just a little tipsy; he could barely stand up. First he slapped her for making too much noise, and then he fell onto the instrument cart, sending everything sprawling. They asked the nursing staff for another doctor, but were told that he was the only one available. Later the nurses testified that their evaluation of Dr. Kleeman was about the same as the Amerson's, but there wasn't anything they could do about it. The baby was coming, and Dr. Kleeman was the only doctor they had.

Fortunately the baby was born healthy, but the episiotomy was a disaster, and the damage was permanent. To the hospital's credit it then fired Dr. Kleeman, apparently concluding that one more trip to rehab wasn't likely to be of much help. But as is usually the case with incompetent or impaired physicians, he just picked up and started a practice elsewhere. After a couple of years in New York he moved to Delaware. They can always find a job somewhere.

The night before the Amerson case went to trial I walked over to the courthouse at four p.m. to get copies of the jury questionnaires that prospective jurors fill out when they are selected for jury duty. When I started practicing law thirty years ago there was lots of information on those questionnaires. By reading them carefully a lawyer had a pretty good idea of who that person was before ever asking him a single question. We also had a good idea as to who might favor our client, and who might favor the defense.

But over the years the questionnaires have grown shorter and shorter, to the point that they are now next to useless. I still read them, but I'm not sure why. I was thinking about that as I read through the questionnaires for the Amerson jury. "They don't even give us their address anymore," I grumbled. "The only information we have is the town where they live." With that, I started flipping through them, looking at the towns where they came from. And then it struck me that there was something really odd about this jury.

The City of Kalamazoo has a population of roughly eighty thousand, about one third of the county. Richland is a small residential community north of Kalamazoo, with a population of around five hundred. But of the thirty-five potential jurors for my case, five lived in Richland, and only one lived in Kalamazoo. The rest came from either the surrounding farms, or from the City of Portage, an affluent bedroom community south of Kalamazoo. The City of Kalamazoo is the only Democratic stronghold in the county, and is also the home of most of the county's black population. If you exclude the City of Kalamazoo from the jury pool you are left with a very conservative all white jury, favorable for the prosecution in criminal cases, and for defendants in civil cases. Somebody was stacking this jury with conservative white jurors, I just didn't know who or how.

The criminal defense attorneys had complained about Kalamazoo juries for years. They knew that there were no blacks on the jury panels, but they had never been able to prove actual discrimination. Every challenge had gone down in failure, and most of the lawyers had given up trying. The next morning before trial I had coffee at a local restaurant frequented by attorneys, and I got nothing but laughter when I told them I was going to get this jury panel disqualified. "Good luck," was the usual response.

When the judge called our case that morning, I told him what I had discovered, and asked to have the jury panel replaced with one that was representative of the county. The judge had also been through many of these challenges, and his response was similar to what I had received earlier from my attorney friends. Many have tried, and many have failed, he told me, but he did grant a brief recess to allow me to go upstairs to talk to the jury clerk to determine how the jurors had been selected. The clerk's office, I discovered, was in the prosecutor's office. And this jury was a prosecutor's dream.

Every challenge in the past had been to the racial makeup of the jury, but try as they might they could never identify any official act of racial discrimination. My focus was different. The clerk wasn't excluding blacks; he was excluding the city where

blacks lived, and in the process he was also excluding most Democrats and most of the Western Michigan University population. Now all I had to figure out was how he was doing it.

The answer wasn't long in coming. In addition to the circuit court, where all felonies and serious civil cases were tried, the city also had four district courts for misdemeanors and traffic offenses. The actual mechanics of the jury selection process were somewhat complicated, but the bottom line was that all of the City of Kalamazoo jurors were being funneled to district court. That left only white conservative jurors to serve on the serious cases in circuit court. It was a blatant violation of both federal and state requirements that juries be selected at random from all segments of the community.

When I returned to the courtroom with my discovery the judge adjourned the trial while he tried to decide what to do next. Eventually the entire court system was closed down for a month until new jury panels were selected to accurately reflect the county's population. In the meantime we settled the Amerson's case. The insurance company was happy to try that case in front of the first jury. They were much less interested in trying it in front of a randomly selected jury.

That wasn't quite the end of the matter, however. The next day I was back in the courthouse to file some papers, and when I looked in the courtroom I saw the same judge swearing in that same jury to hear a felony case against an alleged drug dealer. Jim Hills was the defense lawyer, and after the court recessed for the day I told Jim that a day earlier I had gotten that same jury disqualified by the same judge. Eventually the criminal case was adjourned also, and a visiting judge was brought in to decide what to do with it. After hearing all the evidence the visiting judge agreed that the jury selection was unconstitutional. Additionally he ruled that all the charges against the drug dealer had to be dismissed under the theory of double jeopardy because both the judge and the prosecutor had participated in the misconduct. They both knew the jury was illegal, but were more than willing to swear in the jury without revealing what they knew to the defendant or his attorney. I wasn't very popular in the courthouse for a while after that.

In the long run it was a Pyrrhic victory. That all took place fifteen years ago, and there are still almost no blacks on Kalamazoo County juries, even though blacks make up twenty percent of the county's population. We have city residents on juries now, but almost no blacks. And I have no idea how they're doing it. Maybe it's just a coincidence. I believe in coincidences now more than I used to. Some years ago I had an appointment with a new client I had never met before. Mike Reynolds was a local small businessman who wanted to start a malpractice claim against a radiologist for failing to recognize an obvious wrist fracture. He made an early morning appointment to show me his medical records and his x-rays.

While he was sitting in my office my secretary knocked on the door to tell Mike that one of his customers was asking for him on our private telephone line. Mike looked stunned, telling me that he had not told anyone he was coming to my office that morning. Plus neither he nor anyone else knew the number for that private line. Eventually we figured out that our private phone number was just one digit off from Mike's business phone number, and the customer had accidentally misdialed our number at the very time that Mike was sitting in my office for his first visit. If that can happen, anything can happen.

On the other hand, coincidences don't happen every day. Sometimes you have reason to be suspicious. Whenever I investigate a possible medical malpractice case one of my first acts is to order a copy of my client's hospital chart. Most cases are won or lost based on what is in that chart. My client can say anything, but if it isn't documented no one is going to convince any jury that the hospital record is wrong. For the first few years I ordered hospital charts, and assumed that what they sent me was complete. Then I got involved in a death case of a woman who died of a heart attack a few days after being hospitalized for chest pains. The hospital had sent her home, and its defense was that they had given her a heart stress test that came back as totally normal. How could I blame them for not running more tests after she passed something like that with flying colors? And, indeed, the hospital chart had a report saying that the cardiologist found no abnormalities during the stress test.

Somewhere in the middle of that case I had reason to be in the hospital, and while I was there I asked to see my client's original chart. When I looked through it I discovered that they had sent me every record except one. The one page they left out had the handwritten notes of the stress test, and those notes stated that because of my client's arthritis she had been unable to get her heart rate high enough to run a meaningful test. It was true that her test was normal so far as it went, but as a medical screening test it was absolutely useless. So in effect they then sent her home with chest pains without having any idea if they were heart related or not. When I asked why they had not sent me that page along with the other records the hospital representative shrugged her shoulders, and said it must have been an oversight.

It might have been an oversight, but once bitten, twice shy. The next case I had with that hospital concerned an elderly woman who was sent directly from the hospital to a nursing home. Within a few hours of her arrival she wandered out the back door of the nursing home and froze to death in the snow. She was clearly somewhat senile, but the nursing home denied that it had any knowledge about that, and nothing showed up in the records that I received from either the nursing home or the hospital. So once again I asked to see the hospital's original chart. Hospital charts often run for several hundred pages, and there is no way to go through them except one page at a time. It can be a laborious process, but when I did that I once again discovered that when the chart was copied they just happened to leave out the five page transfer record. One of those pages warned the nursing home that she was senile, and needed to be either restrained or monitored, because she was not safe if left unattended.

Again the hospital representative was apologetic, saying that the omission must have been just an innocent oversight, and promised to mail me a copy of the transfer record the next day. And a couple of days later I did receive the transfer record, or at least four fifths of it. This time they left out the one page that said the patient had to be closely monitored. Not until my third request did I finally receive the one page that would make or break the case. And I suppose it could have been just a coincidence, but since then I have always made it a point to look at the original record, and more often than not I find they have sent me everything except the one or two pages that are most critical. It might just be a coincidence, but that's probably not the way to bet. As my children say, I don't trust anyone.

Chapter Twenty-Eight

I didn't win every case, but over the years I either settled or won most of the cases I filed, because I tried to be extremely careful to only take cases that were legitimate. All competent trial lawyers follow that rule. Taking a case that is frivolous is a short road to the poor house. Insurance companies like to make noise about frivolous cases, but any lawyer who takes one is a fool. He won't win, and he will lose a lot of time and money in the process. There are fools in this profession, but they don't stay around long.

Unfortunately I don't always know how strong a case is when I start it. Doctors won't talk to a lawyer voluntarily before suit is filed, and the medical records can be misleading, because they often reflect only the tip of the iceberg. Once I start taking depositions I begin to learn all that facts that they didn't put into the record, and those facts can change the picture dramatically. Some cases that look weak initially suddenly turn into winners, and some apparent winners go up in smoke.

A few of the cases that I lost were lost because the facts changed as the case progressed, but other losses were cases that any law school student should have been able to win. Those are the cases that remind us what a gamble it is to walk into a courtroom. There is often no rhyme or reason for what juries believe, or how they think. But as unpredictable as they are, I would never give up the right to trial by jury, because trial by judge is even more unpredictable. There are as many nutty judges as there are nutty jurors, and with juries the numbers tend to have a moderating effect. One bad judge can do great damage, but one bad juror is usually neutralized by the other jurors.

Still, there are times when entire juries come up with decisions that are beyond all comprehension. Think O.J. Simpson as an example, and unfortunately there are more O.J. Simpson juries out there than we might like to believe.

Barbara Collins was a sixty-five year old woman who lived in Paw Paw, about fifteen miles west of Kalamazoo. She had a long history of heart problems which culminated in a heart attack one evening just before midnight. Her husband rushed her to the local hospital in Paw Paw, and from there they called Dr. Winter, her cardiologist in Kalamazoo, to request instructions. The hospital in Paw Paw wasn't equipped to treat a heart attack, so Dr. Winter ordered a helicopter to fly her to Kalamazoo where he would be waiting.

When they arrived in Kalamazoo they were met by a young resident, but there was no sign of Dr. Winter. The resident ordered blood work and a series of other tests, but did nothing to actually treat the heart attack. An hour went by, and then another, and then another, and the family was still waiting. Finally in desperation her daughter requested a transfer to another hospital where she hoped to actually get some treatment for her mother. When that request was made the hospital called Dr. Winter who finally did show up about six hours after the heart attack had started, but by then the damage was done. Mrs. Collins survived the initial episode, but suffered substantial damage, and died of heart failure six months later.

The trial followed a familiar pattern. A parade of defense experts testified that Dr. Winter and the hospital followed the standard of care in all respects. It was necessary to perform hours of testing before treating a heart attack. Cardiologists can't run to the hospital to see every heart attack patient, because if they did they would never get any rest. Besides, the resident did everything just as well as the cardiologist would have. While there may be drugs, and stents, and various surgeries to treat heart attacks, the standard of care doesn't require a physician to do any of those things. They are purely optional. The only thing the standard of care requires is bed rest. So long as the resident put Mrs. Collins in bed he fulfilled all of his professional obligations, and if she died it wasn't his fault. And then finally the "so what" defense. So what if Dr. Winter and the resident violated the standard of care? It didn't make any difference because she was going to die anyway.

Dr. Winter testified that he was waiting by the telephone that night, monitoring and directing her care from home, and that he was prepared to come in as soon as all of the tests were completed. Furthermore, the resident did everything Dr. Winter would have done if he had been there himself. Mrs. Collins' death was regrettable, but certainly not the result of substandard medical care.

Hostile doctors can be very difficult witnesses for a lawyer to manage, but I looked forward to the chance to cross examine Dr. Winter, and it didn't require any great oratorical skills, or even much imagination. Dr. Winter had talked to the family that night after he finally did arrive at the hospital, but what he didn't know was that they had tape recorded the meeting. And what he said that night bore no resemblance to his testimony under oath.

When Dr. Winter arrived at the hospital he checked on Mrs. Collins, and then met with her husband and two of her adult daughters in a hospital conference room. One of them had a small tape recorder, and taped the conversation so they would be able to remember what he said. He told them that after the initial phone call he had gone back to sleep, expecting that the hospital would call him when her helicopter arrived. But no one did call until several hours later when the family requested a transfer, and by the time he got to the hospital too much time had elapsed to successfully reopen the blocked artery. He was also upset with the resident. He told the family that the resident should have known how to treat a heart attack, and that his lack of care was not up to acceptable standards for a major hospital. He also promised them that the resident would never again ignore a patient in their mother's condition. Finally, he told them that the lack of care had caused significant heart damage, and that only time would tell how serious it would be. When I played the tape for the jury I expected that the case would be over, especially after the doctor had told a completely different story from the witness stand.

What I didn't take into consideration was the overwhelming public perception that doctors are the victims in malpractice suits. Most jurors in these cases have great sympathy for the doctor before they ever hear a word of testimony, and we all tend to hear what we want to hear. It takes an extraordinarily strong case to overcome that prejudice. I felt certain that the doctor's confession on tape would be enough, but I thought wrong. In short order the jury returned a verdict that neither the doctor nor the hospital had done anything wrong. The family got nothing.

I always talk to jurors after a trial, whether I win or lose, and I inevitably learn something that I can use the next time around. When I talked to this jury I discovered that they weren't impressed with the doctor's confession of malpractice on the tape, and they weren't impressed that he had lied in his testimony. But they were very upset that the family had secretly tape recorded him, and they weren't about to award compensation to anyone who would do something like that. They started the trial wanting to put an end to frivolous lawsuits, and the secret tape was enough for them to conclude that Dr. Winter was the real victim.

A few years later I tried another case against a hand surgeon who severed my client's median nerve while performing carpal tunnel surgery. The median nerve is the main nerve to the hand, and this was a devastating injury for her. She had no effective use of the hand, and the unrelenting pain was so severe that she was contemplating amputation.

At trial the surgeon testified that he didn't know how he could have cut the nerve, although he admitted that he did it. He looked at my client sitting beside me, and told her in front of the jury that he wanted to publicly apologize to her. He said that he had no excuse for cutting the nerve, and that he accepted responsibility for it. He tried to be a good doctor, but this operation had gone terribly wrong.

It was a brilliant ploy. The jury was out less than an hour before finding him not responsible for the injury. When I spoke with the jurors after the trial they were unanimous on one thing. They refused to find the doctor guilty of malpractice just because he made one mistake. It is an attitude that I had seen before. Jurors would have little hesitation in finding against A. J. Foyt if he rear ended one car in his life, but doctors have a special status. Jurors are very reluctant to enter a verdict against a doctor unless they believe he is so incompetent that he shouldn't be practicing medicine at all.

That isn't the law, but it is the burden that plaintiffs usually must overcome, and it is a very heavy burden.

Perhaps my most painful loss was a case that I took all the way to the U.S. Supreme Court, for free. It was a pro bono case that I accepted from West Michigan Legal Aid, and it was worse than just for free. Before it was over I spent thousands of dollars of my own money for filing fees and court reporters, but it was a case that someone had to take.

Antoine Jennings was a Western Michigan University college student when President George W. Bush made an appearance here a few months after his first inauguration. At that time Democrats were still up in arms over the belief that the election had been stolen by the Republican members of the U. S. Supreme Court, and the administration was determined to avoid any public displays of opposition. So before the President arrived the Secret Service ordered the Western Michigan University Police Department to arrest anyone who displayed a protest sign along the parade route. Antoine was the first person arrested, and he needed someone to represent him when the case went to trial. I had not defended a criminal case in many years, but the facts of this case were so egregious that I agreed to take it.

Antoine was actually arrested several hours before the motorcade arrived on campus, but crowds were already beginning to gather, including Antoine and several other members of the Young Democrats, most of them carrying signs. Antoine's sign read "Welcome to Western Governor Bush." It was a not so subtle suggestion that, but for the stealing of the election, Bush should still be the Governor of Texas instead of President of the United States. The Secret Service understood the message, and told the WMU police to do something about it.

When the police officers confronted Antoine they told him that he had two choices. If he wanted to stay along the parade route he had to get rid of the sign. If he wanted to keep his sign he had to go behind a building where no one would be able to see him. Otherwise he would be arrested for trespassing on a public street. When Antoine objected that he had a Constitutional right to protest he was arrested. Seeing what had happened to Antoine, his friends then left, but not before the Secret Service confiscated and destroyed some of their signs.

Kalamazoo wasn't the first town where the Secret Service directed the arrest of protestors during presidential visits, but in all other cities the protestors were only held until the President left town. Then they were released, and the charges were dropped. But Kalamazoo County was a conservative Republican area, with an aggressive prosecutor, and he decided to go for a conviction.

The right to protest is of course protected by the Constitution, and by many Supreme Court opinions. In the early 1970s Richard Nixon tried to prohibit anyone from protesting the Vietnam War in his presence, and the Supreme Court repeatedly found the arrests to be illegal. In 1993 Bill Clinton's advisors wanted protestors to be banned from his inaugural parade down Pennsylvania Avenue, and that was also found to be illegal. The only exception is if the protest presents a physical threat to the safety of the President, and certainly there was no one who could think that Antoine was a physical threat. Well, almost no one.

The arresting officer, Captain Castor, testified that he arrested Antoine for yelling and screaming, and disturbing the peace. But once again I had a secret videotape of the arrest made by one of Antoine's friends, and the tape clearly showed that the officer was lying. Antoine had been quiet and cooperative, and this time the jury believed the videotape instead of the officer's testimony. He was acquitted of disorderly conduct, but that still left the prosecutor with the claim that Antoine was a physical threat to the President.

The problem with that claim was that Antoine carried only a paper sign, and even the arresting officers said that he was not a physical danger. He was arrested only because the Secret Service demanded it. In fact, there was no witness who testified that Antoine was a threat to anyone, and I was confident that the jury would also decide that fact in Antoine's favor. He was clearly guilty of nothing except exercising his Constitutional rights.

I have no doubt that the jury would have found Antoine to be no threat to the President if they had been given a chance to decide that issue, but they never got that chance. In criminal cases there is always a right to trial by jury, but not for Antoine. Judge Ann Hannon declared that in this case she intended to be the finder of fact because the case involved Constitutional issues, and it was her conclusion that a criminal defendant is not entitled to have a jury decide factual issues relating to Constitutional rights. So she alone would decide if Antoine was a threat to the President. Not surprisingly, she concluded that he was a threat. In a written opinion she wrote that she disagreed with the testimony of the arresting officers who said he wasn't a threat. In her opinion the small sign that Antoine held could have distracted the President's limo driver as the motorcade drove by, and Antoine therefore had no Constitutional right to hold the sign on a public street. If he was standing on the sidewalk with a sign he was guilty.

I was stunned by the decision, but I had no doubt that it would be reversed on appeal. After all, it denied Antoine both his Constitutional right to protest, and his Constitutional right to trial by jury. I remained confident even after the conviction was upheld by the local circuit court. I even retained some hope after the Michigan Court of Appeals and the Michigan Supreme Court ruled that the case was not important enough for them to even consider an appeal. But there was no hope when the U.S. Supreme Court also ruled that it was too busy to consider this case. So now Antoine has a permanent criminal record for trespassing.

A few months after this case was decided the American Civil Liberties Union filed suit against the Secret Service, challenging similar arrests in other states. Before the case got to trial the Secret Service admitted that the practice was unconstitutional, and entered into a voluntary agreement to cease and desist. But Antoine's conviction stands, and he remains possibly the only person in the country to have a criminal record because of the Secret Service's illegal conduct. And I did not have the legal skill to do anything about it. It is just one example of how the politics of judges can trump any facts or any law. We call ourselves a country of laws, and not men, but it is a false boast. So long as men interpret the laws their biases will mean more than the Constitution or any law passed by the legislature.

Chapter Twenty-Nine

Insurance companies use shady tactics because there is virtually no penalty when they get caught. Usually the worst that happens is that they have to pay what they owe, and if the tactics work they pay nothing. Over the years I had grown to expect almost anything from corporate defendants and insurance companies, but I naively assumed that the U. S. Justice Department would play by different rules. Then I met Trent Long. Trent was a young boy whose hands were severely scalded by tap water at the Fort Huachuca Army base in Arizona when he was two years old. I represented Trent, and sued the Army for maintaining water temperatures that were far higher than they should have been. Many federal regulations specify that water temperatures in residential housing should not exceed one hundred twenty degrees, and the water in Trent's residence was at least thirty degrees hotter than that. At those temperatures skin will scald in only a few seconds.

Suits against the Army must be filed in federal court, and are defended by the local U.S. Attorney. This case was defended by the U.S. Attorney for the Western District of Michigan, and soon after the case was filed I arranged to fly out to Arizona with an engineering expert to examine the water heater that caused the injury. The U.S. Attorney scheduled the examination, but left the supervision to the army's attorneys who were stationed at the base.

I met my expert at the Phoenix airport, and rented a car to drive to Ft. Huachuca where we were greeted by two army attorneys who had been assigned as our escorts. It was noon, so they invited us to join them for lunch at the officer's club before we conducted our inspection. They had some knowledge of the case, but not a lot, and we spent about an hour in casual conversation before going to officer housing where Trent's father had lived while he was stationed there.

The home where Trent was burned was a large old two story wooden home that probably dated back to the days of the Indian Wars. The water heater was located in a shed attached to the back of the home, and was locked so that only the base engineers had access to it. Our two attorney escorts had a key to the padlock so my expert could get in, and as soon as he took the cover off the water heater he told me that the thermostat was brand new, and had obviously been replaced since the date of the injury. The two attorneys shrugged their shoulders to indicate their ignorance of any such change. They were just there to show us around.

Without the original thermostat the whole trip was pretty much a waste of time. I was discussing what to do when the current resident came home for a late lunch. I caught him walking into the house, and asked him if anyone had worked on the water heater recently. "Yea," he said, "they came out yesterday and replaced the thermostat, but I don't know why."

As soon as he told me that, the feigned ignorance of the army's attorneys was abandoned. They admitted that they knew about the change in thermostats, but also had no idea why the change had been made. We then drove over to the base engineers to ask why they had changed the thermostat, but no one had an answer there either. The reason for the change was as much of a mystery to them as it was to us. Maybe we were just unlucky that we hadn't arrived a day earlier.

Despite being unable to test the water heater, the case remained strong. We knew that the water temperature was far higher than the Army's own regulations allowed, and Trent had significant functional and cosmetic injuries. Over the next year we exchanged the names of experts, took depositions, and provided all of Trent's medical history to the U.S. Attorney who would try the case. Then shortly before trial the U.S. Attorney hit us with a surprise motion to add additional experts, and to require Trent to be seen by a burn specialist at the University of Michigan. The U.S. Attorney said she needed to add these additional experts because of new information that had just come to her attention.

She told the court that she had recently submitted Trent's photographs to three independent plastic surgeons around the country, who all came to the same conclusion; the burns could not have been an accident. According to these experts, the only way an infant could be burned like that was if his mother deliberately held his hands under scalding water. Faced with that new allegation the judge granted the U.S. Attorney's motion, and suddenly the whole complexion of the case changed. I was now as worried about defending the mother as I was about pursuing the case against the army. The best defense is often a good offense, and this new claim rocked me back on my heels.

Trent was examined by the burn specialist at the University of Michigan, and then we waited for the U.S. Attorney to send us a copy of his report as required by the Federal Court Rules. A couple of weeks later she sent me that report, and it largely confirmed the opinions of the three independent experts. He didn't come right out and allege that the mother deliberately scalded her son, but he did say that the burn patterns were consistent with that kind of an injury. My case was in serious trouble.

The next step was to take the depositions of the three new plastic surgeons who had all independently concluded that Trent was intentionally burned. But before I did that I arranged for the mother to take a polygraph exam at the Kalamazoo County Sheriff's Department. Polygraphs are not admissible in court, but they are still probably the most reliable test we have to determine if someone is lying. I believed her when she told me that she had not scalded her son, but I felt a lot better when the polygraph operator told me that she passed the test convincingly.

Shortly thereafter I flew down to Miami to take the deposition of the first plastic surgeon. The U.S. Attorney had received permission to add these three experts by telling the judge that she had only discovered their opinions late in the case, and it didn't take me long to discover that that claim wasn't close to the truth. Nor was it true that the three plastic surgeons had independently concluded that the burn patterns showed an intentional injury. The doctor readily admitted that when I originally filed the case all three plastic surgeons were army doctors stationed at Walter Reed Hospital in Washington D.C.. When the Army asked them to help prepare a defense the three of them sat down together and came up with the argument that the burns could have been intentional. Contrary to what the U.S. Attorney had represented to the court, they weren't three experts who independently came up with the same opinion, and the opinion wasn't new. The U.S. Attorney had known about it for years, but by the time the U.S. Attorney disclosed these experts to the judge they had all left the Army, and had taken up practice in various parts of the country.

I thought the U.S. Attorney might be in trouble with the judge for misrepresenting where these experts came from, but I soon had evidence that was even more damning when I asked to see the doctor's file. Going through his records I found the report from the burn specialist at the University of Michigan, and a copy of his cover letter to the U.S. Attorney. To be more accurate, I found two reports. In the cover letter the University of Michigan doctor told the U.S. Attorney that he was sending her two different reports. The first report, for her eyes only, said that he did not think this was an intentional injury. The second report, for her to file with the court, said the burns were consistent with an intentional injury.

I don't think any insurance company lawyer would have made that mistake. He would never send a smoking gun like that to his other experts, and if he did he would remove it from the file before I started the deposition. But U.S. Attorneys don't handle many civil suits, and I can only presume that it never occurred to her that I would ask to see the doctor's file. One thing that was pretty clear, however, was that she could never go to trial after lying to the judge, and she quickly made a settlement offer that was substantially higher than what I had hoped for when the case began. Crime often pays, but not always.

Chapter Thirty

The last Ford to live in Hillsdale was my Grandmother Leithel, and she left almost thirty years ago, but occasionally I took my kids to Hillsdale to visit the family cemetery, or to show them the old family farm. I didn't expect any of them to go to college there, but they knew that Hillsdale had a special significance in our family's history, and during John's senior year in high school he surprised me by indicating that he had an interest in going to Hillsdale College. He was dating Beverly that year, and during the winter they both skipped school one day without permission. They missed school, they missed dinner, they missed play practice that evening, and Hattie and I were alarmed, as were Bev's parents. Finally they showed up around eight o'clock in the evening, and naturally we wanted to know where they had been.

They told us that they were both considering where to attend college, and had taken the day off to tour the campus at Hillsdale. Bev's parents bought that story. I didn't. I asked John if he had picked up any literature while he was there, but he said he hadn't. Like any good lawyer I had some follow up questions. "A whole day is a long time to tour that campus. What else did you do?" He said he had taken Beverly out to show her the old family farm. "That's nice. I sometimes have trouble finding that farm. What road is it on?" John said he couldn't remember the name of the road, but he knew how to get there. "Really?" I handed him a sheet of paper. "Draw me a map."

Not one to give up easily John drew a box at the top of the page, marked "college," and a straight line to an "X" at the bottom marked "farm." "Not even close," I told him.

"Now where were you?" He then confessed that they had spent the day in Chicago. That I could believe.

When Jim said he wanted to attend college at Hillsdale he was serious. He spent one year at Michigan State and decided that a big school just wasn't for him. I encouraged him to look at Albion College, but a sense of history made him lean towards Hillsdale instead. By then Hillsdale had become a far more conservative bastion than it was when my parents attended, but it is a good school, and if that's where Jim wanted to go I didn't try to discourage him. He was admitted for the winter semester in 1997.

When the college moved to Hillsdale in the eighteen fifties my Great-Great Grandfather Darwin donated stones and lumber to help construct Central Hall. In return the college gave him a "Perpetual Scholarship" guaranteeing the holder of the certificate free tuition forever for one pupil at a time. That certificate has been handed down from generation to generation, and was in my possession when I took Jim to Hillsdale to enroll in January 1997. But the certificate had not sat dormant all those years. Many members of the family had attended Hillsdale College over the previous hundred and fifty years, and all of them used that certificate, but I knew that the college had stopped honoring it early in the Twentieth Century. The generations who attended after that were only given a token three dollar credit towards their tuition, three dollars being the value of tuition when the certificate was first issued. On the other hand, it did say free tuition forever. When it came time to pay for Jim's tuition I offered the certificate instead.

The business manager said that she had never seen a certificate such as this, but that it looked valid to her. So she accepted it subject to approval by the college administration. A week later I received a letter from the vice president for finance advising me that the administration did not approve. He explained that the college trustees who issued the certificate had not considered the effects of inflation, and that, "The trustees of a later era found it necessary to revoke the previous decision." This started a series of letters back and forth regarding the ability of the college to revoke a certificate issued in perpetuity for value received. I didn't think they could. The vice president argued otherwise.

The vice president presented several rationales for his position. One was the effect of inflation, another was that honoring the certificate was commercially impracticable, and a third was that tuition had a different meaning in the nineteenth century than it has today. Back then, he argued, tuition only covered a portion of the student fees, instead of the full cost of admission as it does today. I was in no position to argue that point, but the certificate did say "free tuition forever." It didn't say free tuition as calculated in eighteen-fifty.

Little by little we moved towards a compromise. The vice president offered a twenty-five percent reduction off Jim's tuition if I surrendered the certificate. I proposed a fifty percent reduction without surrender. I also suggested the possibility of arbitrating the dispute as an alternative to litigation. Eventually we settled on a compromise that seemed to me to be better than my initial offer. The college agreed to honor the certificate for all of Jim's tuition for as long as he attended the college if I agreed to cancel the certificate when he graduated. I had some concern that I was selling out future generations, but not enough to pass up thousands of dollars of savings in the short run. I also thought it unlikely that there would be any more Fords interested in attending Hillsdale. Most of my extended family has now migrated to other parts of the country, and there are few connections left with Michigan, much less Hillsdale.

So at Jim's graduation I cancelled the certificate, and presented it to the vice president just as I promised, hoping that Great-Great-Grandfather Darwin and all future generations would forgive me. I suspect they will. What I didn't tell the vice president was that Darwin received two "Perpetual Scholarships." I still have one in reserve. It was a Pyrrhic victory though, and the College got the last laugh. They turned this young man, with so much potential, into a committed free market conservative, and not even my best efforts have been able to deprogram him.

Chapter Thirty-One

The law is full of convenient fictions. Sometimes life is easier if we just ignore reality, and choose to believe whatever we want to believe, and the law is no different. Courts don't allow the use of polygraphs, because they aren't foolproof, but they do allow juries to determine a witness's credibility, despite numerous studies that have convincingly demonstrated that most of us are very bad at recognizing when someone is lying. At the end of every trial the judge instructs the jury on the law, and we pretend that juries understand and remember all of those instructions even though lawyers themselves can argue for hours over the meaning of many of them. I don't have a solution for those dilemmas, but I know from painful experience that juries usually have only a vague understanding of the legal standards they are asked to apply.

Another fiction is that eye witnesses are reliable. An eye witness will usually trump objective evidence any day. If a crime victim picks you out of a lineup it's time to start packing your bags, because life is going to be very unpleasant for the foreseeable future. When the witness says, "He did it," your goose is just about cooked. Clever lawyers in years gone by countered that testimony by having an imposter sit next to them at the counsel table, and more often than not the victim would confidently identify the imposter as the person who committed the crime. It happened so often that the Michigan Supreme Court finally declared that it was unethical for a lawyer to use an imposter. It was simply too difficult to get a conviction when the eye witness looked like a fool, and the Supreme Court wasn't about to tolerate that.

It isn't just that eye witnesses occasionally lie; the bigger problem is that they often have no real idea what they saw. When I was quite young, a high school teacher asked me to help her conduct an experiment in one of her classes. She smeared ketchup on my arm, and had me rush into her classroom in a panic saying that I had cut myself. I stayed for a short time before she ushered me out. Then she went back in and asked her class to write down what they had just seen. They had to describe what I looked like, and repeat what I had said. Most of them had no idea what I was wearing, and only the vaguest memory of what I had said. They all thought they knew, but were more often wrong than right.

I remembered that exercise years later while representing a woman who suffered a significant arm injury when her husband drove in front of a train at a downtown crossing. Unsure of just how the accident occurred I filed suit against both the husband and the railroad. I didn't expect that the case would be too difficult to figure out, because there were numerous eye witnesses. There were cars stopped on the opposite side of the crossing, there were cars following my client, and there were a couple of pedestrians standing beside the tracks who saw the whole thing unfold. All we had to do was sit them down and have them tell us what they saw.

The defense lawyers and I scheduled all of the depositions for the same afternoon. Witnesses often have strong motivation to distort the truth, but none of these witnesses had a dog in this fight. They were just trying to remember as honestly as they could, and they all had a front row seat. Plus it was a dramatic event, so it was burned in their memories. They all remembered the day clearly, and knew exactly what had happened.

By the end of the afternoon the other lawyers and I could barely keep a straight face as we walked one witness after another through the accident. My client's car was going five mph; it was going twenty-five mph. The train was northbound; it was southbound. It was just an engine; it was an engine and a couple of cars; it was an engine with fifty cars. It was going fast; it was going slow. The train blew its whistle; it didn't blow its whistle. The flashing lights at the crossing were on; they were off. Every witness was telling this story to the very best of his ability, and when they were done we had just about every factual combination that one could think of. They had no idea what they had seen.

Fortunately there was enough factual evidence to reconstruct the accident somewhat accurately without the eye witnesses. Although some witnesses said the flashing lights were not operating, we had conclusive evidence that they did work, because when the train hit the car it also knocked over the flashing lights, and they were still blinking in the ditch when the police arrived. But without that evidence a single witness who said they were not operating would have certainly carried the day.

Eventually the case settled, and it came time to distribute the money. As always, I provided my client with an itemized list of payments for court reporters, transcripts, filing fees and other expenses so she would know where her money had gone. That has always been sufficient for any of my other clients, but not this couple. My client called me, and said that she and her husband wanted to see the receipts. I told them they were welcome to do so, and scheduled a time the next day for them to come in. When they arrived I handed them a folder with the receipts for every expense on the list, and told them that they were welcome to spend as much time as they wanted going through them. I then left them in the waiting area, and went back to my office.

A short time later my secretary suggested that I should check on them. When I walked back to the reception area I found them both down on their knees with the receipts spread all over the floor, as they marked them off one by one. I could only assume that they knew what they would have done with the list of expenses if they had been in my shoes, and they must have assumed that I would do the same thing to them. A year later I was visited by an IRS agent who was investigating them for tax fraud, and it didn't surprise me when they were convicted.

Chapter Thirty-Two

There are a thousand ways for judges to put their thumbs on the scales of justice when they want to. If a judge is afraid that a jury might decide a fact the wrong way he can simply declare that a question of fact is a question of law, and then make the decision himself. The Constitution says that juries must decide questions of fact, but if a judge just calls it a question of law he doesn't have to worry about pesky juries. The Michigan Supreme Court is a master at that game, and very few cases get to a jury under their rule.

It wasn't always that way. Up until 1999 the Michigan Supreme Court was more or less neutral. It tended to be somewhat conservative, with corporations and insurance companies winning over fifty percent of the cases, but only slightly, something like fifty-three percent to forty-seven percent. That changed overnight in January 1999 when two Democratic Justices retired, and the Republicans gained a five to two advantage. In the year that followed corporations and insurance companies won ninety-three percent of their cases in front of the Michigan Supreme Court, and the numbers haven't changed much since. Over the last nine years the Court has been so highly partisan in protecting business interests that private individuals have had virtually no chance.

The outrageous decisions by this Court are too numerous to list, but a few examples can give some indication of how they operate. In premises liability cases the Court has forbidden any claim where the danger is "open and obvious," although no such language appears in the statute. On the surface that sounds like a reasonable rule, until one sees how it has been enforced. According to the Court anything visible to the naked eye is deemed open and obvious as a matter of law. In other words, the Court will decide, not a jury. Clear water on a tile floor is open and obvious because it is not impossible to see. A hole in a walkway at night is open and obvious because it would have been visible during the day, so why should there be a different rule for the nighttime hours. Water on the floor should be open and obvious to a blind man, because it isn't the restaurant owner's fault that the blind man can't see. These are all actual cases.

A few years ago the Michigan Legislature passed a law giving a woman the right to sue if a physician negligently injures her by failing to diagnose breast cancer, thereby depriving her of a chance to survive. Then the Michigan Supreme Court got its hands on it. A woman dying of breast cancer can't sue, said the Court, because cancer isn't an "injury." Only death is an injury. She therefore must wait until after she is dead to sue. Of course if she doesn't die within two years of the date of the misdiagnosis then the case is barred by the statute of limitations.

There is also a state statute requiring road commissions to maintain highways in a condition reasonably safe for travel. But if they design a defectively dangerous highway they get a free pass according to this Court. After all, the statute says the road commission must "maintain" a safe highway, it doesn't say they have to design or build a safe highway. Even if the road commission knows the highway is defectively designed, it still has no duty to fix it because that can't be considered maintenance. There is also no duty for the road commission to maintain traffic lights or stop signs. According to this Court traffic signs and signals aren't part of the "highway," so as a matter of law road commissions have no duty to repair them. In Michigan you'd better be careful when you approach an intersection.

The Michigan Civil Rights Act makes it illegal for employers to sexually harass female employees, but when a female employee was harassed and eventually killed because her co-employees did not like women, the Court gave the employer a free pass, concluding that the statute only prohibits sexual advances. There is nothing in that statute, ruled the Court, that prevents an employer from harassing women so long as he does it out of hate instead of lust.

This is just the tip of the iceberg. The Michigan Supreme Court claims that it is just interpreting statutes literally, but it is like Humpty Dumpty in *Alice in Wonderland;* words mean what the Court says they mean. There is an old story about Abraham Lincoln regaling his colleagues when he was riding the circuit in Illinois. According to legend he asked his friends how many legs a horse would have if you called its tail a leg. "Five," they responded. "Not so," said Lincoln. "No matter what you call a tail it is still a tail." But in Michigan words almost always mean that corporations win, and individuals lose. There aren't any Lincolns on the Michigan Supreme Court.

It's a court that also takes umbrage at criticism, as I discovered shortly after the Republican members took control in 1999. After a fifteen year battle the court ruled in one of my cases that an automobile insurer in Michigan was not required to cover its insured when he was driving someone else's vehicle. The Court made that ruling despite the clear language of the statute that requires insurance companies to cover their policy holders whenever they drive "a motor vehicle." "A" motor vehicle, the court concluded, could only mean the insured's own vehicle. So once again words meant what the Court said they meant, and not what the dictionary or the legislature said they meant.

A dissenting Republican justice called the decision unconscionable, and when I was contacted by a newspaper I went even further, calling the decision absurd. I also said that, "Until widows and orphans can donate as much money as insurance companies we will continue to see these types of decisions."

My comments were not appreciated by the Republican majority on the Court, or by their Republican friends. The Republican members of the Court and their corporate sponsors had worked a long time to gain control of Michigan's legal system, and they didn't want criticism to jeopardize what they had attained. So a couple of weeks after my comments appeared in the paper my secretary, Amy Arver, was waiting for me when I returned from lunch. "The Supreme Court didn't like what you said," she told me, as she handed me a grievance from the Michigan Attorney Grievance Commission.

When I opened it I saw that it wasn't filed by the Supreme Court. It had been filed by a lawyer named Eric Doster, someone I had never heard of, and my first response was, "Who the hell is Eric Doster?" Then turning to the Michigan Bar Directory I discovered that he was the general counsel for the Michigan Republican Party, and it all became clear. In a highly partisan court the party's supporters wanted to solidify their control by intimidating any attorney intrepid enough to voice criticism. Mr. Doster alleged that it was a violation of attorney ethics for me to suggest that a decision of the Supreme Court could be absurd, or that politics or money played any part in their decisions.

Most attorneys who have a grievance filed against them want to keep it as quiet as possible, but never having learned that discretion is the better part of valor I sent a copy of the grievance to the newspapers. Things went downhill fairly quickly for Mr. Doster and his allies after that. Lawyers around the state rallied to my support, and most of the state's newspapers, including even those with Republican leanings, were critical of the effort to stifle free speech about public officials who did, after all, have to run for election.

As my support picked up momentum I received a message from Mr. Doster that if I would simply apologize all would be forgiven. There wasn't a chance in the world that I would accept that offer. Then the Grievance Commission suggested that the grievance should focus just on whether or not attorneys have the same First Amendment rights as any other citizen, and I also declined that offer. My defense wasn't that I had a First Amendment right to free speech. My defense was that every word I spoke was true.

The Grievance Commission then argued that even if my statements were true, it was rude and unprofessional to describe a court opinion as absurd. The opinion I was criticizing was written by Justice Clifford Taylor, and when I received this latest complaint from the Grievance Commission I went back through Justice Taylor's previous dissents, and found one, when he was in the minority, where he himself had described a majority opinion as absurd. I was almost starting to enjoy this.

Along the way approximately one hundred lawyers in the Detroit Area took out a full page add in the Detroit Free Press, and signed their names to the exact quote that had generated my grievance. Now if the Supreme Court or the Grievance Commission intended to discipline me they would have to go after all the other lawyers also, and there would be more where they came from.

The final straw came when the Grievance Commission sent me a questionnaire demanding to know every organization I had ever belonged to, my political views on a range of topics, and various other questions with very heavy Joe McCarthy overtones. When I sent those questions to the press the reaction was so strong that the Grievance Commission investigator offered his resignation, and soon thereafter the grievance was dropped. As a parting shot, however, the letter dismissing the grievance admonished me that it was unethical for me to suggest that insurance companies contributed money to judicial campaigns, because there is a specific Michigan statute that makes such contributions illegal. I also sent that letter to the press, along with my response. In it I traced money from several insurance companies to the American Tort Reform Association, and from there to the Michigan Lawsuit Abuse Watch which sets up shop in Michigan every two years to campaign for Republican Supreme Court candidates. I supplied IRS documents confirming this money trail, and concluded by saying that these contributions, which the Supreme Court justices surely knew about, were illegal no matter how many times the money got laundered along the way. I never heard another word from them.

When Justice Taylor learned that the grievance had been dismissed it obviously didn't sit well with him. A month or two later he spoke to a seminar for workers compensation attorneys, and the subject of my grievance came up during the question and answer session at the end of his speech. He expressed his displeasure that I was allowed to criticize him, and warned that he would get his revenge by destroying my career. He said that if I could criticize him, then he could criticize me, and that as a Supreme Court justice his criticism would have enough clout to put me out of business.

One of the attendees at the seminar sent me a videotape of his threats, but I didn't take them seriously. Then about a week later I received a call from a reporter at the Kalamazoo Gazette. She told me that Justice Taylor had driven down unannounced from Lansing to talk to the Gazette's editorial board, and that the only thing he wanted to talk about was what a poor lawyer I was, suggesting in no subtle terms that I was just a greedy trial lawyer after money. The Gazette did print a few of his comments, but it never affected my practice. Several lawyers around the state recommended that I file a grievance against Justice Taylor with the Judicial Tenure Commission, but I wasn't interested in that. Justice Taylor was right about one thing; he had as much right to criticize me as I had to criticize him.

Chapter Thirty-Three

When Mark Zarbock and I became partners in 1983 I was thirty-seven and Mark was fifty-seven, but Mark was an old fifty-seven. He had lived life in the fast lane for a long time, and it took a toll on him. He was no longer drinking when I joined him, but he was living with the consequences of years of abuse, and he was lucky to still be alive. There are drinkers, and there are hard drinkers, and Mark had been a hard drinker. Lawyers who knew him in his prime told me that he always had a bottle in his briefcase, but despite that he was one of the brightest and most successful lawyers in Kalamazoo for many years.

Mark was as sharp as ever when I joined him, and he still had many cases and many clients, but the fire was gone. Trial law can do that to you. It is very rare to see a trial lawyer in his sixties. Litigation at a high level just takes too much out of you, physically and emotionally. An active litigation practice involves unrelenting pressure and constant battles. It is also frustratingly petty. Lawyers can and do fight over everything, and trials are like a marathon, in court all day and then working late into the night to prepare for the next day. After a week or two of that I am completely spent. I can't imagine how any lawyer survives a trial that lasts for months.

I enjoyed practicing with Mark. He was a brilliant lawyer from Harvard, but he was more than that. He spoke German fluently, had an insatiable curiosity, and could talk about anything. He was generous to a fault, and had a million stories, many of them true. Life with Mark was never boring, but it did become frustrating, because at that stage of his life he just couldn't motivate himself to do anything productive. He knew life was short, and he hated to squander any of it with the routine but necessary nonsense that takes up so much of a lawyer's time. Mark had the ability, but I was carrying ninety percent of the load, and eventually it had to end.

In 1988 I finally told Mark that I wanted to dissolve the partnership, and practice by myself. We continued to share office space for a while after that, but that was all. I did well on my own, but it was a struggle for Mark, and after a year or two he retired and moved to New Mexico where he died broke a few years later. Since then I have carried a fair amount of guilt for abandoning him when he probably needed my help. He did, after all, give me a place to go when I left my former firm, and he was always fair with me. Perhaps I owed him more, and I think I should have been more understanding of his age and his fatigue. I am more sympathetic now, twenty years later, when I am the same age as Mark was back then, and as it becomes progressively more and more difficult to force myself to do the things I did easily when I was forty. I wish I could tell Mark that now I understand. And I would like to confess to him that these days when I wake up in the morning and look in the mirror, I see Mark looking back at me.

I'm not practicing law as actively as I once did. The Michigan Supreme Court has made cases against doctors and insurance companies far more difficult and expensive, resulting in fewer and fewer cases that a lawyer can afford to take, but even if the law had not changed it is still a young man's game, and I'm not a young man. I'm more interested now in my grandchildren than I am in the law, and I hope to have a few more years to enjoy them. Given the longevity that runs in my family I may last for a while yet, but the finish line is starting to come into view, and I think about what comes after. I don't have Grandfather Henry's confidence that there will be a reunion in heaven, but I do have that hope, not just for a reunion with the people I loved, but also with Darwin and Henry and Robert and the others who came before. I have no control over that, but I do have something to say about my mortal remains, and one of these days I would like my bones to rest in Oak Grove Cemetery next to Edna and Henry and Sarah and Dad, and only a short distance from Benjamin and Darwin and Alton. It will complete not only my own journey, but also the family odyssey that started in

Hillsdale one hundred and seventy-three years ago when Darwin and Julia first set foot in an untamed wilderness.

Index

C

D

G

H

J

K

N

O

P

R

S

T

U

Made in the USA
Columbia, SC
30 March 2021